OUTLINES OF LECTURES ON
JURISPRUDENCE

LONDON : HUMPHREY MILFORD
OXFORD UNIVERSITY PRESS

OUTLINES OF LECTURES

ON

JURISPRUDENCE

By

ROSCOE POUND

FIFTH EDITION

CAMBRIDGE
HARVARD UNIVERSITY PRESS
1943

PREFACE TO THE FIFTH EDITION

THESE Outlines represent over fifty years' study and forty-three years' teaching of jurisprudence. The first edition (1903) was chiefly from the English analytical standpoint, and so on its systematic side from the standpoint of the Continental Pandectists. It contained little more than references to the English texts, but gave some translations from Continental jurists and philosophers. The second edition (1914), being meant for use by more mature students, included an Outline of a Course in Theory of Law and Legislation published in two parts in 1912 and 1913, and references to Roman law sources, to the text books of the modern Roman law, and to Continental historical and philosophical jurists. Also it contained a short bibliography. In the third edition (1920) the references to the literature of jurisprudence in all languages were greatly expanded and the bibliography was made to cover the materials for analytical and historical jurisprudence, and comparative law, as well as the writings on jurisprudence from all standpoints. The fourth edition (1928) was a thorough revision of the third.

In the present edition there has again been a thorough revision and the systematic part has been wholly rewritten and much amplified. It is neither easy nor profitable to draw a sharp line between analytical jurisprudence and comparative law. Hence the bibliography has been made somewhat full on the side of comparative law. As to what is more strictly within the scope of a science of law, the bibliography has been made as complete as possible.

Like the English books on jurisprudence, and the treatises of the civilians and commentators on the civil codes, the Outlines deal only with private law, excluding conflict of laws, public law, criminal law, and international law, except as they bear incidentally on general problems of the legal order, of the authoritative precepts and technique and ideals of private law, and of the judicial and administrative processes in relation thereto. Like the Continental introductions to the study of law and treatises on the science of law, the Outlines are not confined to one approach, but take up each subject and topic from the analytical, the historical, the philosophical, and the sociological standpoint. Also, while made to the exigencies of my course on jurisprudence and so presenting materials for developing my own views, the Outlines endeavor to present all other views by full references to the writings in which they are expounded.

What I have expected students to read as the minimum for serious study of the subject is put in large type. What is available as to details, and what may be looked into by the teacher or by the student pursuing some particular point, is printed in small type. The bibliography has been brought down as nearly to date as conditions since 1939 would permit.

As to the citation of articles in the periodicals, I can only say that all that I have read are included, but it is quite possible that something worth while has escaped here and there. Unhappily, some of the best things which have been written have been the hardest to find.

In preparation of this edition I had hoped to have the cooperation of Dr. Julius Stone, Professor in Auckland University College (University of New Zealand), who, as Instructor and afterward Assistant Professor, assisted me in teaching jurisprudence from 1932 to 1936. He went through the legal periodicals from 1928 to 1936 to find articles which deserved my notice, but was called to another position before we could begin work upon what I had planned as a joint production. I am therefore solely responsible.

ROSCOE POUND

17 October 1942

OUTLINE OF THE COURSE

OUTLINES OF LECTURES ON JURISPRUDENCE

THEORY OF LAW AND LEGISLATION

PART 1

JURISPRUDENCE

I. WHAT IS JURISPRUDENCE?

Holland, Jurisprudence, chap. 1; Salmond, Jurisprudence, §§ 1–4;
Gray, The Nature and Sources of the Law, §§ 288–321, 2 ed. pp.
133–151; Amos, Science of Law, chap. 2; Austin, Jurisprudence,
lect. 1; Bryce, Studies in History and Jurisprudence, essay 12;
Pollock, Essays in Jurisprudence and Ethics, essay 1; I Clark,
Roman Private Law: Jurisprudence, 1–39; Gareis, Science of Law
(transl. by Kocourek) 13–28, §§ 3–4; Korkunov, General Theory of
Law (transl. by Hastings) §§ 2–4; Brown, The Austinian Theory of
Law, §§ 640–669; Allen, Legal Duties, 1–27.

Rottschaeffer, Jurisprudence: Philosophy or Science, 11 Minn. L. Rev. 293;
Cohen, Philosophy and Legal Science, 32 Columbia L. Rev. 1103, reprinted in
his Law and the Social Order, 219; id. Law and Scientific Method, in Law and
the Social Order, 184; Thorne, Concerning the Scope of Jurisprudence, 35
American L. Rev. 546.

Uses of the term "jurisprudence."
Is there a "science of law"?

Rueff, From the Physical to the Social Sciences (transl. by Green).

The theory of "normative sciences."
Methods of legal science.
A developed system of law may be looked at from four points of
view:

1. *Analytical.* — Examination of its structure, subject-matter, and
precepts in order to reach by analysis the principles, theories, and
conceptions which it logically presupposes, and to organize the
authoritative materials of judicial and administrative determinations
on this logical basis.

2. *Historical.* — Investigation of its historical origin and development, and of the origin and development of its institutions and
doctrines, in order to discover its general principles, and to organize

the authoritative materials on the basis of these historically developed principles.

3. *Philosophical.* — Study of the philosophical bases of its institutions and doctrines; an attempt to reach its fundamental principles through philosophy, and to understand and organize the ideal element in the authoritative materials.

4. *Sociological.* — Study of the system of law functionally as a part or phase of social control, and of its institutions and doctrines with respect to the social ends to be served.

Applied to the study of legal systems generally, these four methods are the methods of jurisprudence. The propriety of naming a comparative method as a method of jurisprudence may be doubted. The analytical, historical, and philosophical methods, as methods of jurisprudence, must be comparative.

II. HISTORY OF JURISPRUDENCE

(To the Nineteenth Century)

A. The Beginnings of a Science of Law in Antiquity

1. Greek philosophical theories of justice and the social order.

Aristotle, Nicomachean Ethics, bk. v, bk. viii, 7, 2–4 (there is a convenient transl. by Browne in Bohn's Libraries); Aristotle, Politics, i, 1, 9, i, 13, iii, 1, iii, 4–5, iv, 12 (Jowett's transl. should be used); Plato, Republic, ii, 368, iii, 397–398 (Jowett's transl. should be used).

See Berolzheimer, The World's Legal Philosophies, 46–77; II Vinogradoff, Historical Jurisprudence, chaps. 2–3; Pound, Introduction to the Philosophy of Law, 15–26; McIlwain, The Growth of Political Thought in the West, chaps. I, II, III.

2. The secularization of social control (in Roman law 304–253 B.C.) — lawyers and law teachers.

Girard, Manuel élémentaire du droit romain (8 ed.) 47–51; Jolowicz, Historical Introduction to Roman Law, 86–91.

3. The beginnings of legal analysis — the "taking of differences" and framing of maxims.

III Jhering, Geist des römischen Rechts, §§ 49–50; Jörs, Römische Rechtswissenschaft zur Zeit der Republik. Compare The Hedaya (Hamilton's transl.) bk. 16, chap. 1 (Grady's ed. 244); Picot's Case, Y.B. Mich. 33 Edw. I (Horwood ed.) 22–23; The Executor's Case, id. 63; Note, Keilway, 41; Note, 2 Dyer, 111b in margin; 2 Dyer, 143b (pl. 57).

See also Pound, The Maxims of Equity, 34 Harv. L. Rev. 809; id. On Certain Maxims of Equity, Cambridge Legal Essays, 259–277.

4. Greek philosophy and Roman law — the beginnings of a general science of law.

Dareste, La science du droit en Grèce, 1–18, 29–34; Cicero, De oratore, i, 41, § 189.

(a) The *Ius Gentium* — rules universally applicable among civilized men, and hence applicable to foreigners. "A combination of comparative jurisprudence and rational speculation."

Buckland, Text Book of Roman Law (2 ed.) 52–55; Bruns-Lenel, Geschichte und Quellen des römischen Rechts, § 19 (in I Holtzendorff, Enzyklopädie der Rechtswissenschaft, 7 ed.); Cicero, De officiis, iii, 17, 69; id. Oratoriae partitiones, 37, 130; Gaius, i, 1; Inst. i, 2, pr. and §§ 1–2; Dig. i, 1, 1–6, 9.

See I Voigt, Das Ius naturale, aequum et bonum, und Ius Gentium der Römer, §§ 13–15, 42, 43, 79–88, 103; I Karlowa, Römische Rechtsgeschichte, §§ 59–60; I Kuhlenbeck, Entwicklungsgeschichte des römischen Rechts, 205–235.

(b) The *Ius Naturale* — a speculative body of principles, serving as the basis of lawmaking, juristic doctrine, and criticism, of potential applicability to all men, in all ages, among all peoples, derived from reason and worked out philosophically.

Cicero, De officiis, iii, 5, 23; id. De republica, iii, 23, 33 (transl. by Sabine and Smith as Cicero on the Commonwealth); id. Tusculan Disputations, i, 13, 30; Inst. i, 2, pr. and §§ 1–2; Dig. i, 1, 1–6, 9.

See Burle, Essai historique sur le développement de la notion de droit naturel dans l'antiquité grecque; Bryce, Studies in History and Jurisprudence, essay 11; Maine, Ancient Law, chaps. 3–4 and Sir Frederick Pollock's notes E and F; Pollock, Essays in the Law, 31–79; Ritchie, Natural Rights, chap. 2; Salmond, The Law of Nature, 11 L. Q. Rev. 122; I Carlyle, History of Medieval Political Theory, chaps. 3–7; I Voigt, Das Ius naturale, aequum et bonum, und Ius Gentium der Römer, §§ 15–41, 52–64, 98.

See also Sabine and Smith, Cicero on the Commonwealth, chaps. II, III; McIlwaine, The Growth of Political Thought in the West, chap. IV.

5. Roman jurists and law teachers.

(a) The schools of lawyers: teachers and writers.

Dig. i, 2, 2, §§ 47–53 (Monro's transl. may be used); Roby, Introduction to the Study of Justinian's Digest, chap. 9; Jolowicz, Historical Introduction to the Study of Roman Law, 384–387; Krüger, Geschichte der Quellen und Literatur des römischen Rechts (2 ed.) § 20; Kipp, Geschichte der Quellen des römischen Rechts, § 18; Baviera, Le due scuole dei giureconsulti romani.

(b) The classical jurists.

Jolowicz, Historical Introduction to the Study of Roman Law, 387–399; Roby, Introduction to the Study of Justinian's Digest, chaps. 10–15; Girard, Manuel élémentaire du droit romain (8 ed.) 68–77.

(c) The fifth-century teachers.

Collinet, Histoire de l'école de droit de Beyrouth; id. The General Problems Raised by the Codification of Justinian, IV Revue d'histoire du droit, 1, 16–27; Jolowicz, Historical Introduction to the Study of Roman Law, 469–471.

B. THE BEGINNINGS OF A SCIENCE OF LAW IN THE MODERN WORLD ROMAN LAW AND SCHOLASTIC THEOLOGY

The history of modern legal science begins with the revival of the study of Roman law in the twelfth century.

See I Continental Legal History Series, General Survey, 128 (§ 38)–175, 178 (§ 77)–199; 2 Holdsworth, History of English Law, 124–142; Sohm, Institutes of Roman Law (transl. by Ledlie) Grueber's Introduction (in first ed. only) i–xxxvi; Sohm, Institutes of Roman Law (transl. by Ledlie, 3 ed.) §§ 24–28; Westlake, Chapters on the Principles of International Law, 17–51; Hastie, Outlines of Jurisprudence, 237–253, 260–271.

There are two parallel lines of juristic development from the twelfth century to the seventeenth, one legal, the other philosophical.

(a) The lawyers.

(1) The glossators.

I Continental Legal History Series, General Survey, 124–142 (transl. from Calisse, Storia del diritto italiano); Vinogradoff, Roman Law in the Middle Ages, 44–58; Kantorowicz, Studies in the Glossators of the Roman Law (1938); V Savigny, Geschichte des römischen Rechts im Mittelalter, 222–240; I Stintzing, Geschichte der deutschen Rechtswissenschaft, 102 ff.; Salvioli, Storia del diritto italiano (8 ed.) §§ 105–112, with full bibliography. See also II Pertile, Storia del diritto italiano (2 ed.) § 61; Del Vecchio, Di Irnerio e la sua scuola (1869); Besta L'opera di Irnerio (2 vols. 1896); Landsberg, Die Glosse des Accursius (1883); Pescatore, Die Glossen des Accursius (1888); Kantorowicz, Accursio e la sua biblioteca, 2 Rivista di storia del diritto italiano, 35.

(2) The commentators.

I Continental Legal History Series, General Survey, 356–378 (transl. from Calisse, Storia del diritto italiano); V Savigny, Geschichte des römischen Rechts im Mittelalter, 225–228, 353–356; VI ibid. 1–25; I Stintzing, Geschichte der deutschen Rechtswissenschaft, 106–133; Salvioli, Storia del diritto italiano (8 ed.) §§ 113–115, with full bibliography.

As to Bartolus, see II Continental Legal History Series, Great Jurists of the World, 58–108; Woolf, Bartolus of Sassoferrato; Van de Kamp, Bartolo da

Sassoferrato; Beale, Bartolus on the Conflict of Laws, contains a translation of the Commentary of Bartolus on Code, i, 4 — a good example of his method.

(3) The humanists.

The forerunner is Alciatus. See Viard, André Alciat, 1492–1550.

The French school — Jacobus Cujacius (Jacques Cujas, 1522–1590); Hugo Donellus (Doneau, 1527–1591).

I Continental Legal History Series, General Survey, 147–154 (transl. from Calisse, Storia del diritto italiano); ibid. 252–259 (transl. from Brissaud, Manuel d'histoire du droit français); II Continental Legal History Series, Great Jurists of the World, 58–108; I Stintzing, Geschichte der deutschen Rechtswissenschaft, 133–154; Salvioli, Storia del diritto italiano (8 ed.) §§ 124–131, with full bibliography; Gentili, De Iuris Interpretibus (ed. by Astuti); Astuti, Mos Italicus e Mos Gallicus.

(b) The philosophical jurist-theologians.

McIlwain, The Growth of Political Thought in the West, chap. VII.

(1) The schoolmen.

Thomas Aquinas (1225 [or 1227]–1274).

II DeWulf, History of Medieval Philosophy, §§ 269–289; Lachance, Le concept de droit selon Aristote et S. Thomas; Lottin, Le droit naturel chez S. Thomas et ses prédecesseurs.

(2) The Protestant jurist-theologians.

The emancipation of jurisprudence from theology.

Hemmingsen (Hemmingius) De lege naturae apodictica methodus (1562) Q. 9. This passage may be found also in II Kaltenborn, Die Vorläufer des Hugo Grotius, 31. Compare Grotius, De iure belli ac pacis, prolegomena (1625) § 11.

See I Hinrichs, Geschichte der Rechts und Staatsprincipien seit der Reformation, 28–37; I Höffding, History of Modern Philosophy (transl. by Meyer) 42 ff.

There were sixteenth-century attempts to free international law from theology: Belli, De re militari et bello tractatus (1563) — see introduction to Nutting's transl. (Classics of International Law Series) 25a–26a; Gentile, De iure belli (1598) bk. I, cap. 1 (transl. in Classics of International Law Series).

(3) The Spanish jurist-theologians.

Universal as against nationalist theories.

Figgis, Studies of Political Thought from Gerson to Grotius, lect. 6; Scott, Francisco Suarez, His Philosophy of Law and of Sanctions, 22 Georgetown L. J. 405.

Sources: Soto, De iustitia et iure (1589); Suarez, De legibus ac deo legislatore (1619).

Suarez, De legibus, i, 8, §§ 1–2, i, 9, § 2, ii, 19, § 9, xii, 13; Soto, De iustitia et iure, i, q. 5, art. 2.

C. The Modern Science of Law
(From the Seventeenth to the Nineteenth Century)

1. Emancipation of law from the text of the Corpus Iuris.

François Hotman (Hotomannus, 1524–1590); Hermann Conring (1606–1681). Hotman, Anti-Tribonianus (1567) chaps. 1–2, 7–9, 12–13; Conring, De origine iuris germanici (1643) chaps. 21–27, 32–34.

See I Brissaud, Cours d'histoire générale du droit français, 353; Dareste, Étude sur François Hotman, II Revue de législation et de jurisprudence (1850) 257; II Stintzing, Geschichte der deutschen Rechtswissenschaft, 1–31, 165–188; I Continental Legal History Series, General Survey, 428–429 (transl. from II Stobbe, Geschichte der deutschen Rechtsquellen, 418–420); Brunner, Grundzüge der deutschen Rechtsgeschichte (8 ed.) § 64; Stobbe, Hermann Conring, der Begründer der deutschen Rechtsgeschichte (1870).

2. The law-of-nature school.

(a) The seventeenth century.

Hugo Grotius (De Groot) 1583–1645.

II Continental Legal History Series, Great Jurists of the World, 169–184, 305–344; Lysen, Hugo Grotius (1925); Vreeland, Hugo Grotius (1917); Knight, Life and Works of Hugo Grotius (1925); Pound, Grotius in the Science of Law (1925) 19 Am. Journ. of International Law, 685.

Sources: Grotius, De iure belli ac pacis (1625) — Whewell's transl. (1853) is convenient, there is also an abridged transl. by Campbell (1901), and a transl. in the Classics of International Law Series; Pufendorf, De iure naturae et gentium (1672) — Kennet's transl. (1703) may be found in several editions, and there is an abridged transl. by Spavan (1716).

Grotius, De iure belli ac pacis, prolegomena, 30, 40, bk. I, chap. I, 9–12; Pufendorf, De iure naturae et gentium, bk. II, chap. III, § XIII.

Gierke, Natural Law and the Theory of Society (transl. by Barker) introduction, § 3.

(b) The eighteenth century.

II Continental Legal History Series, Great Jurists of the World, 447–476.

Sources: Burlamaqui, Principes du droit naturel (1747) — Nugent's transl. in several editions is useful; Wolff, Institutiones iuris naturae et gentium (1750); Rutherforth, Institutes of Natural Law (1754–1756); Vattel, Le droit des gens, préliminaires (1758). There are many translations of Vattel.

Wolff, Institutiones iuris naturae et gentium, chap. II, §§ 38, 41; Vattel, Le droit des gens, preface (1802 ed.) iii–iv (Chitty's transl. 5 Am. ed.) v ff.; Burlamaqui, Principes du droit naturel, pt. I, chap. I, 3–12, chap. II, chap. V, chap. VIII, 1–2; Rutherforth, Institutes of Natural Law, bk. I, chap. I, chap. VII; I Blackstone, Commentaries, 38–43.

(c) The law-of-nature school in the nineteenth century.

(1) The classical French public law.

Hauriou, Précis de droit constitutionnel (1923) liv. I, chap. 1; I Duguit, Traité de droit constitutionnel (2 ed. 1921) §§ 14–16; I Esmein, Éléments de droit constitutionnel (7 ed. 1921) 539–563.

(2) Neo-Rousseauists.

Wilson, The State, §§ 1415–1460; Acollas, Introduction à l'étude du droit (1885) 1, 2, 7; id. L'idée du droit (1889) 29; Beaussire, Les principes du droit (1888) introduction, especially 1, 7, but compare 25 ff.

(3) The law of nature in Italy.

See Perticone, Die italienische Rechtsphilosophie im letzten Vierteljahrhundert, XXIII Archiv für Rechts- und Wirthschaftsphilosophie, 275.

(4) The law of nature in Spain.

See Legaz y Lacambra, Die Hauptrichtungen der Rechts-, Staats-, und Sozial-philosophie in Spanien, XXVI Archiv für Rechts- und Wirthschaftsphilosophie, 29.

(5) The law of nature in Scotland.

See Lorimer, Institutes of Law (2 ed.) bk. I, chaps. 1, 3, 5–9; Miller, The Data of Jurisprudence, chap. 1.

(6) The law of nature in England.

I Blackstone Commentaries, 38–43; Calvin's Case, 7 Co. 1, 46; Bonham's Case, 8 Co. 114, 118; Day v. Savadge, Hob. 856; Captain Streater's Case, 5 How. St. Tr. 365, 386; City of London v. Wood, 12 Mod. 669, 687; Jefferys v. Boosey, 4 H.L.C. 815; Lee v. Bude & Torrington Jct. R. Co., L. R. 6 C.P. 576, 582.

Plucknett, Bonham's Case and Judicial Review, 40 Harv. L. Rev. 30; Corwin, The "Higher Law" Background of American Constitutional Law, 42 Harv. L. Rev. 169–185, 365, 370–371, 380, 409; Dunoyer, Blackstone et Pothier.

(7) The law of nature in America.

Haines, The Law of Nature in State and Federal Decisions, 25 Yale L. J. 617; Corwin, The "Higher Law" Background of American Constitutional Law, 42 Harv. L. Rev. 380–381, 388–409; Green, J. in State Bank v. Cooper, 10 Tenn. (2 Yerger) 599, 602–603; Hosmer, C. J. in Goshen v. Stonington, 4 Conn. 209, 225; Jackson, J. in Holden v. James, 11 Mass. 396, 405.

Marshall, C. J. in Fletcher v. Peck, 6 Cranch, 87, 135; Chase, J. in Calder v. Bull, 3 Dall. 386, 388; Field, J. in Butchers Union Co. v. Crescent City Co., 111 U. S. 746, 762; Harlan, J. in Chicago R. Co. v. Chicago, 166 U. S. 226, 237; Cobb, J. in Pavesich v. Life Ins. Co., 122 Ga. 190, 194; Winslow, J. in Nunemacher v. State, 129 Wis. 190, 198–203.

Mason, J. in White v. White, 5 Barb. (N. Y.) 474, 484–485; Knowlton, J. in Com. v. Perry, 155 Mass. 117, 121; Barculo, J. in Benson v. Mayor, 10 Barb. (N. Y.) 223, 244–245; Per Curiam in Ham v. McClaws, 1 Bay (S. C.) 93, 98. But see Andrews, J. in Bertholf v. O'Reilly, 74 N. Y. 509, 514–516; Moody, J. in Twining v. New Jersey, 211 U. S. 78, 106–107.

Story, J. in Wilkinson v. Leland, 2 Pet. 627, 657; Miller, J. in Loan Assn. v. Topeka, 20 Wall. 655, 662; Fuller, C. J. in In re Kemmler, 136 U. S. 436, 448; Deemer, J. in State v. Barker, 116 Ia. 96, 105; Brewer, J. in State v. Nemaha County, 7 Kan. 542, 555–556; Cooley, J. in People v. Hurlbut, 24 Mich. 44, 97–98; Allen, J. in People v. Albertson, 55 N. Y. 50, 57; Gibson, C. J. in Norman v. Heist, 5 Watts & S. 171, 173; Hines, C. J. in Barbour v. Board of Trade, 82 Ky. 645, 648–649; Brown, J. in Rasmusen v. United States, 197 U. S. 516, 531. But see Garrison, J. in Attorney General v. McGuiness, 78 N. J. L. 346, 369 ff.; 1 Dillon, Municipal Corporations (5 ed.) § 98.

See Tucker, A Few Lectures on Natural Law (1844); Bishop, Non-Contract Law (1889) § 85; Smith, The Law of Private Right (1890) pt. 3, chap. 3; I Andrews, American Law (2 ed. 1908) §§ 103–104; Pound, Introduction to the Philosophy of Law, 49–50; Haines, The Revival of Natural Law Concepts, chaps. 3–6; Dodd, Extra-Constitutional Limitations Upon Legislative Power, 40 Yale L. J. 1188; Grant, The Natural Law Background of Due Process, 31 Columbia L. Rev. 56; Miller, Fundamental Law in the American Revolution, 1760–1776; Wright, American Interpretations of Natural Law; Pound, The Revival of Natural Law (1942) 17 Notre Dame Lawyer, 287, 328–342.

III. SCHOOLS OF JURISTS: THE NINETEENTH-CENTURY SCHOOLS

1. Methods and schools.

Berolzheimer, The World's Legal Philosophies, chaps. 5–7; Charmont, La renaissance du droit naturel, chaps. 1–5 (chap. 5 is translated in Modern French Legal Philosophy, 65–73); I Vinogradoff, Historical Jurisprudence, 103–160 (Methods and Schools of Jurisprudence); Vinogradoff, Aims and Methods of Jurisprudence, 24 Columbia L. Rev. 1; Isaacs, The Schools of Jurisprudence, 31 Harv. L. Rev. 373; Pound, Jurisprudence, in 8 Encyclopaedia of the Social Sciences, 477, 477–485.

2. The nineteenth-century schools.

(a) In general.

Pollock, Oxford Lectures, 1–36; Pollock, Essays in Jurisprudence and Ethics, 1–30; Bryce, Studies in History and Jurisprudence, essay 12; Munroe Smith, Jurisprudence, 30–42; Brown, The Austinian Theory of Law, excursus F; Korkunov, General Theory of Law (transl. by Hastings) 23–30, 116–138; Lightwood, The Nature of Positive Law, chaps. 12–13; Lorimer, Institutes of Law (2 ed.)

38–54; Miller, Lectures on the Philosophy of Law, appendix E; Leonhard, Methods Followed in Germany by the Historical School of Law, 7 Columbia L. Rev. 573; Pound, The Scope and Purpose of Sociological Jurisprudence, 24 Harv. L. Rev. 591; id. The Philosophy of Law in America, VII Archiv für Rechts- und Wirthschaftsphilosophie, 213, 385; id. The Spirit of the Common Law, lect. 6.

Clark, Practical Jurisprudence, 1–6; Amos, Systematic View of the Science of Jurisprudence (1872) 40–43; Holland, Elements of Jurisprudence (13 ed.) 1–13; I Puchta, Cursus der Institutionen (1841) §§ 33–35 (English transl. by Hastie, Outlines of Jurisprudence, 124–132); Fichte, Grundlage des Naturrechts (1796) introduction, § 2 (English transl. by Kroeger as Fichte's Science of Rights, 16–21); Hegel, Grundlinien der Philosophie des Rechts (1820) §§ 1–3 (English transl. by Dyde as Hegel's Philosophy of Right, 1–10); Boistel, Cours de philosophie du droit (1899) §§ 1–2; Miller, Data of Jurisprudence (1902) 1–2.

For France see I Bonnecase, La pensée juridique française, 285–508; for Germany, see Berolzheimer, The World's Legal Philosophies, 180–259. See also the series of papers on nineteenth-century schools of jurists in particular countries in the Archiv für Rechts- und Wirthschaftsphilosophie: XXIII, 275 (Italy by Perticone); XXIV, 37 (Hungary by Horváth); XXVI, 289 (Russia by Laserson); XXVI, 29 (Spain by Legaz y Lacambra).

(b) Doctrines and methods.

The nineteenth-century schools represent different phases of a reaction from the philosophical method of the seventeenth and eighteenth centuries.

I Austin, Lectures on Jurisprudence (5 ed.) 215–218; I Bentham, Traités de législation, chap. 13, § 10 (1802 ed. I, 133).

Bluntschli, Die neueren Rechtsschulen der deutschen Juristen (1862); Bekker, Ueber den Streit der historischen und der filosofischen Rechtsschule (1886); Pound, Interpretations of Legal History, lect. I.

(1) The historical school.
Forerunners: Jacques Cujas (1522–1590).
     Gustav Hugo (1764–1844).
     Edmund Burke (1729–1797).
     Vicenzo Cuoco (1770–1823).
Founder: Friedrich Carl von Savigny (1779–1861).

II Continental Legal History Series, Great Jurists of the World, 561–589; Stintzing, Friedrich Carl von Savigny (1862); Bethmann-Hollweg, Erinnerung an Friedrich Carl von Savigny (1867); Enneccerus, Friedrich Carl von Savigny und die Richtung der neueren Rechtswissenschaft (1879); Stoll, Der junge Savigny (1927); id. F. C. v. Savigny, Professorenjahre in Berlin (1929).

Monroe Smith, Four German Jurists, 10 Political Science Q. 664–

669, 11 id. 278–309; Vinogradoff, Introduction to Huebner, History of German Private Law (transl. by Philbrick) xvii–xli; Small, Origins of Sociology, chap. 2, The Thibaut-Savigny Controversy: Continuity as a Phase of Human Experience (this chapter was first printed in 28 Am. Journ. of Sociology, 711); Kantorowicz, Savigny and the Historical School of Law, 53 L. Q. Rev. 326.

Savigny, Vom Beruf unsrer Zeit für Gesetzgebung und Rechtswissenschaft (1814) chaps. 1, 2 (use 3 ed. 1840 or Hayward's transl.); II Berolzheimer, System der Rechts- und Wirthschaftsphilosophie, 230–231 (World's Legal Philosophies, 204); Dernburg, Pandekten (8 ed.) § 12.

For critiques of the historical school, see Pound, Interpretations of Legal History, lect. 1; Korkunov, General Theory of Law (Hastings' transl.) 116–122; Harrison, Jurisprudence and the Conflict of Laws, 70–97, and Lefroy's note, 173–179; Charmont, La renaissance du droit naturel, 74–94; Stammler, Ueber die Methode der geschichtlichen Rechtstheorie; Bekker, Recht des Besitzes, § 1; Kantorowicz, Lehre von dem richtigen Rechte, 8; Manigk, Savigny und der Modernismus im Recht; Anderssen, Die Wert der Rechtsgeschichte; I Lambert, Études de droit commun législatif, 127–141; Bonnet, La philosophie du droit chez Savigny; Gierke, Natural Law and the Theory of Society (transl. by Barker) introduction, § 4.

For the influence of the historical method on the application of the German Civil Code, see Jung, Die sogenannte Gewohnheitsrecht, XXII Archiv für Rechts- und Wirthschaftsphilosophie, 228–259.

For American parallels, see Carter, On the Proposed Codification of our Common Law (1884); id. Provinces of the Written and the Unwritten Law (1889), reprinted in part in 24 Am. L. Rev. 1; Field, Short Response to a Long Discourse: An Answer to James C. Carter's Proposed Codification of our Common Law (1884); id. Codification — Mr. Field's Answer to Mr. Carter, 24 Am. L. Rev. 255; Miller, Destruction of our Natural Law by Legislation (1882); Franklin, The Historic Function of the American Law Institute, 40 Harv. L. Rev. 1367; Williston, The Written and the Unwritten Law, 17 Am. Bar Assn. Journ. 39.

The English historical school is partly a development of the foregoing and partly a reaction from the English analytical school.

Sir Henry Maine (1822–1888). See bibliography, *post*, 196.

Duff, Sir Henry Maine (1892); Vinogradoff, The Teaching of Sir Henry Maine (1904) 20 L. Q. Rev. 119; Robson, Sir Henry Maine Today, in Modern Theories of Law, 160–180; Smellie, Sir Henry Maine, Economia, no. 22, 64 (March 1928).

(2) The English analytical school.

Forerunners: Thomas Hobbes (1588–1679).

Jeremy Bentham (1748–1832).

Founder: John Austin (1790–1859). See bibliography, *post*, 194.

On Hobbes, see Robertson, Hobbes (1886); Stephen, Hobbes (1904); Tönnies, Hobbes Leben und Lehre (1896); Woodbridge, The Philosophy of Hobbes (1903); Catlin, Thomas Hobbes as Philosopher, Publicist, and Man of Letters (1922).

On Bentham, see *infra*, (3).

On Austin, see preface (by Sarah Austin) to 3d and subsequent editions of Austin, Lectures on Jurisprudence; Schwartz, John Austin and the German Jurisprudence of his Time, Politica, no. 2, 178 (August 1934).

Austin, Lectures on Jurisprudence, Outline of the Course of Lectures, Preliminary Explanations, and lect. 1; Gray, Nature and Sources of the Law, §§ 1–19 (2 ed. pp. 1–5); II Berolzheimer, System der Rechts- und Wirthschaftsphilosophie, 18–20 (World's Legal Philosophies, 9–11); Kocourek, The Century of Analytical Jurisprudence Since John Austin, in II Law: A Century of Progress (New York University Publication) 195.

Bergbohm, Jurisprudenz und Rechtsphilosophie, 12–20; Somló, Juristische Grundlehre, 33–37; Dowdall, The Present State of Analytical Jurisprudence, 42 L. Q. Rev. 451. See also the comparison of analytical jurisprudence with the classical economics in Cooke, Adam Smith and Jurisprudence, 51 L. Q. Rev. 326, 331.

(3) In the nineteenth century the philosophical method was continued by: (i) the Benthamite utilitarians, (ii) the metaphysical school, (iii) the positivists.

i. The Benthamite utilitarians.

See bibliography, *post*, 197.

On Bentham see: Albee, History of English Utilitarianism; Allen, The Young Bentham, 44 L. Q. Rev. 492; Alexander, Bentham: Philosopher and Reformer, 7 N. Y. Univ. L. Rev. 141, 405; Atkinson, Jeremy Bentham, His Life and Work; Berolzheimer, The World's Legal Philosophies, 134–141; Cohen, Jeremy Bentham (Fabian Tracts, no. 221); Dicey, Lectures on the Relation between Law and Public Opinion in England in the Nineteenth Century, lect. 6; Dillon, Laws and Jurisprudence of England and America, lect. 12, reprinted (revised) as Bentham's Influence in the Reforms of the Nineteenth Century, 1 Select Essays in Anglo-American Legal History, 492; Everett, The Education of Jeremy Bentham; Geiser and Jaszi, Political Philosophy from Plato to Bentham, chap. 13; Halévy, La formation du radicalisme philosophique (English transl. by Morris as The Growth of Philosophic Radicalism) contains also a full bibliography of Bentham's writings and of accounts of Bentham and estimates of his work; Judson, Modern View of the Law Reforms of Jeremy Bentham, 10 Columbia L. Rev. 41; Kayser, The Grand Social Enterprise: A Study of Jeremy Bentham in his Relation to Liberal Nationalism; MacCann, Bentham and His Philosophy of Reform; Mitchell, Bentham and His School, 35 Juridical Review, 248; Mitchell, Bentham's Felicific Calculus, 33 Political Science Q. 161; Ogden, Introduction (in his ed. of

Bentham's Theory of Legislation); id. Bentham's Theory of Fictions; Phillipson, Three Criminal Law Reformers, pt. II, Bentham; I Stephen, The English Utilitarians; Solari, L'idea individuale e l'idea sociale nel diritto privato, §§ 31–36; Wallas, Jeremy Bentham; id. Jeremy Bentham, 38 Political Science Q. 161.

Atkinson, Jeremy Bentham, 126–155, 212–237; Phillipson, Three Criminal Law Reformers, pt. II, Bentham, 26–106; Dicey, The Relation between Law and Public Opinion in England in the Nineteenth Century, 69–210; Montague, Bentham's Fragment on Government, 1–58.

Bentham, Theory of Legislation (Hildreth's transl. 5 ed.) 1–87, 88–124, 239–295; Bentham, Indications concerning Lord Eldon, V Works (Bowring's ed.) 349–381; Bentham, Truth Against Ashhurst, id. 234; Ogden, Bentham's Theory of Legislation, xxxi–xli, 511–512.

ii. The metaphysical school.

See bibliography, *post*, 198–199.

Bonnecase, La notion de droit en France au dix-neuvième siècle, chaps. 1–3; Tourtoulon, Philosophy in the Development of Law (transl. by Read) 474–520.

Kant, Metaphysische Anfangsgründe der Rechtslehre (2 ed.) xxxi–xlvii (Kant's Philosophy of Law, transl. by Hastie, 43–58); Hegel, Grundlinien der Philosophie des Rechts, § 1; Ahrens, Cours de droit naturel (8 ed.) I, 1, II, 17–20; Lorimer, Institutes of Law (2 ed.) 353; Miller, Lectures on the Philosophy of Law, 9, 71–73; Boistel, Cours de philosophie de droit, §§ 1–2.

Geyer, Geschichte und System der Rechtsphilosophie, § 2; Prins, La philosophie du droit et l'école historique (1882); Stace, The Philosophy of Hegel, 374–438; Binder, Busse und Lorenz, Einführung in Hegel's Rechtsphilosophie; Singh, The Jurisprudence of Lorimer, 44 Internat. Journ. of Ethics, 332.

See Gray, Nature and Sources of the Law (1 ed.) §§ 7–9; Bryce, Studies in History and Jurisprudence (Am. ed.) 631–634; Pollock, Essays in Jurisprudence and Ethics, 28–30; Korkunov, General Theory of Law (Hastings' transl.) § 4; Bergbohm, Jurisprudenz und Rechtsphilosophie, §§ 6–15; I Berolzheimer, System der Rechts- und Wirthschaftsphilosophie, vii.

In the latter part of the nineteenth century there was a tendency to bring the different methods together and to broaden the basis of both the historical and the philosophical schools.

Maine, Ancient Law, chap. 1; Jenks, Law and Politics in the Middle Ages, 1–4; Brown, The Austinian Theory of Law, § 629; Salmond, Jurisprudence, § 17; id. The Underlying Principles of Modern Legislation, 64–67; Carter, Law: Its Origin, Growth, and Function, 336–338.

Dahn, Rechtsphilosophische Studien, 288; Schuppe, Rechtswissenschaft und Rechtsphilosophie, I Jahrbuch der internationalen Vereinigung für vergleichende

Rechtswissenschaft, 215; Kohler, Rechtsphilosophie und Universalrechtsgeschichte, § 8.

iii. The positivists.
See *post*, V, 4, VI, 1–3.

On positivism generally: Comte, Cours de philosophie positive (1830–1842, 5 ed. 1892–1894, abridged transl. by Martineau, 3 ed. 1893). See Mill, Auguste Comte and Positivism (5 ed. 1907); Lévy-Bruhl, La philosophie d'Auguste Comte (there is an English transl. by Beaumont-Klein). On Spencer: Duncan, Life and Letters of Herbert Spencer; Elliot, Herbert Spencer; Barker, Political Thought in England from Herbert Spencer to the Present Day, chap. 4.

Spencer, Social Statics; Spencer, Justice, chaps. 1–5; Durkheim, On the Division of Labor in Society (transl. by Simpson) introduction and bk. 1; Ardigò, Opere filosofiche, vols. 3, 4; Duguit, Theory of Objective Law Anterior to the State — Prevailing Misconceptions of the State and of Law, in Modern French Legal Philosophy, 236–257.

Berolzheimer, The World's Legal Philosophies, 308–323.

(4) The "comparative method."
See bibliography, *post*, 205.

Meili, Institutionen der vergleichenden Rechtswissenschaft (1898) — a bibliography only.

Maine, Village Communities, lect. 1; Bryce, Studies in History and Jurisprudence, essay 11; Pollock, Essays in the Law, 1–30; Gray, Nature and Sources of the Law, §§ 292–314 (2 ed. 134–148); Jenks, The New Jurisprudence, 59–65; II Berolzheimer, System' der Rechts- und Wirthschaftsphilosophie, 21; Schuppe, Die Methoden der Rechtsphilosophie, V Zeitschrift für vergleichende Rechtswissenschaft, 209; Capitant, Conception, méthode, et fonction du droit comparé d'après R. Saleilles, L'oeuvre juridique de Raymond Saleilles, 65; Wenger, Römisches Recht und Rechtsvergleichung, XIV Archiv für Rechts- und Wirthschaftsphilosophie, 1, 106; Rheinstein, Comparative Law and the Conflict of Laws in Germany, 2 Univ. of Chicago L. Rev. 232.

IV. THE SOCIAL PHILOSOPHICAL SCHOOLS

Pound, The Scope and Purpose of Sociological Jurisprudence, 25 Harv. L. Rev. 140; Tourtoulon, Les principes philosophiques de l'histoire du droit, 7–79 (transl. by Read as Philosophy in the Development of Law, 5–73); I Jhering, Der Zweck im Recht (6–8 ed.) 442–445 (transl. by Husik as Law as a Means to an End, 330–332); Stammler, Theory of Justice (transl. by Husik) 3–14 (transl. from pp. 1–11 of the first ed. of the Lehre von dem richtigen Rechte — now somewhat altered in 2 ed. pp. 39–43); Kohler, Rechtsphilosophie und Universalrechtsgeschichte, §§ 8–10; Hocking, The Present

Status of the Philosophy of Law and of Rights, chaps. 1–5; Drake, Introduction to Jhering, Law as a Means to an End (transl. by Husik) xv–xx; Kocourek, Introduction to Jhering, The Struggle for Law (transl. by Lalor 2 ed.); Saleilles, L'école historique et droit naturel d'après quelques ouvrages récents (1902) 1 Revue trimestrielle de droit civil, 80; Jones, The Aims of Legal Science, 47 L. Q. Rev. 62.

See Cohen, A Critical Sketch of Legal Philosophy in America, in II Law: A Century of Progress (New York Univ. Publication) 266.

At the end of the nineteenth century a revolt from the historical school, which had all but supplanted philosophical jurisprudence, and a new development of the philosophical school, resulted in three well-marked types of social philosophical jurisprudence.

(a) The social utilitarians.
Rudolf von Jhering (1818–1892).

II Continental Legal History Series, Great Jurists of the World, 590–599; Munroe Smith, Four German Jurists, 10 Political Science Q. 664, 11 id. 278, 12 id. 21; Rudolf von Jhering in Briefen an seine Freunde (1913).

Jhering, Law as a Means to an End (transl. by Husik) preface, lviii–lix, chap. 1, § 1 (pp. 1–3), chap. 3, § 5 (pp. 32–35), chap. 7 (pp. 71–74); id. Scherz und Ernst in der Jurisprudenz, pt. 3 (Im juristisches Begriffshimmel); I id. Geist des römischen Rechts, Einleitung; III id. 1, § 60; Jhering, Law as a Means to an End, chap. 5, § 4 (pp. 49–51), chap. 8, § 10 (pp. 239–246), chap. 8, § 12 (pp. 325–423).

I Sternberg, Allgemeine Rechtslehre, 190–191; Saleilles, Individualization of Punishment (transl. by Jastrow) 8–10; Cardozo, The Growth of the Law, lect. 2; Heck, Interessenjurisprudenz (1933) in Recht und Geschichte der Gegenwart, no. 97; Josserand, Les mobiles dans les actes juridiques (essais de téléologie juridique, II) 1–41.

Critiques of Jhering: Merkel, Rudolf von Jhering, appendix I to Law as a Means to an End (transl. by Husik, the original may be found in II Merkel, Gesammelte Abhandlungen, 733); II Berolzheimer, System der Rechts- und Wirthschaftsphilosophie, § 43, The World's Legal Philosophies, 337–351; Berolzheimer, Rechtsphilosophische Studien, 143–148; Stammler, Wirthschaft und Recht, § 100; id. Theory of Justice (transl. by Husik) 148–155 (translated from Lehre von dem richtigen Rechte, 1 ed. 191–195, in 2 ed. this is much altered); Korkunov, General Theory of Law (transl. by Hastings) §§ 13–14; Tanon, L'évolution du droit et la conscience sociale (3 ed.) 44–81 (transl. in appendix II to Jhering, Law as a Means to an End, transl. by Husik); Radbruch, Grundzüge der Rechtsphilosophie, 18–21.

(b) The neo-Kantians.
Rudolf Stammler (1856–1938).
Stammler, Wirthschaft und Recht, §§ 32–33; id. Theory of Justice

(transl. by Husik) 9–11 (§ 2), 19–21, 72–73, 89–91, 152–155 (§ 5), 160–166; Kantorowicz, Zur Lehre vom richtigen Recht, 9; Gény, The Critical System (Idealistic and Formal) of R. Stammler, appendix I to Theory of Justice (transl. by Husik of II Gény, Science et technique en droit privé positif, 127–190); Croce, Historical Materialism and the Economics of Karl Marx, chap. 2.

Stammler's writings: Ueber die Methode der geschichtlichen Rechtstheorie (1888) reprinted in I Rechtsphilosophische Abhandlungen, 1–40; Wirthschaft und Recht (1896, 5 ed. 1924); Die Gesetzmässigkeit in Rechtsordnung und Volkswirthschaft (1902), reprinted in I Rechtsphilosophische Abhandlungen, 169–184; Lehre von dem richtigen Rechte (1902, 2 ed. 1926); Wesen des Rechts und der Rechtswissenschaft, in Die Kultur der Gegenwart (1906); Systematische Theorie der Rechtswissenschaft (1911, 2 ed. 1923); Rechts und Staatstheorien der Neuzeit (1917); Lehrbuch der Rechtsphilosophie (1922, 3 ed. 1928); Fundamental Tendencies of Modern Jurisprudence, 21 Mich. L. Rev. 623, 765.

Critiques of Stammler: deBustamente y Montoro, Stammler; Paz, La filosofia del derecho de Rodolfo Stammler; Ginsberg, Stammler's Philosophy of Law, in Modern Theories of Law, 38; Sabine, Rudolf Stammler's Critical Philosophy of Law, 18 Cornell L. Q. 321; Drake, Juristic Idealism and Legal Practice, 25 Mich. L. Rev. 571, 752; Wu, Stammler and his Critics, Theory of Justice (transl. by Husik) appendix II; II Berolzheimer, System der Rechts- und Wirthschaftsphilosophie, § 48, World's Legal Philosophies, 398–422; Kantorowicz, Zur Lehre vom richtigen Recht; Binder, Rechtsbegriff und Rechtsidee (1915); id. Kritische und metaphysische Rechtsphilosophie, IX Archiv für Rechts- und Wirthschaftsphilosophie, 142, 267; Wielikowski, Die Neukantianer in der Rechtsphilosophie (1914); Radbruch, Grundzüge der Rechtsphilosophie, 21–24.

See also Richard, La question sociale et le mouvement philosophique au XIXe siècle, chaps. 4, 5; Picard, La philosophie sociale de Renouvier, chap. 3.

On the relation of Kelsen's neo-Kantianism to that of Stammler, see Kallab, Le postulat de justice dans la théorie du droit, 1 Revue internationale de la théorie du droit, 89, 91–94; Küry, Kritische Bemerkungen zu Stammler's Lehre, 6 Revue internationale de la théorie du droit, 158.

On Stammler's influence on the "Freirecht" movement, see Kantorowicz and Patterson, Legal Science — A Summary of its Methodology, 28 Columbia L. Rev. 679; Kantorowicz, Vorgeschichte der Freirechtslehre, 5–6. Compare, in the United States, Nelles, Towards Legal Understanding, 34 Columbia L. Rev. 862, 1041.

Kelsen's writings on jurisprudence: Ueber Grenzen zwischen juristischer und soziologischer Methode (1911); Hauptprobleme der Staatsrechtslehre (1911, 2 ed. 1923); Zur Soziologie des Rechtes (1912) 34 Archiv für Sozialwissenschaft und Sozialpolitik, 601; Eine Grundlegung der Rechtssoziologie (1915) 39 id. 839; Die Rechtswissenschaft als Norm- oder als Kulturwissenschaft (1916) 40 Schmollers Jahrbuch für Gesetzgebung, Verwaltung, und Volkswirthschaft, 1181 (there is a Japanese translation); Zur Theorie der juristischen Fiktionen (1919) 1 Annalen der Philosophie, 630; Das Problem der Souveränität und die Theorie des Völkerrechtes (1920, 2 ed. 1928); Der Staatsbegriff der "verstehenden Soziologie" (1921) 1 Zeitschrift für Volkswirthschaft und Sozialpolitik, 104; Das Verhältnis von Staat und Recht im Lichte der Erkenntniskritik (1921) 2

Zeitschrift für öffentliches Recht, 453; Staat und Recht: Zum Problem der soziologischen oder juristischen Erkenntnis des Staates (1922) 2 Kölner Viertel-jahrschrift für Soziologie, Reihe A, 18; Der Begriff des Staates und die Sozial-psychologie in 8 Imago, Zeitschrift für Anwendung der Psychoanalyse auf die Geisteswissenschaften (1922) 97 (there is an English translation); Rechtswissen-schaft und Recht (1922) 3 Zeitschrift für öffentliches Recht, 103; Der sozio-logische und der juristische Staatsbegriff (1922, 2 ed. 1928 — there is a Japanese translation in two editions); Allgemeine Staatslehre (1925 — there are transla-tions into French and Spanish); Grundriss einer allgemeinen Theorie des Staates (1926 — there are translations into Czechish, French, Greek, Hungarian, Italian, Japanese, Roumanian, and Spanish); Das Wesen des Staates (1926) 1 Interna-tionale Zeitschrift für Theorie des Rechts, 5; Staatsform als Rechtsform (1926) 5 Zeitschrift für öffentliches Recht, 73; Aperçu d'une théorie générale de l'état (1926) 33 Revue du droit public, 561; Naturrecht und positives Recht (1927) 2 Internationale Zeitschrift für Theorie des Rechts, 71; Die Idee des Naturrechtes (1927) 7 Zeitschrift für öffentliches Recht, 221 (there is an Italian translation); Die philosophischen Grundlagen der Naturrechtslehre und des Rechtspositivismus (1928 — there is a Japanese translation); Rechtsgeschichte gegen Rechtsphiloso-phie (1928); Juristischer Formalismus und reine Rechtslehre (1929) 58 Juris-tische Wochenschrift, 1723 (there are translations into Czechish and Italian); Allgemeine Rechtslehre im Lichte materialistischer Geschichtsauffassung (1931) 66 Archiv für Sozialwissenschaft und Sozialpolitik, 449; Zur Theorie der Inter-pretation (1934) 8 Internationale Zeitschrift für Theorie des Rechts, 9; La méthode et la notion de la théorie pure du droit (1934) 41 Revue de metaphysique et de morale, 183; Reine Rechtslehre (1934); The Pure Theory of Law (1934) 50 L. Q. Rev. 474; L'âme et le droit (1936) 2 Annuaire de l'institut international de philosophie du droit et de sociologie juridique, 60; The Function of the Pure Theory of Law in II Law: A Century of Progress (New York University Publica-tion, 1937) 231.

Expositions and critiques of Kelsen: Lauterpacht, Kelsen's Pure Science of Law in Modern Theories of Law (1933) 105–138; Voegelin, Kelsen's Pure Theory of Law (1927) 42 Pol. Sci. Q. 268; id. Die Souveränitätstheorie Dickinsons und die reine Rechtslehre (1929) 8 Zeitschrift für öffentliches Recht, 413; Kunz, The Vienna School and International Law (1934) 11 N. Y. U. L. Q. Rev. 370; Wilson, The Basis of Kelsen's Theory of Law (1934) 1 Politica, 54; Recaséns Siches, Direcciones Contemporáneas del Pensamiento Jurídico (1929) 108–164; id. Estudios sobre la teoría pura del derecho y del estado (prologue to the Spanish transl. of Kelsen's Allgemeine Staatslehre, 2 ed. 1934); id. Estudio de filosofia del derecho (1936) 519–521; 2 Bonnecase, La pensée juridique française (1933) §§ 375–384; Davy, Le problème de l'obligation chez Duguit et chez Kelsen in Archives de philosophie du droit et de sociologie juridique (1933) 7; Weyr, Reine Rechtslehre und Verwaltungsrecht in Festschrift für Hans Kelsen (1933) 366.

Mention should be made specially of the writings of Fritz Sander: I and II Staat und Recht (1922); Rechtsdogmatik oder Theorie der Rechtserfahrung (1921); Kelsens Rechtslehre (1923); Die transzendentale Methode der Rechts-philosophie und der Begriff des Rechtsverfahrens (1920); Prolegomena zu einer Theorie der Rechtserfahrung (1922); Zur Methodik der Rechtswissenschaft (1923); Staatssubjekt und Staatsakt (1937) 30 Archiv für Rechts und Sozial-philosophie, 363.

There is a full bibliography of the literature which has grown up about

Kelsen's pure theory of law: Métall, Bibliographie der reinen Rechtslehre (1934). See also 2 Bonnecase, La pensée juridique française (1933) § 376.

(c) The neo-Hegelians.

Josef Kohler (1849–1919).

Kohler, Rechtsphilosophie und Universalrechtsgeschichte (in Holtzendorff, Enzyklopädie der Rechtswissenschaft, 7 ed.) § 8; id. Lehrbuch der Rechtsphilosophie (3 ed.) 1–21, 28–32; id. Philosophy of Law (transl. by Albrecht) 25–27 (altered in 3 ed. of original); II Berolzheimer, System der Rechts- und Wirthschaftsphilosophie, § 48, iv (The World's Legal Philosophies, 422–431); Pound, Interpretations of Legal History, 141–151.

Kohler's writings on jurisprudence and philosophy of law: Shakespeare vor dem Forum der Jurisprudenz (1883, 2 ed. 1919); Recht, Glaube und Sitte (1892); Zur Urgeschichte der Ehe (1897); Einführung in die Rechtswissenschaft (1902, 5 ed. 1919); Rechtsphilosophie und Universalrechtsgeschichte (in Holtzendorff, Enzyklopädie der Rechtswissenschaft, 6 ed. 1904, 7 ed. 1915); Moderne Rechtsprobleme (1907, 2 ed. 1913); Lehrbuch der Rechtsphilosophie (1908, 3 ed. by Arthur Kohler 1923), the first ed. transl. by Albrecht as Kohler's Philosophy of Law (1914); Recht und Persönlichkeit in der Kultur der Gegenwart (1914).

Heymann, Seeberg, Klee, und Schmidt, Josef Kohler zum Gedächtniss (1920); Osterrieth, Josef Kohler (1920); Rabel, Josef Kohler, 10 Reinische Zeitschrift für Zivil und Prozessrecht, 123; Adam, In Memoriam, Josef Kohler, 38 Zeitschrift für vergleichende Rechtswissenschaft, 1; Fleischmann, Josef Kohler zum Gedächtniss, 11 Zeitschrift für Volkerrecht, 1; Biographical Note by Arthur Kohler, XXVI Archiv für Rechts- und Wirthschaftsphilosophie, 212–217.

Kohler, Moderne Rechtsprobleme (2 ed.) § 1; 1 Kohler, Lehrbuch des bürgerlichen Rechts, §§ 38, 39; Berolzheimer, Zum Methodenstreit in der Rechtsphilosophie der Gegenwart, IV Archiv für Rechts- und Wirthschaftsphilosophie, 56; Sauer, Stand und Zukunftsaufgaben der Rechtsphilosophie, XXVI id. 3, 20–28; id. Hegel und die Gegenwart, XXV id. 1, 1–5.

For critiques of Kohler, see: Pound, Interpretations of Legal History, 141–151; II Gény, Science et technique en droit privé positif, 111–126; Hocking, The Present Status of the Philosophy of Law and of Rights, chaps. 3–4; Lasson, Kohler's Philosophy of Law, appendix II to Albrecht's transl. (transl. of review in II Archiv für Rechts- und Wirthschaftsphilosophie, 318); Castillojo y Duarte, Kohler's Philosophical Position, appendix III to Albrecht's transl. of the Lehrbuch der Rechtsphilosophie (transl. from the introduction to the Spanish transl. of Kohler's Rechtsphilosophie und Universalrechtsgeschichte).

(d) Recently a neo-idealist social-philosophical school seems to be arising — a logical-psychological relativist idealism.

Pound, Fifty Years of Jurisprudence, 51 Harv. L. Rev. 444, 454–462.

Tourtoulon, Principes philosophiques de l'histoire du droit, bk. ii, chap. 13 (English transl. Philosophy in the Development of Law, 416–472); Radbruch,

Grundzüge der Philosophie des Rechts, 29–42, 82–104, 184–211; id. Rechtsphilosophie, §§ 4, 7, 9–15; Binder, Philosophie des Rechts, 118–288; id. Grundlegung zur Rechtsphilosophie; Recaséns Siches, La filosofia del diritto in Germania, 8 Rivista internazionale di filosofia del diritto, 1.

For a critique of Radbruch see Gurvitch, Une philosophie antinomique du droit: Gustav Radbruch (1932) Archives de philosophie du droit, 530.

(e) Phenomenology.

As a philosophy, phenomenology derives from Edmund Husserl (1859–).

Reinach, Die apriorischen Grundlagen des bürgerlichen Rechtes (1922); Schapp, Die neue Wissenschaft vom Recht (1931–1932); Kaufmann, Logik und Rechtswissenschaft (1922); id. Die Kriterien des Rechtes (1924); id. Die philosophischen Grundprobleme der Lehre von der Strafrechtsschuld (1929); Schreier, Grundbegriffe und Grundformen des Rechts (1927); G. Husserl, Recht und Welt (1930).

See also Spiegelberg, Gesetz und Sittengesetz (1934).

For applications, see G. Husserl, Der Rechtsgegenstand (1933); id. Rechtskraft und Rechtsgeltung (1925); Engisch, Zur phänomenologischen Methode im Strafrecht (1937) 30 Archiv für Rechts und Sozialphilosophie, 130.

(f) In France the same movement took the form of a revival of natural law.

Pound, Fifty Years of Jurisprudence, 51 Harv. L. Rev. 444, 463–472.

Charmont, La renaissance du droit naturel (1910) — see Modern French Legal Philosophy, §§ 43–103, for translation of part of this book — §§ 78–103 are important in the present connection; Haines, The Revival of Natural Law Concepts, chap. 10.

Beudant, Le droit individuel et l'état (1891, 3 ed. 1920); II Gény, Science et technique en droit privé positif, §§ 134–140, 177; Demogue, Notions fondamentales du droit privé, 21–22; Leroy, Le temps présent et l'idée du droit social (1932) Archives de philosophie du droit et de sociologie juridique, 215–228; Gurvitch, Le temps présent et l'idée du droit social (1931).

See Jung, Das Problem des natürlichen Rechts (1912).

There are two outstanding types: (1) neo-scholastic, (2) positivist-sociological.

(1) Neo-scholastic.

François Gény (1861–). See bibliography, *post*, 203.

Wortley, François Gény, in Modern Theories of Law, 139–159; Saleilles, Preface to Gény, Méthode d'interprétation (1 ed.) i–xiii; Gény, Méthode d'interprétation (1 ed.) 1–44, 174–175, 178–205, 456–473; id. Science et technique en droit privé positif, I, 11–21, II, 1–20, III, 1–31, IV, 142–157.

See Saleilles, L'école historique et droit naturel d'après quelques ouvrages récents, 1 Revue trimestrielle de droit civil, 80, 89–90.

Compare with Gény, Dabin, La philosophie de l'ordre juridique, 254–397.

Compare the suggestion of a neo-Aristotelian jurisprudence: Adler, Legal Certainty, 31 Columbia L. Rev. 91 (1931); Hutchins, Legal Education, 4 Univ. of Chicago L. Rev. 357 (1937).

(2) Positivist-sociological.

Léon Duguit (1859–1928). See bibliography, *post*, 203.

Laski, Introduction to Duguit, Law in the Modern State, ix–xxxiv; Stone, Review of Durkheim, The Division of Labor in Society (transl. by Simpson) 47 Harv. L. Rev. 1450; Laski, M. Duguit's Conception of the State, in Modern Theories of Law, 52–68.

Duguit, L'état, le droit objectif, et la loi positive, chaps. 1–2 (transl. in Modern French Legal Philosophy, 258–359); id. Les transformations générales du droit privé depuis le Code Napoléon, 24–29 (transl. in XI Continental Legal History Series, Progress of Continental Law in the Nineteenth Century, 65–146); id. Law and the State, 31 Harv. L. Rev. 180; Jordan, Forms of Individuality, chaps. 5–9.

Critiques of Duguit: II Gény, Science et technique en droit privé positif, 190–272; Allen, Law in the Making, 336–348 (2 ed. 351–362, 3 ed. 482–494); Spencer, Editorial Preface to Modern French Legal Philosophy, pp. xliv–xlvii; Bonnard, Léon Duguit, ses oeuvres, sa doctrine (1929); Bonnecase, La pensée juridique française, I, 348–588, II, 225–261; Bonnard, Les idées de L. Duguit sur les valeurs sociales (1932) Archives de philosophie du droit et de sociologie juridique, 1; Réglade, Théorie générale du droit dans l'oeuvre de Léon Duguit (1932) Archives de philosophie du droit et de sociologie juridique, 21; Politis, L'influence de la doctrine de L. Duguit sur le développement du droit international, id. 69; Jèze, L'influence de L. Duguit sur le droit administratif français, id. 135; Morin, L'oeuvre de Duguit et le droit privé, id. 153; Mestre, Remarques sur le notion de propriété d'après Duguit, id. 163; Le Fur, Le fondement de droit dans la doctrine de L. Duguit, id. 175; Ionescu, Léon Duguit et le droit subjectif, id. 269.

Comparisons of Duguit and Kelsen: Bonnard, La doctrine de Duguit sur le droit et l'état, 1 Revue internationale de la théorie du droit, 18; Kunz, Die Rechts- und Staatslehre Léon Duguits, id. 140, 204; Davy, Le problème de l'obligation chez Duguit et chez Kelsen (1933) Archives de philosophie du droit et de sociologie juridique, 7; Scheuner, Dynamik und Statik in der Staatsrechtslehre, eine Untersuchung zur Staats- und Rechtstheorie Léon Duguits und Hans Kelsens, 3 Revue internationale de la théorie du droit, 220.

(g) In different forms, the revived natural law has recently become strong on the Continent generally.

(1) In Germany since 1920.

i. In public law.

Mattern, The Constitutional Jurisprudence of the German Republic, 614–635; Anschutz und Thoma, II Handbuch des deutschen Staatsrechts (1932) 137–159;

Jellinek, Grenzen des Verfassungsgesetzgebung (1931); Leibholz, Les tendences actuelles du droit public en Allemagne (1931) Archives de philosophie du droit et de sociologie juridique, 207–224; Mainzer, Gleichheit vor dem Gesetz, Gerechtigkeit und Recht (1929); I Hölscher, Sittliche Rechtslehre (1928) 287–300. See the letter of the German judges to the government in 1924, Juristische Wochenschrift (1924) 90.

ii. In private law.

Hedemann, Die Flucht in Generalklausen (1933); I Hölscher, Sittliche Rechtslehre (1928) §§ 25–33; Von Bieberstein, Vom Kampf des Rechts gegen die Gesetze (1927) 1–21; Darmstaedter, Rechtsstaat oder Machtstaat, Archiv für Rechts- und Wirthschaftsphilosophie, beiheft no. 26.
See also the commentaries on §§ 242, 826 of the German Civil Code.

(2) In Italy.

Perticone, Die italienische Rechtsphilosophie im letzten Vierteljahrhundert, XXIII Archiv für Rechts- und Wirthschaftsphilosophie, 275; Carlo, Il diritto naturale nell' attuale fase del pensiero italiano (1932).

(3) In Spain.

Mendizábal y Martin, El indestructible derecho natural, in II Studi Filosofico-Giuridici Dedicati a Giorgio Del Vecchio, 100.
See also Mendizábal y Martin, Tratado de derecho natural (7 ed. revised by Mendizábal Villalba 3 vols. 1928–1931).

(4) In America recently — ethical-rationalist.

Cohen, Law and the Social Order, bk. III, Law and Reason, 165–247 (1933, but reprint of papers published 1914, 1915, 1916, 1927, 1932).

(h) Of late there is a clear tendency toward synthesis of the social-philosophical approaches.

Gény, La notion de droit en France (1933) Archives de philosophie du droit et de sociologie juridique 9–41. See also the comparative studies referred to under Stammler and Duguit.

Swoboda, Das Privatrecht der Zukunft, XXV Archiv für Rechts- und Wirthschaftsphilosophie, 458, 470–472 (the same paper in Italian, Il diritto civile dell' avvenire, 10 Rivista internazionale di filosofia del diritto, 333) — neo-Kantian and neo-Hegelian; Sauer, Lehrbuch der Rechts- und Sozialphilosophie (1929) 101–122; id. Stand- und Zukunftsaufgaben der Rechtsphilosophie, XXVI Archiv für Rechts- und Wirthschaftsphilosophie (1933) 3–10, 17, 20, 23; Petrashek, System der Rechtsphilosophie (1932) — neo-Kantian, neo-scholastic, and neo-Hegelian; Edlin, Rechtsphilosophische Scheinprobleme (1932), vorwort, v–vi (beiheft No. 27 to XXVI Archiv für Rechts- und Wirthschaftsphilosophie); Sauer, Die Wirklichkeit des Rechts, XXII Archiv für Rechts- und Wirthschaftsphilosophie, 1, 1–4. See also the observations on Chicherin's philosophy of law in Laserson, Russische Rechtsphilosophie, XXVI Archiv für Rechts- und Wirthschaftsphilosophie, 289, 300–302 — neo-Hegelian, neo-Kantian.

THE PHILOSOPHICAL SCHOOLS COMPARED

Law-of-Nature	Metaphysical	Social-Philosophical
Sought to deduce a complete system of principles, of universal validity, from the nature of man in the abstract, and to develop these principles into an all-sufficient code of legal rules.	Sought to deduce from some single fundamental idea a complete system of principles of universal validity to which jurists should endeavor to make the actual law conform.	Studies the ideal element of the actual law and seeks materials for criticism, for constructive law-making, and for guidance of judicial and administrative determinations, on the basis of some form of social philosophy.

THE TYPES OF THE SOCIAL-PHILOSOPHICAL SCHOOL

	Social-Utilitarians	Neo-Kantians	Neo-Hegelians
Tendency	Analytical and social-philosophical	Critical-logical and sociological	Historical and sociological
Leading Representative	Rudolf von Jhering (1818–1892)	Rudolf Stammler (1856–1938)	Josef Kohler (1849–1919)
Achievements	(1) Overthrow of the "jurisprudence of conceptions." (2) Insistence upon the interests which the legal system secures rather than upon the rights by which it secures them. (3) The theory of punishment as something to be adjusted to the criminal rather than to the nature of the crime. (4) Recognition in recent Continental thought of the imperative idea of law. (5) Giving us a theory of the administrative element in the legal order.	(1) Turning attention from the relation of morals and ethics to abstract rules and directing it to the relation of these matters to the administration of justice through rules. (2) The theory of the social ideal as the criterion of justice through rules. (3) Adding a theory of the just decision of causes to the theory of making just rules. (4) Giving us a theory of the application of legal precepts.	(1) The theory of law as the product of the civilization of a people. (2) The theory of the relation of comparative legal history and the philosophy of law. (3) Theory of the sociological interpretation and application of legal rules. (4) The method of formulating the jural postulates of the civilization of the time and place.

V. REALIST SCHOOLS

1. Introductory excursus — Interpretations of Legal History.

Pound, Interpretations of Legal History, lects. 2–5; Simkhovitch, Approaches to History, 44 Political Science Q. 481, 45 id. 481, 47 id. 410, 48 id. 23.

(a) Interpretations of history.

See Seligman, The Economic Interpretation of History (2 ed.); Small, General Sociology, 44–62; Shotwell, History of History, chap. 27; Barth, Die Philosophie der Geschichte als Soziologie, 200–346 (2 ed. 483–809, 3 and 4 ed. 511–856). For the religious interpretation see Belloc, History of England. For the geographical interpretation see Semple, Influences of Geographic Environment (1911); Febure, A Geographical Introduction to History (transl. by Mountford and Paxton 1925) with full bibliography. For the ethnological interpretation see Pittard, Race and History (transl. by Collum 1926) with full bibliography; Gumplowicz, Der Rassenkampf (1883). For the economic interpretation see Patten, The Development of English Thought, a Study in the Economic Interpretation of History (1899); Croce, Historical Materialism and the Economics of Karl Marx, chap. 2; Levi, Un' interpretazione del materialismo storico, 22 Rivista di filosofia, 185.

(b) Interpretations of jurisprudence and legal history.

(1) Idealistic interpretations.

II Vinogradoff, Collected Papers, 320–325.

i. Ethical.

Hastie, Outlines of Jurisprudence, 152–153 (transl. of Friedländer, Juristische Enzyklopädie, 65).

ii. Religious.

II Stahl, Philosophie des Rechts (5 ed.) § 5, p. 4; Felix, Der Einfluss der Religion auf die Entwicklung des Eigenthums (1889) — chap. I is translated in Kocourek and Wigmore, Formative Influences in Legal Evolution; De Zulueta, The Girard Testimonial Essays, 30 L. Q. Rev. 214, 216–217; Pound, The Spirit of the Common Law, lect. 2. See also Albertsworth, Current Religious Thought and Modern Juristic Movements, 34 Internat. Journ. of Ethics, 364; Draghiescu, Droit, morale, et religion (1933) Archives de philosophie du droit et de sociologie juridique, 229–245; Weber, Die protestantische Ethik und der Geist der Kapitalismus, 20 Archiv für Sozialwissenschaft und Sozialpolitik, 1–54, 21 id. 1–110; Roberti (and others) Christianesimo e diritto romano; Pound, The Church in Legal History (1939) in Jubilee Law Lectures of Catholic University of America, 3–97; id. Law and Religion (1940) 27 The Rice Institute Pamphlet, 109–172.

iii. Political.

Lorimer, Institutes of Law (2 ed.) 353–356; Hastie, Outlines of Jurisprudence, 5, 7, 24–28 (Puchta, Cursus der Institutionen, §§ 2, 3, 9); Maine, Ancient Law, last two paragraphs of chap. 5.

(2) Geographical interpretations.

Randall, Law and Geography, III Evolution of Law Series, Formative Influences of Legal Development, 198–214; Semple, The Influences of Geographic Environment on Law, State, and Society, id. 215–233 (extracts from Influences of Geographic Environment); Declareuil, Histoire du droit français (1895) chap. 1; Langhans-Ratzeburg, Begriff und Aufgaben der geographischen Rechtswissenschaft, beiheft to Zeitschrift für Geopolitik (1928).

(3) Ethnological interpretations.
i. Idealistic.

I Jhering, Geist des römischen Rechts, § 19; Muirhead, Historical Introduction to the Private Law of Rome, § 1. But see I Voigt, Römische Rechtsgeschichte, § 2; I Cuq, Institutions juridiques des Romains, 29–30; I Kuhlenbeck, Entwicklungsgeschichte des römischen Rechts, 31–40. Compare Hegel, Grundlinien der Philosophie des Rechts, §§ 346–347 (Dyde's transl. 343–344).

ii. Psychological.

Carle, La vita del diritto (2 ed.) bk. V; Fouillée, L'idée moderne du droit (6 ed.) bk. I, introduction and chap. 5 (Modern French Legal Philosophy, §§ 1–45); Duquesne, Sur l'esprit du peuple allemand comme source d'origine du droit allemand in Introduction à l'étude du droit comparé (Recueil d'études en honneur d'Edouard Lambert) pt. V, § 150, pp. 225–239.

iii. Positivist.

Post, Die Grundlagen des Rechts, 8–9.
For critique, see Tourtoulon, Principes philosophiques de l'histoire du droit, 89–131 (Philosophy in the Development of Law, 84–95). See also Lowie, Anthropology and Law, in Ogburn and Goldenweiser, The Social Sciences, 50–57; Mazzarella, La concezione etnologica della legislazione, 6 Rivista internazionale di filosofia del diritto, 520–634; Riemann, Rasse und Recht, 35 Zeitschrift für Geschichtliche Staatswissenschaft, 273; Trimborn, Die Methode der ethnologischen Rechtsforschung, 43 Zeitschrift für vergleichende Rechtswissenschaft, 416.

(4) The economic interpretation.

On another side the same movement that led to the social-philosophical schools led to the economic interpretation — a method which had for a time much vogue, without at first giving us any general treatises on jurisprudence or a general school of jurists.

Loria, Economic Foundations of Law, III Evolution of Law Series, Formative Influences of Legal Development, 234–266 (Keasbey's transl. Economic Foundations of Society, 73–114); Pound, The Economic Interpretation and the Law of Torts, 53 Harv. L. Rev. 365.

Follett, Creative Experience, 257–258; Hocking, Man and the State, 280–299; Hale, Economics and Law, in Ogburn and Goldenweiser, The Social Sciences, 131–142; Cairns, Law and the Social Sciences, chap. 3, especially pp. 121–122; Commons, Value in Law and Economics, in II Law: A Century of Progress (N. Y. Univ. publication) 232.

i. Idealistic — the realization of an economic idea.

Croce, The Philosophy of Hegel, 201–202; Capograssi, Le glosse di Marx a Hegel, I Studi Filosofico-Giuridici Dedicati a Giorgio Del Vecchio, 54; Rappaport, Die Marxistische Rechtsauffassung; Kelsen, Allgemeine Rechtslehre im Lichte materialistischer Geschichtsauffassung, 66 Archiv für Sozialwissenschaft und Sozialpolitik, 449.

ii. Mechanical-positivist.

Centralization and the Law, 23, 31–35, 63–64, 132–133; Adams, The Modern Conception of Animus, 19 Green Bag, 12, 17, 32–33. See Bohlen, Studies in the Law of Torts, 344, 368–377, reprinted from 59 U. Pa. L. Rev. 298, 318–325. For critiques see Stammler, Sozialismus und Christentum (1920) 58–69; Croce, Riduzione della filosofia del diritto alla filosofia dell' economia (1907); Burdick, Is Law the Expression of Class Selfishness? 25 Harv. L. Rev. 349; Laski, Studies in Law and Politics, 276 ff.; id. Review of Coker, Recent Political Thought, 43 Yale L. J. 1200, 1201–1202; Albertsworth, Cases on Industrial Law, 1–5.

As to "class struggle" see Sulzbach, Class and Class Struggle (1940) 6 Journ. of Social Philosophy, 22.

iii. Realist.

See II Berolzheimer, System der Rechts- und Wirthschaftsphilosophie, § 40 (The World's Legal Philosophies, 298–307); Bohlen, Old Phrases and New Facts, 83 U. Pa. L. Rev. 305, 306–307.

In connection with extreme economic interpretations reference may be made to: Machen, Do the Incorporation Laws Allow Sufficient Freedom to Commercial Enterprise? (1909) 14 Rep. Maryland Bar Assn. 78, 81–84, 85, 87–89; People v. Shedd, 241 Ill. 155, 161–162, 163, 165–167 (1909); Chorley, The Conflict of Law and Commerce, 48 L. Q. Rev. 51; W. N. Hillas & Co. Ltd. v. Arcos Ltd., 36 Commercial Cases, 353; May & Butcher v. The King, unreported, discussed in W. N. Hillas & Co. Ltd. v. Arcos Ltd., *supra*, at pp. 366–368; Fanton v. Denville [1932] 2 K. B. 309.

(5) Conceivably, a great-lawyer interpretation.

Pound, Interpretations of Legal History, 124–140; Frankfurter, Mr. Justice Brandeis, 49–50.

2. Economic determinism.

On determinism in jurisprudence generally see Tourtoulon, Principes philosophiques de l'histoire du droit, 658–680 (English transl. as Philosophy in the Development of Law, 567–586).

Beard, An Economic Interpretation of the Constitution of the United States (1935 ed.) 14–18, 156 ff.; Hazard, Soviet Law — An Introduction (1936) 36 Columbia L. Rev. 1236; Pound, Fifty Years of Jurisprudence (1938) 51 Harv. L. Rev. 777, 779–800.

Paschukanis, Allgemeine Rechtslehre und Marxismus (transl. from Russian 3 ed. 1929); Stucka, La fonction révolutionnaire du droit et de l'état (3 ed. 1924); id. Introduction à la théorie du droit civil (1927); Dobrin, Soviet Jurisprudence and Socialism, 52 L. Q. Rev. 402; Gsovski, The Soviet Concept of Law, 7 Fordham L. Rev. 1.

See also *supra* the mechanical-positivist economic interpretation.

3. Psychological realism.

Frank, Law and the Modern Mind (1930) 1–203, 243–252; Robinson, Law and the Lawyers (1935) 1–19, 46–121, 284–323; Arnold, The Symbols of Government (1935) 1–104, 199–288.

See Mechem, The Jurisprudence of Despair (1936) 21 Iowa L. Rev. 669; Arnold, The Jurisprudence of Edward S. Robinson (1937) 46 Yale L. J. 1282.

Cf. Moore, An Institutional Approach to the Law of Commercial Banking (1929) 38 Yale L. J. 703.

See *infra* skeptical neo-realism.

4. Skeptical neo-realism.

Llewellyn, The Bramble Bush (1930) 3; id. A Realistic Jurisprudence — The Next Step (1930) 30 Columbia L. Rev. 431; id. Some Realism About Realism (1931) 44 Harv. L. Rev. 1222; Goodhart, Some American Interpretations of Law (1933) in Modern Theories of Law, 7–20.

See Bingham, What is Law? (1912) 11 Mich. L. Rev. 1, 109; Llewellyn, Präjudizienrecht und Rechtsprechung in Amerika (1933) §§ 1–16; Pound, The Call for a Realist Jurisprudence (1931) 44 Harv. L. Rev. 697; Llewellyn, Legal Tradition and Social Science Method (1931) in Swann (and others) Research in the Social Sciences, 89; Frank, What Courts Do in Fact (1932) 26 Illinois L. Rev. 645; id. Are Judges Human? (1931) 80 U. Pa. L. Rev. 17, 233; Hutcheson, The Judgment Intuitive (1928) 14 Cornell L. Q. 274; Yntema, Rational Basis of Legal Thinking (1931) 31 Columbia L. Rev. 925; Radin, Legal Realism (1931) 31 Columbia L. Rev. 824; Arnold, The Role of Substantive Law and Procedure in the Legal Process (1932) 45 Harv. L. Rev. 615; Frank, Mr. Justice Holmes and Non-Euclidean Legal Thinking (1932) 14 Cornell L. Q. 568; Goble, Law as a Science (1934) 9 Ind. L. Rev. 295; Beutel, Some Implications of Experimental Jurisprudence (1934) 48 Harv. L. Rev. 169; Marx, Juristischer Realismus in den Vereinigten Staaten von Amerika (1936) 10 Revue internationale de la théorie du droit, 28; F. Cohen, Transcendental Nonsense and the Functional Approach (1935) 35 Columbia L. Rev. 809.

See also Cohen, Law and the Social Order, 219–247; id. On Absolutisms in Legal Thought (1936) 84 U. Pa. L. Rev. 681; Dickinson, Legal Rules: Their

Function in the Process of Decision, Their Application and Elaboration (1931) 79 id. 832, 1052; Fuller, American Legal Realism (1934) 82 id. 429; Kantorowicz, Some Rationalism About Realism (1934) 43 Yale L. J. 1240; Harris, Idealism Emergent in Jurisprudence (1934) 10 Tulane L. Rev. 169; Cardozo, Address Before the New York State Bar Assn. (1932) 55 Rep. N. Y. State Bar Assn. 263; Friedrich, Remarks on Llewellyn's View of Law, Official Behavior, and Political Science (1935) 50 Political Science Q. 419; Kennedy, Principles or Facts (1935) 4 Fordham L. Rev. 53; id. Functional Nonsense and the Transcendental Approach (1936) 5 id. 272; id. Realism, What Next? (1938) 7 id. 203.

Lundstedt, Superstition or Rationality in Action for Peace? (1925) 96–119; id. Die Unwissenschaftlichkeit der Rechtswissenschaft (1932–1936); id. The General Principles of Civil Liability in Different Legal Systems (1934) 2^{II} Acta Academiae Universalis Jurisprudentiae Comparativae, 367.

5. Positivist logical realism.

Cook, Scientific Method and the Law (1927) 13 Am. Bar Assn. J. 303; id. The Possibilities of Social Study as a Science (1931) in Swann (and others) Research in the Social Sciences, 27; id. A Scientific Approach to the Study of Law (1937) in Essays in Political Science in Honor of W. W. Willoughby, 201.

> See also Cook, The Logical and Legal Bases of the Conflict of Laws (1924) 33 Yale L. J. 457; Dimock, Le professeur W. W. Cook et le relativisme juridique (1932) Archives de philosophie du droit et de sociologie juridique, 575 — contains a bibliography of Professor Cook's writings.
> Cf. Rueff, From the Physical to the Social Sciences (transl. by Green 1929); Oliphant, Facts, Opinions, and Value Judgments (1932) 10 Texas L. Rev. 127.

VI. SOCIOLOGICAL JURISPRUDENCE

Pound, The Scope and Purpose of Sociological Jurisprudence, 25 Harv. L. Rev. 489; id. The Need of a Sociological Jurisprudence, 19 Green Bag, 107; Amos, Roscoe Pound, in Modern Theories of Law, 86–105; Kantorowicz, Rechtswissenschaft und Soziologie, 1–15, 21–30, 30–34; Tanon, L'évolution du droit et la conscience sociale (3 ed.) 143–176, 196–202; Brugeilles, Le droit et la sociologie, introduction and chaps. 1, 2, 6; Van der Eycken, Méthode positive de l'interprétation, 109–112; Rolin, Prolégomènes à la science du droit, 1–9; Ehrlich, Erforschung des lebenden Rechts, 35 Schmoller's Jahrbuch für Gesetzgebung, 129; id. Fundamental Principles of the Sociology of Law (transl. by Moll) chap. 21; Page, Professor Ehrlich's Czernowitz Seminar of Living Law, Proceedings of Fourteenth Annual Meeting of the Association of American Law Schools, 46; Cardozo, The Nature of the Judicial Process, lects. 2–3; Pound,

Sociology and Law, in Ogburn and Goldenweiser, The Social Sciences, 319–328; Keyser, On the Study of Legal Science, 38 Yale L. J. 418.

The sociological school arose, under the influence of the positivist philosophy, as another phase of the movement considered under III and IV, *supra*.

The forerunner is Montesquieu (1689–1755).

See II Continental Legal History Series, Great Jurists of the World, 417–446; Ehrlich, Montesquieu and Sociological Jurisprudence, 29 Harv. L. Rev. 582.

1. The mechanical stage.

For critiques, see II Berolzheimer, System der Rechts- und Wirthschaftsphilosophie, § 44 (The World's Legal Philosophies, 351–374); Charmont, La renaissance du droit naturel, chap. 5 (Modern French Legal Philosophy, 65–73); Korkunov, General Theory of Law (transl. by Hastings) 265–266; Francis, The Domicile of a Corporation, 38 Yale L. J. 335, 335–339.

2. The biological stage.

Post, Der Ursprung des Rechts, 7; Richard, Origine de l'idée de droit, 5, 54–55; Vaccaro, Les bases sociologiques du droit et de l'état, 450–452.

For critiques, see II Berolzheimer, System der Rechts- und Wirthschaftsphilosophie, §§ 47, 51 (The World's Legal Philosophies, 387–391, 456–466); Tourtoulon, Principes philosophiques de l'histoire du droit, 80–88, 132–173 (Philosophy in the Development of Law, 76–83, 96–133); Cairns, Law and Anthropology, 31 Columbia L. Rev. 32; Cairns, Law and the Social Sciences, chap 2.

3. The psychological stage.
Gabriel Tarde (1843–1904).

II Berolzheimer, System der Rechts- und Wirthschaftsphilosophie, § 49 (The World's Legal Philosophies, 431–446); Tarde, Les transformations du droit; Tourtoulon, Principes philosophiques de l'histoire du droit, 174–253 (Philosophy in the Development of Law, 134–211); Tanon, L'évolution du droit et la conscience sociale (3 ed.) 143–176; Allen, Law in the Making (2 ed. 59–69, 3 ed. 98–106).

I Gierke, Deutsche Genossenschaftsrecht, 1; Gierke, Das Wesen der menschlichen Verbände, 33–34; id. Die Genossenschaftstheorie und die deutsche Rechtssprechung, 10 ff.; id. Die Grundbegriffe des Staatsrecht und die neueste Staatstheorien, 30 Zeitschrift für die gesammte Staatsrechtswissenschaft, 304; Mogi, Otto von Gierke.

Ward, Dynamic Sociology, I, 468–472, 704–706, II, 11–17; id. The Psychic Factors of Civilization, 120; id. Applied Sociology, 13.

Tarde, Laws of Imitation (transl. by Parsons) 2–3, 11–13, 14–15, 310–320.

Brugeilles, Le droit et la sociologie, chap. 6.

Legal method: Science of Legal Method (9 Modern Legal Philosophy Series); Les méthodes juridiques (lectures by French jurists, 1910); Wurzel, Das juristische Denken; Bozi, Die Weltanschauung der Jurisprudenz; Cardozo, The Nature of the Judicial Process, lect. 4.

Since 1920 there has been a renewed emphasis on this approach and important applications have been made.

Hauriou, La théorie de l'institution et de la fondation (1925); Renard, La théorie de l'institution (1930); Jennings, The Institutional Theory (1933) in Modern Theories of Law, 68–85; Gurvitch, L'idée du droit social (1932) 1–46, 535–567.

Gény, La notion de droit (1931) Archives de philosophie du droit et de sociologie juridique, 9, 33–41; Morin, Vers la révision de la technique juridique, id. 73; Delos, La théorie de l'institution, id. 97; Gurvitch, Les idées maîtresses de Maurice Hauriou, id. 155; Hallis, Corporate Personality, 217–238; Jerusalem, Soziologie des Rechts (1925).

In the United States, cf. *supra*, "Psychological determinism." See also Cohen, Justice Holmes and the Nature of Laws, 31 Columbia L. Rev. 352, 357–359; Llewellyn, The Constitution as an Institution, 34 Columbia L. Rev. 1, 28–31.

A logical-psychological intuitionist form of this psychological sociology of law is to be seen in the work of Leo Petrazycki (1864–1931). For the most part his writings are accessible only in Russian or Polish.

Petrazycki, Methodologie der Theorien des Rechts und der Moral (1933) in Opera Academiae Universalis Jurisprudentiae Comparativae, Series II, Studia, Fasciculus 2; id. Ueber die Motive des Handelns und über das Wesen der Moral und des Rechts (1907 — transl. from the Russian by Balson); Meyendorff, Leo Petrazycki (1933) in Modern Theories of Law, 21–37.

For critiques of Petrazycki, see Grouber, Une théorie psychologique du droit (1912) 10 Revue trimestrielle de droit civil, 531; Gurvitch, Une philosophie intuitioniste du droit (1931) Archives de philosophie du droit et de sociologie juridique, 403–420; Laserson, Russische Rechtsphilosophie (1933) XXVI Archiv für Rechts- und Wirthschaftsphilosophie, 289, 324–330; Cornil, À propos d'un livre posthume de L. Petrazycki (1934) Archives de philosophie du droit et de sociologie juridique, 180–196.

Compare with Petrazycki, Stoop, Analyse de la notion du droit (1927).

4. The stage of unification.

Pound, Social Control through Law; Cairns, Law and the Social Sciences; Roguin, La règle de droit, 8; Van der Eycken, Méthode positive de l'interprétation, 112; Kantorowicz, Rechtswissenschaft und Soziologie, 8; Brugeilles, Le droit et la sociologie, 160 ff.; Richard, La philosophie du droit et de sociologie en Angleterre (1932) Archives de philosophie du droit et de sociologie juridique, 377.

The Principal Schools of Jurists Compared

	Analytical	Historical	Philosophical	Sociological
I. What element in the complex we call law and what kind of system of social control do they regard?	Consider developed systems only; and regard only the precept element.	Consider all social control; consider the past rather than the present of law; or the present through the past only.	Seek to understand, organize, and criticize the ideal element in law; seek ideal standards by which to criticize law and direct lawmaking.	Consider the working of law more than its abstract content.
II. How do they answer the question as to the nature of law? How do they answer the question how law comes into existence?	Regard law as something made consciously by lawgivers, legislative or judicial; postulate bodies of law such as Justinian's codification or the Code Napoléon.	Regard law as something that is not and in the long run cannot be made consciously.	Agree with the historical jurist that law is not made, but is found. Find the binding force of a legal precept in its expression of a principle of right and justice.	Regard law as a social institution which may be improved by intelligent human effort, and hold it their duty to discover the best means of furthering and directing such effort.
III. How do they answer the question what makes law obligatory? What do they take to be the source of the authority of law? What do they hold gives efficacy to the legal order?	See chiefly the force and constraint behind legal rules; conceive that the sanction of law is enforcement by the judicial organs of the state, and that nothing which lacks an enforcing agency is law.	See chiefly the social pressure behind legal rules; find sanction in habits of obedience, displeasure of one's fellow-men, public sentiment or opinion, or the social standard of justice.	Look at the ethical bases of rules rather than at their sanction.	Lay stress upon the social purposes which law subserves rather than upon sanction; regard means of making legal precepts effective in action as one of the problems of legal science.
IV. What form of legal precept do they take as the type?	Take statute as the typical law.	Take custom or those customary modes of decision that make up a body of juristic tradition or of case law as the type of law.	Have no necessary preference for any form of law.	Look upon legal institutions, precepts, and doctrines functionally and regard the form as a matter of means only.
V. What are their philosophical views?	Their philosophical views are utilitarian or teleological.	As a rule they have been Hegelians.	Hold very diverse philosophical views. In the XIX century Hegelians or Krauseans. Today some form of the Social-Philosophical School.	Their philosophical views are very diverse. Chiefly they are (a) Social-Philosophical of one type or another, (b) Positivists, (c) Pragmatists.

Vinogradoff, The Crisis of Modern Jurisprudence, 29 Yale L. J. 312.

Ward, Pure Sociology, 12–14; Small, General Sociology, 91; id. The Meaning of Social Science, 87.

Pound, Interpretations of Legal History, 116–140, 151–165.

Aronson, Cardozo's Doctrine of Sociological Jurisprudence (1938) 4 Journ. of Social Philosophy, 5.

5. Since the first world war, the dominant neo-Kantian thinking has made itself felt in sociology in a preoccupation with logical methodology.

Rueff, From the Physical to the Social Sciences (transl. by Green, and Introduction by Oliphant and Hewitt); Keyser, Thinking about Thinking; Michael and Adler, Crime, Law, and Social Science (1933) and the symposium thereon by Ruml, Llewellyn, and McKeon, 33 Columbia L. Rev. 273.

Dunkmann, Lehrbuch der Soziologie und Sozialphilosophie (1931); Horváth, Rechtssoziologie (1934); Sauer, Persönlichkeit und Werk, XXIII Archiv für Rechts- und Wirthschaftsphilosophie, 411–442; Seidler, Die sozialwissenschaftliche Erkenntniss; Jordan, Forms of Individuality (1927) 17–40, 61–80.

The social sciences have to do with techniques for the invention of more useful patterns to be followed in the shaping and control of human behavior. — Allport, Social Psychology and Human Values, 38 Internat. Journ. of Ethics, 369, 373–374.

6. Sociology of law.

Pound, Fifty Years of Jurisprudence, 51 Harv. L. Rev. 777, 809–811.

See also Pound, Preface to Gurvitch, Sociology of Law (1942).

THE PROGRAMME OF THE SOCIOLOGICAL SCHOOL

Sociological jurists insist upon eight points:

(a) Study of the actual social effects of legal institutions, legal precepts, and legal doctrines.

Ehrlich, Grundlegung der Soziologie des Rechts, chap. 21 (transl. by Moll as Fundamental Principles of the Sociology of Law, 486–506); id. Die Erforschung des lebenden Rechts, 35 Schmoller's Jahrbuch für Gesetzgebung, 190; id. Das lebende Recht der Völker von Bukowina (1913); Page, Professor Ehrlich's Czernowitz Seminar of Living Law, Proceedings of Fourteenth Annual Meeting of the Association of American Law Schools, 46; Kantorowicz, Rechtswissenschaft und Soziologie, 7–8; Van der Eycken, Méthode positive de l'interprétation (1907) 109; Moore and Sussman, Legal and Institutional Methods Applied to the Debiting of Direct Discounts, 40 Yale L. J. 380, 555, 752, 928, 1054; Douglas, Vicarious Liability and Administration of Risk, 38 Yale L. J. 584, 720; Schoene and Watson, Workmen's Compensation on Interstate Railways (1934) 47 Harv. L. Rev. 389; Fortas, Wage Assignments in Chicago (1933) 42

Yale L. J. 526; Hamilton, In re The Small Debtor (1933) id. 473; Nehemkis, The Boston Poor Debtor Court — A Study in Collection Procedure (1933) id. 561; Clark, Douglas and Thomas, The Business Failures Project — A Problem in Methodology (1930) 39 Yale L. J. 1013; Douglas and Thomas, The Business Failures Project — An Analysis of Methods of Investigation (1931) 40 id. 1034; Douglas, Some Functional Aspects of Bankruptcy (1932) 41 id. 329; Marshall and May, The Divorce Court, vol. I, Maryland, vol. II, Ohio.

(b) Sociological study in preparation for lawmaking.

Kantorowicz, Rechtswissenschaft und Soziologie, 9; Tanon, L'évolution du droit et la conscience sociale (3 ed.) 196–198; Willcox, The Need of Social Statistics as an Aid to the Courts (1913); Oliphant, The Relation of Current Economic and Social Problems to the Restatement of the Law (reprint from Acad. Pol. Sci. N. Y. 1923); Douglas, Wage Earner Bankruptcies: State v. Federal Control, 42 Yale L. J. 591; Williston, Some Modern Tendencies in the Law (1929) 141–158.

(c) Study of the means of making legal precepts effective in action.

Pound, The Need of a Sociological Jurisprudence, 19 Green Bag, 607; id. Law in Books and Law in Action, 44 Am. L. Rev. 12; id. The Limits of Effective Legal Action, 27 Internat. Journ. of Ethics, 150; id. The Administration of Justice in the Modern City, 26 Harv. L. Rev. 302; Parry, The Law and the Poor, 248–249; Smith, Justice and the Poor (1919); Gurney-Champion, Justice and the Poor in England, chaps. 1–7; Maguire, The Lance of Justice (1928); Schramm, Piedpoudre Courts, a Study of the Small Claims Litigant in the Pittsburgh District (1928).

See, *post*, XX, 3; XX, 6.

(d) Study of juridical method: psychological study of the judicial, legislative, and juristic processes as well as philosophical study of the ideals.

Cardozo, The Nature of the Judicial Process (1921); id. The Growth of the Law, lect. 3; Pound, The Theory of Judicial Decision, 36 Harv. L. Rev. 641, 802, 940; Wigmore, Problems of Law, 65–101; Science of Legal Method, 9 Modern Legal Philosophy Series, especially Wurzel, Juridical Thinking, § 30, pp. 422–428; Morris, How Lawyers Think (1937); Isaacs, How Lawyers Think, 23 Columbia L. Rev. 555; Waite, Caveat Emptor and the Judicial Process, 25 Columbia L. Rev. 131; I Gény, Méthode d'interprétation (2 ed.) § 7; Les méthodes juridiques (lectures by a number of French jurists, 1911); Bozi, Die Weltanschauung der Jurisprudenz (2 ed. 1911); Hellwig, Zur Psychologie der richterlichen Urteilsfindung (1914); Ehrlich, Die juristische Logik (1918); Introduction by Oliphant and Hewitt to Rueff, From the Physical to the Social Sciences (transl. by Green); Moore and Sussman, The Lawyer's Law, 41 Yale L. J. 566; Keyser, The Nature of Doctrinal Function and its Rôle in Rational Thought, 41 Yale L. J. 713; Green, The Duty Problem in Negligence Cases, 38 Columbia L. Rev. 1014; Cook, Substance and Procedure, 42 Yale L. J. 333–336,

355–358; Cook, Scientific Method and the Law, 13 Am. Bar Assn. J. 303; Frank, Law and the Modern Mind; Ross, Theorie der Rechtsquellen.

See, *post*, XVII, D, 5, 6.

(e) A sociological legal history; study of the past social background and past social effects of legal institutions, legal precepts, and legal doctrines, and of how these effects were brought about.

Brugeilles, Le droit et la sociologie, 160; Kantorowicz, Rechtswissenschaft und Soziologie, 33–34; I Wigmore, Evidence, § 865; Salvioli, Storia del diritto italiano (8 ed. 1921) preface; Joüon des Longrais, La conception anglaise de la saisine (1925) 141–148.

(f) Recognition of the importance of individualized application of legal precepts — of reasonable and just solutions of individual cases.

Hollams, Jottings of an Old Solicitor, 160–162; Pound, Enforcement of Law, 20 Green Bag, 401; id. The Administrative Application of Legal Standards (1919) 44 Rep. Am. Bar Assn. 445; Gnaeus Flavius (Kantorowicz), Der Kampf um die Rechtswissenschaft; Kantorowicz, Rechtswissenschaft und Soziologie, 11 ff.; Llewellyn, Some Realism About Realism, 44 Harv. L. Rev. 1237, 1240–1241; Preface by Capitant and Lambert to Espèces choisis empruntés à la jurisprudence (2 ed.) 1, 27; Llewellyn, Legal Illusion, 31 Columbia L. Rev. 82, 87–90.

(g) In English-speaking countries, a ministry of justice.

IX Bentham, Works (Bowring ed.) 597–612; Ferri, Criminal Sociology (transl. by Morrison) 153; I Nash, Life of Lord Westbury, 191; Pound, Juristic Problems of National Progress, 22 Am. J. of Sociology, 721; id. Anachronisms in Law, 3 J. Am. Jud. Soc. 142, 146; Report of Lord Haldane's Committee on the Machinery of Government (1918); Cardozo, A Ministry of Justice, 35 Harv. L. Rev. 113; Pound, Criminal Justice in the American City, Criminal Justice in Cleveland, 605–606; Glueck, The Ministry of Justice and the Problem of Crime, 4 American Rev. 139; Reports of the Commission to Investigate Defects in the Law and its Administration, New York Legislative Documents, nos. 70 (1924), 74 (1925); Mullins, The Quest of Justice, 420–428; Yntema, Legal Science and Reform, 34 Columbia L. Rev. 207, 215–230; The Ministry of Justice and the Statute Law Commission, 5 Law Magazine and Review (2 ser.) 352; Clark, Reform in Bankruptcy Administration, 43 Harv. L. Rev. 1189, 1215; Willoughby, Principles of Judicial Administration, 264–280; Laski, A Grammar of Politics, 579–582; Pound, Judicial Councils and Judicial Statistics, 17 Tenn. L. Rev. 153–167, 28 Am. Bar Assn. J. 98–105; id. A Ministry of Justice (1942) 13 The Bar Bulletin of the City of Boston, 71–80.

For critique see I Birkenhead, Points of View, 92–130; Bacon, A Ministry of Justice, 22 Virginia L. Rev. 175.

(h) That the end of juristic study, toward which the foregoing are but some of the means, is to make effort more effective in achieving the purposes of law.

Kohler's Introduction in Rogge, Methodologische Vorstudien zu einer Kritik des Rechts, viii.

CHARACTERISTICS OF RECENT LEGAL SCIENCE

(a) The functional attitude.

Cohen, The Problems of a Functional Jurisprudence, 1 Modern L. Rev. 1.

(b) Study of law in relation to and as part of the whole process of social control.

(c) The movement for preventive justice.

Pound, Preventive Justice and Social Work, Proceedings of the National Conference of Social Work (1923) 151.
See, *post*, lect. XXXIII, 5(b, 3).

(d) The movement for individualization.

Gény, Méthode d'interprétation en droit privé positif (2 ed. 1919); Pound, Courts and Legislation, Science of Legal Method (9 Modern Legal Philosophy Series) 202–228; Science of Legal Method, chaps. i–v; Ransson, Essai sur l'art de juger (1912); Kantorowicz, Die Kampf um die Rechtswissenschaft (1906); Brütt, Die Kunst der Rechtsanwendung (1907); Saleilles, Individualization of Punishment (transl. by Mrs. Jastrow) chap. 9; Pound, Administrative Application of Legal Standards, 44 Rep. Am. Bar Assn. 445.
See, *ante*, p. 34(f).

(e) The movement for team work with the other social sciences.

See e.g. Columbia University Council for Research in the Social Sciences, Report by the Committee to Study Compensation for Automobile Accidents (1932).
But see, Banco de Portugal v. Waterlow [1932] A. C. 452, and Note in 49 L. Q. Rev. 11–12.
See also Kirsh, Trade Associations: The Legal Aspects (1928).
Compare the movement for unifying the social-philosophical and sociological approaches: Hubert, Science du droit, sociologie juridique et philosophie du droit (1931) Archives de philosophie du droit et de sociologie juridique, 43–71; Zissis, Soziologie und Rechtsphilosophie, 23 Archiv für Rechts und Sozialphilosophie, 1–20. Note the title of the recent Archives de philosophie du droit et de sociologie juridique.
Gurvitch, L'idée du droit social (1932) chap. 4; Piot, Droit naturel et réalisme (1930); LeFur, La théorie du droit naturel depuis le XVIIme siècle et la doctrine moderne, 18 Recueil de l'academie de droit internationale, 263, 353–399; Nast, Du rôle de l'autorité judiciaire, 3 Revue internationale de la théorie du droit, 145–183; id. Materialisme et idealisme juridique, 171–177; Kaufmann, Juristischer und soziologischer Rechtsbegriff, in (1931) Verdross, Staat, Gesellschaft, und Recht, 15.

(a) The valuing of interests.

See, *post,* lect. XV.

(b) The relation of law to administration.

Pound, Introduction to the Philosophy of Law, lect. 3; id. The Administrative
Application of Legal Standards, 44 Rep. A. Bar Assn. 445; Isaacs, The Limits of
Judicial Discretion, 32 Yale L. J. 339; von Laun, Das freie Ermessen und seine
Grenzen (1910); Pound, Administrative Law (1942) lect. I.
See, *post,* lect. XX.

(c) The limits of effective legal action.

See, *post,* lect. XV.

(d) The means of informing judges, jurists and lawmakers as to
the social facts involved in legislation and in the judicial finding,
shaping, and application of legal precepts.

In this connection reference should be made to the well-known briefs of Mr.
Justice Brandeis (when at the bar) in Muller v. Oregon, 208 U. S. 412 and
Ritchie v. Wayman, 244 Ill. 509.
See also the briefs filed by friends of the court in Adkins v. Children's Hospital,
262 U. S. 539 and opinion of Sutherland, J. at 559–560, and of Holmes, J. at
570–571; Brandeis, J. in Burns Baking Co. v. Bryan, 264 U. S. 502, 533–534;
People v. Schweinler Press, 214 N. Y. 395, 412–413. Compare on the Continent,
Sauer, Stand und Zukunftsaufgaben der Rechtsphilosophie, XXVI Archiv für
Rechts- und Wirthschaftsphilosophie, 3, 11–12.
See also Willcox, The Need of Social Statistics as an Aid to the Courts (1913);
Palfrey, The Constitution and the Courts, 26 Harv. L. Rev. 507, 525–530; Pound,
The Task of the American Lawyer, 20 Illinois L. Rev. 439; Glueck, The Social
Sciences and Scientific Method in the Administration of Justice (1933) 167
Annals of the American Academy of Political Science, 106; Galloway, The In-
vestigative Function of Congress, 21 Am. Political Science Rev. 47; Frankfurter,
Hours of Labor and Realism in Constitutional Law, 29 Harv. L. Rev. 353;
Frankfurter and Landis, The Business of the Supreme Court, 43 Harv. L. Rev.
33, 53–57; Beutel, Some Implications of Experimental Jurisprudence, 48 Harv.
L. Rev. 169.
Pound, Jurisprudence (1929) in Research in the Social Sciences (ed. by Gee)
181, 200–206; Holt, Due Process of Law (1926) chaps. 10–11; Landis, Constitutional Limitations on the Congressional Power of Investigation, 40 Harv. L. Rev.
153; Brown, Police Power, 42 Harv. L. Rev. 866, 897–898; Hurwitz and Mulli-
gan, The Legislative Investigating Committee, 33 Columbia L. Rev. 1.

(e) Improvement in the form of the law — "restatement," codification.

See, *post,* lect. XIX.

DEFINITIONS OF JURISPRUDENCE FOR DISCUSSION IN CONNECTION WITH THE FOREGOING

The formal science of positive law. — Holland, Elements of Jurisprudence (13 ed.) 13.

Scientific knowledge of the history and system of right (law). — I Puchta, Cursus der Institutionen, § 33.

The ultimate object of jurisprudence is the realization of the idea in the ideal of humanity, the attainment of human perfection, and this object is identical with the object of ethics. . . .

The proximate object of jurisprudence, the object which it seeks as a separate science (i.e. from ethics) is liberty. But liberty, being the perfect relation between human beings, becomes a means towards the realization of their perfection as human beings. Hence jurisprudence, in realizing its special or proximate object, becomes a means towards the realization of the ultimate object which it has in common with ethics. The relation in which jurisprudence stands to ethics is thus a subordinate one, the relation of species to genus. — Lorimer, Institutes of Law (2 ed.) 353, 355.

The science of the human will, in the distinction of the particular from the universal, and in the relation of the particular to the universal. — Herkless, Jurisprudence, 1.

Jurisprudence has for its subject law, that is, an aggregate of norms which determine the mutual relations of men living in a community. — Arndts, Juristische Encyklopädie, § 1.

Juristic encyclopedia, accordingly, is a systematic, unified survey of the means of peaceable adjustment of the external relations of mankind and social communities. — Gareis, Science of Law (transl. by Kocourek) 26.

It is at once a philosophy, a science, and an art. As a philosophy, its desire is to understand justice; as a science, its purpose is to explain the evolution of justice; as an art, its aim is to formulate those rules of conduct essential to the realization of justice. Conceived in this manner, jurisprudence forms the background of all associated activity; it provides the framework that limits and controls the exercise of liberty; it reflects the color and resounds the tone of those unconscious premises of action which give character to a civilization. The law is neither a schoolmaster for instruction nor a guardian for command; it is rather the expression of the ethical sense of a com-

munity crystallized about the problem of common living. — Adams,
Economics and Jurisprudence, 8.

The science of law in the wider sense is our whole knowledge of
law. But this knowledge is on the one hand practical, on the other
hand philosophical. Accordingly it may be divided into the science
of law in its narrower and more proper sense, called jurisprudence,
and the philosophy of law. — I Sternberg, Allgemeine Rechtslehre,
§ 12.

General theory of law investigates the formal (constructive) side
of fundamental juristic conceptions and legal institutions; the philosophy of law investigates their material kernel and basis. — II Berolzheimer, System der Rechts- und Wirthschaftsphilosophie, 20.

The Science of Justice as practiced in civilized nations. — Beale,
The Development of Jurisprudence during the Nineteenth Century,
I Select Essays in Anglo-American Legal History, 558.

The theory of law may set itself narrower or wider limits for its
task. Accordingly it is either jurisprudence in the narrower sense, or
philosophy of law.

In its narrower limitation, jurisprudence has to do primarily with
the immediate application of law, the carrying out of the existing
law, juristic technique. . . . It inquires only with respect to the law
as to which we can say that it obtains, that it is in force, that is, that
it is generally recognized as furnishing a measure for the events of
life, for legal transactions, for wrongs, for tax administration, for
acts of police, for affairs of international intercourse and the like.
In the modern state this is chiefly the written law. — Schmidt,
Einführung in das Recht (2 ed.) § 4.

The field of the science of law is not nature, but civilization. The
fundamental conception with which the jurist must work is not
causality, what must be, but freedom, what ought to be. The rules
with which the science of law has to do are not theoretical but practical, and the world which comes under its investigation is that of
ideas. — Binder, Philosophie des Rechts, 852.

Rule, idea, and life — jurisprudence has a share in all three of
these. It has for its subject-matter the imperative of the lawgiver, a
will, and so it is equally near to and far from the world of what ought
to be and of values and the world of what is practicable and of what
is. — Radbruch, Grundzüge der Rechtsphilosophie, 211.

Law is a social phenomenon, like religious, moral, political and economic phenomena. . . .

It is evident that there can be no question here of a science in the sense of the natural sciences. They have for their object the study of material things, and the phenomena of material things are their theatre. These things are animate or inanimate, and the role of natural science is to study their constitution and the forces of life which are active in them or upon them. Now the law looks upon man not as a material being submitted to physical laws of life, but as a thinking man, a reasonable man, creating rules to limit his activity for the profit of the activity of others. The law considers this faculty of moral order in man, which we call reason, which, so to speak, has inspired him to create the law. It is for this reason that we classify the science of law among the so-called moral sciences.

But the law looks upon man not only as a moral being, but as a social being living in the midst of a social group. Now there are beside the law other manifestations of social life which may be studied scientifically. There is a science of religions, a science of morals, a science of intellectual products, political science, economic science, a science of human groups. Law is no exception. . . . The science of law is part of the group of sciences called social since they study social life under its different aspects. — May, Introduction à l'étude du droit (2 ed.) 53–54.

PART 2

THE END OF LAW

VII. THE END OF LAW AS DEVELOPED IN LEGAL PRECEPTS AND DOCTRINES

1. Theories of justice.

Miller, The Data of Jurisprudence, chap. 6; Salmond, Jurisprudence, § 9; Pulszky, Theory of Law and Civil Society, § 173; Bentham, Theory of Legislation, Principles of the Civil Code, pt. I, chaps. 1–7; Holland, Jurisprudence, chap. 6.

Kant, Philosophy of Law (Hastie's transl.) 45–46 (§ C): Spencer, Justice, chaps. 5, 6; Willoughby, Social Justice, chap. 2; Sidgwick, The Methods of Ethics, chap. 5; Paulsen, Ethics (Thilly's transl.) chap. 9; Lotmar, Vom Rechte das mit uns geboren ist — Die Gerechtigkeit (1893); Gareis, Vom Begriff Gerechtigkeit; Demogue, Notions fondamentales du droit privé, 119–135; Picard, Le droit pur, liv. ix (le but de droit: la justice); Radbruch, Grundzüge der Rechtsphilosophie, 82–158 (3 ed. Rechtsphilosophie, §§ 7–9); Binder, Philosophie des Rechts (1 ed.) § 12; Vacca, Il diritto sperimentale, 163–189; Pound, Social Justice and Legal Justice, 75 Central L. J. 455; Duncan, The End and Aim of Law, 47 Juridical Rev. 154.

2. Development of the idea of the end of law in legal institutions, precepts and doctrines.

Pound, The End of Law as Developed in Legal Rules and Doctrines, 27 Harv. L. Rev. 195. See Leonhard's review transl. in 28 Harv. L. Rev. 337–339.

(a) Primitive law.

Not social control in primitive societies, but a more or less differentiated legal order which is primitive relatively to social control by systematic application of the force of a politically organized society as it has been known since the Roman law.

Holmes, The Common Law, lect. 1; Hartland, Primitive Law; Seagle, The Quest for Law (1941) 27–149.

II Post, Ethnologische Jurisprudenz, bk. iv; Fehr, Hammurapi und das Salisches Recht, 135–138; Hobhouse, Friede und Ordnung bei den primitivsten Völkern innerhalb der Gruppe, V Zeitschrift für Völkerpsychologie und Soziologie, 40; Hogbin, Law and Order in Polynesia, introduction by Malinowski (1934); Llewellyn and Hoebel, The Cheyenne Way (1941).

I Vinogradoff, Historical Jurisprudence, 163–369.

Jenks, Law and Politics in the Middle Ages, chap. 4; Maine, Ancient Law, chap. 10; Strachan-Davidson, Problems of the Roman Criminal Law, chap. 3; Leist, Graeco-Italische Rechtsgeschichte, §§ 28–53; Amira, Grundriss des germanischen Rechts, chaps. 4, 6; Coleman Phillipson, The Trial of Socrates; Bonner and Smith, The Administration of Justice from Homer to Aristotle.

Code of Hammurabi, §§ 196–214 (Harper's transl.); Laws of Manu, viii, 279–280 (Bühler's transl.); Twelve Tables of Gortyna, ii, 4–5, and ix (Roby's transl. in 2 L. Q. Rev. 125); Law of Draco, quoted by Demosthenes against Aristocrates, § 96 — "If any one is killed violently, reprisals by seizing men (τὰς ἀνδροληψίας) to be a right of his nearest relatives until justice is done for the murder or the murderers are surrendered. But this right of reprisal to extend to three men and no more;" Law of Draco, quoted by Plutarch, Life of Solon — "He [Draco] likewise enacted a law for reparation of damage received from beasts. A dog that had bit a man was to be delivered up bound to a log four cubits long;" Twelve Tables, viii, 2–3, 12–13, xii, 2a (transl. in Goodwin, Twelve Tables, 13, 14); Gaius, iii, §§ 183–192, 222–223, iv, §§ 75–78 (transl. by Abdy and Walker, and by Poste); Salic Law, xiv, 1–3, xxx, 4–7, xl (transl. in Henderson, Historical Documents of the Middle Ages); Laws of Ethelbert, §§ 33–61 (transl. in I Thorpe, Ancient Laws of England, 13–18); Laws of Alfred, § 24 (transl. in I Thorpe, 79); Maitland, The Laws of Wales — the Kindred and the Blood Feud, I Collected Papers, 202; Evans, Mediaeval Welsh Law (Laws of Howel the Good), 185–187, 190–191; Abdur Rahim, Muhammadan Jurisprudence, 358–359.

Dareste, Le droit des représailles, Nouvelles études d'histoire du droit, 38; Leist, Altarisches Jus Gentium, § 68; V Maurer, Altnordische Rechtsgeschichte, pt. I; Maine, Early History of Institutions, lect. 2; Dareste, Le prix du sang, Nouvelles études d'histoire du droit, 1; Strachan-Davidson, Problems of the Roman Criminal Law, chap. 1; Wilda, Strafrecht der Germanen, 278–280; I Jhering, Geist des römischen Rechts (5 ed.) §§ 18–18a; Danz, Der sakrale Schutz im römischen Rechtsverkehr, 47 ff.; Greenidge, Infamia, chaps. 3, 4; Thayer, Preliminary Treatise on Evidence, 9–10; Letts, The Sachsenspiegel and its Illustrators, 49 L. Q. Rev. 555; Cairns, Law and the Social Sciences, chap. II (Anthropology) reprinting Law and Anthropology, 31 Columbia L. Rev. 32.

Reinsch, The English Common Law in the American Colonies, II Bulletin of the University of Wisconsin, Historical Series, no. 4, reprinted in I Select Essays in Anglo-American Legal History, 367–463; I Massachusetts Colonial History, 174–175.

(b) The strict law.

II² Jhering, Geist des römischen Rechts (5 ed.) §§ 44–47d.

Gaius, iii, § 168, iv, §§ 116–117; I Heusler, Institutionen des deutschen Privatrechts, § 12; Justinian, Institutes, ii, 23 (transl. by Abdy and Walker and by Moyle); Doctor and Student, dial. II, chaps. 6, 7, 11, 24; Hargrave, Law Tracts, 324–325; Finch, Law, chap. 3; Coke, Fourth Institute, 82–84; Kerly, History of Equity, 113–115; Ames, Specialty Contracts and Equitable Defenses, 9 Harv. L. Rev. 49; Anonymous, Y. B. Mich. 13 Ric. 3, 1 (Plucknett's ed.) p. 31; Belsheim, The Old Action of Account, 45 Harv. L. Rev. 466, 475–486; Sayre, Mens Rea, 45 Harv. L. Rev. 974, 975–982.

Pollock, Genius of the Common Law, 36; II Danz, Lehrbuch der Geschichte des römischen Rechts, § 142; Gray, Restraints on the Alienation of Property,

§ 74b; Coke on Littleton, 214b; I Spence, History of the Equitable Jurisdiction of the Court of Chancery, 629, 654.

Aristotle, Politics, bk. ii, chap. 8 (Jowett's transl. vol. I, 47–49, Welldon's transl. 71–72); Mirror of Justices, bk. 5, chap. 1, § 19 (Selden Society ed. 157); Letter of Thomas Jefferson to John Tyler, I Tyler, Letters and Times of the Tylers, 35; Loyd, Early Courts of Pennsylvania, 162–163, 189–190, 193–195, 196–197, 209–210; Radin, The Conscience of the Court, 48 L. Q. Rev. 506; Marriott and Pascal's Case, 1 Leon. 159.

Wohlhaupter, Studien zur Rechtsgeschichte der Gottes und Landfrieden in Spanien (1933).

(c) Equity and natural law.

I Voigt, Das Jus naturale, aequum et bonum und Jus Gentium der Römer, 321–323; Pound, A Comparison of Ideals of Law, 47 Harv. L. Rev. 1, 12–14.

Holland, Jurisprudence (13 ed.) 31–40; Markby, Elements of Law (6 ed.) §§ 116–124; Miller, Data of Jurisprudence, 381–387, 391–407; Salmond, Jurisprudence, § 13; Korkunov, General Theory of Law (transl. by Hastings) § 17; Pulszky, Theory of Law and Civil Society, § 220; Goadby, Introduction to the Study of Law (2 ed.) 127–134; Siegel, Deutsche Rechtsgeschichte, § 53; Maine, Ancient Law, chaps. 2, 3; Buckland, Equity in Roman Law; Maitland, Equity, lects. 1, 2; I Erdmann, History of Philosophy (transl. by Hough) 190; Zeller, Stoics, Epicureans and Sceptics (transl. by Reichel) 287–290; Holdsworth, Blackstone's Treatment of Equity, 43 L. Q. Rev. 1; references under ius naturale, *ante*, II, 4 (b).

(1) Identification of law with morals.

Digest of Justinian, i, 1, 1, pr. (transl. by Monro); id. i, 1, 11; Institutes of Justinian, ii, 7, 2; Code of Justinian, viii, 55 (56), 1 and 10; id. iv, 44, 2; III Planiol, Traité élémentaire de droit civil (11 ed.) § 2638; Grueber, Introduction to Sohm, Institutes of Roman Law (1 ed.) xxv; Russell, International Law, 19 Rep. Am. Bar Assn. 253–268; Year Book, 4 Hen. VII, 5; III Blackstone, Commentaries, 429–430; Drew v. Hansen, 6 Ves. 675, 678; Lambe v. Eames, L. R. 6 Ch. App. 597; I Story, Equity Jurisprudence, § 247; Maitland, Equity, 104.

(2) Human beings as subjects of legal rights.

Institutes of Justinian, i, 3, § 2, 8, §§ 1, 2; Digest, i, 5, 17 (transl. by Monro); Salkowski, Institutes of Roman Law (transl. by Whitfield) 160, 162, 248–253, 280–285; Gaius, i, §§ 144–145; Grotius, bk. ii, chap. 5, §§ 1–7; Maine, International Law (Am. ed.) 126–127; Bryce, Studies in History and Jurisprudence (Am. ed.), 786–824; Ehrlich, Die Rechtsfähigkeit.

(3) Substance rather than form.

Digest of Justinian, iv, 5, 2, § 1 (transl. by Monro); Gaius, i, § 158, ii, §§ 40–41, 101–104, 115–117, 119, iv, § 36; Muirhead, Historical Introduction to the Private Law of Rome (3 ed.) 216; Phelps, Juridical Equity, §§ 194–204.

(4) Good faith.

Gaius, iv, §§ 61–62; Muirhead, Historical Introduction to the Private Law of

Rome (3 ed.) 256–257; Sohm, Institutes of Roman Law (transl. by Ledlie, 3 ed.) 101–103; Gaius, ii, § 43; Digest of Justinian, xxii, 1, 25, § 1, xli, 1, 40, xli, 1, 48, pr. and § 1; Code of Justinian, iii, 32, 22; Digest of Justinian, xli, 3, 4, § 20; Gaius, ii, § 43; Digest, l, 17, 84, § 1; Sext. 1, 18; Grotius, bk. iii, chap. 11, §§ 3–4 (transl. by Whewell); Pufendorf, Law of Nature and Nations (transl. by Kennet) bk. iii, chap. 4; Burlamaqui, Principles of Natural and Politic Law (transl. by Nugent) bk. ii, pt. 4, chap. 10, § 4, bk. i, pt. 1, chap. 7; Maine, Ancient Law, chap. 9; Ames, Law and Morals, 22 Harv. L. Rev. 97, 106; Gorphe, Le principe de bonne foi; Schulz, Principles of Roman Law, chap. 11; Ellerman Lines Ltd. v. Read [1928] 2 K. B. 144; The Idea of Good Faith (1939) in Jubilee Law Lectures of Catholic University of America, 47–71.

(5) Unjust enrichment.

Digest, l, 17, 206, xii, 6, 1, xii, 6, 66; Moses v. Macferlan, 2 Burr. 1005; Ames, Law and Morals, 22 Harv. L. Rev. 97, 106; Mosoiou, De l'enrichissement unjuste, Étude de droit comparé (1932).

(d) The maturity of law.

Pound, The Decadence of Equity, 5 Columbia L. Rev. 20; Progress of Continental Law in the Nineteenth Century, XI Continental Legal History Series, chaps. 1, 2 (Alvarez); First Reports of the Real Property Commissioners (1924) 6–7; Bryant Smith, Legal Relief Against the Inadequacies of Equity, 12 Texas L. Rev. 109; Hanbury, The Field of Modern Equity, 45 L. Q. Rev. 196, 207–213; Paulsen, Ethics (transl. by Thilly) 8.

(1) Equality.

Digest, i, 1, 4; Bentham, Theory of Legislation, Principles of the Civil Code, pt. I, chap. 2; Clark, Practical Jurisprudence, 110–114; I Austin, Jurisprudence (3 ed.) 97–98 (5 ed.) 94–96; Stephen, Liberty, Equality, Fraternity, 189–255; Maine, Early History of Institutions (Am. ed.) 398–400; Miller, Data of Jurisprudence, 379–381; Lorimer, Institutes of Law (2 ed.) 375–414; II Röder, Grundzüge des Naturrechts, §§ 106–119; Lasson, System der Rechtsphilosophie, 376–377; Ritchie, Natural Rights, chap. 12; Demogue, Notions fondamentales du droit privé, 136–142.

(2) Security.

Bentham, Theory of Legislation, Principles of the Civil Code, pt. I, chaps. 2, 7; Lorimer, Institutes of Law (2 ed.) 367–374; Gareis, Science of Law (transl. by Kocourek) 33; Demogue, Notions fondamentales du droit privé, 63–110; Massachusetts Bill of Rights, art. 10 (1780); Schulz, Principles of Roman Law, chap. 12.

(e) The socialization of law.

As to this name see Stein, Die soziale Frage im Lichte der Philosophie (2 ed.) 457 ff. (1 ed. 1897); Vinogradoff, *infra*; Charmont (1903) cited by Valeur, *infra*, cxiii–cxiv.

I Vinogradoff, Historical Jurisprudence, 157–159; Dicey, Lectures on the Relation Between Law and Public Opinion in England, 62–65; Sharp, The Movement in Supreme Court Adjudication, 47 Harv. L. Rev. 361, 593, 795; II Recent Social Trends, 1446–1448.

Jhering, Scherz und Ernst in der Jurisprudenz (13 ed. 1924) 408–425; Charmont, Le droit et l'esprit démocratique, chap. 2; Pound, Social Justice and Legal Justice (1912) Proc. Mo. Bar Assn. 110, 75 Central L. J. 455; Duguit, Les transformations générales du droit privé depuis le code Napoléon (transl. in XI Continental Legal History Series, chap. 3); Barasch, Le socialisme juridique et son influence sur l'évolution du droit civil en France à la fin du XIXᵉ siècle et au XXᵉ siècle (1923); Beale, Social Justice and Business Costs: A Study in the Business Organization of Today, 49 Harv. L. Rev. 593; Darmstaedter, Der Strukturwandel des Rechts, XXV Archiv für Rechts- und Wirthschaftsphilosophie, 180–211; Radbruch, Du droit individualiste au droit social (1931) Archives de philosophie du droit et de sociologie juridique, 387; Charmont, Les transformations du droit civil; id. La socialisation du droit (1903) Revue de métaphysique et de morale, 380 ff.; Leroy, Les transformations de la puissance publique; Hedemann, Das bürgerliche Recht und die neue Zeit; Morin, La révolte des faits contre le code; id. La loi et le contrat: la décadence de leur souveraineté; Valeur, L'enseignement du droit en France et aux États Unis (1928) 89–92.

(1) Limitations on the use of property: anti-social exercise of rights.

German Civil Code, § 226; English Law of Property Act (1925) § 84; I Cosack, Lehrbuch des deutschen bürgerlichen Rechts (8 ed.) § 124, II, 2; II Planiol, Traité élémentaire de droit civil (11 ed.) §§ 870–872bis; Walton, Motive as an Element in Torts in the Common and in the Civil Law, 22 Harv. L. Rev. 501; id. Delictual Responsibility in the Civil Law, 49 L. Q. Rev. 70, 86–89; Charmont, L'Abus du droit, I Revue trimestrielle de droit civil, 113; Porcherot, De l'abus du droit; Salanson, De l'abus du droit; Josserand, De la relativité des droits, 2 Revue internationale de la théorie du droit, 142–150; id. De l'abus des droits; id. De l'esprit des lois et de leur relativité; Campion, De l'abus des droits; Huffcut, Percolating Waters: The Rule of Reasonable User, 13 Yale L. J. 222; Ames, How Far An Act May Be a Tort Because of the Wrongful Motive of the Actor, 18 Harv. L. Rev. 411, 414 ff.; Stoner, The Influence of Social and Economic Ideals on the Law of Malicious Torts, 8 Mich. L. Rev. 468; II Wigmore, Cases on Torts, app. A, §§ 262, 271–272; Gutteridge, Abuse of Rights (1933) 5 Cambridge L. J. 22; Leake, The Abuse of Rights in Louisiana (1933) 7 Tulane L. Rev. 626; Lauterpacht, The Development of International Law by the Permanent Court of International Justice, 53–54; Dunshee v. Standard Oil Co., 152 Ia. 618; Hollywood Silver Fox Farm v. Emmett [1936] 2 K. B. 468 and notes in 52 L. Q. Rev. 461 (Goodhart) and 53 id. 1 (Holdsworth).

Village of Euclid v. Ambler Realty Co., 272 U. S. 365; Windsor v. Whitney, 95 Conn. 357; State v. Houghton, 144 Minn. 1; Piper v. Ekern, 180 Wis. 586. See Note by Professor T. P. Hardman, The Social Interest in the Aesthetic and the Socialization of the Law, 29 W. Va. L. Q. 195; Note in 8 Canadian Bar Rev. 384.

Jenks, Governmental Action for Social Welfare, 81; II Recent Social Trends, 1440–1441; General Outdoor Advertising Co. v. Department of Public Works, 289 Mass. 149, 201; Gardner, The Massachusetts Billboard Decision, 49 Harv. L.

Rev. 869; Advertisements Regulation Act [1907] 7 Edw. 7, c. 27, § 2; Terry, Constitutionality of Statutes Forbidding Advertising Signs on Property, 24 Yale L. J. 1; Billboard and Other Forms of Outdoor Advertising, Chicago City Club Bulletin V, no. 24; St. Louis Advertisement Co. v. City, 235 Mo. 99, 249 U. S. 269, 274; People v. Oak Park, 266 Ill. 365; Bill Posting Co. v. Atlantic City, 71 N. J. Law 72; Bryan v. City, 212 Pa. St. 259.

American Law Institute, Restatement of the Law of Torts, § 339.

(2) Limitations on freedom of contract.

I Wyman, Public Service Corporations, § 331; Thompson, The Relation of Common Carrier of Goods and Shipper, 38 Harv. L. Rev. 869; Dicey, Law and Public Opinion in England, lect. 8; Pound, Liberty of Contract, 18 Yale L. J. 454; Jastrow, Was ist Arbeiterschutz? VI Archiv für Rechts- und Wirthschafts-philosophie, 133, 317, 322, 501; Brown, Underlying Principles of Modern Legislation, 316–321; Isaacs, The Standardizing of Contracts, 27 Yale L. J. 34; Patterson, Administrative Control of Insurance Policy Forms, 25 Columbia L. Rev. 253; id. The Insurance Commissioner in the United States, 244–268; Llewellyn, What Price Contract? 40 Yale L. J. 704, 731–734; Posner, Liability of the Corporate Trustee, 42 Harv. L. Rev. 201, 212, 227–230, 244–248; Scott, Fifty Years of Trusts, 50 Harv. L. Rev. 60, 68.

Noble State Bank v. Haskell, 219 U. S. 104; Chicago B. & Q. R. Co. v. McGuire, 219 U. S. 549, 566–575; Nebbia v. New York, 291 U. S. 502; Note in 44 Harv. L. Rev. 1287.

(3) Limitations on the *ius disponendi*.

Gray, Restraints on the Alienation of Property (2 ed.) viii–ix; Thompson, Homesteads and Exemptions, § 465; Massachusetts Acts of 1908, chap. 605; Illinois, Act of June 5, 1889, Laws of 1889, p. 208; New Jersey, Laws of 1893, p. 97; id. 1902, p. 489; New Zealand Family Protection Act, 1908; Allardice v. Allardice [1911] A. C. 730; III Huber, System und Geschichte des schweizer-ischen Privatrechtes, §§ 82–83; Perticone, La proprietà e sui limiti (1930).

(4) Limitations on the power of the creditor or injured party to exact satisfaction.

Thompson, Homesteads and Exemptions, §§ 40, 379; Bureau, Le Homestead; German Civil Code, §§ 528–529, 829; German Code of Civil Procedure (Zivil-prozessordnung) § 850; Munch Petersen, Procedure From a Social Point of View, 5 N. C. L. Rev. 322, 325; Central Bank v. Hume, 128 U. S. 195; Wood-bridge, Wage Earners' Receiverships (1940) 23 J. Am. Jud. Soc. 242.

Smith, Justice and the Poor, 56, 57; In re Davis, 103 Neb. 703; Note, 47 Harv. L. Rev. 299.

Compare Digest, xlii, 3, 4, pr.; Code, vii, 71, 1; Code, ii, 11, 11; Digest, xlii, 1, 16–17; Digest, xlii, 1, 19, § 1; Digest, l, 17, 173; II Roby, Roman Private Law, 129, note 1; Buckland, Text Book of Roman Law, 687–688; I Baudry-Lacantinerie, Précis de droit civil (10 ed.) § 529, toned down somewhat in later editions — see 13 ed. I § 550; Lavet, La bénéfice de la compétence (1927).

As to statutory moratoria see Feller, Moratory Legislation, A Comparative Study, 46 Harv. L. Rev. 1061; Stone, Mortgage Moratoria, 11 Wisconsin L. Rev.

203. As to restrictions on foreclosure of mortgages in equity, see Carey, Brabner-Smith and Sullivan, Studies in Realty Mortgage Foreclosures, 27 Illinois L. Rev. 848, 861–864 and cases cited; Brabner-Smith, Economic Aspects of the Deficiency Judgment, 20 Virginia L. Rev. 719; Federal Title & Mtge Guaranty Co. v. Lowenstein, 113 N. J. Eq. 200; White v. Wielandt, 259 App. Div. 676, 680, 681.

(5) Liability without fault; responsibility for agencies employed.

Wambaugh, Workman's Compensation Acts, 25 Harv. L. Rev. 129; Boyd Workmen's Compensation, 27–29, 81; Arizona Workmen's Compensation Cases, 250 U. S. 400, 435, 436, 449; Opinion of the Justices, 209 Mass. 607; State v. Clausen, 65 Wash. 156; Borgnis v. Falk, 147 Wis. 327. See Ives v. South Buffalo R. Co., 201 N. Y. 271.

Ballantine, A Compensation Plan for Railway Accident Claims, 29 Harv. L. Rev. 705; Marx, Compulsory Compensation Insurance, 25 Columbia Law Rev. 164; Report of the Committee to Study Compensation for Automobile Accidents, Columbia University Council for Research in the Social Sciences (1932) and review by Thurston, 43 Yale L. J. 160.

Pilotage Act (1913) § 15 (England); Connecticut Public Acts (1925) chap. 195, § 21; Bowerman v. Sheehan, 242 Mich. 95 (1928).

Compare 1 Bishop, Criminal Law, §§ 285–291, with Hobbs v. Winchester Corporation [1910] 2 K. B. 471, 482 ff.; United States v. Balint, 258 U. S. 250; State v. Keller, 8 Idaho 699; State v. Turner, 54 Ohio L. Bull. 409, 410; Sayre, Public Welfare Offences, 33 Columbia L. Rev. 55.

(6) Change of *res communes* and *res nullius* into *res publicae*.

See statutes in 1 Wiel, Water Rights (3 ed.) §§ 6, 170, 347; Wiel, Natural Communism, Air, Water, and the Seashore, 47 Harv. L. Rev. 425; Ex parte Bailey, 155 Calif. 472; Greer v. Connecticut, 161 U. S. 519; Missouri v. Holland, 252 U. S. 416, 434; Gallatin v. Corning Irr. Co., 163 Calif. 405; Greaves v. Dunlap, 87 Wash. 648; Water Code of Washington (1913) §§ 1–2. See also *post*, XIV, 3, iv.

(7) Interest of society in dependents.

Mack, The Juvenile Court, 23 Harv. L. Rev. 104; Flexner, Juvenile Courts and Probation, 9, 68; Eliot, The Juvenile Court, 89, 90; Young, Social Treatment in Probation and Delinquency, chaps. 8–13; Polish Draft Code on Juvenile Courts, French transl. in Recueil des projets des lois de la Revue Polonaise de législation civile et criminelle, no. 1; Cardozo, J. in Loucks v. Standard Oil Co., 224 N. Y. 89, 103–106; Gothard v. Lewis, 235 Ky. 117; Oliver v. Birmingham Omnibus Co. [1933] 1 K. B. 35; Note, 42 Harv. L. Rev. 42–44. But see McReynolds, J. in Pierce v. Society of Sisters, 268 U. S. 510, 535.

English Guardianship of Infants Act (1925) § 1; New Zealand Family Protection Act (1908); Newman v. Newman [1927] N. Z. L. Rep. 418; Note, 45 L. Q. Rev. 378; Note on statutory rights of pretermitted children, 44 Yale L. J. 842.

Magnussen, Norwegian Law of Illegitimacy (1918) U. S. Children's Bureau, Leg. Set no. 1, publ. no. 31; Arizona Laws (1921) chaps. 114, 238.

(8) Tendency to hold that public funds should respond for injuries to individuals by public agencies.

Maguire, State Liability for Torts, 30 Harv. L. Rev. 20; Borchard, State Indemnity for Errors of Criminal Justice; Crane, Jurisdiction of the Court of Claims, 34 Harv. L. Rev. 161, 163–165, particularly 165 and citations; Borchard, Government Liability in Tort, 34 Yale L. J. 1, 129, 229, 36 id. 1, 757, 1039, 28 Columbia L. Rev. 577, 734. See Fowler v. City of Cleveland, 100 Ohio St. 158; Aldrich v. City of Youngstown, 106 Ohio St. 342.

(9) Replacing of the purely contentious conception of litigation by one of adjustment of interests.

Pound, The Causes of Popular Dissatisfaction With the Administration of Justice, 29 Rep. Am. Bar Assn. 395, 404–406; I Wigmore, Evidence, § 21; II id. § 1503; IV id. § 2251; Arnold, Trial by Combat and the New Deal, 47 Harv. L. Rev. 913; Kohler, Philosophy of Law (transl. by Albrecht) 262; Pound, Some Principles of Procedural Reform, 4 Illinois L. Rev. 491, 498–505; id. Canons of Procedural Reform, 51 Rep. Am. Bar Assn. 290, 300–301; id. Organization of Courts (1940) 253–254; Millar, Notabilia of American Civil Procedure 1887–1937, 50 Harv. L. Rev. 1017, 1067–1070.

(10) Reading of reasonableness into the obligation of contracts — equitable-izing of the terms as fixed by the parties.

Building and Loan Assn. v. Blaisdell, 290 U. S. 398; 1 Williston, Contracts, §§ 60, 60a; 2 id. § 794; Stull, Die Lehre von den Leistungsstörungen (1936) 6–12 and appendix §§ 24, 33, pp. 137–138, 142.

(11) Increasing legal recognition of groups and relations as legal units instead of exclusive recognition of individuals and of certain associations as their analogues.

Ehrlich, Fundamental Principles of the Sociology of Law (transl. by Moll) chaps. 2, 3.

Magruder, A Half Century of Legal Influence Upon the Development of Collective Bargaining (1937) 50 Harv. L. Rev. 1071; National Labor Relations Board v. Jones & Laughlin Steel Corp., 301 U. S. 1 (1937); Note, The Present Status of Collective Labor Agreements, 51 Harv. L. Rev. 520; Jaffe, Law Making by Private Groups (1937) 51 Harv. L. Rev. 201.

Great Britain, Ministry of Labor, I Report on Collective Agreements Between Employers and Workpeople in Great Britain and Northern Ireland (1934); Foenander, Towards Industrial Peace in Australia (1937) 9–11.

Barassi, Diritto sindicale e corporativo (1934); Coniglio, Lezioni di diritto corporativo (2 ed. 1934); Mazzoni, L'ordinamento corporativo: Contributo alla formulazione di una domestica del diritto corporativo (1934); Cioffi, Istituzioni di diritto corporativo (1935); Cesarini Sforza, Curso di diritto corporativo (4 ed. 1935); Pergolesi, Istituzioni di diritto corporativo (2 ed. 1935); Chiarelli, Lo stato corporativo (1936); Zanelli Quarantini, Le fonti del diritto corporativo (1936); Lescure, Le nouveau régime corporatif italien (1934); Pitigliani, The Italian Corporative State (1933).

Aunós Pérez, Principios de derecho corporativo (1929); Caballero, La legis-lación vigente sobre organización corporativa nacional (1929); Aunós Pérez, La organización corporativa y su posible desenvolvimiento (1929); Aunós Pérez, Estudios de derecho corporativo (1931); Zancada, Programa de derecho corporativo (1931).

Florinsky, Fascism and National Socialism, chap. 5; Gesetz zur Ordnung der nationalen Arbeit, I Reichsgesetzblatt (1934) 45; Muenz, Das Gesetz zur Ord-nung der nationalen Arbeit (1934); Pelcovits, The Social Honor Courts of Nazi Germany, 53 Political Science Q. 350. For the older regime of collective bargain-ing in Germany see Oertmann, Deutsches Arbeitsvertragsrecht (1923).

(12) Tendency to relax the rules as to trespassers.

Compare the older views as set forth in Maynard v. Boston & Maine R., 115 Mass. 458 (1874); Grand Trunk R. Co. v. Barnett [1911] A. C. 361; Sheehan v. St. Paul & D. R. Co., 76 Fed. 201 (1896); Lary v. Cleveland R. Co., 78 Ind. 323 (1881); Buch v. Amory Mfg. Co., 69 N. H. 257 (1897); Frost v. Eastern R., 64 N. H. 220 (1886), with 2 Restatement of Torts, §§ 334–339. Compare Barker v. Bates, 13 Pick. (Mass.) 255 (1832) and South Staffordshire Water Co. v. Sharman [1896] 2 Q.B.D. 44 with Weeks v. Hackett, 104 Maine 264 (1908), Groover v. Tippins, 51 Ga. App. 47 (1935), and Gaither v. Jones (1935) Warren, Cases on Property (2 ed.) 129.

VIII. THE END OF LAW AS DEVELOPED IN JURISTIC THOUGHT

Pound, The End of Law as Developed in Juristic Thought, 27 Harv. L. Rev. 605, 30 Harv. L. Rev. 201; id. Twentieth Century Ideas as to the End of Law, Harvard Legal Essays, 357–375; Yntema, The Rational Basis of Legal Science, 31 Columbia L. Rev. 925, 934–955.

1. Greek philosophy.

II Berolzheimer, System der Rechts- und Wirthschaftsphilosophie, §§ 13–16 (World's Legal Philosophies, 46–77).

Aristotle, Nicomachean Ethics, bk. v (convenient transl. by Browne in Bohn's Libraries) bk. viii, 7, 2–4; Aristotle, Politics, i, 1, 9, i, 13, iii, 1, iii, 4–5, iv, 12 (Jowett's transl. is preferable; there is also a convenient transl. by Well-don); I Erdmann, History of Philosophy (transl. by Hough) 37, 52, 123, 190–191; Hildenbrand, Geschichte und System der Rechts- und Staatsphilosophie, §§ 1–121; Dunning, Political Theories, Ancient and Mediaeval, 28, 105; Mc-Ilwain, The Growth of Political Thought in the West, chaps. 1–3; Sauter, Die philosophischen Grundlagen des Naturrechts, chaps. 1–2; II Zeller, Aristotle and the Earlier Peripatetics (transl. by Costelloe and Muirhead) 175, 197.

Shall we not then find that in such a city . . . a shoemaker is only a shoe-maker, and not a pilot along with shoemaking, and that the husbandman is only a husbandman, and not a judge along with husbandry; and that the soldier is a soldier, and not a money-maker besides; and all others in the same way? He admitted it. And it would appear that if a man, who through wisdom were able to become everything and to imitate everything should come into our city and should wish to show us his poems, we should honor him . . . but we should tell him that there is no such person with us in our city, nor is there any such allowed to be, and we should send him to some other city. — Plato, Republic, iii, 397–398. See also id. iv, 423.

Justice is doing one's own business and not being a busybody. — Plato, Republic, iv, 433. Compare St. Paul in Eph. v, 22 ff. and vi, 1–5.

2. Roman law.

II Berolzheimer, System der Rechts- und Wirthschaftsphilosophie, §§ 17–20 (World's Legal Philosophies, 78–92).

Institutes of Justinian, i, 1, pr. and § 3; Cicero, De Officiis, ii, 12, De Republica, i, 32; Hildenbrand, Geschichte und System der Rechts- und Staatsphilosophie, §§ 131–135, 143–147; I Voigt, Das Ius Naturale, aequum et bonum und Ius Gentium der Römer, §§ 16, 35–41, 44–64, 89–96; I Savigny, System des heutigen römischen Rechts, 407–410, § 59; Affolter, Das römische Institutionensystem, 421–430; Donati, Il primo precetto del diritto "vivere con honestà" (1926); McIlwain, The Growth of Political Theory in the West, chap. 4.

3. Mediaeval philosophical theology.

II Berolzheimer, System der Rechts- und Wirthschaftsphilosophie, §§ 21–23 (World's Legal Philosophies, 93–111).

Thomas Aquinas, Summa Theologica, prima secundae, qu. 90–97, secunda secundae, qu. 57–80, 120, 122; I Erdmann, History of Philosophy (transl. by Hough) 229; Sauter, Die philosophischen Grundlagen des Naturrechts, 57–85; Dunning, Political Theories, Ancient and Mediaeval, 158, 196; III Carlyle, History of Mediaeval Political Theory, 3–14; McIlwain, The Growth of Political Theory in the West, chap. 6.

4. The Protestant jurist-theologians.

II Berolzheimer, System der Rechts- und Wirthschaftsphilosophie, § 24 (World's Legal Philosophies, 112–114).

Sources: Oldendorp, Iuris naturalis gentium et ciuilis εἰσαγωγή (1539); Hemmingius (Hemmingsen), De lege naturale apodictica methodus (1562); Winckler, Principiorum iuris libri V (1615). These may be found conveniently in Kaltenborn, Die Vorläufer des Hugo Grotius.

I Hinrichs, Geschichte der Rechts- und Staatsprincipien seit der Reformation, 1–60; Gierke, Johannes Althusius (2 ed.) 18–49, 142–162, 321; Johannes Althusius, Politica methodice digesta (transl. with introduction by Friedrich); Dunning, Political Theories from Luther to Montesquieu, chaps. 1–3.

5. The Spanish jurist-theologians.

Figgis, Studies of Political Thought from Gerson to Grotius, lect. VI.

Sources: Soto, De iustitia et iure (1589); Suarez, De legibus ac deo legislatore (1619).

Suarez, De legibus, iii, 9, § 4, iii, 11, iii, 35, § 8; Soto, De iustitia et iure, iii, q. 3, art. 2; I Franciscus de Victoria, Relectiones theologicae (1557), 354, 375.

Dunning, Political Theories from Luther to Montesquieu, 132–149; Westlake, Chapters on the Principles of International Law, 25–28; Scott, On the Spanish Origin of International Law (1928).

6. The seventeenth century.

II Berolzheimer, System der Rechts- und Wirthschaftsphilosophie, §§ 25–27 (World's Legal Philosophies, 115–134).

Sources: Grotius, De iure belli ac pacis (1625); Hobbes, Leviathan (1651); Pufendorf, De iure naturae et gentium (1672).

Grotius, i, 1, 3–6, 8–11, ii, 1, 1, ii, 1, 11, ii, 10, 1, ii, 17, 2, § 1; Pufendorf, De iure naturae et gentium, i, chap. 7, §§ 6–17, iv, 4; Hobbes, Leviathan, chap. 15; Rutherforth, Institutes of Natural Law, I, 2, § 3.

II Stintzing, Geschichte der deutschen Rechtswissenschaft, 1–111; I Hinrichs, Geschichte der Rechts- und Staatsprincipien seit der Reformation, 60–274, II, III, 1–318; Sauter, Die philosophischen Grundlagen des Naturrechts, 91–98, 113–151; Dunning, Political Theories from Luther to Montesquieu, 164–171, 318–325; Duff, Spinoza's Political and Ethical Philosophy, chap. 22.

That is unjust which is contrary to the nature of rational creatures. — Grotius, i, 1, 3, § 1.

From that law of nature by which we are obliged to transfer to another such rights as being retained hinder the peace of mankind, there followeth a third, which is this: "that men perform their covenants made;" without which covenants are in vain and but empty words, and the right of all men to all things remaining, we are still in a condition of war. And in this law of nature consisteth the fountain and original of justice. For where no covenant hath preceded, there hath no right been transferred and every man has right to everything, and consequently no action can be unjust. But when a covenant is made, then to break it is unjust; and the definition of injustice is no other than the not performance of covenant. And whatsoever is not unjust is just. . . . And therefore where there is no "own," that is, no property, there is no injustice; and where there is no coercive power erected, that is where there is no commonwealth, there is no property, all men having right to all things; therefore where there is no commonwealth, there nothing is unjust. So that the nature of justice consists in keeping of valid covenants; but the validity of covenants begins not but with the constitution of a civil power sufficient to compel men to keep them; and then it is also that property begins. — Hobbes, Leviathan, chap. 15.

Again, in the state of nature no one is by common consent master of anything, nor is there anything in nature which can be said to belong to one man rather than another. Hence in the state of nature we can conceive of no wish to render to every man his own or to deprive a man of that which belongs to him; in other words, there is nothing in the state of nature answering to justice and injustice. Such ideas are only possible in a social state, when it is decreed by common consent what belongs to one man and what to another. — Spinoza, Ethics, pt. iv, pr. 37, n. § 2 (Elwes' transl.).

7. The eighteenth century.

II Berolzheimer, System der Rechts- und Wirthschaftsphilosophie, § 29 (World's Legal Philosophies, 141–156); Korkunov, General Theory of Law (transl. by Hastings) § 7; Ritchie, Natural Rights, chap. 3; Charmont, La renaissance du droit naturel, 10–43.

Burlamaqui, Principles of Natural and Politic Law (Nugent's transl.) pt. i, chap. 5, § 10 and chap. 10, §§ 1–7; Rousseau, Social Contract, bk. ii, chap. 6 (transl. by Barrington and by Tozer); Montesquieu, Spirit of Laws, bk. i (Nugent's transl. ed. by Prichard, vol. I, 1–7); Vattel, Law of Nations, bk. i, chap. 2, §§ 15–17 (there are several English versions); I Blackstone, Commentaries, 38–43; Rutherforth, Institutes of Natural Law, bk. ii, chap. 5, §§ 1–3; Wolff, Institutiones juris naturae et gentium, §§ 74–102.
Sauter, Die philosophischen Grundlagen des Naturrechts, 151–196.

I shall close this chapter and this book with a remark which ought to serve as a basis for the whole social system; it is that instead of destroying natural equality, the fundamental pact, on the contrary, substitutes a moral and lawful equality for the physical inequality which nature imposed upon men, so that though unequal in strength or intellect, they all become equal by convention and legal right. — Rousseau, Social Contract, bk. i, chap. 9 (Tozer's transl.).

8. The nineteenth century.

(a) Metaphysical jurists.

II Berolzheimer, System der Rechts- und Wirthschaftsphilosophie, §§ 35–36 (World's Legal Philosophies, 215–259); Korkunov, General Theory of Law (transl. by Hastings) 320–322; Gray, Nature and Sources of the Law, § 58 (in 2 ed. pp. 23–24).

Lasson, System der Rechtsphilosophie, §§ 24–25; Herkless, Lectures on Jurisprudence, chap. 4; Hegel, Philosophy of Right (Dyde's transl.) §§ 29–33.

Every action is right which in itself, or in the maxim on which it proceeds, is such that it can coexist along with the freedom of the will of each and all in action according to a universal law. — Kant, Rechtslehre, xxxv (Hastie's transl.).

As to the relation of this to the classical economics, see Cooke, Adam Smith and Jurisprudence, 51 L. Q. Rev. 326.

I must in all cases recognize the free being outside of me as such, that is, must limit my liberty by the possibility of his liberty. — I Fichte, Grundlage des Naturrechts, 49.

This is right: that existence generalized is existence of the free will. Accordingly, as a generalization, it is liberty as an idea. — Hegel, Grundlinien der Philosophie des Rechts, 61.

We may define right as a principle . . . governing the exercise of liberty in the relations of human life. — I Ahrens, Cours du Droit Naturel (8 ed.) 107.

Right is the sum of those universal determinations of action through which it happens that the ethical whole and its parts may be preserved and further developed. — Trendelenburg, Naturrecht, § 46.

The fundamental Axiom which forms the basis of the whole system of Natural Justice I conceive to be that one human being has *no* right to control for his own benefit the volition of another. — Phillipps, Jurisprudence, 80–81 (§ 1).

The ultimate object of positive law is identical with the proximate object of natural law — viz. liberty. But being realizable only by means of order, order is the proximate object of positive law. — Lorimer, Institutes of Law (2 ed.) 523.

Reduced to these terms, the difference between morality and right is a difference in degree and not of essence. Yet it is a very important difference, as it *reduces the power of coercion to what is absolutely necessary for the harmonious coexistence of the individual with the whole.* — I Lioy, Philosophy of Right (transl. by Hastie) 121.

Fundamental principles of justice:

(1) The first and highest fundamental principle of justice provides that every one hold every good which he has unhindered by the acts of any other.

(2) That for every value transferred, one receive in return an equal value.

(3) Every newly produced value belongs to the producer.

(4) Every destroyed good is to be destroyed to the destroyer, and if the destroyed good is another's, the destroyer suffers a subtraction from his own good until the injured person is compensated for his injury by an equivalent value. — Lasson, System der Rechtsphilosophie, § 24.

Right . . . [is] the correspondence or harmony of the will of the individual with the universal will. — Herkless, Lectures on Jurisprudence, 69.

The moral principle which protects the right is the inviolability of the human person. . . . This is the fundamental axiom upon which every doctrine of law may be and ought to be established. — I Boistel, Cours de philosophie du droit, 72.

(b) English utilitarians.

II Berolzheimer, System der Rechts- und Wirthschaftsphilosophie, § 28 (World's Legal Philosophies, 134–141); Markby, Elements of Law, §§ 51–59; Mill, On Liberty, chap. 4; Bentham, Theory of Legislation, Principles of the Civil Code, chaps. 1, 7; Dicey, Law and Public Opinion in England, lect. 6.

Bentham, Principles of Morals and Legislation (1780, reprinted by the Clarendon Press, 1879); id. Traités de législation (ed. by Dumont, 1802, transl. as Bentham's Theory of Legislation by Hildreth, 10 ed. 1904); id. I Works, Principles of the Civil Code, 295–364; Mill, On Liberty (1859).
See Albee, History of English Utilitarianism; Stephen, The English Utilitarians; Halévy, The Growth of Philosophic Radicalism (1928 — transl. by Morris) 35–87, 373–431; Solari, L'idea individuale e l'idea sociale nel diritto privato, §§ 31–36.

The ideas which underlie the Benthamite or individualistic scheme of reform may conveniently be summarized under three leading principles and two corollaries.

(1) Legislation is a science. . . .

(2) The right aim of legislation is the carrying out of the principle of utility, or, in other words, the proper end of every law is the promotion of the greatest happiness of the greatest number. . . .

(3) Every person is in the main and as a general rule the best judge of his own happiness. Hence legislation should aim at a removal of all those restrictions on the free action of an individual which are not necessary for securing the like freedom on the part of his neighbors. . . .

From these three guiding principles of legislative utilitarianism
— the scientific character of sound legislation, the principle of utility,
faith in *laissez faire* — English individualists have in practice deduced the two corollaries that the law ought to extend the sphere
and enforce the obligation of contract, and that, as regards the
possession of political power, every man ought to count for one man
and no man ought to count for more than one. — Dicey, Law and
Public Opinion in England (2 ed.) 134–149.

(c) The historical school.

In virtue of freedom man is the subject of right and law. His freedom is the foundation of right and all real relations of right emanate
from it. . . .

In thus founding right upon the possibility of an act of will, the
essential principle of right is indicated as that of equality. Right
implies the recognition of freedom as belonging equally to all men as
subjects of the power of will. It receives its material and contents
from the impulse of man to refer to himself what exists out of himself. The function of right, as manifested in law, is to apply the
principle of equality to the relations which arise from the operation
of this impulse. — I Puchta, Cursus der Institutionen (Hastie's
transl.) § 4.

Law exists for the sake of liberty; it has its basis in this, that men
are beings endowed with a disposition to free exertion of will. It
exists to protect liberty in that it limits caprice. — Arndts, Juristische Encyklopädie, § 12.

Justice is thus the condition of social equilibrium, both with reference to the domain of the rule of the will of persons, that is, with
regard to the harmony of law and [individual] right, and with reference to the maintenance of the limits of action of different persons,
or, in other words, to the mutual accommodation to each other of
the several and distinct existing rights. — Pulszky, Theory of Law
and Civil Society, § 173.

There is a guide which, when kept clearly and constantly in view,
sufficiently informs us what we should aim to do by legislation and
what should be left to other agencies. This is what I have so often
insisted upon as the sole function both of law and legislation, namely,
to secure to each individual the utmost liberty which he can enjoy
consistently with the preservation of the like liberty to all others.
Liberty, the first of blessings, the aspiration of every human soul, is

the supreme object. Every abridgment of it demands an excuse, and the only good excuse is the necessity of preserving it. Whatever tends to preserve this is right, all else is wrong. To leave each man to work out in freedom his own happiness or misery, to stand or fall by the consequences of his own conduct, is the true method of human discipline. — Carter, Law: Its Origin, Growth and Function, 337.

(d) The positivists.

Hence that which we have to express in a precise way is the liberty of each limited only by the like liberties of all. This we do by saying: — Every man is free to do that which he wills provided he infringes not the equal freedom of any other man. — Spencer, Justice, § 27.

Compare: Our theory reconciles the idea of liberty with those of superior power and superior interest; right, concrete and complete, at the same time ideal and real, becomes the maximum of liberty, equal for all individuals, which is compatible with the maximum of liberty, of force and of interest for the social organism. — Fouillée, L'idée moderne du droit (6 ed.) 394.

Courcelle-Seneuil's parallel:

Ancient Ideal	*Nineteenth-Century Ideal*
1. Property founded on conquest.	1. Property founded on labor and saving.
2. Absolute power founded on military force.	2. Empire of laws freely assented to by all.
3. Classification by privilege founded on tradition and the will of the government.	3. Classification founded on personal merit, tested by competition.
4. A stationary society, corrected from time to time by reversion to the ancient type.	4. A progressive society, constantly improving itself by labor and invention.
5. A society ruled by laws, under the supervision of a public authority invested with compulsory powers.	5. A society living by the free initiative of its citizens, regulated by the observance of the moral law.

See Courcelle-Seneuil, Préparation à l'étude du droit, 99, 396.

(e) Economic realists.

II Berolzheimer, System der Rechts- und Wirthschaftsphilosophie, §§ 37–40 (World's Legal Philosophies, 260–307); Brown, The Underlying Principles of Modern Legislation, Prologue (The Challenge of Anarchy).

(1) Anarchist individualism.

Proudhon, Qu'est-ce que la propriété? (1840); id. Idée générale de la révolution au dix-neuvième siècle (1851); id. De la justice dans la révolution et dans l'église (1858); Stirner, Der Einzige und sein Eigenthum (1845 — transl. as The Ego and His Own); Grave, La société future (7 ed. 1895). See Basch, l'individualisme anarchiste: Max Stirner (1904).

Free association, liberty, which is confined to the maintaining of equality in the means of production and of equivalence in exchanges, is the only possible just and true form of society. Politics is the science of liberty; under whatever name it may be disguised, the government of man by man is oppression. The highest form of society is found in the union of order and anarchy. — I Proudhon, Oeuvres Complètes (1873 ed.) Qu'est-ce que la propriété? 224.

(2) Socialist individualism.
(See, *post*, pp. 204–205.)

Socialism in all its forms leaves intact the individualistic ends, but resorts to collective action as a new method of attaining them. That socialism is through and through individualistic in tendency, with emotional fraternalism superadded, is the point I would especially emphasize. Adler, The Conception of Social Welfare, Proceedings of the Conference on Legal and Social Philosophy (1913) 9.

It is the function of the state to further the development of the human race to a state of freedom. . . . It is the education and evolution of the human race to a state of freedom. Lassalle, Arbeiterprogram (1863) I Werke (ed. by Blum) 156.

See also Radbruch, Rechtsphilosophie (3 ed. 1932) § 6.

9. The social-philosophical and recent sociological schools.

II Berolzheimer, System der Rechts- und Wirthschaftsphilosophie, §§ 43–48, 52 (World's Legal Philosophies, 336–431, 466–477); Pound, How Far Are We Attaining a New Measure of Values in Twentieth-Century Juristic Thought? (1936) 42 W. Va. L. Q. 81; id. Fifty Years of Jurisprudence (1938) 51 Harv. L. Rev. 444, 448–472.

Stammler, Wesen des Rechts und der Rechtswissenschaft (in Systematische Rechtswissenschaft i–lix); Kohler, Lehrbuch der Rechtsphilosophie (1 ed.) 38–43 (Albrecht's transl. 58–65); id. Rechtsphilosophie und Universalrechtsgeschichte, in I Holtzendorff, Enzyklopädie der Rechtswissenschaft (7 ed.) §§ 13–16, 33–34, 51; Ehrlich, Grundlegung der Soziologie des Rechts, chaps. 9, 10, Moll's transl. (as Fundamental Principles of the Sociology of Law) 192–244; Radbruch, Grundzüge der Rechtsphilosophie, 82–138; id. Rechtsphilosophie (3 ed.) 54–55; Gurvitch, Une philosophie antinomique de droit — Gustav Radbruch (1932) Archives de philosophie du droit, 530, 531–538; Binder, Philosophie des Rechts (1925) 282–287; id. System der Rechtsphilosophie (2 ed. 1937) § 9; I Gény, Science et technique en droit privé positif, 9–11, II, § 117 (1914, 1915); Duguit, Les transformations générales du droit privé depuis le code Napoléon (1912) 1–81.

Take any demand, however slight, which any creature, however weak, may make. Ought it not for its own sole sake to be satisfied?

If not, prove why not. The only possible kind of proof you could adduce would be the exhibition of another creature who should make a demand that ran the other way. . . . Any desire is imperative to the extent of its amount; it makes itself valid by the fact that it exists at all. Some desires, truly enough, are small desires; they are put forward by insignificant persons, and we customarily make light of the obligations which they bring. But the fact that such personal demands as these impose small obligations does not keep the largest obligations from being personal demands. . . . After all, in seeking for a universal principle, we inevitably are carried onward to the most universal principle — that *the essence of good is simply to satisfy demand.* . . . Since everything which is demanded is by that fact a good, must not the guiding principle for ethical philosophy (since all demands conjointly cannot be satisfied in this poor world) be simply to satisfy at all times *as many demands as we can?* That act must be the best act, accordingly, which makes for the *best whole,* in the sense of awakening the least sum of dissatisfactions. In the casuistic scale, therefore, those ideals must be written highest which *prevail at the least cost,* or by whose realization the least number of other ideals are destroyed. . . . The course of history is nothing but the story of men's struggle from generation to generation to find the more inclusive order. Invent some manner of realizing your own ideals which will also satisfy the alien demands — that and that only is the path of peace! . . . Though some one's ideals are unquestionably the worse off for each improvement, yet a vastly greater total number of them find shelter in our civilized society than in the older savage ways. . . . As our present laws and customs have fought and conquered other past ones, so they will in their turn be overthrown by any newly discovered order which will hush up the complaints that they still give rise to without producing others louder still. — James, The Will to Believe, 195–206.

Justice to the individual, then, must according to these principles consist in the rendering to him, so far as possible, all those services, and surrounding him with all those conditions, which he requires for his highest self, for the satisfaction of those desires which his truest judgment tells him are good. Conversely, opportunity for fulfilment of highest aims is all that may be justly claimed as a right. — Willoughby, Social Justice, 20–21.

The satisfaction of every one's wants so far as they are not outweighed by others' wants. — Adapted from Ward, Applied Sociology, 22–24.

The old justice in the economic field consisted chiefly in securing to each individual his rights in property or contracts. The new justice must consider how it can secure for each individual a standard of living, and such a share in the values of civilization as shall make possible a full moral life. — Dewey and Tufts, Ethics, 496.

Justice . . . may be described as the effort to eliminate from our social conditions the effects of the inequalities of nature upon the happiness and advancement of man, and particularly to create an artificial environment which shall serve the individual as well as the race and tend to perpetuate noble types rather than those which are base. — Kelly, Government or Human Evolution: Justice, 360.

Fundamental principles of just law:

The principles of respect. — 1. The content of a person's will must not be subjected to the arbitrary will of another. 2. A rightful demand can only be maintained in the sense [i.e. in such manner, to such extent] that the person bound can still be "his own neighbor" [i.e. an end in himself, so as to make "just volition possible"].

The principles of participation. — 1. No person legally bound is to be excluded from the common interest arbitrarily. 2. A legally conferred power of disposition can only be exclusive in the sense that [i.e. so far as] the person excluded may still be "his own neighbor" [i.e. an end in himself]. — Stammler, Lehre von dem richtigen Rechte (2 ed.) 148, 150.

As to the phrase "his own neighbor" see Lehre von dem richtigen Rechte (2 ed.) 194–196 (Husik's transl. 217–218).

Man has no rights, nor has the collectivity any rights. But every individual has a function to fulfill in society, a certain task to execute. This is the foundation of the principle of right and law which is imposed upon all, great and small, governors and governed. . . .

Every man has a social function to fulfill, and in consequence he has a social duty to fulfill it. He has the duty of developing his individuality, physical, intellectual and moral as fully as possible so as to fulfill it as well as possible, and none may hinder that free development. But one has no power of remaining inactive, of hindering the free development of his individuality. He has no right of inactivity, of idleness. Those who govern may intervene to impose work upon him. They may even regulate his work; for those who govern do no more in such case than impose upon him the obligation of fulfilling the social function incumbent upon him. — Duguit, Les transformations générales du droit privé depuis le code Napoléon, 20–21.

For the individualist conception, work values and collective values are at the service of the personality values. Civilization is but a means of personal education. The state and the law are but institutions to guarantee the security and the development of the individual. For the superindividualist conception, personal values and work values are at the service of collective values. Morals and civilization are put at the service of the state and of the law. . . . For the transpersonalist conception, personal values and collective values are at the service of work values. Morals, law and the state are at the service of civilization. . . . For individualism the highest end is freedom, for superindividualism the highest end is the nation or state, for transpersonalism it is civilization. — Radbruch, Rechtsphilosophie (3 ed.) 54–55.

I do not think so ill of our jurisprudence as to suppose that its principles are so remote from the ordinary needs of civilized society and the ordinary claims it makes upon its members as to deny a legal remedy where there is so obviously a social wrong. — Lord Atkin in Donoghue v. Stevenson [1932] A.C. 562, 583.

The only possible objective . . . is the welfare of the community. — p. 24.

There can never be a question of public benefit in any higher ethical sense, but only in the sense of what is to be considered useful for the community according to the estimate actually prevailing in the community. — p. 135.

Lundstedt, Superstition or Rationality in Action for Peace? Introduction and "General Remarks on My Theory of Public Welfare as the Basis of Law" (1925).

PART 3

THE NATURE OF LAW

IX. THEORIES OF LAW

Pound, Theories of Law, 22 Yale L. J. 114.

The different meanings of the term "law": (1) The legal order — a regime of adjusting relations and regulating conduct; (2) the body of authoritative grounds of or guides to decision and administrative action under a legal order; (3) the judicial and the administrative process under a legal order.

Unification of these by the idea of social control.

Law as a body of precepts or norms.

Standpoints and resulting conception of law in the second sense.

The standpoint of the individual subject to the law — (a) a body of rules or norms of conduct; (b) a body of threats of application of the force of politically organized society.

The standpoint of the judge or of the administrative official — a body of rules or norms of decision.

The standpoint of the counselor — bases of prediction.

The standpoint of the entrepreneur — a body of business devices.

Two ideas of law as a body of rules or norms of conduct, illustrated by two sets of words:

Greek	τὸ δίκαιον	νόμος
Latin	ius	lex
German	Recht	Gesetz
French	droit	loi
Italian	diritto	legge
Spanish	derecho	ley

Compare English, law, a law.

1. Greek definitions.

What the ruling part of the state enacts after considering what ought to be done, is called law. — Xenophon (B.C. c.429–c.356) Memorabilia, i, 2, § 43.

Law is a definite statement according to a common agreement of the state giving warning how everything ought to be done. — Anaximenes (B.C. c.560–c.500) quoted by Aristotle, Rhetoric to Alexander, i.

Law seeks to be the finding out of reality. — [?] Plato (B.C. 427–347) Minos, 315A.

The common law, going through all things, which is the same with Zeus who administers the whole universe. — Chrysippus (B.C. 287–209) quoted by Diogenes Laertius, vii, 88.

This is law, which all men ought to obey for many reasons, and chiefly because every law is both a discovery and a gift of God and a teaching of wise men and a setting right of wrongs, intended and not intended, but also a common agreement of the state, according to which every one in the state ought to live. — Demosthenes (B.C. 384–322) Against Aristogeiton, 774.

2. Roman definitions.

Law (*lex*) is the highest reason, implanted in nature, which commands what ought to be done and prohibits the contrary. — Cicero (B.C. 106–43) De Legibus, i, 6.

Law (*lex*) is the right reason of commanding and prohibiting. — Id. i, 5.

For law (*lex*) is nothing else than right reason derived from the gods commanding what is honorable and forbidding the contrary. — Id. Philippic. xi, 12.

Compare: A *lex* is a general command of the people or of the *plebs* upon question by a magistrate. — Capito (ob. A.D. 22) quoted by Aulus Gellius, x, 20, 2.

Moreover the laws (*iura*) of the Roman people consist of statutes (*leges*), enactments of the plebeians (*plebiscita*), resolves of the senate (*senatus consulta*), enactments of the emperor, edicts of those who have authority to issue them, and the answers of those learned in the law (*responsa prudentium*). — Gaius, i, § 2.

When about to study law we ought first to know whence comes the word law (*ius*). Moreover it is called law (*ius*) from justice (*iustitia*) for, as Celsus [a jurist of the end of the first or beginning of the second century A.D.] well defines it, law (*ius*) is the art of what is right and equitable. — Ulpian (third century A.D.) in Digest, i, 1, 1, pr.

3. The earlier Middle Ages.

As to the use of *lex* to mean law in general in this period, see I Savigny, Geschichte des römischen Rechts im Mittelalter, § 37 (Cathcart's transl. 115–121).

Fas is divine law (*lex*), *ius* is human law (*lex*). . . . *Lex* is a written enactment. *Mos* is usage approved by time or unwritten law (*lex*). . . . Moreover usage is a certain law (*ius*) instituted by observance which is held for enactment (*lex*) when enacted law (*lex*) is wanting. — Isidore of Seville (ob. 636) II Bruns, Fontes Iuris Romani Antiqui (6 ed.) 83.

Ius is the art of what is right and equitable. *Lex* is *ius* enacted by wise princes. — Petri Exceptiones Legum Romanorum, app. I; Fitting, Juristische Schriften des früheren Mittelalters, 164 (11th century).

Ius is the general term, so called because just; *lex* moreover is a species of *ius* and is so called from *legere* (to read) because it is written. Now all *ius* consists of *leges* and customs. *Lex* is an enactment of princes written down for the common good; custom is ancient usage derived from conduct (*moribus*), or unwritten *lex*. — Libellus de Uerbis Legalibus, 1, appended to the foregoing; Fitting, 181.

4. Development of the conception and definition of law from the revival of legal study at Bologna (twelfth century) to the time of Grotius (seventeenth century).

Pound, A Comparison of Ideals of Law, 47 Harv. L. Rev. 1, 5–11.

Corpus iuris ciuilis believed to be binding statute law, and hence *lex*.
Law made up of the *corpus iuris* as interpreted by jurists and contemporary enactment, on the one hand, and of customary law of various peoples on the other.

Ius is the genus and *lex* the species. All *ius* consists of enactments and customs. *Lex* is a written enactment. Custom is long usage. Usage is a certain kind of law (*lex*), instituted by observance, which is held for enactment (*lex*) when enacted law (*lex*) is wanting. — Gratian, cc. 2–5, dist. I (about 1150).

For the English laws (*leges*), although not written, may as it should seem, and that without any absurdity, be termed laws (since this itself is a law — that which pleases the prince has the force of law). . . . For if from the mere want of writing only they should not be considered as laws, then unquestionably writing would seem to confer more authority upon laws themselves than either the equity of the persons constituting or the reason of those framing them. — Glanvill, De Legibus et Consuetudinibus Regni Angliae, Preface (Beames' transl.) xi (about 1189).

Theory of St. Thomas Aquinas (1225 [or 1227]-1274):
 The old *ius naturale* divided into
 lex aeterna (eternal law) the "reason of the divine wisdom, governing the whole universe."
 lex naturalis (natural law) the law of human nature proceeding ultimately from God, but immediately from human reason, and governing the actions of men only.
Positive law a mere recognition of the *lex naturalis*, which is above all human authority.
 See Summa Theologica, 1, 2, qq. 92–95 (transl. in Rickaby, Aquinas Ethicus, 274–288).

A law is a rule and measure of acts, whereby one is induced to act or is restrained from action. Now the rule and measure of human acts is reason: it being the part of reason to direct to the end, which is the first principle of conduct. Hence a law must be some function of reason. — Thomas Aquinas, Summa Theologica, 1, 2, q. 90, art. 1 (Rickaby's transl.).

A law is . . . an ordinance of reason for the general good, emanating from him who has the care of the community, and promulgated. — Id. 1, 2, q. 90, art. 4.

Every law framed by man bears the character of a law exactly to that extent to which it is derived from the law of nature. But if on any point it is in conflict with the law of nature, it at once ceases to be a law: it is a mere perversion of law. — Id. 1, 2, § 95, art. 2.

Law (*lex*) is a holy sanction, commanding what is right and prohibiting the contrary. — Fortescue, De Laudibus Legum Angliae, cap. 3 (about 1468).

As natural law was discoverable by reason, the obvious effect was to require all rules of positive law to be tested by reason. Hence: "The first is the law eternal. The second is the law of nature of reasonable creatures, the which, as I have heard say, is called by them that be learned in the law of England, the law of reason." — Doctor and Student (Temp. Henry VIII) Intr.

A law (*lex*) of nature is a rule of reason; wherefore a human law (*lex*) partakes of the reason of law (*lex*) in so far as it is derived from a law of nature. And if they disagree in anything, there is no law but a corruption of law. — R. Suarez, Repetitiones, 272–273 (1558).

The proper signification of *ius* is one, namely, when *ius* is used to mean an enactment directing on behalf of the government those things which are right. . . . From this signification other less proper meanings have sprung. — Donellus, De iure civili, I, 3, § 2 (1589).

Ius from *iussum*. And hence the word *ius*. For I agree with those who consider that we say *ius* from *iubere* so that *ius* is as if you should say *iussum*. . . . For all law (*ius*) commands as is expressed in the definition of *ius*. . . .

Some [he cites Alciatus] hold that *ius* is said by metathesis, so that *ius* is, as it were, *uis* with the letters reversed. This does not agree with the fact. — Id. I, 4, §§ 1–2.

5. Development of the conception and definition from Grotius to Kant (seventeenth and eighteenth centuries).

Pound, A Comparison of Ideals of Law, 47 Harv. L. Rev. 1, 12–15.

Grotius puts natural law on a rational instead of a theological basis.
Hotman, Antitribonianus, cap. 12 (1567) had attacked the authority of Justinian.
Conring (1643) overturns the mediaeval notion of the statutory authority of the *corpus iuris*.
Thus natural law became once more *ius naturale*, the dictates of reason in view of the exigencies of human constitution and human society, no longer *lex naturalis*, the enactments of a supernatural legislator.
And positive law became the application of reason to the civil relations of men, of which the *corpus iuris* was an exponent only because and to the extent of its inherent reasonableness.

[After defining *ius* in the ethical sense, that which is right, and *ius* in the sense of a right.] There is also a third signification in which it means the same as *lex* when that word is used in its broadest sense, so that it is a rule of moral actions obliging to that which is right. — Grotius, De iure belli ac pacis, i, 1, 9, § 1 (1625).

Law (*la loi*) in general is human reason. — Montesquieu, L'esprit des lois (1748) i, 3.

A rule to which men are obliged to make their moral actions conformable. — I Rutherforth, Institutes of Natural Law (1754) 1, § 1.

In England following the period of legislative energy during the Commonwealth, Hobbes saw chiefly the imperative element.

Civil law is to every subject those rules which the commonwealth hath commanded him . . . to make use of for the distinction of right and wrong; that is to say of what is contrary and not contrary to the rule. — Hobbes, Leviathan (1651) chap. 26.

With the rise of a national law on the Continent, *lex* begins to stand for the rules of the civil law in each state.

A law (*lex*) is an enactment by which a superior obliges one subject to him to direct his actions according to the command of the former. — Pufendorf, Elementa iurisprudentiae universalis (1672) def. 13.

* In the eighteenth century the effect of an age of absolute government in reviving the conception of law as enactment becomes marked.

A rule prescribed by the sovereign of a society to his subjects. — Burlamaqui, Principes du droit naturel (1747) 8, 2.

Law is the expression of the general will. — Rousseau, Contrat social (1762) ii, 6.

Blackstone attempted to combine the two ideas.

A rule of civil conduct, prescribed by the supreme power in a state, commanding what is right and prohibiting what is wrong. — I Blackstone, Commentaries (1765) 44.

See I Blackstone, 41, 43, 47, 123, 160–161; Finch, Law (1613) bk. i, chap. 6.

6. Further development from Kant to Jhering.

(a) Metaphysical.

The sum of the circumstances according to which the will of one may be reconciled with the will of another according to a common rule of freedom. — Kant, Metaphysische Anfangsgründe der Rechtslehre (1797) 27.

Man stands in the midst of the external world, and the most important element in his environment is contact with those who are like him in their nature and destiny. If free beings are to co-exist in such a condition of contact, furthering rather than hindering each other in their development, invisible boundaries must be recognized within which the existence and activity of each individual gains a secure free opportunity. The rules whereby such boundaries are determined and through them this free opportunity is secured are the law. — I Savigny, System des heutigen römischen Rechts (1840) § 52.

The organic whole of the external conditions of life measured by reason. — Krause, Abriss des Systemes der Philosophie des Rechtes (1828) 209.

The recognition of the just freedom which manifests itself in persons, in their exertions of will and in their influence upon objects. — I Puchta, Cursus der Institutionen (1841) § 6.

An aggregate of rules which determine the mutual relations of men living in a community. — Arndts, Juristische Encyklopädie (1850) § 1.

The rule or standard governing as a whole the conditions for the orderly attainment of whatever is good, or assures good for the individual or society, so far as those conditions depend on voluntary action. — Ahrens, Rechtsphilosophische Einleitung, in Holtzendorff, Encyklopädie der Rechtswissenschaft (1 ed. 1871 — transl. by Pollock).

The expression of the idea of right involved in the relation of two or more human beings. — Miller, Philosophy of Law (1884) 9.

The aggregate of the rules which provide for the employment of the force of society to restrain those who infringe the liberty of others. — Acollas, Introduction à l'étude du droit (1885) 2.

The sum of the conditions of social coexistence with regard to the activity of the community and of individuals. — Pulszky, Theory of Law and Civil Society (1888) 312.

The sum of moral rules which grant to persons living in a community a certain power over the outside world. — Sohm, Institutes of Roman Law (1 ed. 1889, § 7 — transl. by Ledlie).

(b) Eighteenth-century and Neo-Rousseauist.

Those rules of intercourse between men which are deduced from their rights and moral claims; the expression of the jural and moral relations of men to one another. — Woolsey, International Law (1871) § 3.

The recognition of the law of nature by special enactments and its vindication in special circumstances and relations. — Lorimer, Institutes of Law (1880) 9.

The aggregate of received principles of justice. — Smith, Elements of Right and of the Law (1887) § 231.

The will of the state concerning the civic conduct of those under its authority. — Woodrow Wilson, The State (1898) § 1415.

A rule agreed upon by the people regulating the rights and duties of persons. — Andrews, American Law (1900) § 72.

Law is a body of rules for human conduct within a community which by common consent of this community shall be enforced by external power. — I Oppenheim, International Law (1905) § 5.

(c) Later historical.

The sum of the rules which fix the relations of men living in society — or at least of the rules which are sanctioned by the society — imposed upon the individual by a social constraint. — Brissaud, Manuel d'histoire du droit français (1898) 3.

The rule of conduct to which a society gives effect in respect to the behavior of its subjects toward others and toward itself and in respect to the forms of its activity. — Merkel in Holtzendorff, Encyklopädie der Rechtswissenschaft (5 ed. 1890) 5.

A rule expressing the relations of human conduct conceived as subject to realization by state force. — II Wigmore, Cases on Torts (1911) app. A, § 3.

(d) Analytical.

(1) French. Influence of the French Code.

The civil law is, therefore, a rule of conduct upon a subject of common interest prescribed to all citizens by their lawful sovereign. It is the solemn declaration of the legislative power, by which it commands, under certain penalties or subject to certain rewards, what each citizen ought to do or not to do or to permit for the common good of society. — I Toullier, Droit civil français (1808) § 14.

A law (*loi*) is a rule established by the authority which, according to the political constitution, has the power of commanding, or prohibiting, or of permitting throughout the state. A law truly and properly so-called, therefore, . . . is a rule sanctioned by the public power, a rule civilly and juridically obligatory. Law (*droit*) is the result, or better, the aggregate or totality of these rules. — I Demolombe, Cours de Code Napoléon (1845) § 2.

Law (*loi*) is a rule established by a superior will in order to direct human actions. . . . The law (*droit*) . . . sometimes the rules of law (*lois*) seen in their aggregate, or more often the general result of their dispositions. — I Demante, Cours analytique de code civil (1849) §§ 1–2.

What is law (*droit*)? It is the aggregate, or rather the resultant, of the dispositions of the laws (*lois*) to which man is subjected, with the power of following or of violating them. . . . Now these laws (*lois*) are rules of conduct established by a competent authority. — I Marcadé, Explication du Code Napoléon (5 ed. 1859) § 1.

One may say with Portalis that law (*la loi*) is a solemn declaration of the will of the sovereign upon an object of common interest. — I Laurent, Principes du droit civil français (1878) § 2.

Obligatory rules of conduct, general and permanent, established for men by the temporal sovereign. — Vareilles-Sommières, Principes fondamentaux de droit (1889) 12.

Law (*droit*) is the aggregate of precepts or laws (*lois*) governing the conduct of man toward his fellows, the observance of which it is possible, and at the same time just and useful, to assure by way of external coercion. — Baudry-Lacantinerie, Précis de droit civil (10 ed. 1908) i, § 1.

The *ensemble* of the rules to which the external conduct of man in his relations with his fellows is subjected, and which, under the inspiration of the natural idea of justice, in a given state of the collective consciousness of humanity, appearing susceptible of a social sanction where coercion is required, are or tend to be provided with such a sanction and thenceforth take the form of categorical injunctions governing particular wills for the purpose of assuring order in society. — I Gény, Science et technique en droit privé positif (1914) 51.

The *ensemble* of precepts, rules, or laws which govern human activity in society, the observance whereof is sanctioned in case of need by social constraint, otherwise called public force. — I Colin et Capitant, Droit civil français (1914) 1.

(2) Anglo-American.

First Stage. — The imperative theory perfected; eighteenth-century ideas eliminated.

Of the laws or rules set by men to men, some are established by *political* superiors, sovereign and subject: by persons exercising supreme and subordinate *government* in independent nations or independent political societies. The aggregate of the rules thus established, or some aggregate forming a portion of that aggregate, is the appropriate matter of jurisprudence, general or particular. To the aggregate of the rules thus established, or to some aggregate forming a portion of that aggregate, the term *law*, as used simply and strictly, is exclusively applied. — Austin, The Province of Jurisprudence Determined (1832) 2.

A command proceeding from the supreme political authority of a state and addressed to the persons who are the subjects of that authority. — Amos, Science of Law (1874) 48.

The general body of rules which are addressed by the rulers of the political society to the members of that society, and which are generally obeyed. — Markby, Elements of Law (1871) § 9.

A law is a command; that is to say it is the signification by a lawgiver to a person obnoxious to evil of the lawgiver's wish that such person should do or forbear to do some act, with an intimation of an evil that will be inflicted in case the wish be disregarded. — Poste, Gaius (1871) 2.

Second Stage. — Influence of the historical school: enforcement substituted for enactment.

A general rule of external human action enforced by a sovereign political authority. — Holland, Jurisprudence (1880) chap. 3.

Rules of conduct defined by the state as those which it will enforce, for the enforcement of which it employs a uniform constraint. — I Anson, Law and Custom of the Constitution (1886) 8.

The sum of the rules of justice administered in a state and by its authority. — Pollock, First Book of Jurisprudence (1896) 17.

The aggregate of rules administered mediately or immediately by the state's supreme authority, or regulating the constitution and functions of that supreme authority itself; the ultimate sanction being in both cases disapproval by the bulk of the members of that state. — Clark, Practical Jurisprudence (1883) 172.

Third Stage. — Enforcement by tribunals substituted for enforcement by the sovereign.

The law of every country . . . consists of all the principles, rules, or maxims enforced by the courts of that country as being supported by the authority of the state. — Dicey, Private International Law as a Branch of the Law of England (1890) 6 L. Q. Rev. 3.

The law or laws of a society are the rules in accordance with which the courts of that society determine cases, and by which, therefore, the members of that society are to govern themselves; and the circumstance which distinguishes these rules from other rules for conduct, and which makes them the law, is the fact that courts do act upon them. — Gray, Definitions and Questions in Jurisprudence (1892) 6 Harv. L. Rev. 24.

The sum of the rules administered by courts of justice. — Pollock and Maitland, History of English Law (1 ed. 1895) Introduction, xxv.

The rules recognized and acted on in courts of justice. — Salmond, Jurisprudence (1902) § 5.

The rules and principles recognized and applied by the state's authorities, judicative and executive. — I Clark, Roman Private Law: Jurisprudence (1914) 75.

7. German definitions after Jhering: influence of German legislation.

The sum of the rules of constraint which obtain in a state. — I Jhering, Der Zweck im Recht (1877) 320.

The rule armed with force first gives us the conception of law. That which does not possess the guarantee lying in force cannot be called law. — Lasson, System der Rechtsphilosophie (1882) 207.

Law is a peaceable ordering (*Friedensordnung*) of the external relations of men and their communities to each other. It is an ordering (*norma agendi*), a regulating through the setting up of commands and prohibitions. — Gareis, Encyklopädie der Rechtswissenschaft (1887) § 5.

The purpose of all law is a determinate external behavior of men toward men. The means of attaining this purpose, wherein alone the law consists, are norms or imperatives. — I Bierling, Juristische Prinzipienlehre (1894) § 3.

The legal order is an adjustment through coercion of the relations of human life arising in a social manner from the social nature of man. — Kohler, Einführung in die Rechtswissenschaft (1902) § 1.

Law is the ordering of the relations of life guaranteed by the general will. — I Dernburg, Das bürgerliches Recht des deutschen Reichs und Preussens (1903) § 16.

Law is the ordering (*Ordnung*) based upon autonomous government in a state of civilization. — III Berolzheimer, System der Rechts- und Wirthschaftsphilosophie (1906) § 17.

8. Recent definitions from present-day standpoints.

Pound, Progress of the Law — Analytical Jurisprudence, 1914–1927, 41 Harv. L. Rev. 174; id. Fifty Years of Jurisprudence, 50 Harv. L. Rev. 557, 566–571.

(a) Philosophical.

In the present, with its political storms which have shaken the consciousness-of-right of men and of peoples, in a time of confusion which looks upon law sometimes as sheer force, sometimes only as ideal powerlessness, we must call mankind back to a consciousness that law is neither the one nor the other, but rather might in the service of the idea of society, external coercion as the basis of freedom, form of the national community life, in which alone the individual may be free and may strive to fulfill in his person the idea of humanity. — Binder, Philosophie des Rechts (1925) 1063.

(b) Normative-analytical.

The norms of a customarily followed, comprehensive, and permanent supreme power. — Somló, Juristische Grundlehre (1917) 105.

Law is the legitimate order given to a human subject, individual or collective, bound to execute to the profit of another subject (entitled to claim from him the execution thereof) that an external fact be followed by another external fact, in default thereof by a third, and so on, with prescribed application of physical constraint to certain links in this chain. — I Roguin, La science juridique pure (1923) 122.

The delimitation of what men and groups of men are at liberty to do or not to do without incurring a condemnation, an execution, or some particular putting in play of force. — Lévy-Ullmann, La définition du droit (1917) 165.

Legislation and custom . . . rest upon the constitution, which in the sense of legal logic is the ultimate norm, the final source of the system of law. The decisive element for the positivity of law which gives law the character of a self-sufficient system, distinct from all other systems of norms, independent, and closed within itself, lies in this norm [i.e. the constitution] as the highest, derivable from nothing beyond, through the quality of sovereignty lent by this ultimate norm to the whole system of law raised out of it. — Kelsen, Das Problem der Souveränität (1920) 94.

The legal norm refers to the conduct of two entities: the citizen, against whose delict the coercive measure of the sanction is directed; and the organ that is to apply the coercive measure to the delict. The function of the legal norm consists in attaching the sanction as a consequence to certain conditions among which the delict plays a leading part. Looked at from a sociological point of view, the essential characteristic of law, by which it is distinguished from all other social mechanisms, is the fact that it seeks to bring about socially desired conduct by acting against contrary socially undesired conduct — the delict — with a sanction which the individual involved will deem an evil. — Kelsen, The Pure Theory of Law and Analytical Jurisprudence (1941) 55 Harv. L. Rev. 44, 58.

(c) Sociological.

The reason why people will pay lawyers to argue for them or to advise them, is that in societies like ours the command of the public force is intrusted to the judges in certain cases, and the whole power of the state will be put forth, if necessary, to carry out their judgments and decrees. People want to know under what circumstances and how far they will run the risk of coming against what is so much stronger than themselves, and hence it becomes a business to find out when this danger is to be feared. The object of our study, then, is prediction, the prediction of the incidence of public force through the instrumentality of the courts. . . . For the most important and pretty nearly the whole meaning of every new effort of legal thought is to make these prophecies more precise and to generalize them into a thoroughly connected system. . . . The prophecies of what courts will do in fact, and nothing more pretentious, are what I mean by the law. — Holmes, The Path of the Law (1897) 10 Harv. L. Rev. 457, 460, 461.

The limitations imposed upon the free activity of each in the interest of the general peace are expressed in the form of rules of conduct which every man ought to observe in his relations with his fellows. These rules, these precepts to be observed by men in their relations with each other, constitute the law. — May, Introduction à la science du droit (2 ed. 1925) 5.

A system of canons of valuation of social relations. — Perassi, Introduzione alle scienze giuridiche (1922) 23.

A principle or rule of conduct so established as to justify a prediction with reasonable certainty that it will be enforced by the courts if its authority is challenged. — Cardozo, The Growth of the Law (1924) 52.

Law is the ensemble of rules, imperative or permissive, the violation of which will provoke such feelings of dissatisfaction of a special nature in the social group where they are in force that the speedy appeasement of those feelings will be desirable in the interest of maintaining the peaceful character of social relations in that group. — Stoop, Analyse de la notion du droit (1927) 229.

(d) Realist.

From the point of view of the judge, the law may fairly be said to be the judging process or the power to pass judgment. — Frank, Law and the Modern Mind (1930) 274, note.

This doing of something about disputes, this doing of it reasonably, is the business of the law. And the people who have the doing of it in charge, whether they be judges or sheriffs or clerks or jailers or lawyers, are officials of the law. *What these officials do about disputes* is, to my mind, the law itself. — Llewellyn, The Bramble Bush (1930) 3.

X. THE NATURE OF LAW

Pound, More About the Nature of Law, in Legal Essays in Tribute to Orrin Kip McMurray (1935) 513: id. Social Control Through Law (1942) 35–62; id. What is Law? (1940) 47 W. Va. L. Q. 1.

A practical not a mere academic question.

(a) Cases where a state constitution or a state statute having been construed by the highest court of the state, and legal transactions having been entered into on the faith of the interpretation, the state court changes its view in later decisions with the effect that the transactions will not be upheld in the state courts.

Rowan v. Runnels, 5 How. (U. S.) 134, 139; Insurance Co. v. Debolt, 16 How. (U. S.) 415; Gelpcke v. Dubuque, 1 Wall. (U. S.) 175; Butz v. Muscatine, 8 Wall. (U. S.) 573, 575, 583; Douglass v. Pike County, 101 U. S. 677, 686–687; Anderson v. Santa Ana, 116 U. S. 356; German Savings Bank v. Franklin County, 128 U. S. 526; Los Angeles v. Los Angeles City Waterworks Co., 177 U. S. 558; Tidal Oil Co. v. Flanagan, 263 U. S. 444, 454. See also Hackett v. Maxey, 134 Ind. 162, 190–192.

Cf. Jefferson Branch Bank v. Skelly, 1 Black (U. S.) 436, 443; Bridge Proprietors v. Hoboken Co., 1 Wall. (U. S.) 116, 145; Wright v. Nagle, 101 U. S. 791, 793; McGahey v. Virginia, 135 U. S. 662, 667.

(b) Cases where federal courts, called on to apply the law of a state, finding the rule on some point undetermined by the state courts, determine the applicable rule, and after conveyances have been made relying on the decision, the state courts take a different view which would invalidate the conveyances.

Kuhn v. Fairmont Coal Co., 215 U. S. 349, 370–371, citing Gray, Nature and Sources of the Law (1 ed.) §§ 535–550.

(c) Cases where federal courts, administering the law of a state, formerly exercised an independent judgment as to what that law is.

Swift v. Tyson, 16 Pet. (U. S.) 1, 18; Salem Trust Co. v. Manufacturers' Finance Co., 264 U. S. 182, 191–192; Schofield, Swift v. Tyson, Uniformity of Judge-Made Law in State and Federal Courts (1909) 4 Ill. L. Rev. 533; Green, Law as Precedent, Prophecy and Principle: State Decisions in Federal Courts (1924) 19 Ill. L. Rev. 217.

But see Erie R. Co. v. Tompkins, 304 U. S. 64; Wichita Royalty Co. v. City National Bank, 306 U. S. 103, 106–110; West v. American Tel. & Tel. Co., 311 U. S. 211 (1940).

(d) Cases of application of the doctrine as to mistake of law where legal transactions are entered into in reliance on judicial decisions which are afterwards overruled.

Kenyon v. Welty, 20 Cal. 637; Harris v. Jex, 55 N. Y. 421.

(e) Cases where a penal statute having been held unconstitutional, some one acts in contravention of the statute, relying on the decision, and the decision is later overruled.

State v. Longino, 109 Miss. 125, 133–134; Freeman, The Protection Afforded Against the Retroactive Operation of a Judicial Decision (1918) 18 Columbia L. Rev. 230.

(f) Cases as to the operation of statutes with respect to acts abroad.

American Banana Co. v. United Fruit Co., 213 U. S. 347.

1. Analytical.

Austin, Jurisprudence, Analysis of Lectures 1–6 (5 ed. 81–85) lect. 1; Hobbes, Leviathan, pt. II, chap. 26, par. 6; Bentham, A Comment on the Commentaries, §§ I–VI, VIII; Holland, Jurisprudence, chaps. 2, 3; Markby, Elements of Law, §§ 1–26; Pollock, First Book of Jurisprudence, chap. 1; Salmond, Jurisprudence, §§ 5, 16, 17; Brown, The Austinian Theory of Law, §§ 552–639; I Clark, Roman Private Law: Jurisprudence, § 2; Jhering, Law as a Means to an End (transl. by Husik) 233–246.

Difficulties in the way of analytical theories:

(a) No analytical definition of anything undergoing evolution will adequately apply to all stages of development.

(b) Analysis of one element of a system of legal precepts has been made to stand for an analysis of law.

Hence the analytical theory does not cover the legal order nor all of the body of authoritative grounds of or guides to decision; it excludes the element of finding grounds of decision outside of the body of authoritative precepts, even if not outside of the legal order, and excludes the discretionary or administrative element in the judicial process.

(c) The analytical theory has been worked out chiefly from the standpoint of the individual, at the crisis of action, seeking a rule of conduct, or of the judge, at the crisis of decision, seeking a rule of or guide to decision. It ignores other standpoints which require to be considered.

Austin's analysis.

(a) Its presuppositions:

(1) That law is an aggregate of laws.

I Bentham, Works (Bowring ed.) 141.

(2) That a law is a rule of human action.

(3) An analytical separation or distribution of powers.

(b) Its details — laws are found to be:

(1) Commands set by a sovereign to subjects.

Meaning of "command," of "sovereign."

Difficulty of reconciling the origin of legal precepts through adjudication with the theory of a law as a command.

The doctrine of "tacit command."

Pope, English Common Law in the United States, 24 Harv. L. Rev. 6; Williams v. Miles, 68 Neb. 463, 470.

(2) Rules set by a determinate authority.

(3) Rules of general application.

(4) Rules dealing with external human action.

(5) Rules backed by sanctions.

"A legal proposition without legal compulsion behind it is a contradiction in itself; a fire that burns not, a light that shines not." I Jhering, Der Zweck im Recht (3 ed.) 322.

Modification by later analytical jurists: Law as that which is *enforced* by the state or by its judicial organs, not as that which is *set* by the state.

The norm theory: Law as a body of norms (models or patterns) of conduct or of decision established or recognized by the state in the administration of justice.

The hierarchy of norms.

See the reports on this subject presented before the International Congress of Comparative Law in 1933, II[II] Acta Academiae Universalis Jurisprudentiae Comparativae, 1–68; Pound, Hierarchy of Sources and Forms in Different Systems of Law (1933) 7 Tulane L. Rev. 475.

The threat theory.

I Binding, Die Normen und ihre Uebertretung (2 ed.) §§ 5–20; Thon, Rechtsnorm und subjektives Recht, 1–11; I Bierling, Juristische Principienlehre, § 3; Jellinek, Allgemeine Staatslehre (3 ed.) 332–337; I Gény, Science et technique en droit privé positif, § 22; Lévy-Ullmann, La définition du droit; Roguin, La règle de droit (1889); I id. La science juridique pure, 118–130; Kelsen, The Pure Theory of Law, 50 L. Q. Rev. 474; id. Das Problem der Souveränität, 85–101; Pound, Progress of the Law, Analytical Jurisprudence, 41 Harv. L. Rev. 174. See also Kelsen, Aperçu d'une théorie générale de l'état (1926) 33 Revue du droit public, 562, 571–578; Voegelin, Kelsen's Pure Theory of Law, XLII Political Science Q. 268; Wilson, The Basis of Kelsen's Theory of Law (1934) I Politica, 54; Jones, The Aims of Legal Science, 47 L. Q. Rev. 62, 78–84.

Duguit, Objective Law, 20 Columbia L. Rev. 817, 21 id. 17, 126, 142; Duguit, Le droit positif et la loi positive, 502–612.

May, Introduction à la science du droit (2 ed.) 3–9.

Hold von Ferneck, Ein Kampf ums Recht (1927).

The prediction theory.

Holmes, The Path of the Law (1897) 10 Harv. L. Rev. 457, 457–461; Cardozo, The Growth of the Law, 52.

The business device theory — charts of devices for the conduct of business activities.

"Rules for the creation of machinery and instrumentalities for accomplishing certain purposes." Bohlen, Old Phrases and New Facts (1934) 83 U. Pa. L. Rev. 305, 307, 311.

Theories in terms of the judicial process.

Llewellyn, The Bramble Bush; Frank, Law and the Modern Mind, 42–47.

Suggested analysis:

(a) The legal order — a regime of adjusting relations and ordering conduct.

(b) The body of authoritative grounds of or guides to judicial decision and administrative action.

   (1) The precept element.

     i. Rules.

     ii. Principles.

     iii. Precepts defining conceptions.

     iv. Precepts defining standards.

(2) The technique element — a received technique of finding grounds of decision in the body of authoritative precepts and of developing and applying them.

(3) The ideal element — received ideals of the social and legal order, of the end of law and so of what legal precepts should be and how they should be developed and applied in the light thereof.

(c) The judicial and administrative processes.

Pound, Juristic Science and the Law (1918) 31 Harv. L. Rev. 1047, 1060–1063; id. Theory of Judicial Decision (1923) 36 Harv. L. Rev. 641, 643–653; id. The Administrative Application of Legal Standards (1919) 44 Rep. Am. Bar Assn. 443, 454–458; id. The Supreme Court and Minimum Wage Legislation, compiled by the National Consumers' League (1925) Introduction; id. The Ideal Element in American Judicial Decision (1931) 45 Harv. L. Rev. 136; id. A Comparison of Ideals of Law (1933) 47 Harv. L. Rev. 1; id. Hierarchy of Sources and Forms in Different Systems of Law (1934) II^{II} Acta Academiae Universalis Jurisprudentiae Comparativae, published also (1933) in 7 Tulane L. Rev. 475.

See also Fehr, Recht und Wirklichkeit (1927); Al Sanhoury, Les réstrictions contractuelles à la liberté individuelle de travail dans la jurisprudence anglaise, 23–75; Hauriou, Police juridique et fond du droit; Cardozo, The Growth of the Law, 31–39.

As to standards, see Mutual Film Co. v. Industrial Commission, 236 U. S. 230, 245–246; Drake, The Rule, the Principle, the Standard in Fluctuating Exchange, 25 Mich. L. Rev. 860; Richards, Insurance (3 ed.) X; Merrill, Covenants Implied in Oil and Gas Leases, §§ 72 ff.

Characteristics of law in developed systems:

(a) Generality.

(b) Universality.

(c) Predictability.

Jahrreiss, Berechenbarkeit und Recht (1927).

The body of precepts in accordance with which justice is administered by the authority of the state.

The body of authoritative materials for the guidance of judicial and administrative action.

See Cardozo, The Growth of the Law, 36–55.

2. Historical.

Clark, Practical Jurisprudence, pt. I, chaps. 7, 11–16; I id. Roman Private Law: Jurisprudence, § 5; Maine, Early History of Institutions, lect. 13; Carter, Law: Its Origin, Growth, and Function, lects. 1–8.

Jenks, Law and Politics in the Middle Ages, 1–6; Rattigan, Science of Jurisprudence, §§ 8–11a; Wigmore, Problems of Law, 5–10.

Results of philological investigation.

Clark, Practical Jurisprudence, 11–89; Noyes, The Institution of Property, 562–569.

Results of legal history:

Primitive law:

(a) has no imperative element or, at least, that element is not well differentiated;

(b) is not set by a determinate authority;

(c) has no sanction or, at least, sanction is feebly developed;

(d) is recognized rather than enforced.

Historical view of sanction:

The habit of obedience (Maine, International Law, 50–52).

The displeasure of one's fellow men (Clark, Practical Jurisprudence, bk. 1, chap. 16).

Public sentiment and opinion (see Lightwood, The Nature of Positive Law, 362, 389).

The social standard of justice (Carter, The Ideal and Actual in Law, 13 Rep. Am. Bar Assn. 217, 224–225).

Hartland, Primitive Law, chap. 6; I Vinogradoff, Historical Jurisprudence, 353–361; Note, The National Industrial Recovery Act, 47 Harv. L. Rev. 85, 96–98.

Malinowski's historical-anthropological theory: Malinowski, Crime and Custom in Savage Society (1926); id. Introduction to Hogbin, Law and Order in Polynesia (1934). See review by Cairns, 34 Columbia L. Rev. 1379. Cf. Redcliffe Browne, Primitive Law, 9 Encyclopedia of the Social Sciences, 202.

3. Philosophical.

Miller, Data of Jurisprudence, chaps. 4, 5; id. Lectures on the Philosophy of Law, appendix A; Lorimer, Institutes of Law, 255–259; Korkunov, General Theory of Law (transl. by Hastings) 40–165.

Binder, Philosophie des Rechts (1925) § 6; Del Vecchio, Leçons de philosophie du droit, 177–249; Sauer, Rechts und Staatsphilosophie, § 43.

Law as an expression of ideas of right.

Law as a securing of interests.

Law as a delimitation of interests.

The "jural postulates" of civilization.

Philosophical jurists regard the sources of law rather than the nature of law; they consider the ideal element rather than the precept element.

4. Sociological.

Gray, Nature and Sources of the Law (1 ed.) §§ 191–247; Gareis, Science of Law (transl. by Kocourek) § 5; Dicey, Law and Public Opinion in England (2 ed.) 483–494; Willoughby, The Fundamental Concepts of Public Law, chap. 10; Cardozo, The Growth of the Law, 21–55; Ehrlich, Fundamental Principles of the Sociology of Law (transl. by Moll) 26–38.

The functional view of law — law as a social mechanism.

The legal order a phase of social control.

Emge, Ueber den Charakter der Geltungsproblem in der Rechtswissenschaft, XIV Archiv für Rechts- und Wirthschaftsphilosophie, 146, 277, XV, 54; Levi, Contributi ad una teoria filosofica dell' ordine giuridico, §§ 21–25; Perassi, Introduzione alle scienze giuridiche, chap. 1.

The body of precepts and received ideals, and the technique of using them, established or recognized by organized human society for the delimitation and securing of interests.

The formation and maintenance of a set of habits with respect to persons and property upon which the individual may rely and through which he may command security in his day's occupation and plans for the future. — Adapted from Allport, Social Psychology and Human Values, 38 Internat. Journ. of Ethics, 369, 373.

5. Bodies or types of precepts with reference to which theories of the nature of law must be tried.

(a) "Municipal" (civil) private law.

(b) Public law.

(1) Constitutional law.

(2) Administrative law.

See Dicey, Law of the Constitution (8 ed.) 1–34, 324–401, 413–434; Frankfurter, The Task of Administrative Law, 75 U. Pa. L. Rev. 614 (also as General Introduction in Patterson, The Insurance Commissioner in the United States, xi–xviii); Berthélemy, Traité élémentaire de droit administratif (13 ed.) 1–8; Hauriou, Précis de droit administratif (10 ed.) 1–12; I Jèze, Les principes généraux de droit administratif (3 ed.) 1–2; Frankfurter and others, A Symposium on Administrative Law, 18 Iowa L. Rev. 129; Pound, Administrative Law (1942) lect. 1.

(c) International law.

See Austin, Jurisprudence (4 ed.) 177; Holland, Jurisprudence (13 ed.) 133–135; I Savigny, System des heutigen römischen Rechts, § 11; Zorn, Völkerrecht (2 ed.) § 2.

Maine, International Law, 47–53; Hall, International Law, Introductory chapter; I Westlake, International Law, 5–13.

Liszt, Völkerrecht (10 ed.) 8–10; I Mérignhac, Droit public international,

18–26; Bonfils, Droit international public (7 ed.) §§ 26–31; I Hyde, International Law, 1–13. Triepel, Völkerrecht und Landesrecht, 1–10 (French translation Droit international et droit interne, 1–10); Wenzel, Der Begriff des Gesetzes, 344–468; Oppenheim, The Future of International Law (1921); Lauterpacht, The Function of Law in the International Community (1933) 3, 51, 60, 111–127, 245–248, 385–398, 407–439; Wright, The Enforcement of International Law through Municipal Law in the United States (1916) Introduction; Mirkine-Guetzévitch, Droit international et droit constitutionnel (1931) 38 Académie de droit international, 307, chaps. 1, 2, 6, also reprinted (1931).

(d) The conflict of laws.

Harrison, Jurisprudence and the Conflict of Laws, 98–148.

What have these in common?
How far are some of these to be called "law"?

6. Analogous uses of the term "law."

Laws of nature or of science.

Kelsen, The Pure Theory of Law and Analytical Jurisprudence (1942) 55 Harv. L. Rev. 44, 51–52.

Laws of grammar, etc.
Laws of morals, fashion, etc.
Laws of games.

See Carter, The Ideal and the Actual in the Law, 13 Rep. Am. Bar Assn. 217, 225–227.
Analogies to legislation in rules governing modern games.

XI. LAW AND MORALS — JURISPRUDENCE AND ETHICS

Pound, Law and Morals (2 ed.) contains full bibliography.
Austin, Jurisprudence, lect. 5; Bentham, Theory of Legislation, Principles of Legislation, chap. 12; Pollock, First Book of Jurisprudence, pt. I, chap. 2; Gray, Nature and Sources of the Law (1 ed.) §§ 642–657; I Clark, Roman Private Law: Jurisprudence, § 3. Carter, Law: Its Origin, Growth, and Function, lect. 6; Amos, Science of Law, chap. 3; Green, Principles of Political Obligation, §§ 11–31; Korkunov, General Theory of Law (transl. by Hastings) §§ 5–7; Gareis, Science of Law (transl. by Kocourek) § 6; Lorimer, Institutes of Law (2 ed.) 353–367; Kohler, Philosophy of Law (transl. by Albrecht) 58–60; Del Vecchio, The Formal Bases of Law (transl. by Lisle) §§ 96–111; Modern French Legal Philosophy

(7 Modern Legal Philosophy Series) §§ 190, 206–207; Hocking, Ways of Thinking About Rights: A New Theory of the Relation between Law and Morals in II Law: A Century of Progress, 1835–1935, 242.

Ames, Law and Morals, 22 Harv. L. Rev. 97; Rattigan, Science of Jurisprudence, §§ 4–4a; Dillon, Laws and Jurisprudence of England and America, 12–20; Woodrow Wilson, The State, §§ 1449–1456; Lightwood, The Nature of Positive Law, 362–368; Miraglia, Comparative Legal Philosophy (transl. by Lisle) §§ 119–127; Hegel, Philosophy of Right (transl. by Dyde) §§ 105–114; Miller, Philosophy of Law, lect. 13; Hastie, Outlines of Jurisprudence, 17–20; Winfield, Ethics in English Case Law, 45 Harv. L. Rev. 112; F. Cohen, The Ethical Bases of Legal Criticism, 41 Yale L. J. 201, reprinted in Ethical Systems and Legal Ideals, chap. 1; Hewart, Law, Ethics and Legislation, in Essays and Observations, 43; Radin, The Lawful Pursuit of Gain (1931); Williston, Modern Tendencies in Law, 1–59.

II Jhering, Zweck im Recht (5 ed.) 15–103, 135–351; Jellinek, Die sozial-ethische Bedeutung von Recht, Unrecht und Strafe, chap. 2; Stammler, Theorie der Rechtswissenschaft, 450–481; Binder, Rechtsbegriff und Rechtsidee, 214–229; Pagel, Beiträge zur philosophischen Rechtslehre, 60–81; Roeder, Die Untrennbarkeit von Sittlichkeit und Recht, 29 Archiv für Rechts und Sozialphilosophie, 29; Petrazycki, Introduction to Law and Morals, in Russian (3 ed. in Polish) (1930), well summarized by Gurvitch, Une philosophie intuitioniste du droit (1931) Archives de philosophie du droit et de sociologie juridique, 404, 407–413; Radbruch, Rechtsphilosophie (3 ed. 1932) § 6, well summarized in Gurvitch, Une philosophie antinomique du droit — Gustav Radbruch, in (1932) Archives de philosophie du droit, 530, 531 ff., and more briefly in Pound, Fifty Years of Jurisprudence, 51 Harv. L. Rev. 444, 455–457; Edlin, Rechtsphilosophische Scheinprobleme und der Dualismus im Recht (beiheft No. 27 to XXVI Archiv für Rechts- und Wirthschaftsphilosophie).

Kocourek, Subjective and Objective Elements in Law, 21 Ill. L. Rev. 689; Cohen, Change of Position in Quasi Contracts, 45 Harv. L. Rev. 1333, 1333–1338, 1356; Osborne v. Osborne, 40 Fed. (2d) 800 (1930) and note 44 Harv. L. Rev. 276.

As to the terminology of ethics in this connection see Eckstein, Die Entwertung ethischer Ausdrücke, XXII Archiv für Rechts- und Wirthschaftsphilosophie, 434. As to the meaning of "morals," "morality," "ethics," see Lee, Morals and Morality, 38 Internat. Journ. of Ethics, 450.

1. Historical view.

Law and morality have a common origin, but diverge in their development.

Four stages in the development of law in this respect may be noted:

(a) The stage of undifferentiated ethical custom, custom of popular action, and law.

(b) The stage of strict law — codified or crystallized custom which in time is outstripped by morality.

(c) The stage of infusion of morality and morals into law.

(d) The stage of conscious lawmaking.

2. Philosophical view.

Older views.

Natural law and positive law.

Practical results of this notion in legal history.

The theory can be held with safety only at a time when absolute theories of morals obtain.

Newer views.

Teleological (Jhering).

The ideals of an epoch (Stammler).

Evolutionary (Kohler).

Antinomic (Radbruch).

Justice has to do with the relations between men; the moral ideal with men themselves. Justice looks to an ideal social order; the moral ideal to an ideal man.

Revived natural law.

Moór, Das Problem des Naturrechts, 28 Archiv für Rechts und Sozialphilosophie, 325.

Sociological.

See Cardozo, The Nature of the Judicial Process, lect. 3; Ehrlich, Grundlegung der Sociologie des Rechts, chap. 4; Kornfeld, Soziale Machtverhältnisse, § 16; Wurzel, Das juristische Denken, 62–66 (transl. in Science of Legal Method, 371–377); Gurvitch, L'idée du droit social, 95–113; Petrazycki, Ueber die Motive des Handelns und über das Wesen der Moral und des Rechts, 50–58.

3. Analytical view.

Contact of law and morals in:

(a) Judicial choice of starting points for legal reasoning;

(b) interpretation of laws;

(c) application of standards;

(d) judicial discretion.

So far as a complete separation of judicial and legislative functions is possible, the distinction is —

law is for the judge;

morals are for the lawmaker.

Distinction between law and morals in respect of application and subject-matter:

(a) Morals look to thought and feeling, law looks to acts.

Ethics aims at perfecting the individual character of men.

Law seeks only to regulate the relations of individuals with each other and with the state.

As to the Good Samaritan doctrine, see Dutch Penal Code, Art. 450; German Civil Code, § 826; Stammler, Lehre von dem richtigen Rechte, 489–490; 2 Planck, Bürgerliches Gesetzbuch (3 ed.) 995 (§ 826 note e); Bentham, Principles of Morals and Legislation (Clarendon Press Reprint) 322–323; id. Theory of Legislation (transl. by Hildreth, 5 ed.) 65–66; Livingston, Draft Code of Crimes and Punishments for the State of Louisiana, II, 126–127; Macaulay, Notes to Draft of Indian Penal Code, chap. XVIII, § 294, and note M, pp. 53–56; American Law Institute, Restatement of the Law of Torts, § 192.

(b) Moral principles must be applied with reference to circumstances and individuals; legal rules are typically of general and absolute application.

Laws must act in gross and so more or less in the rough.

(c) Law does not necessarily approve what it does not condemn.

(d) Rules may be required for cases where there is no fault, or is equal or contributing fault, and where there is equal moral claim.

(e) Resistance to law may be moral but cannot be legal.

The "right of revolution." I Wilson, Works (Andrews' ed.) 18; I Andrews, American Law (2 ed.) § 103.

Developed law is and must be scientific.

XII. LAW AND THE STATE — JURISPRUDENCE AND POLITICS

Austin, Jurisprudence, lect. 6; Salmond, Jurisprudence, §§ 59–69; Holland, Jurisprudence, chap. 4; Bryce, Studies in History and Jurisprudence, essay 10; Markby, Elements of Law, §§ 31–38; Maine, Early History of Institutions, lect. 12; Jenks, Law and Politics in the Middle Ages, 68–71; Gray, Nature and Sources of the Law (1 ed.) §§ 169–183; Korkunov, General Theory of Law (transl. by Hastings) §§ 43–48; Gareis, Science of Law (transl. by Kocourek) § 46; Pollock, First Book of Jurisprudence (5 ed.) 261–279; I Clark, Roman Private Law: Jurisprudence, § 4; Duguit, The Law and the State, 31 Harv. L. Rev. 1; Harrison, Jurisprudence and the Conflict of Laws, 1–36, and Lefroy's note, 149–161; Lowie, The Origin of the State, 43–50; Cairns, Law and the Social Sciences, 220–261.

Borchard, The Relation Between State and Law (reprint from 36 Yale L. J.); Radin, The Intermittent Sovereign, 39 Yale L. J. 514.

Clark, Practical Jurisprudence, 157–176; Carter, Law: Its Origin, Growth, and Function, 187–190; Amos, Science of Law (2 ed.) 118–123; Hegel, Philosophy of Right (transl. by Dyde) §§ 257–360; Miller, Philosophy of Law, lect. 7; Kohler, Recht und Staat, in Handbuch der Politik (2 ed.) 120; Heller, Die Souveränität, 13–117; McIlwain, A Fragment on Sovereignty, 48 Political Science Q. 94.

I Vinogradoff, Historical Jurisprudence, 84–99; Krabbe, The Modern Idea of the State (transl. by Sabine and Shepard) translators' introduction, author's introduction, chaps. 1–4, 9.

Kelsen, Hauptprobleme der Staatsrechtslehre (2 ed.) 97–188; id. Das Problem der Souveränität, chaps. 1–4; id. Aperçu d'une théorie générale de l'état (1926) 33 Revue du droit public, 561.

1. The legal theory of the state.

Willoughby, The Fundamental Concepts of Public Law, chaps. 1–3, 5–7.

The purpose is to set forth the legal theory of the state.

Not political theories of the state.

Not philosophical theories of the state.

The legal theory has reference to the immediate practical source of rules and sanctions.

Political theories have reference to the ultimate practical source of rules and sanctions.

Philosophical theories have reference to the ultimate moral source of rules and sanctions.

A state is a permanent political organization, supreme within and independent of *legal* control from without.

"The subject of will which imposes a legal order." Del Vecchio, Sulla Statualitá del Diritto, 9 Rivista internazionale di filosofia del diritto (1929) 1; see English transl. The Statuality of the Law, 19 Journal of Comparative Legislation and International Law, 1, 8; German version Ueber die Staatlichkeit des Rechts, 8 Zeitschrift für öffentliches Recht, 510, 517 (there is also a French version).

The state as a person.

Willoughby, The Fundamental Concepts of Public Law, chap. 4; I Wolff, Organschaft und juristische Person (1933) 232–441.

For a full exposition and critique of theories of state and law from the beginning of the nineteenth century to the present, see Sander, Staat und Recht, (2 vols. 1922).

2. Anglo-American theory of sovereignty.

Dickinson, A Working Theory of Sovereignty, 42 Political Science

Q. 524; 43 id. 32; Willoughby, The Fundamental Concepts of Public Law, chaps. 8, 9, 12–15.

See also Hallis, Corporate Personality, Introduction, i-lxiii; Brown, The Austinian Theory of Law, Excursus A, B, 254–285; McIlwain, The Growth of Political Thought in the West, chap. 7; Ward, Sovereignty (1928); Orfield, Sovereignty and the Federal Amending Powers, 16 Iowa L. Rev. 391, 504.

The state is the whole of the political society in its corporate aspect.

The sovereign is that organ or that complex of organs which exercises its governmental functions.

"Consent of the governed" is a political, not a legal theory.

Sovereignty is the aggregate of powers possessed by the ruler or the ruling organs of a political society.

"By sovereignty is meant the aggregate of all civil and political power." Harper, J. in State v. Hunt, 20 S. C. Law (2 Hill, Law) 1, 250.

It may be:

(a) Internal — the sovereign is legally paramount over all action within.

(b) External — the sovereign is independent of all legal control from without.

Willoughby, The Fundamental Concepts of Public Law, chap. 20.

Powers of internal sovereignty.

The separation of powers.

Pound, Administrative Law (1942) 4–46.

Aristotle, Politics, iv, 14 (Jowett's transl. I, 133; Welldon's transl. 292); Montesquieu, L'esprit des lois, bk. 2, chap. 6 (Nugent's transl. may be used); Locke, Treatise on Civil Government, chap. 12; I Blackstone, Commentaries, 296; Federalist no. 417 (Madison); Dickinson, Administrative Justice and the Supremacy of the Law, chap. 2; I Goodnow, Comparative Administrative Law, chap. 3; Sidgwick, Elements of Politics, 363; Bondy, The Separation of Governmental Powers, V Columbia University Studies in History, Economics and Public Law, no. 2, 133; Fuzier-Hermann, La séparation des pouvoirs, 181 ff.; Hauriou, Principes de droit public (2 ed.) 692–700; Berthélemy, Traité élémentaire de droit administratif (13 ed.) 9–28; Esmein, Éléments de droit constitutionnel (7 ed.) 457–538; II Duguit, Traité de droit constitutionnel (2 ed.) §§ 63–64; Jellinek, Recht des modernen Staates (3 ed.) 496–504, 595–624; I Schmidt, Allgemeine Staatslehre, 209–217; Duff and Whiteside, Delegata potestas non potest delegari, A Maxim of American Constitutional Law, 14 Cornell L. Q. 168.

Wade, Consultation of the Judiciary by the Executive, 46 L. Q. Rev. 169, 47 id. 58; Allen, Administrative Consultation of the Judiciary, 47 L. Q. Rev. 43.

As to legislation conditioned on administrative action, see Queen v. Burah, 3 App. Cas. 889; Cargo of Brig Aurora v. United States, 7 Cranch, 382; Field v. Clark, 143 U. S. 649; J. W. Hampton, Jr. & Co. v. United States, 276 U. S. 394; People v. Klinck Packing Co., 214 N. Y. 121, 138–140.

As to devolution of rate making power upon commissions, see Intermountain Rate Cases, 234 U. S. 476 (compare s.c. below, Atchison T. & S. F. R. Co. v. United States, 191 Fed. 856); Eulogy of Chief Justice Taft on Chief Justice White, 257 U. S. xxv; German Alliance Ins. Co. v. Kansas, 233 U. S. 389; State v. Chicago M. & St. P. R. Co., 38 Minn. 281 (reversed on other grounds in Chicago M. & St. P. R. Co. v. Minnesota, 134 U. S. 418); Village of Saratoga Springs v. Saratoga Gas, Elec. Lt. & P. Co., 191 N. Y. 123; State v. Whitman, 196 Wis. 472, 512–517.

See also Powell, Separation of Powers, 27 Political Science Q. 215, 222–225.

The sovereign is incapable of legal limitation, but separate organs may be held to certain spheres or modes of action.

The mandate theory.
See Vattel, bk. i, chap. 3, § 4; Coxe, Judicial Power and Unconstitutional Legislation, 114–121; Brown v. Leyds, 14 Cape Law J. 94; Haines, The American Doctrine of Judicial Supremacy (1932); Jennings, The Law and the Constitution (1932).

Legal and political sovereignty must be distinguished.

Sabine, Political Science and the Juristic Point of View, 22 Am. Pol. Sci. Rev. 553.

Sovereignty is a modern development.

3. Duguit's theory of sovereignty.

Duguit, Les transformations du droit public, chaps. 1, 2, and conclusion (Laski's transl. Law and the Modern State, 1–67, 243–245); id. L'état, les gouvernants, et les agents; id. The Concept of Public Service, 32 Yale L. J. 425; Brown, The Jurisprudence of M. Duguit, 32 L. Q. Rev. 168; Laski, The Problem of Sovereignty, chap. 1; Jèze, Cours de droit public, liv. 2; Gavet, Individualism and Realism, 29 Yale L. J. 523; Kunz, Die Rechts- und Staatslehre Léon Duguits, 1 Revue internationale de la théorie du droit, 140; Chen, Recent Theories of Sovereignty (1929); Coker, Pluralistic Theories and the Attack on State Sovereignty, in IV Dunning, History of Political Theories; Laski, The Foundations of Sovereignty, 1–29, 209–249.

4. Hauriou's institutional theory.

Hauriou, La théorie de l'institution et de la fondation, in La cité moderne et les transformations du droit (1925); Renard, La théorie de l'institution (1930); Gurvitch, Les idées maîtresses de Maurice Hauriou (1931) Archives de philosophie du droit et de sociologie juridique, 155–259; Viehweg, Husserl, Hauriou und die deutsche Rechtswissenschaft, 31 Archiv für Rechts und Sozialphilosophie, 84.

5. Kelsen's theory of sovereignty as a postulate of the legal order.

Kelsen, Das Problem der Souveränität, chaps. 1–6.

6. Theory of sovereignty in the corporative state.

Pitigliani, The Italian Corporative State (1935) chap. 1.

XIII. JUSTICE ACCORDING TO LAW

Pound, Justice According to Law, 13 Columbia L. Rev. 696, 14 id. 1, 103.

Pollock, First Book of Jurisprudence, pt. I, chap. 2; Salmond, Jurisprudence, §§ 6, 7, 9, 10, 18–20, 26–29; Markby, Elements of Law, § 201; Amos, Science of Law, chap. 14; Korkunov, General Theory of Law (transl. by Hastings) §§ 41, 49; Demogue, Les principes fondamentales du droit privé, pt. I, chaps. 2–3.

1. The administration of justice — the legal order.

Systems of social control in the society of today:
(a) Religion.
(b) Public opinion.
(c) Ethics of professions and trade and business organizations.
(d) Administration of justice by the state.

2. Justice without law.

Law is not theoretically essential to the administration of justice. Examples of justice without law:
In legal history.
In modern states.

Salmond, First Principles of Jurisprudence, 89–90; Grotius, De jure belli ac pacis (Whewell's transl.) ii, 26, 1; I Ahrens, Cours de droit naturel (8 ed.) 177; Lasson, Rechtsphilosophie, 238–239; Gareis, Science of Law (transl. by Kocourek) § 6; Pulszky, Theory of Law and Civil Society, § 174; Stammler, Theorie der Rechtswissenschaft, 134–136. See Laws of Kansas (1913) chap. 170.
See also Simpson and Quinn, Popular Justice, XIX Archiv für Rechts- und Wirthschaftsphilosophie, 433.

Marx's theory of disapearance of law in the socialist state.

Dobrin, Soviet Jurisprudence and Socialism, 52 L. Q. Rev. 402; Gsovski, The Soviet Concept of Law, 7 Fordham L. Rev. 1; Paschukanis, Allgemeine Rechtslehre und Marxismus, introduction and chaps. 4, 5; Pound, Fifty Years of Jurisprudence, 51 Harv. L. Rev. 777, 780–782.

Administration of justice in the corporative state.

Pound, Fifty Years of Jurisprudence, 51 Harv. L. Rev. 777, 782–783.

Commercial arbitration.

Kellor, Arbitration in the New Industrial Society and review by Phillips, 48 Harv. L. Rev. 141; id. Arbitration in Action (1941); Phillips, Rules of Law or Laissez Faire in Commercial Arbitration, 47 Harv. L. Rev. 590; id. Commercial Arbitration under the N.R.A., 1 Univ. of Chicago L. Rev. 424; id. The Function of Arbitration in the Settlement of Industrial Disputes, 33 Columbia L. Rev. 1366; id. The Paradox in Arbitration Law: Compulsion as Applied to a Voluntary Proceeding, 46 Harv. L. Rev. 1258; id. Arbitration and Conflict of Laws, 19 Cornell L. Q. 197; id. A Practical Method for the Determination of Business Fact, 82 U. Pa. L. Rev. 230.

3. Justice according to law, i.e. according to authoritative precepts applied by an authoritative technique.

Law means uniformity of judicial and magisterial action — generality, equality, and certainty in the administration of justice.

Advantages of law:

(a) Law makes it possible to predict the course which the administration of justice will take.

(b) Law secures against errors of individual judgment.

(c) Law secures against improper motives on the part of those who administer justice.

(d) Law provides the magistrate with standards in which the settled ethical ideas of the community are formulated.

(e) Law gives the magistrate the benefit of all the experience of his predecessors.

(f) Law prevents sacrifice of ultimate interests, social and individual, to the more obvious and pressing but less weighty immediate interests.

Disadvantages of law:

(a) Rules are made for cases in gross and men in the mass and operate impersonally and more or less arbitrarily.

(b) Science and system carry with them a tendency to make law an end rather than a means.

(c) Law begets more law, and a developed system tends to attempt rules where rules are not practicable and to invade the legitimate domain of justice without law.

(d) As law formulates settled ethical ideas, it cannot, in periods of transition, accord with the more advanced conceptions of the present; there is always an element, greater or less, that does not wholly correspond to present needs or to present conceptions of justice.

Salmond, First Principles of Jurisprudence, 90–92; Korkunov, General Theory of Law (transl. by Hastings) 326–327, 394–395; Pound, Causes of Popular Dissatisfaction with the Administration of Justice, XXIX Rep. Am. Bar Assn. 395, 397–402.

4. Legislative justice.

Sidgwick, Elements of Politics, 355–356, 360, 482–484.

Examples of legislative justice:

(a) Greek trials before popular assemblies.

See II Vinogradoff, Historical Jurisprudence, 150–152.

(b) Roman capital trials before the people and appeals to the people in criminal causes.

(c) Germanic administration of justice by assemblies of free men.

(d) Judicial power of the English parliament.

(1) Relief against duress and fraud.

See I Rogers, Protests of the Lords, 17, 19, 22, 30, 39.

(2) Error and appeal in the House of Lords.

See Holdsworth, The House of Lords, 1689–1783, 45 L. Q. Rev. 307, 326–330.

(3) Impeachments.

(4) Parliamentary declaration of treason.

Rezneck, Parliamentary Declaration of Treason, 46 L. Q. Rev. 80.

(5) Bills of attainder and of pains and penalties.

(6) Divorce bills.

(e) Jurisdiction of the French senate to "pass judgment upon the President of the Republic and the ministers and to take cognizance of attacks upon the security of the state." Cf. Untersuchungausschüsse of the German Reichstag. See Scheffer, Die deutsche Justiz (1928) 286–295.

(f) Judicial powers of American colonial legislatures and state legislatures immediately after the Revolution. Pound, Organization of Courts (1940) 22–29, 33–34, 64–65, 110–111.

(1) Bills of attainder.

(2) Bills of pains and penalties.

See Tanner, Tudor Constitutional Documents, 423–432.

(3) Legislative appellate jurisdiction.

(4) Legislative granting of new trials.

See Merrill v. Sherburne, 1 N. H. 199, 216; Calder v. Bull, 3 Dall. (U. S.) 386; Wheeler's Appeal, 45 Conn. 306; Norwalk St. Ry. Co.'s Appeal, 69 Conn. 576; Chipman's Reports (Vt.) preface, 20 ff.; Taylor v. Place, 4 R. I. 324.

(5) Legislative equitable relief in Pennsylvania.

Loyd, Early Courts of Pennsylvania, 191–192; Cowan, Legislative Equity in Pennsylvania, 4 Univ. of Pittsburgh L. Rev. 1.

(6) Legislative jurisdiction in divorce.

(7) Legislative jurisdiction in insolvency.

(g) Legislative justice in America today.

(1) Impeachment.

See Potts, Impeachment as a Remedy, 12 St. Louis L. Rev. 15, 31–38.

(2) Claims against the state.

Defects of legislative justice:

(a) In practice legislative justice has proved unequal, uncertain, and capricious.

II Wooddesson, Lectures, lect. 41; I Tucker's Blackstone, 292–294; Thompson, Anti-Loyalist Legislation During the American Revolution, 3 Ill. L. Rev. 81, 147, 171; Eaton, The Development of the Judicial System in Rhode Island, 14 Yale L. J. 148, 153.

(b) The influence of personal solicitation, lobbying, and even corruption has been very marked.

Eaton, The Development of the Judicial System in Rhode Island, 14 Yale L. J. 148, 153; Pierce v. State, 13 N. H. 536, 557; III Debates of Pennsylvania Constitutional Convention (1873) 5–20.

(c) Legislative justice has always proved highly susceptible to the influence of passion and prejudice.

Thompson, Anti-Loyalist Legislation During the American Revolution, 3 Ill. L. Rev. 147, 157, 162; I Tucker's Blackstone, 293; Trial of Judge Addison, 7–15; Loyd, Early Courts of Pennsylvania, 143, 146; I Trial of Andrew Johnson (official ed.) 674, 693, 696–697, 698–700; I Stephen, History of the Criminal Law, 160; Lovat-Fraser, The Impeachment of Lord Melville, 24 Juridical Rev. 235; Rezneck, The Parliamentary Declaration of Treason, 46 L. Q. Rev. 80–103; Park, Biographical Sketch of Judge Emory Spear, 36 Rep. Georgia Bar Assn. 101, 114–115.

(d) Purely partisan or political motives have preponderated as grounds of decision.

See the last four citations next above; I Atlay, Victorian Chancellors, 144–145; VIII Campbell, Lives of the Lord Chancellors, 144–146; Browne, The New York Court of Appeals, 2 Green Bag, 277–278.

(e) Legislators who have not heard all the evidence have habitually participated in argument and decision; and those who have not heard all the arguments have habitually taken part in the decision.

See the record of attendance and voting in the Impeachment of Cox (Minnesota, 1881). Cf. Owens v. Battenfield, 33 Fed. (2d) 753, 757–758.

On the psychology of legislative justice, see Ross, Social Psychology, 57; Le Bon, The Crowd, chap. 5; Sidis, Psychology of Suggestion, 299.

5. Executive justice.

Pound, Executive Justice, 55 Am. Law Reg. 137; id. The Revival of Personal Government (1917) Proc. N. H. Bar Assn. 13; id. Administrative Law: Its Growth, Procedure, and Significance (1942); Goodnow, The Growth of Executive Discretion, II Proc. Am. Pol. Sci. Assn. 29; Dickinson, Administrative Justice and the Supremacy of Law; Powell, Judicial Review of Administrative Action in Immigration Proceedings, 22 Harv. L. Rev. 360; McClintock, The Administrative Determination of Public Land Controversies, 9 Minnesota L. Rev. 420, 542, 638–656; Patterson, The Insurance Commissioner in the United States, chap. 1; National Commission on Law Observance and Enforcement, Report on the Enforcement of the Deportation Laws of the United States (1931); Franklin, Administrative Law, 8 Tulane L. Rev. 483, 484–485; Dimock, The Development of American Administrative Law, XV J. Soc. Comp. Leg. 3 ser. 35; Lillienthal, Public Utilities During the Depression, 46 Harv. L. Rev. 745, 774–775; Jennings, Courts and Administrative Law — The Experience of English Housing Legislation, 49 Harv. L. Rev. 426; Hyneman, Administrative Adjudication: An Analysis, 51 Pol. Sci. Q. 383, 516; Vanderbilt, The Bar and the Judge, 23 A. B. A. J. 871, 873; Allen, Some Aspects of Administrative Law (1929) Journal of the Society of Public Teachers of Law, 10; Oppenheimer, Recent Developments in the Deportation Process, 36 Michigan L. Rev. 355; II Recent Social Trends, 1467–1480; Note, Development in the Law of Unfair Competition, 46 Harv. L. Rev. 1171, 1200–1202.

Wheat, The Regulation of Interstate Telephone Rates, 51 Harv. L. Rev. 846; Konitz, Administrative Law and Democratic Institutions, 3 Journ. of Social Philosophy, 139; Landis, Business Policy and the Courts, 27 Yale Rev. 235.

Bonnard, Précis élémentaire de droit administratif, 79-80; Andréadès, Le contentieux administratif, with preface by Jèze (1934).

In legal history.

In the Anglo-American polity.

Law and administration in nineteenth-century America.

The reaction in America.

Boards of Health, etc.
Public Utility Commissions.
Boards of Engineers, etc.
Industrial Commissions.
Probation and Parole Commissions.
Pure Food Commissions.
Administrative powers in immigration.
The Federal Trade Commission.
The Securities and Exchange Commission.
The Federal Communications Commission.
The Bituminous Coal Commission.
The National Labor Relations Board.

Also administration orders in the nature of adjudication by the Secretary of Agriculture, by the Board of Governors of the Federal Reserve System, by the Secretary of Commerce, of the Post Office Department, and of the Treasury Department.

As to the same movement in England, see Local Government Board v. Arlidge [1915] A. C., 120, [1914] 1 K. B. 160; Dicey, Law and Opinion in England (2 ed.) xli-xliv; id. Law of the Constitution (8 ed.) xxxvii-xlvii; Hewart, The New Despotism; id. Essays and Observations, 122-123; Allen, Bureaucracy Triumphant; Willis, The Parliamentary Powers of English Government Departments; Report of the Committee on Ministers' Powers (1932) 72-75; Robson, Justice and Administrative Law; Gordon, Administrative Tribunals and the Courts, 49 L. Q. Rev. 94.

As to Germany, see Scheffer, Die deutsche Justiz, 277-286.

Analogy in English law in the sixteenth century.

See Maitland, English Law and the Renaissance, 21 ff.; Marriott, The Crisis of English Liberty: a History of the Stuart Monarchy and the Puritan Revolution, 1-18; Tanner, Tudor Constitutional Documents, 245-247, 279-286, 299-300, 336.

The balance between law and administration.

The advantages claimed for executive justice are those claimed for justice without law.

(a) Directness.
(b) Expedition.

(c) Conformity to popular will for the time being.

(d) Freedom from the bonds of purely traditional rules.

(e) Freedom from technical rules of evidence and power to act upon the everyday instincts of ordinary men.

Bonnard's reasons why France does not commit review of administrative action to the civil courts:

(a) A certain spirit of judicial hostility to administrative action.

(b) Administrative disputes frequently have a technical character, calling for special judges.

(c) Administrative experiments give rise to a great mass of disputes which would prove too much for the civil courts.

(d) Administrative courts can be organized so as to offer the same guarantees of independence and impartiality as the ordinary courts.

(e) The judges in the civil courts are accustomed to applying written texts and codified law, and hence are not adapted to dealing with an uncodified administrative law.

Bonnard, Précis élémentaire de droit administratif, 79, 80.

The defects of executive justice are those of justice without law. Pound, Administrative Law (1942) lect. 3 (Administrative Procedure).

Report of the Special Committee on Administrative Law (1938) 63 Rep. Am. Bar Assn. 331–362; Pound, Administrative Law (Institute on Modern Federal Administrative Law, 1939) 51 Rep. Va. State Bar Assn. 8; id. The Place of the Judiciary in a Democratic Polity (1941) 27 A. B. A. J. 133; id. For the Minority Report, 27 id. 664; Administrative Procedure in Government Agencies, Report of the Committee on Administrative Procedure, Appointed by the Attorney-General, Senate Document No. 8, 77th Congress, 1st Session (1941); Dickinson, The Acheson Report: A Novel Approach to Administrative Law (1942) 90 U. Pa. L. Rev. 757; Montague, Reform of Administrative Procedure (1942) 40 Mich. L. Rev. 501 — contains full references to all the recent literature of the subject.

Defects of administrative justice in the common-law world:

(a) A tendency to decide without a hearing or without hearing one of the parties.

In re Evans, 52 New South Wales Weekly Notes, 1; Roche, L. J. in Errington v. Minister of Health [1935] 1 K. B. 249, 280–281; Rex v. Housing Appeal Tribunal [1920] 3 K. B. 334, 342, 344; Cooper v. Wilson [1937] 2 K. B. 309, 345; Lamar, J. in Interstate Commerce Commission v. Louisville & N. R. Co., 227 U. S. 88, 93; Tri-State Broadcasting Co. v. Federal Communications Commission, 96 Fed. (2d) 564, 566 (1938). See cases from state courts cited in Pound, Administrative Law (1942) 68.

(b) A tendency to decide on the basis of matters not before the tribunal or on secret reports or evidence not produced.

Cardozo, J. in United States v. Chicago, M. & St. P. R. Co., 294 U. S. 499, 510; IX Wigmore, Evidence (3 ed.) § 2569; Morgan v. United States, 304 U. S. 1, 14–15, 17, 19–20; and cases cited in Pound, Administrative Law (1942) 69–72.

(c) A tendency to make decisions on the basis of preformed opinions and prejudices.

Scott, L. J. in Cooper v. Wilson [1937] 2 K. B. 309, 345.

(d) A tendency to consider the administrative determining function one of acting rather than of deciding; to apply to the determining function the methods of the directing function.

See Vanderbilt, The Bar and the Public, 23 A. B. A. J. 871, 873.

(e) A tendency to disregard jurisdictional limits and seek to extend the sphere of administrative action, and to set up and give effect to policies beyond or even at variance with the statutes or the general law governing the action of the administrative agency.

See Doran v. Eisenberg, 30 Fed. (2d) 503; Charles D. Kaier Co. v. Doran, 42 Fed. (2d) 923, 924; Motsinger v. Perryman, 218 N. C. 15, 21 (1940); In re Atchison, T. & S. F. R. Co.'s Protest, 44 N. M. 608, 613 (1940); Puhl v. Pennsylvania Public Utilities Commission, 139 Pa. Super. Ct. 152, 158 (1939).

(f) A tendency to make determinations without a basis in evidence of rational probative force.

Taylor v. Cornett Lewis Coal Co., 281 Ky. 366, 368 (1940); and cases discussed in Pound, Administrative Law (1942) 68–73.

(g) A tendency to do "what will get by"; to yield to political or other pressure at the expense of the law.

(h) A tendency to arbitrary rule making for administrative convenience at the expense of important interests.

See Doran v. Eisenberg, 30 Fed. (2d) 503, 504.

(i) A tendency at the other extreme to fall into a perfunctory routine.

See Criminal Justice in Cleveland, 616, 623, 631, 647; Young, Social Treatment in Probation and Delinquency, 468.

(j) A tendency to exercise the deciding function by deputies and to rubber stamp review of the acts of subordinates by the subordinates themselves.

(k) A tendency to mix up rule making, investigation, prosecution, the advocate's function, the judge's function, and the function of enforcing the judgment, so as to make a proceeding one to give effect to a complaint.

See Vanderbilt, The Bar and the Public, 23 A. B. A. J. 871, 873.

Forms and rules, by compelling deliberation, guard against suggestion and impulse and insure the application of reason to the cause.

See Stephens, Administrative Tribunals and the Rules of Evidence, chap. 7; Pittman, The Doctrine of Precedents and the Interstate Commerce Commission, 5 George Washington L. Rev. 543, 578–579. As to the results of want of rules of evidence in criminal trials before laymen, see Chandler, American Criminal Trials, 137–138.

In time administrative tribunals have turned into ordinary courts.

Hyneman, The Case Law of the New York Public Service Commission, 33 Columbia L. Rev. 67, 104–105.

6. Judicial justice.

Bluntschli, Theory of the State (3 Oxford ed.) 523; Lieber, Civil Liberty and Self-Government, chaps. 18, 19; II Burgess, Political Science and Constitutional Law, 356–366; Baldwin, The American Judiciary, 1–98; Brown, Judicial Independence, XII Rep. Am. Bar. Assn. 265; Root, Judicial Decisions and Public Feeling, Addresses on Government and Citizenship, 445; Pound, Social Problems and the Courts, 18 Am. J. Sociol. 331; 2 Beard, Rise of the American Constitution, 587.

Setting off of the judicial function has been a gradual process. Objections urged against judicial justice:

(a) That it is too rigid and does not allow sufficient play to the non-legal conscience in the ascertaining or in the applying of the law.

(b) That the premises employed in judicial justice are too narrow and pedantic and the fundamental principles too fixed, so that judicial justice is too slow in responding to the environment in which it must operate.

See Wyatt v. Kreglinger & Fernau [1933] 1 K. B. 793.

(c) That it is characterized by a tendency to reduce to rule, along with those things which demand rule, those with respect to which detailed rules are not practicable.

See Lord Shaw in Local Government Board v. Arlidge [1915] A. C. 120, 137–138; Crownhart, Labor Law Enforcement through Administrative Orders, 4 American Labor Legislation Rev. 13; Commons and Morehouse, Legal and Economic Job Analysis, 37 Yale L. J. 139; Rosenberry, Power of the Courts to Set Aside Administrative Rules and Orders, 24 A. B. A. J. 279; Vanderbilt, The Place of the Administrative Tribunal in our Legal System, id. 267.

These objections amount to this: That judicial justice realizes justice according to law most completely and so brings out its defects as well as its excellencies.

Advantages of judicial justice:

(a) It combines the possibilities of certainty and of flexibility better than any other form of administering justice.

(b) There are checks upon the judge which do not obtain or are ineffective in case of legislative and executive officers. Pound, Administrative Law (1942) 60–68.

(c) Because of training in and habit of seeking and applying principles when called on to act and because their decisions are subject to expert criticism, judges will stand for the law against excitement and clamor.

Rutgers v. Waddington, 1 Thayer Cas. Const. L. 63; Bayard v. Singleton, 1 Martin (N. C.) 42; Brown v. Leyds, 14 Cape L. J. 71, 84; Littleton v. Fritz, 65 Ia. 488; Sims' Case, 7 Cush. 285; The Case of Thomas Sims, 14 Monthly L. Reporter, 1; The Removal of Judge Loring, 18 Monthly L. Reporter, 1.

As to the achievements of an independent common-law bench and its importance in a constitutional polity, see Holdsworth, The Constitutional Position of the Judges, 48 L. Q. Rev. 25, 31 ff.

PART 4

THE SCOPE AND SUBJECT MATTER OF LAW

XIV. INTERESTS

A. The Subject Matter of Law as Determined by the Civilization of the Time and Place

Kohler, Philosophy of Law (transl. by Albrecht) 4–5, 58–62; Pound, A Comparison of Ideals of Law, 47 Harv. L. Rev. 1.

Hocking, The Present Status of the Philosophy of Law and of Rights, §§ 41–48; I Recent Social Trends, xi-xv, lxx-lxxv, and review by Laski, 47 Harv. L. Rev. 1086; Lerner, The Social Thought of Mr. Justice Brandeis, 41 Yale L. J. 1, 11–17, reprinted in Frankfurter, Mr. Justice Brandeis, 9–45; Frankfurter, The Public and its Government, 1–35; Beard, The American Leviathan, 20–52; Jordan, Forms of Individuality, 54–55.

Lerner, The Supreme Court and American Capitalism, 42 Yale L. J. 668, 696–701; Dickinson, The Law Behind Law, 29 Columbia L. Rev. 285, 296–307; Hamilton, The Problem of Anti-Trust Reform, 32 Columbia L. Rev. 173; Winfield, Public Policy in the English Common Law, 42 Harv. L. Rev. 76, 92–93, 99–100; Brown, Legislation for Health and Safety, 42 Harv. L. Rev. 866, 866–872; Keyser, On the Study of Legal Science, 38 Yale L. J. 413.

Duguit, Les transformations du droit privé; Gülland, Stellung und Aufgaben des Richters im Spiegel der Zeit, 69 Gruchot, Beiträge zur Erläuterung des deutschen Rechts, 857; Gurvitch, L'idée du droit social, 27–31.

B. The Jural Postulates of the Civilization of the Time and Place as a Measure of Interests to be Recognized and Secured

Kohler, Philosophy of Law (transl. by Albrecht) 4; Pound, The Ideal Element in American Judicial Decision, 45 Harv. L. Rev. 136, 146–147.

Sauer, Die Wirklichkeit des Rechts, XXII Archiv für Rechts- und Wirthschaftsphilosophie, 9–18, 30–42; Oppenheimer, Die beiden Wurzeln des Rechts, XXIII id. 178–179.

Dodd, For Whom are Corporate Managers Trustees? 45 Harv. L. Rev. 1145; Berle and Means, The Modern Corporation and Private Property; Gardner, Inquiry into the Principles of Contract, 46 Harv. L. Rev. 1, 20–39; Llewellyn, What Price Contract? 40 Yale L. J. 704; Heilman, Judicial Method and Economic

Objections in the Conflict of Laws, 43 Yale L. J. 1082, 1108; Green, The Duty Problem in Negligence Cases, 28 Columbia L. Rev. 1014, 29 id. 255; Llewellyn, Behind the Law of Divorce, 32 Columbia L. Rev. 1281, 1287–1296, 33 id. 249; Tugwell, The Industrial Discipline and the Governmental Courts (1933).

C. Theory of Interests

Jhering, Law as a Means to an End (Husik's transl.) 28–35, 325; Gray, Nature and Sources of the Law (1 ed.) §§ 48–50; II Gény, Méthode d'interprétation (2 ed.) §§ 173–175; Cardozo, The Nature of the Judicial Process, 112–115; Pound, The Spirit of the Common Law, 91–93, 197–203; id. Introduction to the Philosophy of Law, 90–96; id. Interpretations of Legal History, 158–164; id. Social Control Through Law (1942) 63–80; Stone, A Critique of Pound's Theory of Interests, 20 Iowa L. Rev. 531; Green, Judge and Jury, 3–12; 1 Beale, Conflict of Laws, 58–64.

Adams, Some Remarks on Carnelutti's System of Jurisprudence (1939) 50 Ethics, 84–95.

An interest is a demand or desire which human beings either individually or in groups seek to satisfy, of which, therefore, the ordering of human relations in civilized society must take account.

The law does not create interests. It classifies them and recognizes a larger or smaller number; it defines the extent to which it will give effect to those which it recognizes, in view of (a) other interests, (b) the possibilities of effectively securing them through law; it devises means for securing them when recognized and within the determined limits.

Hence in determining the scope and subject matter of a legal system we have (1) to take an inventory of the interests which press for recognition and generalize and classify them; (2) to determine the interests which the law should recognize and seek to secure; (3) to determine the principles upon which such interests should be defined and limited for the purpose of securing them; (4) to consider the means by which the law may secure them when recognized and delimited; and (5) to take account of the limitations upon effective legal action which may preclude complete recognition or complete securing of interests which otherwise we should seek to secure.

D. Inventory and Classification of Interests

The interests which the legal order secures may be (1) demands or desires involved in or regarded from the standpoint of the individual life immediately as such (*individual interests*); (2) demands or desires involved in or looked at from the standpoint of life in a politically organized society, asserted in title of political life (*public interests*); or (3) those wider demands or desires involved in or looked at from the standpoint of social life in civilized society and asserted in title of social life (*social interests*).

INTERESTS TO BE SECURED

Ritchie, Natural Rights; Spencer, Justice, chaps. 9–18; Paulsen, Ethics (Thilly's transl.) 633–637; Green, Principles of Political Obligation, §§ 30–31; Lorimer, Institutes of Law, chap. 7; Demogue, Notions fondamentales du droit privé, 405–443.

II Ahrens, Cours de droit naturel (8 ed.) §§ 43–88; Hegel, Philosophy of Right (Dyde's transl.) §§ 34–104; Fichte, Science of Rights (Kroeger's transl.) 298–343, 391–469; Beaussire, Les principes du droit, bk. iii; Lasson, System der Rechtsphilosophie, §§ 48–56; I Boistel, Philosophie du droit, §§ 96–241; Kohler, Lehrbuch der Rechtsphilosophie (3 ed.) 109–185.

1. Individual.

Jethro Brown, The Underlying Principles of Modern Legislation, chaps. 7, 8; Jordan, Forms of Individuality, chap. II, pp. 56–57, and chap. IV.

II Lioy, Philosophy of Right (Hastie's transl.) chap. 1. The public good is in nothing more essentially interested than in the protection of every individual's private rights. — I Blackstone, Commentaries, 139. Two fundamental tendencies, which are characteristic of English thinking with respect to the relation of the individual to the state and have found more marked expression in English law-making than in any other, put their stamp upon Locke's philosophy of law and of the state: unlimited high valuing of individual liberty and respect for individual property. — II Berolzheimer, System der Rechts- und Wirthschaftsphilosophie, 160 (The World's Legal Philosophies, 137).

Man *in abstracto*, as assumed by philosophies of law, has never actually existed at any point in time or space. — III Wundt, Ethics (transl. by Titchener and others) 160.

Aulard et Mirkine-Guetzévitch, Les déclarations des droits de l'homme de tous pays; Resch, Zur Soziologie der Freiheit, XXIII Archiv für Rechts- und Wirthschaftsphilosophie, 28–39; Renner, Die Menschenrechte, ihre geschichtliche Rolle und ihre zukunftige Geltung, 1 Zeitschrift für soziales Recht, 225; von Keller, Freiheits Garantien für Person und Eigenthum im Mittelalter.

(a) Personality.

Pound, Interests of Personality, 28 Harv. L. Rev. 343, 445, Selected Essays on the Law of Torts, 87.

Gareis, Science of Law (Kocourek's transl.) §§ 122–135; Adler, Die Persönlichkeitsrechte im allgemeinen bürgerlichen Gesetzbuch (in the Festschrift zur Jahrhundertsfeier des allgemeinen bürgerlichen Gesetzbuches); Geyer, Geschichte und System der Rechtsphilosophie, 137–142; Stahl, Philosophie des Rechts (5 ed.) 312–350.

Reznek, Parliamentary Declarations of Treason, 46 L. Q. Rev. 80; Note on Entrapment Cases, 49 Harv. L. Rev. 109.

(1) The physical person.
Green, Principles of Political Obligation, §§ 148–156.

Miller, Lectures on the Philosophy of Law, lect. XI; Amos, Systematic View of the Science of Jurisprudence, 287–297; II Post, Ethnologische Jurisprudenz, § 102; I Blackstone, Commentaries, 129–138; Green, "Fright Cases," 27 Ill. L. Rev. and articles cited in note 26, p. 769; Green, Relational Interests, 29 Ill. L. Rev. 460, 1041, 30 id. 1, 314, 31 id. 35; Stallybrass, Public Mischief, 49 L. Q. Rev. 183; Borchard, Convicting the Innocent, Introductory chapter; von Moschzisker, Res Judicata, 38 Yale L. J. 299, 327–329; Eshugbayi Eleko v. Government of Nigeria [1928] A. C. 459; Rex v. Governor of Brixton Prison [1910] 2 K. B. 1056; Territory v. Anduha, 48 Fed. (2d) 171.

(2) Freedom of will —
free choice of location
free determination.
(3) Honor — reputation.

Dewey and Tufts, Ethics, 85–89; Westermarck, Origin and Development of the Moral Ideas, chap. 32; II Post, Ethnologische Jurisprudenz, §§ 17, 103; Institutes of Justinian, iv, 4; Sohm, Institutes of Roman Law (3 ed. Ledlie's transl.) § 36; Buckland, Text Book of Roman Law (2 ed.) 91–92.

De Villiers, The Roman and Roman Dutch Law of Injuries, 82–140, 173–185; Bower, Code of Actionable Defamation, appendix 3; Haymann, Der Schutz gegen wahre üble Nachrede, 70 Gruchot, Beiträge zur Erläuterung des deutschen Rechts, 61; Plucknett, New Light on the Old County Court, 42 Harv. L. Rev. 639, 668–669; Peck v. Tribune Company, 214 U. S. 185; E. Hulton and Company v. Jones [1909] A. C. 20; Cassidy v. Daily Mirror Newspapers, Ltd. [1929] 2 K. B. 331; Withers v. General Theatre Corp. [1933] 2 K. B. 536; New South Wales, Acts of 1912, no. 32, § 7.

(4) Privacy and sensibilities.

Warren and Brandeis, The Right to Privacy, 4 Harv. L. Rev. 193, Selected Essays on the Law of Torts, 122; Pound, Equitable Relief Against Defamation and Injuries to Personality, 29 Harv. L. Rev. 640, 668–677; Green, The Right of Privacy, 27 Ill. L. Rev. 237; Magruder, Mental and Emotional Disturbance in the Law of Torts, 49 Harv. L. Rev. 1033; Gutteridge, Comparative Law of the Right to Privacy, 47 L. Q. Rev. 203; Walton, Comparative Law of the Right to Privacy, id. 219; Bohlen and Polikoff, Liability in New York for the Physical Consequences of Emotional Disturbances, 32 Columbia L. Rev. 409; Bibliography in Note, 43 Harv. L. Rev. 297; New York Civil Rights Law, 1903, §§ 50–51; Damron v. Doubleday, Doran & Co., 133 Misc. (N. Y.) 302; Itzkovitch v.

Whitaker, 115 La. 479; Barnett v. Collection Service Co., 214 Ia. 1303; Tolley v. J. S. Fry & Sons, Ltd. [1930] 1 K. B. 467; Note by Allen, 46 L. Q. Rev. 151; Note, 42 Harv. L. Rev. 107–108; California Penal Code (Deering, 1922) § 258; I Baudry-Lacantinerie, Précis de droit civil, §§ 118–119; Scialoja, Del diritto al nome (1889); Du Boulay v. Du Boulay, L. R. 2 P. C. 430.

See also Brunstein, Namen und Firmenschutz in Oesterreich, Festgabe für Kohler, 28, 38–42; Borchgrave, De la propriété des lettres confidentielles, Festgabe für Kohler, 23; Misch, Der strafrechtliche Schutz der Gefühle (1911); Satku v. Ibrahim, 2 Bombay, 457.

(5) Belief and opinion.

Pollock, Essays in Jurisprudence and Ethics, 144–175; Mill, On Liberty, chap. 2; Stephen, Liberty, Equality, Fraternity, chap. 2; Stimson, American Statute Law, § 6115.

(b) Domestic relations.

Pound, Individual Interests in the Domestic Relations, 14 Mich. L. Rev. 177.

Holbrook, The Change in the Meaning of Consortium, 32 Mich. L. Rev. 1; Warren, The Husband's Right to the Wife's Services, 38 Harv. L. Rev. 421, 622; Feinsinger, Legislative Attack on "Heart Balm," 33 Mich. L. Rev. 979; McCurdy, Torts Between Persons in Domestic Relation, 43 Harv. L. Rev. 1030; Lippman, The Breakdown of Consortium, 30 Columbia L. Rev. 651; Robbins, Familial Property, Rights of Illegitimate Children, 30 Columbia L. Rev. 308; Wright v. Cedzik [1929] Victorian L. R. 117, 43 Com. L. R. 493; Oppenheim v. Kridel, 236 N. Y. 136; Johnson v. Commonwealth, 27 New South Wales S. R. 133; Somberg v. Somberg, 263 N. Y. 1; Nolin v. Pearson, 191 Mass. 283; Pickle v. Page, 252 N. Y. 474; Pyle v. Waechter, 202 Ia. 695.

Miller, Philosophy of Law, lect. 6; II Lioy, Philosophy of Right (Hastie's transl.) chap. 2; Kohler, Rechtsphilosophie und Universalrechtsgeschichte, §§ 17–24; id. Lehrbuch der Rechtsphilosophie, 66–81; Post, Zur Entwicklungsgeschichte des Familienrechts.

(c) Substance.

IV Berolzheimer, System der Rechts- und Wirthschaftsphilosophie.

Kant, Metaphysische Anfangsgründe der Rechtslehre, §§ 1–21 (Hastie's transl. 62–107); Gareis, Science of Law (Kocourek's transl.) §§ 19–23; Schuppe, Grundzüge der Ethik und Rechtsphilosophie, §§ 87–96; Demogue, Notions fondamentales du droit privé, 383–404.

(1) Property.

Noyes, The Institution of Property (1936); Green, Principles of Political Obligation, §§ 211–231; Duguit in Progress of the Law in the Nineteenth Century (II Continental Legal History Series) 129–146; I Vinogradoff, Historical Jurisprudence, 321–343; Pound, Introduction to the Philosophy of Law, lect. 5; Cohen, Property and

Sovereignty, 13 Cornell L. Q. 8, reprinted in Law and the Social Order, 41–68.

Property, Its Duties and Rights, Historically, Philosophically, and Religiously Considered (2 ed.) essays 1–3, 5–8; Ely, Property and Contract in their Relation to the Distribution of Wealth, I, 51, 93, 132–258, 295–443, II, 475–549; Miller, Philosophy of Law, lect. 5; Herkless, Jurisprudence, chap. 10; Amos, Systematic View of the Science of Jurisprudence, chap. 10; de la Grasserie, Les principes sociologiques du droit civil, chap. 13; Kohler, Lehrbuch der Rechtsphilosophie, 81–91 (Albrecht's transl. 120–134).

Letourneau, Property, Its Origin and Development; Coulanges, Ancient City, bk. 2, chap. 6; Maine, Ancient Law (American ed.) 237–294; Maine, Early History of Institutions (American ed.) 98–118; Maine, Early Law and Custom (American ed.) 335–361; Westrup, Joint Family and Family Property in Early Law, in 1 Studi in Memoria di Aldo Albertoni (1922) 143–172; id. Introduction to Early Roman Law, II, Joint Family and Family Property (1934), III, Family Property and Patria Potestas (1935); Jenks, Law and Politics in the Middle Ages, 148–184, 188–241; Larkin, Property in the Eighteenth Century; Hamilton, Property According to Locke, 41 Yale L. J. 864.

Reference may be made to Felix, Entwicklungsgeschichte des Eigenthums (4 vols. 1883–1903).

The literature of this subject is of enormous extent. For discussions from various points of view see:

Proudhon, What is Property? (transl. by Tucker, 1876); George, Progress and Poverty (1881); id. A Perplexed Philosopher (1892); Cathrein, Champions of Agrarian Socialism (transl. and ed. by Heinzle, 1889); Beer, History of British Socialism, vol. 1 (1919) vol. 2 (1920).

Simcox, Primitive Civilization, or Outlines of the History of Ownership in Archaic Communities (1897); Laveleye, Primitive Property (transl. by Marriott, 1878 — the original De la propriété et de ses formes primitives is in 4 ed. 1891); Lowie, Incorporeal Property in Primitive Society, 37 Yale L. J. 551.

Cosentini, La réforme de la législation civile (1913) 371–422; Acollas, La propriété (1886); Budon, La propriété privée et le droit fiscal (1905); Dugast, La propriété devant le droit naturel (1904); Fouillée, La propriété sociale et la démocratie (1884); Hayem, Essai sur le droit de propriété et ses limites (1910); Landry, L'utilité sociale de la propriété individuelle (1901); Marguery, Le droit de propriété et le régime démocratique (1906); Meyer, L'utilité publique et la propriété privée (1893); Parthenin, Le droit social sur les choses: Essai sur la nature des propriétés collectives (1908); Petrucci, Les origines naturelles de la propriété (1905); Tarbouriech, Essai sur la propriété (1901); Thézard, La propriété individuelle: Étude de philosophie historique du droit (1872); Thomas, L'utilité publique et la propriété privée (3 vols. 1904); Hedemann, Die Fortschritte des Zivilrechts im neunzehnten Jahrhundert: Die Entwicklung des Bodenrechts.

Bernstein, Gesellschaftliche- und Privateigenthum (1891); IV Berolzheimer, System der Rechts- und Wirthschaftsphilosophie, §§ 1–13; Karner, Die sociale Funktion der Rechtsinstitute, besonders des Eigenthums (1904).

Conti, La proprietà fondiaria nel passato e nel presente (1905); Cosentini, Filosofia del diritto (1914) 250–279; Fadda, Teoria della proprietà (1907); Labriola, Sul fondamento della proprietà privata (1900); Loria, La proprietà fondiaria e la questione sociale (1897); Piccione, Concetto positivo del diritto di proprietà (1890); Velardita, La proprietà secondo la sociologia (1898); Zini, Proprietà individuale o collettiva (1878).

II Perreau, Cours d'économie politique (1916) §§ 623–695; Wagner, Volkswirthschaft und Recht, besonders Vermögensrecht (3 ed. 1923) (pt. 2 of Grundlegung der politischen Oekonomie).

Succession and testamentary disposition.

Kohler, Rechtsphilosophie und Universalrechtsgeschichte, §§ 25–27; id. Lehrbuch der Rechtsphilosophie, 132–142 (Albrecht's transl. 192–206); de la Grasserie, Les principes sociologiques du droit civil, chaps. 11, 12; Boehmer, Erbfolge und Erbenhaftung, §§ 1–5.

I Vinogradoff, Historical Jurisprudence, 274–295; Coulanges, Ancient City, bk. 2, chap. 7; Maine, Early Law and Custom (American ed.) 78–121; id. Ancient Law (American ed.) 166–208, 209–236; Gaius, iii, § 1, §§ 9–26; Salic Law (transl. in Henderson, Historical Documents of the Middle Ages) tit. 59; Pollock and Maitland, History of English Law, bk. II, chap. 6, §§ 1, 3; Whitelock, Anglo-Saxon Wills.

On inheritance by illegitimate children, see Castberg, Children's Rights Laws and Maternity Insurance in Norway, XVI J. Soc. Compar. Leg. N. S. 283, 285 ff.; Burns, Annotated Statutes of Indiana, § 3333 (Acts of 1901, p. 288); Laws of North Dakota (1917) chap. 70; Freund, Illegitimacy Laws of the United States (1919); Robbins, Familial Property Rights of Illegitimate Children, 30 Columbia L. Rev. 308.

As to inheritance from illegitimate children, see Darrough v. Davis, 135 Okl. 262.

(2) Freedom of industry and contract.

Green, Principles of Political Obligation, § 210; Pound, Liberty of Contract, 18 Yale L. J. 454.

(3) Promised advantages.

Pound, Introduction to the Philosophy of Law, lect. 6; Cohen, The Basis of Contract, 46 Harv. L. Rev. 553, reprinted in Law and the Social Order, 69–111; II Ely, Property and Contract, 576–751.

Amos, Systematic View of the Science of Jurisprudence, chap. 11; Herkless, Jurisprudence, chap. 12; Kohler, Lehrbuch der Rechtsphilosophie, 91–132 (Albrecht's transl. 134–191); de la Grasserie, Les principes sociologiques du droit civil, chap. 6; Collinet, The Evolution of Contract, 48 L. Q. Rev. 488; 1 Parsons, Contracts (1853) 3–5; Wigmore, The Scientific Role of Consideration in Contracts, in Legal Essays in Tribute to Orrin Kip McMurray, 641; Lord Wright, Ought the Doctrine of Consideration to be Abolished from the Common Law? 49 Harv. L. Rev. 1225.

Rice, Collective Labor Contracts, 44 Harv. L. Rev. 572; Note, Some Legal Aspects of the National Industrial Recovery Act, 47 Harv. L. Rev. 85, 114–117.

(4) Advantageous relations with others.

Green, Relational Interests, 29 Ill. L. Rev. 460, 1041; Sharp, The Ethics of

Breach of Contract, 45 Internat. Journ. of Ethics, 27; id. Notes on Contract Problems and Comparative Law, 3 Univ. of Chicago L. Rev. 277; Kennedy and Finkelman, The Right to Trade (1933).

Borden Ice Cream Co. v. Borden's Condensed Milk Co., 200 Fed. 510; Dry Ice Corporation of America v. Louisiana Dry Ice Corp., 54 Fed. (2d) 882; Los Angeles Van & Storage Co. v. Los Angeles Van Transfer & Storage Co., 165 Calif. 89; Westminster Laundry Co. v. Hesse Envelope Co., 174 Mo. App. 228; Vogue Company v. Thomson-Hudson Co., 300 Fed. 509; John Forsythe Co. v. Forsythe Shoe Corp., 234 App. Div. 355, 259 N. Y. 248; Cheney Bros. v. Davis Silk Corp. 35 Fed. (2d) 279; International News Service v. Associated Press, 248 U. S. 215; Glenn, Pre-emption in Connection with Unfair Trade, 19 Columbia L. Rev. 29; Victoria Park Racing Co. v. Taylor [1937] Argus L. R. 597, 58 C. L. R. 479; Note in 54 L. Q. Rev. 319.

> Contractual,
> social,
> business,
> official,
> domestic.

The "Right of Association."

Dicey, Law and Opinion in England, 95–102, 190–200, 266–272, 465–475; Duguit, Le droit social et le droit individuel, 107–143; Nourisson, Histoire de la liberté d'association en France depuis 1789 (2 vols. 1920); Kliwansky, Die strafbaren Verbindungen nach russischen Recht (diss. 1912); Mestre (and others), La liberté d'association (1927); Kirsh, Trade Associations (1928); Foreign Law Series, no. 2, Trade Combinations in U. S. A., France, Germany, Poland (1932); Haslam, The Law Relating to Trade Combinations (1931); International Labour Office, Freedom of Association (5 vols. Studies and Reports, Series A, nos. 28–32, 1927–1930); Witte, The Government in Labor Disputes (1932); Baratier, L'autonomie syndicale et ses limites devant les cours anglaises (1928); Michels, Cartels, Combines and Trusts in Post-War Germany (1928); Frankfurter and Green, The Labor Injunction (1930); Beckner, Labor Agreements in Coal Mines (1931); id. History of Illinois Labor Legislation (1929) chap. II.

Chafee, Internal Affairs of Associations not for Profit, 43 Harv. L. Rev. 993, 1014–1029; Nelles, Commonwealth v. Hunt, 32 Columbia L. Rev. 1128.

Truax v. Corrigan, 257 U. S. 312; National Labor Relations Act, 49 Stat. 449 (1935), 29 U. S. C. §§ 151–166 (Supp. II, 1936).

Qu. Should there be a category of institutional and relational interests?

See Hauriou, La théorie de l'institution et de la fondation, in La cité moderne et les transformations du droit (1925) 10; Renard, La théorie de l'institution (1930) 225–231, 311 ff.; Jennings, The Institutional Theory in Modern Theories of Law (1933) 68–85; Ehrlich, Fundamental Principles of the Sociology of Law (1913 — transl. by Moll, 1936) chaps. 2, 3.

2. Public.

Salmond, Jurisprudence, § 119; Gareis, Science of Law (transl. by Kocourek) § 47; McIlwain, The Growth of Political Thought in the West, chap. 7.

Jellinek, System der subjektiven öffentlichen Rechte (2 ed.); id. Allgemeine Staatslehre (3 ed.) 169–173; Duguit, Manuel de droit constitutionnel (3 ed.) § 15.

(a) Interests of the state as a juristic person.

Fleischmann, The Dishonesty of Sovereignties (1910) 33 Rep. N. Y. State Bar Assn. 229; Singewald, The Doctrine of Nonsuability of the State in the United States (Johns Hopkins University Studies, ser. XXVIII, no. 3); Laski, The Responsibility of the State in England, 32 Harv. L. Rev. 447; Maguire, State Liability for Tort, 30 Harv. L. Rev. 20; Note, Limitations on the Doctrine of Governmental Immunity from Suit, 41 Columbia L. Rev. 1236; Moffatt v. United States, 112 U. S. 24; Borchard, State Indemnity for Errors of Criminal Justice (62d Congress, 3d Session, Senate Document No. 974); id. Government Liability in Tort, 34 Yale L. J. 1, 129, 229, 36 id. 1, 757, 1039; id. Governmental Liability in Tort, 28 Columbia L. Rev. 577, 734; Willoughby, The Fundamental Precepts of Public Law, chap. 25; Freund, Responsibility of the State in Internal (Municipal) Law, 9 Tulane L. Rev. 1; Farrer, A Prerogative Fallacy — "That the Crown Is Not Barred by Estoppel," 49 L. Q. Rev. 511; Borchard, Convicting the Innocent, 375–407 (State Indemnity for Errors of Criminal Justice); Gordon, The Crown as Litigant, 45 L. Q. Rev. 186; Dobrin, A Propos the Soviet Maritime Code, 49 L. Q. Rev. 249, 249–260; Duez, Les actes de gouvernement (1931) Annuaire de l'institut international de droit public, 35; Laun, Les actes de gouvernement, id. 91; Smend, Les actes de gouvernement en Allemagne, id. 192; Faultier, Les actes de gouvernement, id. 733.

Breese, J. in People v. Brown, 67 Ill. 435, 438; Missouri v. Fisk, 290 U. S. 18, 62 Fed. (2d) 150; State v. Cording, 101 Neb. 242; State v. Carr, 191 Fed. 257; Attorney General v. Railroad Co., 68 N. J. Eq. 198; Pittsburgh R. Co. v. Carrick, 259 Pa. 333; Note, 51 Harv. L. Rev. 555.

Lovibond v. Governor General of Canada [1930] A. C. 717; Re Mason [1929] 1 Ch. 1; Civilian War Claims Assn. v. Rex [1932] A. C. 14.

New York Laws of 1929, chap. 467; New York Court of Claims Act, § 12a; U. S. Code, title 31, §§ 209–236.

(1) Personality.

> Security,
> efficient functioning of the political organization,
> dignity.

Compare the distinction between corporate and governmental functions of a municipality.

Note, 46 Harv. L. Rev. 305.

(2) Substance.

Hanbury, Essays in Equity, 114–124; Note, 47 Harv. L. Rev. 841.

Compare the schemes of rights recognized in international law. See Wheaton, International Law (8 ed.) §§ 60, 61, 63, 72, 74, 77, 152, 161, 162, 206, 207, 252.

(b) Interests of the state as guardian of social interests.

3. Social.

Pound, Legislation as a Social Function, VII Publications of the American Sociological Society, 148; id. A Theory of Social Interests, 15 Proceedings of the American Sociological Society, 16; Starr, Individualist and Social Conceptions of the Public, 12 Illinois L. Rev. 1; Green, Principles of Political Obligation, §§ 207–209, 233–246; I Jhering, Der Zweck im Recht (6–8 ed.) 443–465 (Husik's transl. Law as a Means to an End, 330–347).

Egerton v. Earl Brownlow, 4 House of Lords Cas. 1; Broom, Legal Maxims, chap. 1; Greenhood, Doctrine of Public Policy Reduced to Rules (1886); Hale, De Jure Maris, chap. 3, De Portibus Maris (about 1670), in Hargrave Law Tracts, 6–9, 77–78; Munn v. Illinois, 94 U. S. 113 (1876); Tyson v. Banton, 273 U. S. 418, 438 (1927); Wolff Packing Co. v. Court of Industrial Relations, 262 U. S. 522 (1923); McAllister, Business Affected With a Public Interest, 43 Harv. L. Rev. 759, 781–791.

Jhering's classification:

(a) The physical conditions of life of the society — i.e. the external security of its existence.

(b) The economic conditions of life of the society — i.e. the security of trade and commerce.

(c) The ideal conditions of life of the society — those involved in its moral and religious foundations.

I Jhering, Der Zweck im Recht (6–8 ed.) 496–502 (Husik's transl. Law as a Means to an End, 370–374).

(1) General security.

Brown, Police Power Legislation for Health and Safety, 42 Harv. L. Rev. 875, 898; Beard, The American Leviathan, chap. 18.
Com. v. Alger, 7 Cush. 53, 84 (1851); Thorpe v. Rutland & B. R. Co., 27 Vt. 140, 149–151 (1855); Slaughter House Cases, 16 Wall. 36, 61–63 (1872).
i. *Safety.* Grotius, De iure belli ac pacis, iii, 20, 7; Montesquieu, L'esprit des lois, liv. 26, chap. 23 (1748); Noy, Maxims, no. 26 (1641); Governor v. Meredith, 4 T. R. 794 (1792); Case of the King's Prerogative in Saltpetre, 12 Co. 12 (1607).
ii. *Health.* English Local Government Act (1929) § 104, and note by Jennings, 48 L. Q. Rev. 22; Great Britain, Public Health Acts and Other Statutes Relating to Public Health and Allied Subjects, 1875–1930 (1931); Lumley, Public Health Acts Annotated (10 ed. 1930); Glen, Law of Public Health and Local Government (14 ed. 1923); New York (State) Public Health Manual (1925); United States Public Health Service: Citations to Public Health Laws and Regulations (1933); Caffey, Health Laws (1914); Hemenway, Principles of Public Health Administration (1914); Tobey, Public Health Law: A Manual of Law for Sanitarians (1926); Slaughter House Cases, 16 Wall. 36, 61–62.
iii. *Peace and order.* Stat. Westminster I (1273) preamble and chap. 1; Coke, Second Institute (1642) 158; Hale, Pleas of the Crown (1678) 53; I Blackstone, Commentaries, 349–354; 4 id. 142–153.

iv. *Security of transactions.* Strong, J. in Murray v. Charleston, 96 U. S. 432, 449; Federalist, no. 44; 1 Parsons, Contracts, 4–5; Huston, Enforcement of Decrees in Equity (1915) 124–131; Bank v. Dandridge, 12 Wheat. 64, 69–70 (1827); Bell v. Morrison, 1 Pet. 351, 360 (1828); Kneeland v. Milwaukee, 15 Wis. 691, 692–693 (1862); Rothschild v. Grix, 31 Mich. 150, 152 (1875); In re Airey [1897] 1 Ch. 164; Case of Market Overt, 5 Co. 83^b (1597); French Civil Code, arts. 2279–2280; Colin et Capitant, Cours élémentaire de droit civil français (7 ed.) § 865; German Civil Code, §§ 518, 929–932; Thaller, Traité élémentaire de droit commercial (5 ed.) §§ 900–917; Cosack, Lehrbuch des Handelsrechts (7 ed.) § 28(II); English Bills of Exchange Act, § 38(2); Negotiable Instruments Law, § 57; Stat. 29 Car. 2, chap. 3 (1677); Moeneclaey, De la renaissance du formalisme dans les contrats en droit civil et commercial français.

v. *Security of acquisitions.* Grotius, De iure belli ac pacis, iii, 20, 7; Pufendorf, De jure naturae et gentium (1672) iv, 12, 1–3; Broom, Maxims (8 ed.) 737 ff.; Kerfoot v. Farmers and Merchants Bank, 218 U. S. 281, 287–288 (1910); Ayers v. South Australian Banking Co., L. R. 3 P. C. 548, 559 (1871); Rogers v. Goodwin, 2 Mass. 474 (1807); Harrow v. Myers, 29 Ind. 469 (1868); Gaius, ii, § 44; Institutes of Justinian, ii, 7, 2; French Civil Code, art. 931; German Civil Code, § 518; Stat. 39 Car. II, chap. 3; Colin et Capitant, Cours élémentaire de droit civil français (7 ed.) § 866; Lozon v. Pryse, 4 My. & Cr. 600, 617 (1840); Yerger v. Young, 9 Yerger (Tenn.) 37 (1836); Ralston v. Hamilton, 4 Macqueen, 397, 405 (1862); Black, Judicial Precedents, §§ 76–80; Hale, Pleas of the Crown (1676) 54–56; Dumas, Registering Title to Land (1900); Torrens, Essay on the Transfer of Land by Registration (1882).

(2) Security of social institutions.

i. *Domestic.* 1 Story, Equity Jurisprudence, §§ 274–291; 2 id. Equity Jurisprudence, §§ 1427–1428; 2 Bishop, New Commentaries of Marriage, Divorce, and Separation, §§ 249–266; Muirhead, Historical Introduction to the Private Law of Rome (3 ed.) 274–276; I Rudorff, Römische Rechtsgeschichte, § 27; Digest, xxv, 2, 2.

Drummond, Getting a Divorce (1931); Llewellyn, Behind the Law of Divorce, 32 Columbia L. Rev. (1932) 1281, 33 id. (1933) 249; I Birkenhead, Law, Life, and Letters (1927), 197 (The King's Proctor), 179 (Divorce Law Reform); Herbert, Holy Deadlock (1934).

Institutes, i, 10, §§ 12–13; Code, v, 27, 11, § 3; I Colin et Capitant, Droit civil français (7 ed.) §§ 226–252; German Civil Code, § 1699; Schuster, German Civil Law, §§ 425–427; I Blackstone, Comm. 446, 454–458; Stimson, American Statute Law, §§ 6631–6632; In re De Laveaga's Estate, 142 Cal. 158; Pederson v. Christofferson, 97 Minn. 491; Watts v. Owens, 62 Wis. 512.

Maine, Early History of Institutions, lect. 11; Dicey, Law and Public Opinion in England (2 ed.) 371–398; I Colin et Capitant, Droit civil français (7 ed.) 631–670; Barbey, French Family Law, XXXIV Rep. Am. Bar Assn. 431; Schuster, German Civil Law, §§ 413–419; Beale and Others, Marriage and the Domicile, 44 Harv. L. Rev. 501.

Arno v. Arno, 265 Mass. 282; Russell v. Russell [1924] A. C. 687; Nachimson v. Nachimson [1930] P. 85; Hyman v. Hyman [1929] P. 1.

Hegel, Philosophy of Right (transl. by Dyde) §§ 158–181; II Ahrens, Cours de droit naturel (8 ed.) §§ 96–102, 127; Kohler, Philosophy of Law (transl. by Albrecht) 98–119; Miller, Lectures on the Philosophy of Law, 150–175.

Devine, Pensions for Mothers, III Am. Labor Legislation Rev. 191.

ii. *Religious.* Mommsen, Römisches Strafrecht, 902, 918; Girard, Histoire de l'organisation judiciaire des Romains, 33–34; Hermann, Griechische Rechtsalterthümer (4 ed.) 49; 2 Brunner, Deutsche Rechtsgeschichte, 175–177; 2 Post, Grundriss der ethnologischen Jurisprudenz, § 61; I Strachan-Davidson, Problems of Roman Criminal Law, 8–9.

Hegel, Philosophy of Right (transl. by Dyde) § 270; Kohler, Philosophy of Law (transl. by Albrecht) 221, 223; Miller, Lectures on the Philosophy of Law, 365–371; I Lioy, Philosophy of Right (transl. by Hastie) 151–198; II Ahrens, Cours de droit naturel (8 ed.) §§ 130–131; Haring, Grundzüge des katholischen Kirchenrechts (2 ed.) §§ 24–25; I Gareis und Zorn, Staat und Kirche in der Schweiz, §§ 2–3; II Duguit, Traité de droit constitutionnel, §§ 110–112; Desdevises du Désert, L'église et l'état en France (1907–1908); Guerlac, The Separation of Church and State in France, XXIII Political Science Q. 258; Stammler, Recht und Kirche (1917); IV Blackstone, Commentaries, 42–64; Vidal v. Girard, 2 How. 127, 198; Bloom v. Richards, 2 Ohio St. 387, 390–392; Zeisweiss v. James, 63 Pa. St. 465, 470; Bowman v. Secular Society [1917] A. C. 406 (see comment in 31 Harv. L. Rev. 289); Ahrens, Der strafrechtliche Schutz des religiösen Gefühls; Misch, Der strafrechtliche Schutz der Gefühle (diss. 1911); Stuck, Die Religionsvergehen im Reichstrafgesetzbuch (diss. 1912); Tempski, Die Religionsvergehen (diss. 1908); Thümmel, Das Neustrafgesetzbuch und die Religionsvergehen (1927); Lord Coleridge, C.J. in Reg. v. Bradlaugh, 15 Cox C. C. 217.

iii. *Political.* Kant, Philosophy of Law (transl. by Hastie) 174–182; Figgis, Divine Right of Kings (2 ed.) 219–266.

I Strachan-Davidson, Problems of the Roman Criminal Law, 11–19; Liszt, Lehrbuch des deutschen Strafrechts (20 ed.) §§ 104–165; III Garraud, Droit pénal français (3 ed.) § 215; Donogh, History and Law of Sedition and Cognate Offences (1917); Liberty of Speech, 9 Papers and Proceedings of American Sociological Soc. (1914); Chafee, Freedom of Speech in War Time, 32 Harv. L. Rev. 932; id. Freedom of Speech (1920); id. Free Speech in the United States (1941); Nelles, Espionage Act Cases (1918); IV Blackstone, Commentaries, 74–93, 103–118, 119, 126; State v. Haffer, 94 Wash. 136 ["Libel" on George Washington].

iv. *Economic.* Miller v. Race, 1 Burr. 452; Erle, Trade Unions (1869) 5–26; U. S. House of Representatives, Investigation of Communist Propaganda, Hearings (6 vols. 1930); U. S. Congress, Exclusion and Expulsion of Communists: Hearings Before the Committee on Immigration and Naturalization, House of Representatives (1932).

(3) General morals.

1 Bishop, New Criminal Law, §§ 500–506, 1085, 1106, 1113, 1125, 1135; Liszt, Lehrbuch des deutschen Strafrechts (20 ed.) § 103; V Garraud, Droit pénal français (2 ed.) §§ 1795–1800; Stockdale v. Onwhyn, 7 Dowl. & Ry. 625; Greenhood, Public Policy, 136–177, 201–210, 222–237, 292–296, 306–315, 357–367; Code of Justinian, viii, 38, 4; Digest, xlv, 1, 26; French Civil Code, arts. 1133, 1965; German Civil Code, § 138(1); Phelps, Juridical Equity, §§ 256–259; I Savigny, System des heutigen römischen Rechts, 407–410 (Holloway's transl. 332–334); Salkowski, Roman Private Law (transl. by Whitfield) § 57.

See also Misch, Der strafrechtliche Schutz der Gefühle (diss. 1911).

(4) Conservation of social resources.

Use and conservation of natural resources,
protection and education of dependents and defectives,
reformation of delinquents,
protection of the economically dependent.

Schultze, Die Zerstreuung der Weltkraft (1930) XXIII Archiv für Rechts- und Wirthschaftsphilosophie, 460.

Natural resources. Rhinehart, Conservation of Natural Resources and Legal Control, 18 Minn. L. Rev. 168; Ashburn, Conrod, and Plank, Conservation as a National Problem (Arnold Foundation Studies in Public Affairs, 1938).

Digest, xliii, 12, 1, §§ 3–4; Digest, xliii, 14, 1, pr. and §§ 1–6; Digest, xliii, 20, 1, pr. and §§ 1–12; French Civil Code, arts. 538, 642–645; I Planiol, Traité élémentaire de droit civil (12 ed.) § 2428; Wulff und Herold, Wassergesetz vom 7 April, 1913.

Beard, The American Leviathan, chap. 17; English Law of Property Act, 1925, § 84; Improvement of the Land Act, 1864; Housing Acts, 1925 and 1930; Town and Country Planning Act, 1932.

Walls v. Midland Carbon Co., 254 U. S. 300.

Embrey v. Owen, 6 Ex. 353; Lux v. Haggin, 69 Cal. 255; Const. Ariz. art. 17, §§ 1–2; Const. Col. art. 16, §§ 5–6; Const. Idaho, art. 15, § 3; Const. Mont. art. 3, § 15; Const. N. D. § 210; Const. N. M. art. 16, §§ 1–2; Const. Utah, art. 17; Const. Wash. art. 1, § 16, art. 21, § 1; Const. Wyo. art. 8, §§ 1–3. See Swain, Conservation of Water by Storage, chaps. 3–5 and review in 28 Harv. L. Rev. 824.

Ohio Oil Co. v. Indiana, 177 U. S. 190; Manufacturers Gas Co. v. Indiana Natural Gas Co., 155 Ind. 461, 468–474.

Marshall and Meyers, Legal Planning of Petroleum Production, 41 Yale L. J. 33, 42 id. 702; The Oil and Gas Conservation Statutes, U. S. Government Printing Office, 1933; Ely, The Proposed Interstate Compact for Oil Conservation (1933); Hervey, Anti-Trust Laws and the Conservation of Minerals, 147 Annals of the American Academy of Political Science, 67; Note, 43 Harv. L. Rev. 1137; Louisiana, Acts of 1906, no. 71, §§ 1–3.

Case of Mines, Plowd. 310; 1 Lindley, Mines (3 ed.) §§ 200–200c.

Geer v. Connecticut, 161 U. S. 519; American Express Co. v. People, 133 Ill. 649; Haggerty v. Storage Co., 243 Mo. 238; State v. Dow, 70 N. H. 286.

Jennings and Sullivan, Legal Planning for Agriculture, 42 Yale L. J. 878.

Dependents and defectives. I Blackstone, Commentaries, 460–467; I Spence, History of the Equitable Jurisdiction of the Court of Chancery, 611–615; Institutes, i, 13, 15, 18, 20, 22, 23, pr. and § 1; French Civil Code, arts. 388–487.

See Jones and Bellot, Law of Children and Young Persons (1909); Hart, Juvenile Court Laws in the United States (1910); Breckinridge and Abbott, The Delinquent Child and the Home (1912); Flexner and Baldwin, Juvenile Courts and Probation (1914); Eliot, The Juvenile Court and the Community (1914); Lou, Juvenile Courts in the United States (1927) (full bibliography); United States Department of Justice, Supplement to Annual Report for 1914 — First Report of Committee to Study the Need for Legislation Affecting Children in the District of Columbia (1915); Fertig and Hennestad, Compilation of Laws Relating to Juvenile Courts and Dependent, Neglected, and Delinquent Children (1916); Flexner and Oppenheimer, The Legal Aspect of the Juvenile Court,

Children's Bureau Publication No. 99 (1922); London Committee for Investigating Juvenile Delinquency, Report of Committee for Investigating the Causes of the Alarming Increase of Juvenile Delinquency in the Metropolis (1916); Missouri Code Commission, Complete Revision of the Laws for the Welfare of Missouri Children (2 ed. 1917); Annual Reports of the Society for the Reformation of Juvenile Delinquents; Baernreither, Jugendfürsorge und Strafrecht in den Vereinigten Staaten (1905); Stammer, Strafvollzug und Jugendschutz in Amerika (1911); André, Tribunaux pour enfants et liberté surveillée (1914); France, Loi du 22 Juillet, 1912 and Décret du 31 Août, 1913.

See Goldmark, Child Labor Legislation Handbook (in 31 Annals of the American Academy of Political and Social Science, 1908); Scott, Child Labor (Summary of Laws in Force, 1910) American Association for Labor Legislation, Legislative Review, no. 5 (1910); Meyer and Thompson, List of References on Child Labor (United States Children's Bureau, 1916); National Association of Manufacturers, National Education and Employment Program (1927).

Aristotle, Politics, viii, 1–2 (I Jowett's transl. 244–245); I Lioy, Philosophy of Right (Hastie's transl.) 224–226; Lorimer, Institutes of Law (2 ed.) 225–226; Miller, Lectures on the Philosophy of Law, 182–184; II Ahrens, Cours de droit naturel (8 ed.) § 133; Spencer, Social Statics, 153–184; I Spencer, Principles of Ethics, §§ 236–237; Wilson, The State, § 1534; Dicey, Law and Public Opinion in England (2 ed.) 276–279.

I Blackstone, Commentaries, 302–306; I Spence, History of the Equitable Jurisdiction of the Court of Chancery, 618–620; Institutes, i, 23, §§ 3–4; I Colin et Capitant, Droit civil français (7 ed.) 588–630; Schuster, German Civil Law, §§ 28–31; Henderson, Dependents, Defectives, and Delinquents, 169–209.

Delinquents. See Barrows, Indeterminate Sentence and the Parole Law (1899); id. Reformatory System in the United States (1900); Miner, Probation Work in the Magistrates' Courts of New York City (1909); Henderson, Penal and Reformatory Institutions (1910); Brockway, Fifty Years of Prison Service (1912); Ives, History of Penal Methods (1914); Lawes, Twenty Thousand Years in Sing Sing (1932); Leeson, The Probation System (1914); Lewis, The Offender (1917); Herr, Das moderne amerikanische Besserungssystem (1907); Cooley, New Goals in Probation (1926); id. Probation and Delinquency (1927); Young, Social Treatment in Probation and Delinquency (1937); II Recent Social Trends, 1437–1440.

Economically dependent. See Frankfurter and Goldmark, Brief in Oregon Minimum Wage Cases (1917); Frankfurter, Argument and Brief in Adkins v. Children's Hospital, 261 U. S. 525; Brown, Minimum Wage with Particular Reference to the Legislative Minimum Wage under the Minnesota Statute of 1913 (1913); Andrews, Minimum Wage Legislation (1914); Tawney, Establishment of Minimum Rates in the Chainmaking Industry (1914); id. Establishment of Minimum Rates in the Tailoring Industry (1915); Bulkley, Establishment of Legal Minimum Rates in the Boxmaking Industry (1915); Andrews and Hobbs, Economic Effects of the War upon Women and Children in Great Britain (1918); California Industrial Welfare Commission, Report on Wage Board in the Fruit and Canning Industry (1916); Connecticut State Bureau of Labor, Report on Conditions of Wage Earning Women and Girls (1916); Massachusetts Minimum Wage Commission, Reports and Bulletins; Minnesota Minimum Wage Commission, Biennial Report for 1913–1914.

Adkins v. Children's Hospital, 261 U. S. 525; The Supreme Court and Mini-

mum Wage Legislation, Compiled by the National Consumers' League (1925);
Brown, Judicial Regulation of Rates of Wage for Women, 28 Yale L. J. 236.

Ribnik v. McBride, 277 U. S. 350 (1928) and bibliographies in notes on
364–373.

Dicey, Law and Public Opinion in England (2 ed.) 220–240; Ruegg, Changes
in the Law of England Affecting Labour, in A Century of Law Reform (1901);
Commons and Andrews, Principles of Labor Legislation (1916); Annual Review
of Labor Legislation in American Labor Legislation Review (1911). See also
Bulletins of the International Labour Office; Massachusetts State Board of Labor
and Industries, Reports and Bulletins; New York State Department of Labor,
Reports and Bulletins; Pennsylvania Department of Labor and Industry, Re-
ports; Frankfurter and Greene, Labor Injunctions and Federal Legislation, 42
Harv. L. Rev. 766, 778–779; Note: The Federal Wages and Hours Act (1939)
52 Harv. L. Rev. 646; Jennings, Poor Relief in Industrial Disputes, 46 L. Q.
Rev. 225, 229, 233–234; Attorney-General v. Merthyr Tydfil Union [1900] 1
Ch. 516.

Rehabilitation legislation. "Act to create a Commission for the Rehabilitation
of Physically Handicapped Persons" (1919) Laws of New Jersey, chap. 74, p. 138.

Social insurance. Note: Old Age Security, A Problem of Modern Industrial-
ism, 46 Harv. L. Rev. 1012; Jacobson, The Wisconsin Unemployment Insurance
Law, 32 Columbia L. Rev. 420; Douglas, Social Security in the United States
(1936) with bibliography; Hohman, The Development of Social Insurance;
Armstrong, Insuring the Essentials (1932).

Small loans legislation. Gallert, Hilborn and May, Small Loans Legislation
(1932); Beckner, Labor Legislation in Illinois, 111–113; People v. Stokes, 281
Ill. 159; II Recent Social Trends, 1436–1437.

(5) General progress.

{ Economic progress,
political progress,
cultural progress.

Economic progress. Darmstädter, Das Wirthschaftrecht in seiner soziologischen Struktur (1928) (beiheft to XXII Archiv für Rechts- und Wirthschaftsphilosophie).

{ Freedom of property from restrictions on sale or use,
free trade,
free industry,
encouragement of invention.

Freedom of property. Scrutton, Land in Fetters (1886); II Blackstone, Com-
mentaries, 269–274; Digest, viii, 1, 8, pr.; Digest, viii, 1, 15, § 1; Haywood v.
Building Society, 8 Q. B. D. 403; International Tea Stores Co. v. Hobbes [1903]
2 Ch. 165, 172; Brown v. Burdett, 21 Ch. D. 667; Dawkins v. Penrhyn, 4 App.
Cas. 51; Gray, Restraints on Alienation (2 ed.) § 4; Dr. Miles Medical Co. v.
Park, 220 U. S. 373; Park v. Hartman, 153 Fed. 24, 39; Hogg, Tulk v. Moxhay
and Chattels, 28 L. Q. Rev. 73; Bordwell, English Property Reform, 37 Yale
L. J. 1, 1–9; Manning, The Development of Restraints on Alienation Since Gray,
48 Harv. L. Rev. 373; Griswold, Spendthrift Trusts, chaps. 1, 2.

Free trade. Coke, Second Institute, 47; Darcy v. Allen, Moore, 671; Mitchell

v. Reynolds, 1 P. Wms. 181; Act, July 2, 1890, 26 U. S. St. L. 209; II Recent Social Trends, 1432–1436; Jaffe and Tobriner, The Legality of Price Fixing Agreements, 45 Harv. L. Rev. 1164; Beard, The American Leviathan, chap. 14; Raladam v. Federal Trade Commission, 42 Fed. (2d) 430, 435; Hamilton, Affectation with a Public Interest, 39 Yale L. J. 1089, 1106–1109; Clark, The Federal Trust Policy, chaps. 1, 5, 12.

Free industry. Jacobs v. Cohen, 183 N. Y. 207, 219; Erle, The Law Relating to Trade Unions (1869) chap. 1, § 3; Beckner, A History of Labor Legislation in Illinois, chap. 4. See also *ante* XIV, D, 1(c, 4), The Right of Association.

Encouragement of invention. 2 Story, Commentaries on the Constitution, §§ 1151–1152; Bauer v. O'Donnell, 229 U. S. 1; Erman, Wissenschaftliches Eigentum (1929); Ladas, The International Protection of Industrial Property (1929); Note, 47 Harv. L. Rev. 1419; Smith, Protection of Scientific Property (1932) 14 Journ. of Patent Office Society, 336; Chafee, book review, 43 Harv. L. Rev. 1328–1331.

Political progress.
$\left\{ \begin{array}{l} \text{Free criticism,} \\ \text{free opinion.} \end{array} \right.$

English Bill of Rights (1689) Declarations 5, 9; Constitutions: Argentina, pt. I, art. 14; Belgium, tit. I, arts. 14, 18; Brazil, art. 72, §§ 8, 9, 12; Chile, art. 10, §§ 6, 7; Denmark, art. 86; Italy, arts. 28, 32; Mexico, arts. 6–8; Netherlands, arts. 6–8; Norway, art. 100; Switzerland, arts. 49–50, 55.

Cooley, Constitutional Limitations, chap. 12; Liberty of Speech, 9 Papers and Proceedings, American Sociological Society; Chafee, Freedom of Speech in War Time, 32 Harv. L. Rev. 932; id. Freedom of Speech (1920); id. Free Speech in the United States (1941); Eliel, Freedom of Speech During and Since the Civil War, 18 Am. Political Science Rev. 712; Wason v. Walker, L. R. 4 Q. B. 73, 93–94; Heuss, Anreizung zum Klassenkampf (diss. 1909); Herndon v. State, 178 Ga. 832; Chafee, The Inquiring Mind (1928) 3–162; Rosenberg, Censorship in the United States (1928); Whipple, The Story of Civil Liberty in the United States (1928); Note, 41 Yale L. J. 262, 267–271; Wickwar, The Struggle for Freedom of the Press, 1819–1832 (1928); Patterson, Free Speech and a Free Press (1939); Freedom of the Press, Newspaper-Radio Committee (1942).

Cultural progress.
$\left\{ \begin{array}{l} \text{Free science,} \\ \text{free letters,} \\ \text{encouragement of arts and letters,} \\ \text{encouragement of higher education.} \end{array} \right.$

Bury, History of Freedom of Thought (1913); II Blackstone, Commentaries, 406–407; Const. Mass. chap. 5, § 1, art. 1 (1780).

(6) The individual life.

$\left\{ \begin{array}{l} \text{Individual self-assertion,} \\ \text{individual opportunity,} \\ \text{individual conditions of life.} \end{array} \right.$

Cardozo, Paradoxes of Legal Science, lects. 3, 4; Armstrong, Insuring the Essentials (1932).

See also *ante* VII (5).

Individual self-assertion.

> Physical,
> mental,
> economic.

See *ante* XIV, D, 1 (a); Bonham's Case, 8 Co. Rep. 107a--108a; III Blackstone Commentaries, 2, 15; Foster, Crown Law, 273; Stammler, Lehre von dem richtigen Rechte (2 ed.) 148 (Husik's transl. Theory of Justice, 161); Ives, History of Penal Methods, chaps. 11, 19; Lewis, The Offender, pt. I, chap. 8; Gompers, Labor and the Employer, chap. 9; Marot, American Labor Unions, chap. 8; Webb, History of Trade Unionism (rev. ed. 1920) 646–649; Goodrich, The Frontier of Control, 3–50, 104–125. See also *ante* XIV, D, 3 (4) — Economically dependent.

Cf. Brunner, Grundzüge der deutschen Rechtsgeschichte, § 59, with recent labor legislation as to "hiring and firing," see Note, 48 Harv. L. Rev. 648–653.

Individual opportunity.

> Political,
> physical,
> cultural,
> social,
> economic.

Const. U. S. Amendments XIV, XV.

Truxal, Outdoor Recreation Legislation (1929).

Massachusetts, Act of 1641, Lawes and Libertyes of Massachusetts (1648) 47; England, Elementary Education Act (1870) §§ 18, 74(1).

New York Civil Rights Law, § 40; People v. King, 110 N. Y. 418.

Butchers' Union Co. v. Crescent City Co., 111 U. S. 746, 762; Schnaier v. Navarre Hotel Co., 182 N. Y. 83, 87–89; In re Leach, 134 Ind. 165; Cummings v. Missouri, 4 Wall. 277, 321; Wilkinson and Bregy, Shoemakers' Children (1942) II Bill of Rights Rev. 209.

Individual conditions of life. Dig. xlii, 1, 16, 17, 19 § 1; id. xliii, 3, 4, pr.; id. l, 17, 173; Cod. ii, 11, 11; id. vii, 71, 1; Klingemann, Inhalt, Rechtliche Natur und Anwendungsgebiet des Beneficium Competentiae (1904); Charmont, in Progress of the Law in the Nineteenth Century (11 Continental Legal History Series) 162–164; German Civil Code, §§ 528–529; German Code of Civil Procedure, § 850; III Blackstone, Commentaries, 9, 418–419; Thompson, Homesteads and Exemptions, §§ 40–379.

How v. Weldon, 2 Ves. Sr. 516, 518; Taylor v. Rochford, 2 Ves. Sr. 281; Earl of Chesterfield v. Janssen, 2 Ves. Sr. 125; McClure v. Raben, 125 Ind. 139; Pound, Liberty of Contract, 18 Yale L. J. 454, 470–486.

Herbert Morris, Ltd. v. Saxelby [1915] 2 Ch. 57, [1916] A. C. 688; Attwood v. Lamont [1920] 3 K. B. 571.

Com. v. Wormser, 260 Pa. 44; U. S. Fair Labor Standards Act, 1938; Bibliography of Minimum Wage Legislation in Appendix to Brief of Appellants in Adkins v. Children's Hospital, 261 U. S. 525 and Appendix to Brief of Defendant in Error in Bunting v. Oregon, 243 U. S. 426.

U. S. National Housing Act, 1934; California State Housing Act, 1929; Indiana, State Housing and Slum Clearance Laws, 1937; Watson, Housing Problems and Possibilities in the United States; Jennings, Law of Housing

(1936); Henderson and Maddock, Housing Acts, 1899 to 1935 (1935); Whyte and Gordon, Law of Housing in Scotland (1935).

Dana, Two Years Before the Mast, chap. 15; Ives, History of Penal Methods, 147 ff.; 2 Pike, History of Crime in England, 574 ff.

SCHEMES OF INTERESTS TO BE SECURED BY LAW

Hippodamus of Miletus (B.C. c. 408).

He [Hippodamus] also divided his laws into three classes and no more, for he maintained that there are three subjects of law-suits — insult, injury, and homicide. — Aristotle, Politics, ii, 8 (I Jowett's transl. 47).

Justinian, Institutes (A.D. 533).

The precepts of right and law are these: to live honorably, not to injure another, to give to each his own. — Inst. i, 1, § 3.

See I Savigny, System des heutigen römischen Rechts, § 59; Affolter, Das römische Institutionen-System, 421–430.

Bacon (1629).

The use of the law consisteth principally in these three things: 1. To secure men's persons from death and violence. 2. To dispose of the property of their goods and lands. 3. For preservation of their good names from shame and infamy. — Use of the Law, 1. [As to the authorship of this book and its date, see VII Spedding, Bacon's Works, 453–457.]

Bentham (1802).

In the distribution of rights and obligations the legislator . . . should have for his end the happiness of society. Investigating more distinctly in what that happiness consists, we shall find four subordinate ends:

Subsistence,

abundance,

equality,

security.

The more perfect enjoyment is in all these respects, the greater is the sum of social happiness: and especially of that happiness which depends upon the laws.

We may hence conclude that all the functions of law may be referred to these four heads: To provide subsistence; to produce abundance; to favor equality; to maintain security. — Theory of Legislation, Principles of the Civil Code (Hildreth's transl.) chap. 2.

XV. THE SECURING OF INTERESTS

A. Valuing of Interests

Korkunov, General Theory of Law (Hastings' transl.) § 25; Kantorowicz, Rechtswissenschaft und Soziologie, 17–23; Demogue, Notions fondamentales du droit privé, 170–200; Charmont, The Conflict of Interests Legally Protected in French Law, 13 Illinois L. Rev. 461; Brown, Judicial Regulation of Rates of Wage for Women, 28 Yale L. J. 236; Cardozo, Paradoxes of Legal Science, lects. 2, 3; Pound, Social Control Through Law, 103–131.

II Gény, Méthode d'interprétation (2 ed.) § 220; Fehr, Recht und Wirklichkeit.

Walls v. Midland Carbon Co., 254 U. S. 300; Holmes, J. in Olmstead v. United States, 277 U. S. 438, 470; Queensborough Land Co. v. Cazeau, 136 La. 724.

B. Means of Securing Interests

Salmond, Jurisprudence, chaps. 4, 10, 11; Saleilles, The Individualization of Punishment (Mrs. Jastrow's transl.) chaps. 2–7; Bryce, Studies in History and Jurisprudence, essay 9; Stammler, Wirthschaft und Recht, §§ 92–98; Morris, Punitive Damages in Tort Cases, 44.

Bentham, Theory of Legislation (Hildreth's transl.) Principles of Legislation, chaps. 7–11, Principles of the Penal Code, pt. 3; I Austin, Jurisprudence (5 ed.) 91 ff.; Pollock, First Book of Jurisprudence (5 ed.) 21–27; Salmond, Jurisprudence, § 32.

Sayre, Labor and the Courts (1930) 39 Yale L. J. 682, 682–684; Note, Legislative Efforts to Make Insurance Guarantee the Payment of Tort Claims, 46 Harv. L. Rev. 1325; Pound, Law in Books and Law in Action, 44 Am. L. Rev. 12, 16–19; id. Legal Interrogation of Persons Accused or Suspected of Crime, 24 Am. J. Crim. L. and Criminol. 1014; Watts v. Malatesta, 262 N. Y. 80; State ex rel. Smith v. McMahon, 128 Kan. 772; United States v. Cunningham, 37 Fed. (2d) 349; Note, 43 Harv. L. Rev. 1159.

(a) Legal personality (see *post*, XXV).

(b) Legal rights (see *post*, XXI).

(c) Powers (see *post*, XXII).

(d) Liberties and privileges (see *post*, XXIII).

(e) Punishment.

(f) Redress (see *post*, XXXIII).

> (1) Specific,
> (2) Substitutional.

(g) Prevention (see *post*, XXXIII).

Pound, Preventive Justice and Social Work (1923) Proceedings of National Conference of Social Work, 151.

C. Limits of Effective Legal Action

1. Limits in respect of application and subject-matter.

Bentham, Theory of Legislation, Principles of Legislation, chap. 12; Pollock, First Book of Jurisprudence, pt. 1, chap. 2; Amos, Science of Law, chap. 3; Green, Principles of Political Obligation, §§ 11–31; Korkunov, General Theory of Law (Hastings' transl.) §§ 5–7; Gareis, Science of Law (Kocourek's transl.) § 6. See XI, *supra*.

Johnsen (compiler), Selected Articles on Law Enforcement (1930); National Commission on Law Observance and Enforcement, Report on the Enforcement of the Prohibition Laws of the United States, 43–60, 91–98; Radin, The Lawful Pursuit of Gain, 39–46; Note, The Imitation of Advertising, 45 Harv. L. Rev. 542; Handler, False and Misleading Advertising, 39 Yale L. J. 22; Note, The Uniform Small Loan Law, 42 Harv. L. Rev. 689.

2. Social-psychological limitations upon enforcement of legal precepts.

Spinoza, Tractatus Politicus, chap. 10, § 5 (Elwes' transl. p. 381); Duff, Spinoza's Political and Ethical Philosophy, chap. 22; I Bentham, Works, 146; Markby, Elements of Law, §§ 48–59; Salmond, Jurisprudence, § 30; Jellinek, Allgemeine Staatslehre (2 ed.) 89 ff., 324 ff.; Pound, The Limits of Effective Legal Action, XXII Rep. Pa. Bar Assn. 221, III A. B. A. J. 55, XXVII Internat. J. of Ethics, 150; Cohen, Positivism and the Limits of Idealism in the Law, 27 Columbia L. Rev. 237.

Criminal Law — An Agency for Social Control, 43 Yale L. J. 691; May, Social Control of Sex Expression (1931) bks. 2, 3; id. Experiments in the Legal Control of Sex Expression, 39 Yale L. J. 219; Note, Some Legislative Aspects of Birth Control, 45 Harv. L. Rev. 723; Note, Methods of Attacking Invalid Foreign Divorces, 43 Harv. L. Rev. 477; Note, Bribery in Commercial Relationships, 45 Harv. L. Rev. 1248; Chadbourne, Lynching and the Law (1933); Raper, The Tragedy of Lynching (1933); Edlin, Rechtsphilosophische Scheinprobleme, II, 2, Das Problem der Sozialen Gesetzmässigkeit (1932) 75, 185–198 (beiheft to XXVI Archiv für Rechts- und Wirthschaftsphilosophie); Lobe, Die Grenzen der Gesetzgebung (1929) 23 Leipziger Zeitschrift für deutsches Recht, 864.

PART 5

SOURCES, FORMS, MODES OF GROWTH

XVI. SOURCES AND FORMS OF LAW

II Austin, Jurisprudence, lect. 28; Holland, Jurisprudence, chap. 5 to I; Salmond, Jurisprudence, §§ 31–36; Amos, Science of Law (2 ed.) table facing page 76; Pollock, First Book of Jurisprudence (5 ed.) 231–246; Gray, Nature and Sources of the Law (1 ed.) §§ 322–597; Gareis, Science of Law (transl. by Kocourek) §§ 8–12; Korkunov, General Theory of Law (transl. by Hastings) §§ 51–54; Dickinson, The Law Behind Law, 29 Columbia L. Rev. 113, 285.

Carter, The Ideal and the Actual in the Law, 9–11; id. Law: Its Origin, Growth, and Function, lect. 5; Miraglia, Comparative Legal Philosophy (transl. by Lisle) §§ 152–165; Collinet, The General Problems Raised by the Codification of Justinian, IV Tijdschrift vor Rechtsgeschiedenis, 1, 9.

II Austin, Jurisprudence, lect. 30; Holland, Jurisprudence, chap. 5, subdiv. I; Clark, Practical Jurisprudence, 196–201, 324–334; Salmond, Jurisprudence, §§ 42, 43, 46–48; Pollock, First Book of Jurisprudence (5 ed.) 280–290; Gray, Nature and Sources of the Law (1 ed.) §§ 598–641.

Rattigan, Science of Jurisprudence, §§ 72–74; Jenks, Law and Politics in the Middle Ages, 56–63; Hastie, Outlines of Jurisprudence, 37–39.

1. Sources and forms of law in general.
   Ambiguity of "sources of law" as used in the books.
   The source of authority of legal precepts.
   The methods and agencies by which precepts are formulated.
   The authoritative shapes which legal precepts assume; the forms in which they are expressed and to which courts are referred in the decision of controversies.
2. Sources of law.
   (a) Custom as a source of law — customary law.
   Allen, Law in the Making (3 ed.) chaps. 1–2; Sadler, The Relation of Custom to Law (1919).

I Gény, Méthode d'interprétation (2 ed.) §§ 109–137; Ehrlich, Grundlegung der Soziologie des Rechts, 352–380 (English transl. by Moll, Fundamental Principles of the Sociology of Law, 436–471).

Vinogradoff, Custom and Right; id. Customary Law, in Crump and Jacob, The Legacy of the Middle Ages, 288–319; Lambert, La fonction du droit civil comparé, 111–804.

(1) Historical.

Declareuil, Rome the Law Giver, 16–18.

The judge precedes the law; judgments precede customary law.

Maine, Ancient Law, chap. I. But see Ehrlich, Fundamental Principles of the Sociology of Law (transl. by Moll) 37–38; Allen, Law in the Making (3 ed.) 115–119; Malinowski, Crime and Custom in Savage Society, 1–68.

Historical development of customary law.

Relation of customary law to the development of the state.

Bryce, Studies in History and Jurisprudence, 280–284; Markby, Elements of Law, §§ 79–85.

As to non-litigious custom as a form of social control and source of law, see I Vinogradoff, Historical Jurisprudence, 368–369; I id. Collected Papers, 465–478; Seagle, The Quest for Law (1941) 10–12.

(2) Philosophical.

The philosophical basis of customary law.

Lorimer, Institutes of Law (2 ed.) 515–516; Pollock, Essays in Jurisprudence and Ethics, 53–59; Kohler, Einführung in die Rechtswissenschaft, § 5; Stammler, Theorie der Rechtswissenschaft, 114–136; Rümelin, Die bindende Kraft des Gewohnheitsrechts und ihre Begründung (1929).

(3) Analytical.

See Dickinson, Social Order and Political Authority, 23 Am. Pol. Science Rev. 293, 593.

Nature of "customary law."

Customary course of popular action.

1 Lindley, American Law Relating to Mines, §§ 40–45.

Customary course of magisterial action.

Customary course of advice to litigants by those learned in the law.

Customary course of judicial action.

Reaction of law and custom.

Theories of the formulation of law by custom.

Relation of custom to legislation.

Relation of custom to judicial decision.

Customary law and democracy.

Amos, Science of Law (2 ed.) 390.

(4) Customary law in the several legal systems.

i. In Roman law.

Abrogation of a law by posterior contrary custom: Digest, i, 3, 32.

ii. In the civil law.

I Savigny, System des heutigen römischen Rechts, §§ 12, 18, 25. Full bibliography in I Gény, Méthode d'interprétation (2 ed.) §§ 109–139.

Abrogation of legislation by posterior contrary custom: Decretals of Gregory IX, 1, 2, 11; Erskine, Principles of the Law of Scotland, bk. I, tit. 1, § 16; 1 Nathan, The Law of South Africa, § 29; Italian Civil Code, art. 5; Spanish Civil Code, art. 5; 1 Scaevola, Derecho civil, 130–131; I Baudry-Lacantinerie, Traité de droit civil (2 ed.) no. 123; I Planiol, Traité élémentaire de droit civil (12 ed.) no. 231; Acollas, L'idée du droit (2 ed.) 34; Capitant, Introduction à l'étude du droit civil (4 ed.) 91 ff.; I Colin et Capitant, Cours élémentaire de droit civil français (7 ed.) 62–63; I Gény, Méthode d'interprétation (2 ed.) §§ 124–129; I Dernburg, Pandckten (8 ed.) 41, § 20; Esser, Die derogatorische Kraft des Gewohnheitsrecht (1889); Akzin, La désuétude en droit constitutionnel, 35 Revue du droit public, 697.

As to the common law, see Gray, Nature and Sources of the Law (1 ed.) § 419 and appendices VIII and IX; Winfield, The Chief Sources of English Legal History, 78–81; Rex v. Kennedy, 86 Law Times Rep. 753.

iii. In the common law.

Bentham, A Comment on the Commentaries, §§ XII, XVI, XVIII–XX; Livingston, A System of Penal Law (1833 ed.) 54–55; Brown, The Austinian Theory of Law, §§ 569–605; Markby, Elements of Law, §§ 90–91; Clark, Practical Jurisprudence, 316–323.

iv. Custom in international law.

I Oppenheim, International Law, §§ 16–17.

(b) Sources in general.

Sources in archaic law.

Sources in the Roman law.

Sources in the law of Continental Europe.

Sources in Anglo-American law.

Enacted law.

Not enacted.

Judicial.

Non-judicial.
Books of authority.
Writings not of authority.

See Pound, The Formative Era of American Law, 138–167.

As to commercial usage as law, see I Blackstone, Commentaries, 75; III Wooddesson, Lectures on the Law of England, 53; Christian, Note to I Blackstone, 75; Goodwin v. Robarts, L. R. 10 Ex. 337; 1 Morse, Banks and Banking 70n.; President and Directors of Manhattan Company v. Morgan, 242 N. Y. 38, 48–50; Oertmann, Rechtsordnung und Verkehrssitte.

3. Forms of law.
(a) Legislation.
(b) Case law.

See Llewellyn, Präjudizienrecht und Rechtsprechung in Amerika (1933); Allen, Law in the Making (3 ed.) chaps. 3–4.

(c) Textbook law.
Forms in the Roman law.

Legislation $\begin{cases} leges, \\ plebiscita, \\ senatus\ consulta, \\ \text{constitutions of the emperors,} \\ (principum\ placita). \end{cases}$

Edicts of the magistrates.
Responsa of the jurisconsults.
Treatises of the jurisconsults.
Forms in the law of Continental Europe.
Legislation.
Jurisprudence (*Gerichtsgebrauch*).
Doctrine.

I Savigny, System des heutigen römischen Rechts, § 29; I Dernburg, Pandekten (7 ed.) § 29; Gray, Judicial Precedents — A Short Study in Comparative Jurisprudence, 9 Harv. L. Rev. 27; I Gény, Méthode d'interprétation (2 ed.) §§ 39–59; Esmein, La jurisprudence et la doctrine, 1 Revue trimestrielle de droit civil, 1; Capitant, Introduction à l'étude du droit civil (4 ed.) 53–58.

Forms in Anglo-American law.
Legislation — with us, constitutions, treaties, statutes.
Judicial decisions.
Authoritative books.
Forms in international law.

See art. 38 of Statute of the Permanent Court of International Justice;

Cayuga Indian Claims, 20 American Journal of International Law, 574, 581–586 and citations; 1 Hudson, International Legislation, Introduction, §§ 1–9; Wheaton, International Law, pt. I, chap. I, § II; Bergbohm, Staatsverträge und Gesetze als Quellen des Völkerrechts (1877); Jellinek, Die rechtliche Natur der Staatenverträge (1880); Chailley, La nature juridique des traités internationaux selon le droit contemporain (1932).

XVII. THE TRADITIONAL ELEMENT

A. Law as a Priestly Tradition

Maine, Ancient Law, chap. 1, and Sir Frederick Pollock's notes B and C; Maine, Early Law and Custom (American ed.) 45–49; Coulanges, Ancient City, bk. 3, chap. 11; Mayne, Hindu Law, §§ 14–40; Kent, Israel's Laws and Legal Precedents, 8–15; I Vinogradoff, Historical Jurisprudence, 367–368; Hirzel, Themis, Dike und Verwandtes; Nicklin, Review of Glotz, Études sociales et juridiques sur l'antiquité grecque (1907) 22 English Historical Rev. 555, 556.

B. Law as a Popular Tradition

Brunner, Deutsche Rechtsgeschichte, §§ 13, 37; Siegel, Deutsche Rechtsgeschichte, § 2; Allen, Law in the Making (3 ed.) chap. 1; Rümelin, Die bindende Kraft des Gewohnheitsrechts und ihre Begründung (1929); Mokre, Theorie des Gewohnheitsrechts (1932), also in 12 Zeitschrift für öffentliches Recht, 272, 386.

C. Law as a Juristic Tradition

Clark, Practical Jurisprudence, 273–339; Muirhead, Historical Introduction to the Private Law of Rome, §§ 50, 61–64; Maitland, English Law and the Renaissance, 24–35; II Holdsworth, History of English Law, 484–508; Grueber, Introduction to Ledlie's Translation of Sohm, Institutes of Roman Law (1 ed.); I Dernburg, Pandekten, §§ 16–17; I Windscheid, Pandekten, §§ 7–10; Brissaud, Manuel d'histoire du droit civil français, 348–361, 388–400; Stintzing, Geschichte der deutschen Rechtswissenschaft.

Corwin, The "Higher Law" Background of American Constitutional Law, 42 Harv. L. Rev. 149, 365; Schechter, Popular Law and Common Law in Medieval England, 28 Columbia L. Rev. 270; Chorley, The Conflict of Law and Commerce, 48 L. Q. Rev. 51.

D. Modes of Growth

1. Fictions.

Maine, Ancient Law, chap. 2, and Sir Frederick Pollock's note; II Austin, Jurisprudence (5 ed.) 609–611; Gray, Nature and Sources of the Law (1 ed.) §§ 74–89; Phelps, Juridical Equity, § 150; Tourtoulon, Philosophy in the Development of Law, 644–653; Fuller, Legal Fictions, 25 Ill. L. Rev. 6, 363, 518, 817.

III Jhering, Geist des römischen Rechts, § 58; Bernhöft, Zur Lehre von den Fiktionen; Demogue, Notions fondamentales du droit privé, 238–251; Stammler, Theorie der Rechtswissenschaft, 328–333; Lecocq, Fiction comme procédé juridique; Sturm, Fiktion und Vergleich in der Rechtswissenschaft; Kornfeld, Allgemeine Rechtslehre und Jurisprudenz, 45–60; I Vinogradoff, Historical Jurisprudence, 365–367; Mallachow, Rechtserkenntnistheorie und Fiktionslehre; Riccobono, Formulae Ficticiae, A Normal Means of Creating New Law, 9 Revue d'histoire de droit, 1; Bülow, Civilprozessuale Fiktionen und Wahrheit, 62 Archiv für das civilistische Praxis, 1; Krückmann, Wahrheit und Unwahrheit im Rechte, 1 Annalen der Philosophie, 630; Kelsen, Zur Theorie der juristischen Fiktionen, id. 130; Strauch, Die Philosophie des "als ob" und die hauptsächlichsten Probleme der Rechtswissenschaft (1923); Munzer, Ueber Gesetzfiktionen (1927); Baumhoer, Die Fiktion im Straf- und Prozessrecht (1930) (beiheft to XXIV Archiv für Rechts- und Wirthschaftsphilosophie).

Gaius, iv, §§ 32–38; III Blackstone, Commentaries, 43, 44–45, 152–153, 159–165, 200–206, 274–275, 283, 284–287; Gaius, i, §§ 111, 114–115, 119–123, 132, 134, ii, §§ 24, 103–105; Ulpian, Rules, i, §§ 7, 8; II Blackstone, Commentaries, 348–363, particularly 360, 363; Curtis, Jurisdiction of the United States Courts, 127–133.

See also Vaihinger, Philosophy of "As If" (transl. by Ogden) 33–35, 85–95.

2. Interpretation.

Clark, Practical Jurisprudence, 235–244; 1 id. Roman Private Law: Jurisprudence, 115–135; II Austin, Jurisprudence (5 ed.) 989–1001; Bentham, A Comment on the Commentaries, §§ IX, XII; Pound, Spurious Interpretation, 7 Columbia L. Rev. 379; id. Introduction in DeSloovère, Cases on the Interpretation of Statutes; Gray, Nature and Sources of the Law, §§ 370–399 (2 ed. 170–189); Gény, Méthode d'interprétation (2 ed.) I, §§ 92–108, II, §§ 177–187; Allen, Law in the Making (3 ed.) 396–414; Radin, Statutory Interpretation, 43 Harv. L. Rev. 863; Landis, A Note on "Statutory Interpretation," 43 Harv. L. Rev. 886.

Salkowski, Roman Private Law (Whitfield's transl.) § 5; Walton, Introduction to Roman Law (4 ed.) 110–111; Buckland, Text Book of Roman Law, 2; Stammler, Theorie der Rechtswissenschaft, 558–652; Battaglia, L'interpretazione giuridica nella moderna letteratura francese, 9 Rivista internazionale di filosofia del diritto, 185, 376; Heck, Gesetzesauslegung und Interessenjurisprudenz, §§ 1–16; Darmstetter, Recht und Rechtsordnung, Beiträge vom Willen des Gesetzgebers, chaps. 5–7; Degni, L'interpretazione della legge (2 ed.); Schreier, Die Interpretation der Gesetze und Rechtsgeschäfte (1927); DeSloovère, The Functions of Judge and Jury in the Interpretation of Statutes, 46 Harv. L. Rev. 1086; Kantorowicz, Vorgeschichte der Freirechtslehre (1925); Dabin, La technique de l'élaboration du droit positif (1935); Cossio, La plenitud del orden jurídico y la interpretación judicial de la ley (1939).

3. Equity.

Maine, Ancient Law, chap. 3 and Sir Frederick Pollock's note F;

Clark, Practical Jurisprudence, 340–379; Allen, Law in the Making (3 ed.) chap. 5.

II Austin, Jurisprudence, lect. 36; Salmond, Jurisprudence, § 15; Sohm, Institutes of Roman Law (Ledlie's transl. 3 ed.) §§ 15–17; Markby, Elements of Law, §§ 120–122; Pound, The Decadence of Equity, 5 Columbia L. Rev. 20.
Buckland, Equity in Roman Law.

4. Natural law.

Bryce, Studies in History and Jurisprudence, essay 11; Maine, Ancient Law, chaps. 3, 4 and Sir Frederick Pollock's notes, F, G, and H; Pollock, The Expansion of the Common Law, 107–138; Holland, Jurisprudence, chap. 3, subdiv. I; Korkunov, General Theory of Law (transl. by Hastings) §§ 14–17; Pound, The Formative Era of American Law, 3–30.

Pollock, History of the Law of Nature, 1 Columbia L. Rev. 11; id. Essays in the Law, 31–79; Salmond, The Law of Nature, 11 L. Q. Rev. 121; Grotius (Whewell's transl.) i, 1, §§ 10–11; Markby, Elements of Law, §§ 116–117; Rattigan, Science of Jurisprudence, §§ 13, 20b.
For an example of administration of justice according to natural law see preface, chap. 1, Historical-Judicial, to 1 Kyshe (Straits Settlements) iii, ix, xx.

5. Juristic science.

II Austin, Jurisprudence, lect. 32; Gray, The Nature and Sources of the Law (1 ed.) §§ 551–597a; Korkunov, General Theory of Law (Hastings' transl.) § 64; II Jhering, Geist des römischen Rechts, §§ 38–41; IV Bierling, Juristische Prinzipienlehre, §§ 53–58; Stammler, Theorie der Rechtswissenschaft, 262–363; Demogue, Notions fondamentales du droit privé, 225–238.

Cohen, The Place of Logic in the Law, in Law and the Social Order, 165–183; id. Law and Scientific Method, id. 184–197; Gutteridge, Law of Bankers' Commercial Credits (1932).
Gareis, Science of Law (Kocourek's transl.) § 12c; Sohm, Institutes of Roman Law (Ledlie's transl. 3 ed.) §§ 18–20; Beseler, Volksrecht und Juristenrecht, 299–364; I Windscheid, Pandekten, §§ 23–24; I Dernburg, Pandekten, § 38; I Cosack, Lehrbuch des deutschen bürgerlichen Rechts, § 11; Gény, Les procédés d'élaboration du droit civil (in Les méthodes juridiques); Del Vecchio, Il sentimento giuridico; Jellinek, Schöpferische Rechtswissenschaft (1928); Lauterpacht, Analogies in International Law (1927) chap. 1; Riezler, Die Idee der Vereinfachung im Recht, XXIII Archiv für Rechts- und Wirthschaftsphilosophie, 442.
Franklin, The Historic Function of the American Law Institute: Restatement as Transitional to Codification, 47 Harv. L. Rev. 1367; Crane, Law School Reviews and the Courts, 4 Fordham L. Rev. 1; Amos, The Legal Mind, 49 L. Q. Rev. 27; Harrison, Jurisprudence and the Conflict of Laws (1879) 102–124;

Lorenzen, Story's Commentaries on the Conflict of Laws — One Hundred Years Thereafter, 48 Harv. L. Rev. 15, 18, 19.

Maxims. — Gaius, iii, § 180; Digest, De diversis regulis iuris antiqui, 50, 17; Jörs, Römische Rechtswissenschaft zur Zeit der Republik (1888) 282–313; I Jhering, Geist des römischen Rechts, § 3; 2 id. § 40; 3 Savigny, Geschichte des römischen Rechts im Mittelalter, 567–570; 1 Schulte, Geschichte der Quellen und Literatur des canonischen Rechts, 196, 213; 2 id. 84; 3 Savigny, Geschichte des römischen Rechts im Mittelalter, §§ 204–209; 1 Brinz, Pandekten (3 ed.) § 12; Pothier, Pandectae, tit. De diversis regulis iuris antiqui; Fabreguettes, La logique judiciaire et l'art de juger, 192–273; Phillimore, Principles and Maxims of Jurisprudence; Esmein, Cours d'histoire du droit français (13 ed.) 813–814; Chaisemartin, Proverbes et maximes du droit germanique (1891); Amira, Grundriss des germanischen Rechts (3 ed. 1913) 15; Pound, The Maxims of Equity, 34 Harv. L. Rev. 809; id. On Certain Maxims of Equity, Cambridge Legal Essays, 259; Bacon, Maxims (written 1596, published 1630); Broom, A Selection of Legal Maxims (1845, 9 ed. 1924); Tourtoulon, Philosophy in the Development of Law (transl. by Read) 310–327.

6. Judicial empiricism.

II Austin, Jurisprudence, lects. 38 and 39, pt. I; Pollock, Essays in Jurisprudence and Ethics, 237–261; Gray, Nature and Sources of the Law (1 ed.) §§ 420–550; Clark, Practical Jurisprudence, 223–226, 255–265; Dillon, Laws and Jurisprudence of England and America, 229–237, 242–253; Thayer, Judicial Legislation: Its Legitimate Function in the Development of the Common Law, 5 Harv. L. Rev. 172; Pound, Spirit of the Common Law, lect. 7; id. The Formative Era of American Law, 81–127; id. What of Stare Decisis? (1941) X Fordham L. Rev. 1; Cardozo, The Nature of the Judicial Process, lect. 3; id. The Growth of the Law, lects. 3–5; Pound, Theory of Judicial Decision, 36 Harv. L. Rev. 641, 802, 940; Allen, Law in the Making (3 ed.) chaps. 3–4; Pollock, Judicial Caution and Valour, 45 L. Q. Rev. 293.

Markby, Elements of Law, §§ 95–99; Cruet, La vie du droit et l'impuissance des lois; Carter, Law: Its Origin, Growth, and Function; Stammler, Legislation and Judicial Decision, 23 Michigan L. Rev. 362; Cohen, The Process of Judicial Legislation, in Law and the Social Order, 112–147, also in 48 American L. Rev. 161; Goodhart, Determining the Ratio Decidendi of a Case, 40 Yale L. J. 161; Oliphant, A Return to Stare Decisis, 14 A. B. A. J. 71, 159; Llewellyn, Präjudizienrecht und Rechtsprechung in Amerika; Green, The Duty Problem in Negligence Cases, 29 Columbia L. Rev. 255, 280–284; Dickinson, The Law Behind Law, 29 Columbia L. Rev. 285, 296–307; Radin, Case Law and Stare Decisis, 33 Columbia L. Rev. 199, 205–209; Jordan, Theory of Legislation, chap. 12 (The Judicial Process).

As to nineteenth-century method in American law, see Holmes, Collected Papers, 231–232; Pound, Mechanical Jurisprudence, 8 Columbia L. Rev. 605; Holbrook, Epithetical Jurisprudence, 18 Mich. L. Rev. 407; Drake, The Rule of

Law and the Legal Right, 9 Mich. L. Rev. 365; Sturges and Clark, Legal Theories and Real Property Mortgages, 37 Yale L. J. 691, 713–715; Green, Book Review, 37 Yale L. J. 842–843; Tulin, The Role of Penalties in the Criminal Law, 37 Yale L. J. 1049, 1057–1063; Sharp, The Movement in Supreme Court Adjudication, 46 Harv. L. Rev. 745, 809–811; Note, 43 Harv. L. Rev. 926.

As to the English attitude toward *stare decisis*, see Radcliffe v. Ribble Motor Services, Ltd. [1939] A. C. 215; Hill v. Aldershot Corporation [1933] 1 K. B. 259; Note, 49 L. Q. Rev. 155.

As to Continental Europe, see Lambert and Wasserman, The Case Method in Canada and the Possibilities of its Adaptation to the Civil Law, 39 Yale L. J. 11–15; Sauer, Die Wirklichkeit des Rechts, XXII Archiv für Rechts- und Wirthschaftsphilosophie, 1, 24–28; Naste, Du rôle de l'autorité judiciaire, 3 Revue internationale de la théorie du droit, 154; Heinrici, Zur Frage des Einflusses von Richtertum und Ministerial Bürokratie auf die Entwickelung des Privatrechts, 70 Gruchot, Beiträge zur Erläuterung des deutschen Rechts, 577; Dessauer, Recht, Richtertum und Ministerial Bürokratie (1928).

7. Comparative law.

Bryce, Studies in History and Jurisprudence (American ed.) 619–623; Maine, Village Communities (American ed.), 3–6; Demogue, Notions fondamentales du droit privé, 268–285; Pound, The Formative Era of American Law, 145–151; id. Comparative Law in the Formation of American Common Law (1923) I Acta Academiae Universalis Juris Comparativi, 183; Rheinstein, Comparative Law and the Conflict of Laws in Germany (1935) 2 University of Chicago L. Rev. 232; Hug, The History of Comparative Law (1932) 45 Harv. L. Rev. 1027; id. The Progress of Comparative Law (1931) 6 Tulane L. Rev. 68; Lepaulle, The Function of Comparative Law, 35 Harv. L. Rev. 838 (1922).

Meili, Institutionen der vergleichenden Rechtswissenschaft; Lambert, La fonction du droit civil comparé; Bernhöft, Ueber Zweck und Mittel der vergleichenden Rechtswissenschaft; Jitta, La substance des obligations dans le droit international privé, § 7; Wenger, Römisches Recht und Rechtsvergleichung, XIV Archiv für Rechts- und Wirthschaftsphilosophie, 1, 106; Cosentini, La science de droit comparé et l'American Common Law, 62 Bulletin de la Société de Droit Comparé, 322; Rauchhaupt, Die wissenschaftliche Pflege der Rechtsvergleichung, XXIII Archiv für Rechts- und Wirthschaftsphilosophie, 149.

For recent applications see Hallstein, Die Aktienrechte der Gegenwart, Gesetze und Entwurfe in Rechtsvergleichender Darstellung (1931); Siebert, Das rechtsgeschäftliche Treuverhältniss (1933); Lepaulle, Traité théorique et pratique des trusts (1932).

8. Sociological study.

Holmes, The Path of the Law, 10 Harv. L. Rev. 456, 467 ff.; Keasbey, The Courts and the New Social Questions, 24 Green Bag, 114; Kantorowicz, Rechtswissenschaft und Soziologie, 8 ff.; Ehrlich,

Grundlegung der Soziologie des Rechts, 393–409 (Moll's transl. Fundamental Principles of the Sociology of Law, 486–506); II Gény, Méthode d'interprétation (2 ed.) § 221.

Palfrey, The Constitution and the Courts, 26 Harv. L. Rev. 507, 517, 530; Veasey, The Law of Oil and Gas, 18 Mich. L. Rev. 445, 452–455; Heck, Gesetzesauslegung und Interessenjurisprudenz, § 20; Wüstendorfer, Zur Hermaneutik der soziologischen Rechtsfindungstheorie, IX Archiv für Rechts- und Wirthschaftsphilosophie, 170, 289, 422; Drake, Sociological Interpretation of Law, 16 Mich. L. Rev. 599; Gee (editor) Research in the Social Sciences, Introduction and chaps. 1, 6, 9.

XVIII. THE IMPERATIVE ELEMENT

A. LEGISLATIVE LAWMAKING

Korkunov, General Theory of Law (Hastings' transl.) § 54; Salmond, Jurisprudence, §§ 50–54; Miller, Data of Jurisprudence, 238–258; Allen, Law in the Making (3 ed.) chaps. 6, 7 (1939); Freund, Legislative Regulation (1932); Landis, The Study of Legislation in Law Schools, 39 Harvard Graduates' Magazine, 433; Pound, The Formative Era of American Law, lect. 2.

Maine, Early History of Institutions (American ed.) 386–393, 398–400; Clark, Practical Jurisprudence, 202–213.

1. Unconscious legislation.
   Maine, Village Communities (American ed.) 75, 116.

2. Declaratory legislation.
   Maine, Early History of Institutions (American ed.) 26 ff.

Laws of Manu (Bühler's transl.) i, §§ 58–60; Introduction to the Senchus Mor, I Ancient Laws and Institutes of Ireland, 3–41; Prologue to the Lex Salica (Hessels and Kern, Lex Salica, 422–423); Jenks, Law and Politics in the Middle Ages, 7–13.

3. Selection and amendment.
   Carter, Law: Its Origin, Growth, and Function, 255 ff.

Prologue to Alfred's Laws (I Thorpe, Ancient Laws and Institutes of England, 59); Laws of Howel the Good, Introduction (Evans, Welsh Mediaeval Law, 145–146).

4. Conscious constructive lawmaking.

Jenks, Law and Politics in the Middle Ages, 18–21; Dicey, Law and Opinion in England, 45 ff., 48–61; Miller, Philosophy of Law, 38 ff.; Pulszky, Theory of Law and Civil Society, § 245.

5. Codification.
See lecture XIX, *post*.

B. Agencies of Preparation for Legislation

1. Public agencies.
Ilbert, The Mechanics of Law Making, chap. 5.
(a) Legislative committees.

Reinsch, American Legislatures and Legislative Methods, chap. 5; Horack, The Committee System, III Iowa Applied History Series, 535–609; Harlow, Legislative Methods in the Period Before 1825, chaps. 1, 4, 10–12.

(b) Commissions.

Pollock, First Book of Jurisprudence (5 ed.) 359–361; Freund, Standards of American Legislation, 198–301; Webb, Methods of Social Study, chap. 7; Gosnell, British Royal Commissions of Inquiry, 49 Political Science Q. 84.
See Recent Social Trends in the United States, Report of the President's Research Committee on Social Trends (2 vols. 1933).

(c) Legislative councils.

Wisconsin, Laws of 1931, chap. 23; Kansas, Act of March 13, 1933; South Africa Act (1909) 9 Edw. 7, chap. 9, § 87; Christie, The Legislative Council of New Jersey, 6 J. Comp. Leg. 3 ser. 19; Gans, The Wisconsin Executive Council, 26 American Political Science Rev. 914–920.
See 27 American Political Science Rev. 800.

(d) Reference bureaus.
McCarthy, The Wisconsin Idea, chap. 8; Freund, Standards of American Legislation, 303–306.
(e) The Commissioners on Uniform State Laws.

13 Rep. Am. Bar Assn. (1890) 29, 336, and reports of the Committee on Uniform State Laws, or of the Commissioners on Uniform State Laws in each subsequent volume; Terry, Uniform State Laws in the United States; Williston, The Uniform Partnership Act With Some Remarks on Other Uniform Commercial Laws, 63 U. Pa. L. Rev. 196; Vold, Some Reasons Why the Code States Should Adopt the Uniform Sales Act, 5 California L. Rev. 400, 471.
Compare the Conference of Commissioners on Uniformity of Legislation in Canada, 3 Proceedings, Canadian Bar Assn. 229; 17 id. 171.

(f) State bars.

See e.g. Ballantine, Minor Changes in California Corporation Law, 6 California State Bar J. 159.

(g) Executive recommendations.

Reinsch, American Legislatures and Legislative Methods, 283–286; Harlow, Legislative Methods in the Period Before 1825, 244–247.

Reference may be made to the recommendations of legislation in Richardson, Messages and Papers of the Presidents, 1789–1897, new ed. extending over 1898–1918.

(h) Research in administrative departments.

See Thacher, Administration of the Bankruptcy Act, 55 Rep. Am. Bar Assn. 251.

(i) Judicial councils.

Dodge, Judicial Councils, 51 Rep. Am. Bar Assn. 267; Arnold, Judicial Councils, 35 W. Va. L. Q. 193; Ragland, The Kentucky Judicial Council, 17 Kentucky L. J. 373; McClendon, A Review of the Judicial Council Movement, 9 Texas L. Rev. 366, 14 J. Am. Jud. Soc. 93; Ruppenthal, The Work Done by Judicial Councils, 14 J. Am. Jud. Soc. 17, 58; 15 id. 15, 53; Cockerell, Successful Justice, 45–46, 1010–1017; Willoughby, Principles of Judicial Administration, 264–280; Ridgeway, American Judicial Council, Its Powers and Possibilities, 5 Oregon L. Rev. 292; Sunderland, Function and Organization of a Judicial Council, 9 Indiana L. J. 479; id. Purpose, Organization and Powers of a Judicial Council (1935) 41 Rep. Pa. Bar Assn. 392; Hunt, The Judicial Council (1926) Kansas Bar Assn. Proc. 148; Phillips, The Judicial Council, 1 Conn. Bar J. 124; Warner, Role of Courts and Judicial Councils in Procedural Reform, 85 U. Pa. L. Rev. 441; Pound, The Work of a Judicial Council (1939) Proc. Texas Bar Assn. 98; Pirsig, Judicial Councils (1941) Am. Bar Assn. Judicial Administration Monographs, ser. A, no. 2; The Judicial Council, Report of Committee on Judicial Administration of the Merchants' Assn. of New York (1931).

Handbooks, National Conference of Judicial Councils, no. 2 (1940), no. 3 (1941).

(j) Conferences under public authority.

E.g. The Conferences of Governors; the Conferences of Attorneys General; the Conferences of District Attorneys, etc. held in connection with meetings of Bar Associations; the Conferences of Police Chiefs.
See also McCall, The North Carolina Judicial Conference, 15 A. B. A. J. 563.
The Conference of Senior Circuit Judges.
Act of Congress, Sept. 14, 1922, 42 St. L. c. 306, p. 837.

(k) Ministries of Justice.

See *ante* p. 34.

2. Private agencies.

(a) Committees of professional, trade, and business associations.

Beutel, The Pressure of Organized Interests as a Factor in Shaping Legislation (1929) 3 Southern California L. Rev. 1.

Bar association committees.

Miller, Activities of Bar Associations and Legislatures in Connection with Criminal Law Reform (1927) 18 J. of Crim. Law and Criminology, 378; Rutherford, The Influence of the American Bar Association on Public Opinion and Legislation (1937).

(b) Associations and other organizations interested in social and economic problems.

See e.g. Reports of the National Conference on Social Work; Proceedings of the Annual Congress of the American Prison Association; Year Book of the National Probation Association; The American Labor Legislation Review published by the American Association for Labor Legislation.

(c) Private individuals.

See Gilbert, The Municipal Court of Chicago, chap. 3.

(d) The American Law Institute.

See Proceedings, American Law Institute, vols. 1–17 (1923–1940). American Law Institute, Model Code of Criminal Procedure (1930).

(e) Research in universities and institutes.

See Publications of the Institute of Law of The Johns Hopkins University: Monographs in the Study of Judicial Administration in Ohio; Bulletins of the Study of Judicial Administration in Ohio; Monographs in the Study of the Judicial System of Maryland; Bulletins of the Study of the Judicial System of Maryland; Monographs of Survey of Litigation in New York; Bulletins of Survey of Litigation in New York.

See Harron, Current Research in Law, 1928–1929; Iddings, Current Research in Law, 1929–1930.

See Pound, The Task of the American Lawyer, 20 Illinois L. Rev. 439; id. Law and Laws, 28 Univ. of Mo. L. Bull. 25; Research in the Social Sciences (1929, ed. by Gee).

(f) Research by foundations.

See Cleveland Foundation, Survey of Criminal Justice in Cleveland (1923); Missouri Association for Criminal Justice, The Missouri Crime Survey (1926); Illinois Association for Criminal Justice, The Illinois Crime Survey (1929).

See Uniform Crime Reporting (1929).

C. AGENCIES OF LEGISLATION

1. Primary.

(a) Roman law.

Bryce, Studies in History and Jurisprudence (Am. ed.) 708–730; Jolowicz, Historical Introduction to the Study of Roman Law, 83–85, 368–379, 474–478, 484–505; Buckland, Text Book of Roman Law, 1–5, 7–8, 13–21.

Gaius, i, §§ 3–5 (transl. by Poste, by Muirhead, and by Abdy and Walker); Institutes of Justinian, i, 2, §§ 4, 5, 6 (transl. by Moyle and by Abdy and Walker).

(b) The canon law.

Lancelottus, Institutiones Iuris Canonici, I, 3, pr. and §§ 1–8.

(c) English law.

Bryce, Studies in History and Jurisprudence (Am. ed.) 731–739; I Anson, Law and Custom of the Constitution — Parliament (4 ed. rev. 1911) chaps. 3–5; Dicey, Law of the Constitution (8 ed.) xviii–xxiv, 37–48, 58–87; Ilbert, Legislative Methods and Forms, chaps. 2, 4.

(1) Statutes.

Allen, Law in the Making (3 ed.) 357–365.

(2) Royal proclamations.

Dicey, Custom of the Constitution (8 ed.) 48–52.

(3) Resolutions of the Houses.

Dicey, Law of the Constitution (8 ed.) 52–56.

Stockdale v. Hansard, 9 Ad. & Ell. 1.

(d) British dominions and colonies.

Statute of Westminster, 1931 (22 Geo. 5, c. 4); Hudson, Notes on the Statute of Westminster, 1931, 46 Harv. L. Rev. 261.

Ilbert, Legislative Methods and Forms, chap. 9.

(e) American law.

(1) Popular vote.

Opinion of the Justices, 6 Cush. 573; In re the Constitutional Convention, 14 R. I. 649; Koehler v. Hill, 60 Ia. 643.

(2) Constitutional Conventions — ordinances.

Jameson, The Constitutional Convention (3 ed. 1873) chaps. 4–7; Lobingier, The People's Law, chaps. 9–26.

Sproule v. Fredericks, 69 Miss. 898; Wells v. Bain, 75 Pa. St. 39; Woods's Appeal, 75 Pa. St. 59; Frantz v. Autry, 18 Okl. 561.
Smith v. State, 28 Okl. 235.

(3) Legislatures.

Luce, Legislative Assemblies, chaps. 1–16.

   i. Statutes.
      I Kent, Commentaries, 447–451.
   ii. Resolutions and resolves.

Luce, Legislative Procedure, 553–558; Jones, Statute Law Making in the United States, chap. 13.

In re Hague, 105 N. J. Eq. 134; Hawes v. Wm. R. Trigg Co., 110 Va. 165, 201; Swann v. Buck, 40 Miss. 268; In re Lewis, 13 Alta. L. R. 423; Australia, Seat of Government (Administration) Act, 1910, § 12 (3).

(4) Initiative and referendum.

Lobingier, The People's Law, chaps. 27–28.

State v. Thurston County Superior Court, 92 Wash. 16; Beall v. Jenkins, 131 Md. 669; State v. Howell, 107 Wash. 167; Hawke v. Smith, 253 U. S. 221; National Prohibition Cases, 253 U. S. 350; Leser v. Garnett, 258 U. S. 130; State v. Becker, (Mo.) 240 S. W. 229; State v. Whisman, 36 S. D. 260; Moulton v. Scully, 111 Me. 428; Baird v. Burke County, 53 N. D. 140; Norris v. Cross, 25 Okl. 287; In re Opinion of the Justices, 118 Me. 544; State v. Olson, 44 N. D. 614; Hammond Lumber Co. v. Moore, 104 Cal. App. 528; Ralls v. Wyand, 40 Okl. 323, 340; Thompson v. Vaughan, 192 Mich. 512; State v. Erickson, 75 Mont. 429; State v. Stewart, 53 Mont. 18; Dyer v. Shaw, 139 Okl. 165; State v. Mack, 134 Ore. 67; Hopping v. Richmond, 170 Cal. 605; State v. Osborn, 16 Ariz. 247.

(f) The civil law: "statutes" in the civil law.

Story, Conflict of Laws, § 12; Saul v. His Creditors, 5 Mart. N. S. (La.) 569, 576–599; General Survey of Continental Legal History (Continental Legal History Series, vol. 1) 159–175, 263–265, 400–406, 432–445.

Ilbert, Legislative Methods and Forms, 8–19.

(g) Continental Europe and derived systems.

(1) Codes.

Maitland, The Making of the German Civil Code, III Collected Papers, 474–488; Schuster, The German Civil Code, 12 L. Q. Rev. 17.

Le Code Civil, 1804–1904, Livre du centenaire, publié par la Société d'Études Législatives, especially Gény, La technique législative dans la codification civile moderne, in vol. 2, pp. 989–1038, and Moreau, La révision du code civil et la procédure législative, id. 1041–1071; Ilbert, The Mechanics of Law Making, chap. 8; DeColyar, Jean Baptiste Colbert and the Codifying Ordinances of Louis XIV, XIII J. Soc. Comp. Leg. (N. S.) 56; Lobingier, Codification in the Philippines, X J. Soc. Comp. Leg. (N. S.) 239; Progress of Continental Law in the Nineteenth Century (11 Continental Legal History Series) chaps. 5–9; General Survey of Continental Legal History (1 Continental Legal History Series) 279–305, 187–195, 439–451, 690–700.

(2) Statutes.

I Baudry-Lacantinerie, Traité de droit civil, §§ 82–85; Beling, Methodik der Gesetzgebung, 1–92; Bekker, Grundbegriffe des Rechts und Misgriffe der Gesetzgebung, chap. 8.

(3) Executive ordinances.
Freund, Legislative Regulation, § 6.

I Baudry-Lacantinerie, Traité de droit civil, §§ 86–87.

(h) Legislation under an autocracy.

Korkunov, General Theory of Law (transl. by Hastings) § 56.

(i) Comparison of primary lawmaking agencies as to efficiency.

Ilbert, Legislative Methods and Forms, chap. 10.

2. Secondary.

Dicey, Law of the Constitution (8 ed.) 83–133; Ilbert, Legislative Methods and Forms, chap. 3; Allen, Law in the Making (3 ed.) 438–501.

(a) Skeleton legislation, to be filled out by judicial development.

II Hoar, Autobiography of Seventy Years, 363–365.

(b) Devolved legislative power.

Clark, Australian Constitutional Law (2 ed.) 46–51; Quick and Garran, Annotated Constitution of the Australian Commonwealth, 508–510.

American Ins. Co. v. Canter, 1 Pet. 511, 542; Trustees of Vincennes University v. Indiana, 14 How. 268; Miners' Bank v. Iowa, 12 How. 1, 8; Maynard v. Hill, 125 U. S. 190; Mercer v. Williams, Walker (Mich.) 85; Chalfont v. U. S., Morris (Ia.) 284; Terr. v. Guyot, 9 Mont. 46; Whitmore v. Hardin, 3 Utah, 121.

Hodge v. The Queen, 9 App. Cas. 117; King v. Military Governor [1924] 2 Ir. 104.

Delegation by a territorial legislature.

Thallheimer v. Board of Supervisors, 11 Ariz. 431; Thornton v. Territory of Washington, 3 Wash. Terr. 482.

(c) Delegated lawmaking.

Carr, Delegated Legislation; Duguit, Law in the Modern State (transl. by Laski) 95–122; Allen, Law in the Making (3 ed.) chap. 7; Willis, The Parliamentary Powers of English Government Departments, chaps. 1, 2, 4, 5; Chen, Parliamentary Control of Delegated Legislation; Ilbert, The Mechanics of Law Making, 139–149; Shannon, Delegated Legislation, 6 Canadian Bar Rev. 245.

Judicial review in Great Britain.

Willis, The Parliamentary Powers of English Government Departments, 62–106.

The maxim *delegata potestas non potest delegari.*

Duff and Whiteside, Delegata Potestas non Potest Delegari: A Maxim of American Constitutional Law, 14 Cornell L. Q. 168.

(1) Municipal lawmaking.

Freund, Legislative Regulation, § 7.

i. Municipal home rule charters — devolution of legislative power upon municipalities.

Platt v. San Francisco, 158 Cal. 74; Northern Pac. R. Co. v. Duluth, 153 Minn. 122; Walton v. Donnelly, 83 Okl. 233; St. Louis v. Western Union Tel. Co., 149 U. S. 465; Perrysburg v. Ridgway, 108 Ohio St. 245; Fitzgerald v. Cleveland, 88 Ohio St. 338; Laird Norton Yards v. Rochester, 117 Minn. 114; Consumers Coal Co. v. Lincoln, 109 Neb. 51; Los Angeles v. Central Trust Co., 173 Cal. 323; Loop Lumber Co. v. Van Loben Sels, 173 Cal. 228; Ex parte Daniels, 183 Cal. 636; Grant v. Berrisford, 94 Minn. 45; Froelich v. Cleveland, 99 Ohio St. 376; City of Kalamazoo v. Titus, 208 Mich. 252.

Patton, Home Rule in Iowa, II Iowa Applied History Series, 89–210.

ii. Municipal ordinances.

Dillon, Municipal Corporations (5 ed.) chaps. 15, 16, §§ 570–731; I Blackstone, Comm. 475–476; 2 Kent. Comm. 278; Des Moines Gas Co. v. Des Moines, 44 Ia. 505; Trenton Horse R. Co. v. Trenton, 53 N. J. L. 132; St. Johnsbury v. Thompson, 59 Vt. 300; Stetson v. Kempton, 13 Mass. 272; Mobile v. Yuille, 3 Ala. 137.

iii. Resolutions of municipal councils.

Dillon, Municipal Corporations (5 ed.) § 571; Alma v. Guaranty Sav. Bk., 60 Fed. 203; Chicago R. Co. v. Chicago, 174 Ill. 439; Sawyer v. Lorenzen, 149 Ia. 87; Detroit v. Detroit United R. Co., 215 Mich. 401; Campbell v. Cincinnati, 49 Ohio St. 463, 470; Mackenzie v. Maplewood Min. Co., 20 Ont. L. 615.

(2) Judicial rule making.

Erskine, Principles of the Law of Scotland, 40–41; Pound, Regulation of Judicial Procedure by Rules of Court, 10 Illinois L. Rev. 163.

Beers v. Haughton, 9 Pet. 329, 358; Wayman v. Southard, 10 Wheat. 1, 42–50; Bank of United States v. Halstead, 10 Wheat. 51, 61.

Clark, The Proposed Federal Rules of Civil Procedure, 22 A. B. A. J. 447; Clark and Moore, A New Federal Civil Procedure, I The Background, 44 Yale L. J. 387; Gertner, The Inherent Power of Courts to Make Rules, 10 Univ. of Cincinnati L. Rev. 32; Pound, The Rule-making Power of the Courts, 12 A. B. A. J. 599; Sunderland, The Grant of Rule-making Power to the Supreme Court of the United States, 32 Mich. L. Rev. 1116; Wheaton, Procedural Improvements and the Rule-making Power of Our Courts, 22 A. B. A. J. 642.

(3) Administrative lawmaking.

Brown, The Executive Department's Exercise of Quasi Judicial and Quasi Legislative Functions in Wisconsin, 3 Wisconsin L. Rev. 385, 449; Gibbon, Gwyer, and Andersen, The Powers of Public Departments to Make Rules Having the Force of Law, 5 Journal of Public Administration, 399, 404, 414; Stamp, Recent Tendencies Towards the Devolution of Legislative Functions to the Administration, 2 Journal of Public Administration, 23.

i. Legislation conditioned on administrative action.

The Queen v. Burah, 3 App. Cas. 889; Cargo of Brig Aurora v. United States, 7 Cranch, 382; Field v. Clark, 143 U. S. 649; J. W. Hampton, Jr. & Co. v. United States, 276 U. S. 394; Fox River Butter Co. v. United States, 59 Treasury Decisions, 485; United States v. Fox River Butter Co., 20 Ct. Cust. & Pat. App. (Cust.) 38 (Application for certiorari denied, 287 U. S. 628); People v. Klinck Packing Co., 214 N. Y. 121, 138–140.

Powell, Separation of Powers, 27 Political Science Q. 215, 222–225.

ii. Devolution of rate-making power upon commissions.

Intermountain Rate Cases, 234 U. S. 476 (compare s.c. below, Atchison, T. & S. F. R. Co. v. United States, 191 Fed. 856); Eulogy of Chief Justice Taft on Chief Justice White, 257 U. S. xxv; German Alliance Ins. Co. v. Kansas, 233 U. S. 389; State v. Chicago, M. & St. P. R. Co., 38 Minn. 281 (rev'd on other grounds in Chicago, M. & St. P. R. Co. v. Minnesota, 134 U. S. 418); Village of Saratoga Springs v. Saratoga Gas, Electric Light & Power Co., 191 N. Y. 123; State v. Whitman, 196 Wis. 472, 512–517.

iii. Delegation of fixing of standards to administrative officials.

Harmon v. Ohio, 66 Ohio St. 249; Schaezlein v. Cabanios, 135 Cal. 466.

iv. Administrative rules and orders.

Landis, The Administrative Process, 47–88; Port, Administrative Law, chap. 5; Hart, The Ordinance Making Power of the President, chaps. 2, 3, 6; Fairlie, Administrative Legislation, 18 Mich. L. Rev. 90; Foster, The Delegation of Legislative Power to Administrative Officers, 7 Ill. L. Rev. 397; Parker, Executive Judgments and Executive Legislation, 20 Harv. L. Rev. 116; Wickersham, Delegation of Power to Legislate, 11 Va. L. Rev. 183; Macassey, Law Making by Government Departments, 5 J. Soc. Comp. Leg. 3 ser. 73.

Buttfield v. Stranahan, 192 U. S. 470; United States v. Grimaud, 220 U. S. 506; United States v. Antikamnia Chemical Co., 231 U. S. 654; Mutual Film Corporation v. Ohio Industrial Commission, 236 U. S. 230; Waite v. Macy, 246 U. S. 606; International R. Co. v. Davidson, 257 U. S. 506.

State v. Whitman, 196 Wis. 472, 490–512.

Institute of Patent Agents v. Lockwood [1894] A. C. 347; The King v. Halliday [1917] A. C. 260; Minister of Health v. The King [1931] A. C. 494; Carbines v. Powell, 36 C. L. R. 88.

Powell, Separation of Powers, 27 Political Science Q. 215, 225–232.

v. Administrative interpretation.

Work v. United States, 267 U. S. 175.

vi. Administrative codes.

Willis, The Parliamentary Powers of English Government Departments, 110–115.

vii. The mechanics of administrative rule making.

Final Report of Attorney General's Committee on Administrative Procedure, 25–29, 224–232; Report of Committee on Administrative Law, 63 Rep. Am. Bar Assn. 331, 360–361; Pound, For the Minority Report, 27 A. B. A. J. 664, 671–672, 674–675 (1941).
English Local Government Act (1929) 19 Geo. V, c. 17, § 130.
State v. Whitman, 196 Wis. 472, 482–490.

(d) "Autonomic" lawmaking.

Salmond, Jurisprudence, § 51; Gray, Nature and Sources of the Law (2 ed.) 155–159; Allen, Law in the Making (3 ed.) 451–458; Chafee, The Internal Affairs of Associations Not For Profit, 43 Harv. L. Rev. 993.

Com. v. Power, 7 Met. (Mass.) 596; Miller v. Georgia Railroad & Banking Co., 88 Ga. 563; Del Ponte v. Società Italiana, 27 R. I. 1; 2 Thompson, Corporations (3 ed.) §§ 1066, 1068.
Compare Huebner, History of Germanic Private Law (transl. by Philbrick) 7–8, 97–99.

D. Relation of the Imperative to the Traditional Element

Savigny, On the Vocation of Our Age for Legislation and Jurisprudence (Hayward's transl.); Carter, Law: Its Origin, Growth, and Function, 204–220; Dicey, Law and Opinion in England, 393–396; Pound, Common Law and Legislation, 21 Harv. L. Rev. 383; Holland, Jurisprudence (13 ed.) 76–78; Landis, Statutes and the Sources of Law, Harvard Legal Essays, 213; Mulder, Some Obstacles to Effective Legislation, 31 Illinois L. Rev. 24; James, Statutory Doubts and Legislative Intention, 40 Columbia L. Rev. 957; Fowler, A Psychological Approach to Procedural Reform (1934) 43 Yale L. J. 1254.

1. Mutual reaction of the traditional and imperative elements.

Dicey, Law and Opinion in England, 369–392, 396. See Smart v. Smart [1892] A. C. 425, 432; Note, 44 Harv. L. Rev. 280, 283.

2. The traditional element as a means of interpretation.

Carter, Law: Its Origin, Growth, and Function, 309 ff.; Baldwin, The American Judiciary, 81–97; Charmont et Chausse, Les interprètes du code civil, I Livre du centenaire du code civil français, 133–172; I Endemann, Lehrbuch des bürgerlichen Rechts, § 12.
Commercial Nat. Bank v. Canal Bank, 239 U. S. 520; Holmes, J. in Panama R. Co. v. Rock, 266 U. S. 209, 215; id. in Johnson v. United States, 163 Fed. 30,

32; Lord Birkenhead in Bourne v. Keane [1919] A. C. 815, 856–857; Agar v. Orda, 246 N. Y. 248; Thomas G. Jewett, Jr. Inc. v. Keystone Driller Co., 282 Mass. 469, 476, 480.

3. Analogical reasoning from legislation.

Schuster, German Civil Law, § 17; Stammler, Theorie der Rechts-wissenschaft, 633–641; Capitant, Introduction à l'étude du droit civil (4 ed.) 109–114.

Cases of "extension of legislative principles," instead of superseded common law, to new situations: United Mine Workers v. Coronado Co., 259 U. S. 344, 385–392 (1922); McGibbon v. Abbott, L. R. 10 App. Cas. 653, 662–663 (1885); Smart v. Smart [1892] A. C. 425, 431–436; Edwards v. Porter [1925] A. C. 1; Encarnacion v. Jamison, 251 N. Y. 218, 221–224 (1929); Jamison v. Encarna-cion, 281 U. S. 635 (1930); Com. v. Rutherfoord, 160 Va. 524, 531–543 (1933).

4. Adjustment of the traditional element to legislation and vice versa.

Gray, Nature and Sources of the Law (1 ed.) §§ 369–399 (2 ed.) pp. 171–189; II Gény, Méthode d'interprétation (2 ed.) §§ 138–154; Cohen, Law and Facts in the New York Court of Appeals, 33 Columbia L. Rev. 953.

XIX. CODIFICATION

II Austin, Jurisprudence, lect. 39 and Notes on Codification (5 ed.) 1021–1039; Savigny, Vom Beruf unsrer Zeit für Gesetzgebung und Rechtswissenschaft (transl. by Hayward as On the Vocation of Our Age for Legislation and Jurisprudence); Carter, Law: Its Origin, Growth, and Function, lects. 11, 12; Clark, Practical Juris-prudence, 380–394; Dillon, Laws and Jurisprudence of England and America, 178–187; Goadby, Introduction to the Study of Law, chap. 4; I Birkenhead, Points of View, 150–190; Isaacs, The Aftermath of Codification (1920) 45 Rep. Am. Bar Assn. 524; Williston, Modern Tendencies in the Law (1929) chap. 2; id. Written and Unwritten Law (1931) 17 A. B. A. J. 39.

Amos, Science of Law, chap. 13; id. Systematic View of the Science of Juris-prudence, 471–490; Bryce, Studies in History and Jurisprudence (American ed.) 103–105; Clarke, The Science of Law and Lawmaking (this whole book is an argument against codification); Matthews, Thoughts on Codification of the Common Law (2 ed. 1881); Walker, Introduction to American Law (1 ed. 1837) §§ 52–53 (§ 19 in 3d and subsequent editions); Danz, Die Wirkung der Codificationsformen auf das materielle Recht; Bethmann-Hollweg, Ueber

Gesetzgebung und Rechtswissenschaft als Aufgaben unserer Zeit; Müller-Essert, Vom Beruf unsrer Zeit für Gesetzgebung; Demogue, Notions fondamentales du droit privé, 207 ff.; and recent French literature cited in note 2; I Gény, Méthode d'interprétation (2 ed.) §§ 37–50; Livre du Centenaire du code civil français; Festschrift zur Jahrhundertsfeier des allgemeinen bürgerlichen Gesetzbuches; Goudy, Mackay and Campbell, Addresses on Codification of Law; Carss, The Codification of Laws, 40 Canadian L. Times, 14, 126, 216, 292, 379, 451; Gregory, Benthamite Codification, 13 Harv. L. Rev. 374; Holland, Essays Upon the Form of the Law; Hearn, Theory of Legal Rights and Duties, chap. 17; Pollock, First Book of Jurisprudence (5 ed.) 365 ff.; Pulszky, Theory of Law and Civil Society, §§ 246–247; Salmond, Jurisprudence, § 53; Bentham, Letters to the Citizens of the Several American United States (on codification); Report of Joseph Story, Theron Metcalf, Simon Greenleaf, Charles E. Forbes, and Luther S. Cushing, Commissioners "to take into consideration the practicability and expediency of reducing to a written and systematic code the common law of Massachusetts or any part thereof," (1836 — reprinted by David Dudley Field, 1882); Fowler, Codification in the State of New York (2 ed. 1884); Bacon, Proposition to His Majesty Touching the Compilation and Amendment of the Laws of England, VI Spedding, Letters and Life of Bacon, 61–71; Terry, Leading Principles of Anglo-American Law, §§ 606–612; Rauchhaupt, Die Kodifikation als Etappe des Rechtsentwicklung, 58 Juristische Wochenschrift, 402; id. Kodifiziertes und Nichtkodifiziertes Recht in Europa und Amerika, 70 Gruchot, Beiträge zur Erläuterung des deutschen Rechts, 218.

Sharswood, Law Lectures, lect. 9; Pollock, Essay on Codification (prefaced to 4 ed. of his Digest of the Law of Partnership); Amos, An English Code: Its Difficulties and the Mode of Overcoming Them; Bower, Code of Actionable Defamation, Preface; Warren, History of the American Bar, chap. 19; Hoadly, Annual Address before the American Bar Association, XI Rep. Am. Bar Assn. 219 (1889); Sherman, One Code for all the United States, 25 Green Bag, 460; Boston, Law — Anachronistic, Progressive (1918) XXIV Rep. Pa. Bar Assn. 315, 344–345; Chalmers, An Experiment in Codification, 2 L. Q. Rev. 125; Acharyya, Codification in British India.

Schuster, The German Civil Code, 12 L. Q. Rev. 17; Maitland, The Making of the German Civil Code, III Collected Papers, 474; I Endemann, Lehrbuch des bürgerlichen Rechts, §§ 3, 4. Reference should be made also to the various papers in the Livre du centenaire du code civil français; De Colyar, Jean Baptiste Colbert and the Codifying Ordinances of Louis XIV, XIII J. Soc. Comp. Leg. (N. S.) 56; Lobingier, Codification in the Philippines, X J. Soc. Comp. Leg. (N. S.) 239; Progress of Continental Law in the Nineteenth Century (Continental Legal History Series, vol. 11) chaps. 5–9.

1. The so-called ancient codes, more or less authoritative publications of traditional law, are generically distinct. They come before a period of legal development. Codes in the modern sense come after a full legal development and simplify the form of the law.

2. Codification in Roman law.

The compilations of Gregorius and Hermogenianus (fourth century A.D.)

The Theodosian Code (A.D. 429–438. Took effect 439).
The Codification of Justinian (A.D. 528–534).

> The Code (529, revised and re-enacted 534).
> The Digest (533).
> The Institutes (533).
> The Novels.

3. Modern Codes.

The Constitutio Criminalis Carolina (1532).
Partial codification under Louis XIV in France.
  The project of Colbert (1667–1670).
The Prussian Code.

> The draft code of Frederick the Great (1749).
> The Allgemeines Landrecht (1780–1794).

The French Civil Code (1800–1804).

Adopted in Belgium, Egypt, and Polish Russia.
Taken as the model in:
  Argentina (1869, rev. 1883)
  Bolivia (1830, rev. 1903)
  Chili (1855)
  Colombia (1857, rev. 1872)
  Costa Rica (1886)
  Ecuador (1887)
  Guatemala (1877, rev. 1882)
  Haiti (1826)
  Holland (1838)
  Honduras (1880)
  Italy (1865)
  Louisiana (1808, rev. 1824, 1870)
  Mexico (1870, rev. 1884)
  Montenegro (1873–1886)
  Peru (1851)
  Portugal (1867)
  Quebec (1866)
  Rumania (1864)
  Salvador (1880)
  San Domingo (1884)
  Spain (1889)
  Uruguay (1869)
  Venezuela (1873).

The Austrian Civil Code (1713–1811).

Projected 1713, draft 1767, partial new draft 1787, put in force 1811.
Taken as model in
  Servia (1844, rev. 1879).

The German Civil Code (1874–1900).

First commission appointed 1874, first draft published 1887, new commission 1890, new draft 1896, took effect 1900.
Taken as model in
   Japan (1896, took effect 1900).

The Swiss Federal Codes.

The Civil Code (1907, took effect 1912).
The Code of Obligations (1901).
See the Historical Introduction in Shick, Translation of the Swiss Civil Code.

The Civil Code of Brazil (1917).

As to the history of this code, see Lacerda, Codigo Civil Brasileiro, pp. iv-lxiv.

Codification in Poland.

See Rappaport, The Work of the Commission for Codification in Poland, 1 Rev. of Polish Law and Economics, 16 (1928).

Codification in Soviet Russia.

Les codes de la Russie soviétique, I Code de la famille (transl. by Patoillet) Code civile (transl. by Patoillet et Dufour, 1925).

Codification in China.

The Chinese Civil Code (1930). See Chu, Commentaries on the Chinese Civil Code.

Two classes of countries have adopted codes:

(a) Countries with well-developed legal systems which had exhausted the possibilities of juristic development through the traditional element and required a new basis for a new juristic development.

(b) Countries which had their whole legal development before them, which required an immediate basis for development.

Conditions which have led to codification:

(a) The possibilities of juristic development on the basis of the traditional element were exhausted for the time being, or a new basis was required for a country with no juristic past.

(b) The law was unwieldy, full of archaisms and uncertain.

(c) The growing-point had shifted to legislation and an efficient organ of legislation had developed.

(d) Usually, there was a need for one law in a political community, whose several subdivisions had developed divergent local laws.

4. Codification in Anglo-American law.

In England:

The project under Henry VIII
Bacon's project (1614)
Lord Westbury's plan (1860–1863)
Gradual codification in England:
  The Bills of Exchange Act (1882)
  The Partnership Act (1890)
  The Sale of Goods Act (1894)
  The Marine Insurance Act (1906)
"Private codification."

The Anglo-Indian Codes (1837–1882).

In Australia:

The project in Victoria (1878–1882)
See Hearn, Theory of Legal Duties and Rights, 378–382, and appendix, 385.

In the United States:

The New York Codes (1847–1887)
  The Code of Civil Procedure (1848)
    Codes based on this were adopted in 30 jurisdictions
  The draft Civil Code (1862). See Pomeroy, The True Method of Interpreting the Civil Code, 3 West Coast Reporter, 585, 691, 717; 4 id. 1, 49, 109, 145
  The Penal Code (1864, enacted 1887)
  The draft Political Code (1865)
  The Code of Criminal Procedure (1865)
    Throop's Code of Civil Procedure (1876–1880)
All of Field's drafts were adopted in California, North and South Dakota, and Montana, and the California Civil Code was adopted for the Canal Zone
  The Massachusetts commission (1835)
  The Civil Code of Georgia (1860)
  The Conference of Commissioners on Uniform State Laws
    The Negotiable Instruments Law
    The Warehouse Receipts Act
    The Sales Act
    The Stock Transfer Act
    The Bills of Lading Act
    The Partnership Act
  See Williston, The Uniform Partnership Act, With Some Remarks on Other Uniform Commercial Laws, 63 U. Pa. L. Rev. 196; Vold, Some Reasons Why the Code States Should Adopt the Uniform Sales Act, 5 California L. Rev. 400, 471; Terry, Uniform State Laws in the United States.
    "Private Codification"
      The American Law Institute
        See American Law Institute Proceedings, vols. 1–17 (1923–1940);

Franklin, The Historic Function of the American Law Institute: Restatement as Transitional to Codification (1934) 47 Harv. L. Rev. 1367; Cardozo, The American Law Institute in Law and Literature, 121–141; Goodhart, Law Reform in the United States (1934) Journal of the Society of Public Teachers of Law, 19–27; Clark, The Restatement of the Law of Contracts (1933) 42 Yale L. J. 643.

5. Objections to codification:

(a) Defects of codes in the past.

(1) The codifiers too often had but superficial knowledge of much of the law they attempted to codify.

(2) Most codes in the past have been drawn too hurriedly.

(b) Savigny's objections:

(1) That the growth of the Law is likely to be impeded or diverted into unnatural directions.

Schiffer, Die deutsche Justiz (1927) 80–92.

(2) That a code made by one generation is likely to project directly or indirectly the intellectual and moral notions of the time into times when such notions have become anachronisms.

(c) Austin's objections to the French code:

(1) That it makes no adequate provision for the incorporation of judicial interpretation from time to time.

(2) That it was not complete and was intended to be eked out by pre-existing law.

6. Purposes of codification:

The eighteenth-century idea.

Bentham's idea.

The idea of a code as the basis of a juristic new start.

What a code should attempt.

7. Defects of form in American law:

(a) Want of certainty.

(b) Waste of labor entailed by unwieldy form of the law.

(c) Lack of means of knowledge on the part of those who seek to amend the law.

(d) Irrationality, due to partial survival of obsolete rules.

(e) Confusion between two parallel lines of authoritative grounds of determination (case law and statute law) dealing with the same subjects.

8. The need of new premises in American law.

PART 6

APPLICATION AND ENFORCEMENT OF LAW

XX. APPLICATION AND ENFORCEMENT OF LAW

Pound, The Enforcement of Law, 20 Green Bag, 401; id. Courts
and Legislation, 7 American Political Science Rev. 361–383, IX
Modern Legal Philosophy Series, Science of Legal Method, 202–
228; Science of Legal Method, IX Modern Legal Philosophy Series,
chaps. 1–5; Wigmore, Problems of Law, 65–101; Pollock, Judicial
Caution and Valour (1929) 45 L. Q. Rev. 293, 300–304; Arnold,
Substantive Law and Procedure (1932) 45 Harv. L. Rev. 617; id.
Law Enforcement — An Attempt at Social Dissection (1932) 42
Yale L. J. 1; Willoughby, Principles of Judicial Administration, 91–
206; Isaacs, The Limits of Judicial Discretion (1923) 32 Yale
L. J. 339.

Gény, Méthode d'interprétation (2 ed. 1919); I, II id. Science et technique
en droit privé positif; Saleilles, preface to Gény, Méthode d'interprétation (1 ed.);
Kantorowicz, Legal Science (1928) 28 Columbia L. Rev. 679, 692, 707; Van der
Eycken, Méthode de l'interprétation juridique; Mallieux, L'exégèse des codes;
Perreau, Technique de la jurisprudence en droit privé; Ransson, Essai sur l'art
de juger.

Ehrlich, Freie Rechtsfindung und freie Rechtswissenschaft; Gnaeus Flavius
(Kantorowicz), Der Kampf um die Rechtswissenschaft; Fuchs, Recht und
Wahrheit in unserer heutigen Justiz; id. Die gemeinschädlichkeit der konstruk-
tiven Jurisprudenz; Oertmann, Gesetzeszwang und Richterfreiheit; Rumpf,
Gesetz und Richter; Brütt, Die Kunst der Rechtsanwendung; Gmelin, Quousque?
Beiträge zur soziologischen Rechtfindung; Kantorowicz, Rechtswissenschaft und
Soziologie, 11 ff.; Reichel, Gesetz und Richterspruch; Jellinek, Gesetz, Gesetzes-
anwendung und Zweckmässigkeitserwägung; Somló, Juristische Grundlehre,
§§ 110–122; Stammler, Rechts und Staatstheorien der Neuzeit, § 18; id. Aus der
Vorgeschichte der Freirechtslehre; Holldack, Grenzen der Erkenntnis aus-
ländischen Rechts; Stampe, Grundriss der Wertbewegungslehre: Zur Einleitung in ein freirechtliches System der Schuldverhältnisse; Schulz, Die Persönlichkeit des Richters, 24 Leipziger Zeitschrift für deutschen Recht, 1; Alexeff,
L'état, le droit, et le pouvoir discretionaire des autorités publiques, 3 Revue
internationale de la théorie du droit, 195; Schultze, Von den Grenzen der Rechtssprechung, 35 Deutsche juristische Zeitschrift, 127.

Kübl, Das Rechtsgefühl; Riezler, Das Rechtsgefühl, 123–158.

I Endemann, Lehrbuch des bürgerlichen Rechts, §§ 12, 13; I Kohler, Lehrbuch
des bürgerlichen Rechts, §§ 38–40; Heck, Gesetzesauslegung und Interessen-

jurisprudenz (§ 19 is a critique of Kohler); I Planiol, Traité élémentaire de droit civil (12 ed.) §§ 199–225.

Aristotle, Politics, bk. iii, chap. 15 (Welldon's transl. pp. 148 ff.); Selden, Table Talk tit. Equity.

Doctor and Student, pt. 1, chaps. 16, 45; Spence, History of the Equitable Jurisdiction of the Court of Chancery, bk. II, chap. 1.

I Ahrens, Cours de droit natural (8 ed.) 177; Lasson, Rechtsphilosophie, 238–239.

Chalmers, Trial by Jury in Civil Cases, 7 L. Q. Rev. 15; Phelps, Juridical Equity, § 157 and note.

Pound, Introduction to English translation of Saleilles, Individualization of Punishment; Saleilles, The Individualization of Punishment (transl. by Mrs. Jastrow) chap. 9.

Pound, Administrative Application of Legal Standards, 44 Rep. Am. Bar Assn. 445.

1. Analysis of the judicial function:

(a) Finding the law, ascertaining the legal precept to be applied.

(b) Interpreting the precept so chosen or ascertained, that is, determining its meaning by genuine interpretation.

(c) Applying to the cause in hand the precept so found and interpreted.

Pound, The Theory of Judicial Decision, 36 Harv. L. Rev. 940, 945 ff.

2. The technical and the discretionary in judicial administration:

Agencies in legal history for restoring or preserving the balance of the administrative element:

(a) Fictions.

(b) Executive dispensing power.

(c) Interposition of praetor or chancellor on equitable grounds.

(d) Judicial individualization.

Isaacs, The Limits of Judicial Discretion, 32 Yale L. J. 339.

3. Law in books and law in action.

Pound, Law in Books and Law in Action, 44 Am. L. Rev. 13; Wiel, Public Policy in Western Water Decisions, 1 Calif. L. Rev. 11; II Harvey, Some Records of Crime, 6–7, note 1; Pound, Inherent and Acquired Difficulties in the Administration of Punitive Justice (1907) Proc. Am. Political Science Assn. 223, 234–238; Stammler, Theorie der Rechtswissenschaft, 130–134.

Llewellyn, Some Realism About Realism, 44 Harv. L. Rev. 1222, 1248–1250; Clark, Reform in Bankruptcy Administration, 43 Harv. L. Rev. 1189, 1192–1201; Green, Judge and Jury, chap. 14; Frank, Law and the Modern Mind, chap. 16.

4. The modes of applying legal precepts.

(a) Analytical.

(b) Historical.

(c) Equitable.

5. Individualization of application in Anglo-American law.

(a) In equity through discretion in the exercise of jurisdiction and adaptation of remedies.

(b) Through the jury.

Morris, Punitive Damages in Tort Cases, 44 Harv. L. Rev. 1171, 1188–92; Isaacs, Traffic in Trade Symbols, id. 1210; Green, Judge and Jury, chap. 5, especially pp. 177 ff.; Washington, Damages in Contract at Common Law, 48 L. Q. Rev. 90, 107–108.

(c) Through latitude of application under the guise of choice or ascertainment of a rule.

Hutcheson, Lawyer's Law and the Little Small Dice, 7 Tulane L. Rev. 1; id. Judging as Administration, 7 American Law School Rev. 1069.

(d) Through standards.

(1) At law.

Note, 46 Harv. L. Rev. 838–842; Note, 47 Harv. L. Rev. 494–502; Interstate Commerce Act, § 3, 49 U. S. C. § 3(1).
German Civil Code, §§ 242, 826; Swoboda, Das Privatrecht der Zukunft, XXV Archiv für Rechts- und Wirthschaftsphilosophie, 459, 466–468.

(2) In equity.

Langton, J. in Greenwood v. Greenwood [1937] P. 157, 164; Romilly, M. R. in Haywood v. Cope, 25 Beav. 140, 150–153 (1858); English Common Law Procedure Act (1854) § 81.

(e) In criminal law.

Pound, Criminal Justice in America, 41–43.

(1) Through discretion as to prosecution.

Bettman, Criminal Justice Surveys Analysis, in National Commission on Law Observance and Enforcement, Report on Prosecution, 39, 95–100; Report of the Commission, id. 3, 20–23; Illinois Crime Survey, 42–45, 269–274, 301–307; American Law Institute, Model Code of Criminal Procedure, § 305 and Commentary.

(2) Through power of juries to render general verdicts.

Train, From the District Attorney's Office, chap. 6.

(3) Through judicial discretion in sentence.

2 Harris (editor) Reminiscences of Sir Henry Hawkins, 282–290; Train, From the District Attorney's Office, 167–177; Exner, Studien ueber die Strafprozesszumessungspraxis der deutschen Gerichte (Kriminalistische Abhandlungen, no.

16); Heinitz, Der Strafzweck bei der richterlichen Strafbemessung, XXII Archiv für Rechts- und Wirthschaftsphilosophie, 259; 3 Mendizabal, Tratado de derecho natural (7 ed.) 448–461.

(4) Through suspended sentence and probation.

Glueck (editor) Probation and Criminal Justice; National Commission on Law Observance and Enforcement, Report on Penal Institutions, Probation, and Parole, 184–207; Cooley, Probation and Delinquency, chap. 2; Young, Social Treatment in Probation and Delinquency, 139–250.

(5) Through assessment of punishment by juries (statutory).

Pound, Introduction to Saleilles, The Individualization of Punishment (transl. by Jastrow) xvi f.

(6) Through nominal sentence and leaving the duration or form of penal treatment to an administrative board.

Bruce, Burgess and Harno, The Probation and Parole System, in Illinois Crime Survey, 427–574; National Commission on Law Observance and Enforcement, Report on Penal Institutions, Probation, and Parole, 127–145; Wilcox, Parole of Adults from State Penal Institutions in Pennsylvania; Pigeon, Probation and Parole in Theory and Practice (1942).

(7) Through discretion in an appellate court.

English Criminal Appeal Act (1907) § 4(3); Orfield, Criminal Appeals in America, chap. 5.

(f) In petty courts.

Smith, Justice and the Poor, 56–59; Schramm, Piedpoudre Courts, A Study of the Small Claim Litigant in the Pittsburgh District.

6. Individualization of application in the civil law.
(a) Equity (*aequitas, Billigkeit*).

Rümelin, Die Billigkeit im Recht; I Ahrens, Cours de droit naturel (8 ed.) 177; Lasson, Rechtsphilosophie, 238–239; Stammler, Lehre von dem richtigen Rechte (2 ed.) 242–249 (Husik's transl. 288–299). See Grotius, ii, 16, 26.

(b) "Free judgment" (discretion).

Stammler, Lehre von dem richtigen Rechte (2 ed.) 118–122 (Husik's transl. 123–129).

7. Individualization of application through administrative tribunals.

On administrative discretion, see Freund, Administrative Powers over Persons and Property, chap. 6; Sigler, The Problem of Apparently Unguided Administrative Discretion (1934) 19 St. Louis L. Rev. 261; Carr, English Administrative Law, 115–126; Laun, Das freie Ermessen und seine Grenzen (1910) containing full bibliography; Tezner, Das freie Ermessen der Verwaltungsbehörden.

PART 7

ANALYSIS OF GENERAL JURISTIC CONCEPTIONS

XXI. RIGHTS

1. Introductory Excursus — Juristic Conceptions.

(a) The place of juristic conceptions in historical development of law.

I Jhering, Geist des römischen Rechts, § 3.

(b) The use of conceptions.

I Jhering, Geist des römischen Rechts (5 ed.) 36–43, II, §§ 39–41; I Gény, Science et technique en droit privé positif, 145–164, III, 175–257, IV, 23–46; Hohfeld, Fundamental Legal Conceptions, 63–64; Green, Judge and Jury, chap. 9.

(c) Abuse of conceptions.

Pound, Mechanical Jurisprudence (1908) 8 Columbia L. Rev. 605, 610–621; Jhering, Scherz und Ernst in der Jurisprudenz, pt. 3; I Gény, Méthode d'interprétation (2 ed.) 124–204; Arnold, Criminal Attempts, 40 Yale L. J. 53, 79–80; Fuchs, Gesunder Menschenverstand, Neu-Wiener Begriffsnetz und französische "neue Schule" (1928) 4 Die Justiz, 129.

(d) "Necessary" conceptions and "general" conceptions.

II Austin, Jurisprudence (5 ed.) 1073–1075; I Bierling, Juristische Prinzipienlehre, 1; Somló, Juristische Grundlehre, 33–37; Hohfeld, Fundamental Legal Conceptions, 35–64; I Roguin, La Science juridique pure, 3–55, 81–118; Tourtoulon, Philosophy in the Development of Law (transl. by Read) chap. XIII, § 3; Kelsen, Reine Rechtslehre, 1–9, 39–61; Pound, Progress of the Law: Analytical Jurisprudence (1927) 41 Harv. L. Rev. 174, 176–184, 187–189, 195–196; Lundstedt, Superstition or Rationality in Action for Peace (1925) 117–119; Duguit, Les transformations générales du droit privé depuis le code Napoléon, 24.

2. Meanings of "a right."

Hohfeld, Fundamental Legal Conceptions, 6–12; Pound, Legal Rights, 26 Internat. Journ. of Ethics, 92; I Beale, Conflict of Laws, 62–70, 79–86.

3. History of the conception of "a right."

(a) Origins in Greek philosophy.

τὸ δίκαιον, τοὐμὸν δίκαιον

τὸ καθῆκον

Aristotle, Nicomachean Ethics, v, 2, 8-9, v, 4, 1-8, v, 7, 5-6; Demosthenes against Midias, 572, 14; Diogenes Laertius, vii, 108; Cicero, De Officiis, i, 3.

Justice as applied to a particular case. There is no clear idea of "a right," but rather of a legally established or legally recognized moral duty.

(b) Origins in Roman procedure.

The action for a physical thing.

The action for a person judicially or formally condemned to a payment.

Buckland, Text Book of Roman Law, 668; Gaius, iii, § 174. See Gaius, iv, § 21.

The claim asserted generally.

The claim asserted against a particular person.

Gaius, iv, §§ 1-5; Inst. iv, 6, 1.

(c) *Ius* in Roman law.

I Glück, Ausführliche Erläuterung der Pandekten, § 1.

(a) As what is right and just, in reason, in morals, or in ethical custom. Dig. i, 1, 1, pr. and § 1, i, 1, 10-11.

(b) As law — what is legally established or recognized as right and just. Inst. i, 2; Dig. i, 1, 6, i, 1, 11. In Gaius, the strict law, as distinguished from the praetorian law. Gaius, ii, §§ 146, 198, iii, § 75, iv, § 60.

(c) As *a* law or legal precept. Dig. xxii, 3, 5, 1, 17, 82, i, 3, 35, xii, 1, 1.

(d) As legal institution — rightful or customary institution legally recognized or established. Gaius, i, §§ 55, 112, 129, 158.

(e) As presence of a magistrate — where right and justice may be had. Dig. ii, 3.

(f) As political capacity. E.g. *ius suffragii, ius honorum.*

(g) As authority — legally backed customary or moral authority. E.g. *ius imperandi,* Dig. ix, 2, 37, pr.; *ius patris,* Mosaicarum et Romanarum Legum Collatio, iv, 7; persons *alieno iuri subiecti,* Inst. i, 8, pr.

(h) As power — a legally backed moral or customary power. E.g. *ius donandi uendendi concedendi,* Dig. l, 17, 163; *ius testamenti faciendi,* Dig. xxviii, 1, 6, pr.

(i) As privilege — rightful liberty legally recognized. Dig. l, 17, 55.

(j) As legal position — rightful position under a rule of law, legally conferred advantage. E.g. *ius Latii,* Gaius, i, § 95; *ius trium liberorum,* Gaius, i, §§ 145, 194, iii, § 44; Ulpian, Regulae, iii, 1, xix, 3; *ius cognationis,* Dig. i, 1, 12.

There is no clear differentiation and no clear conception of a right.

(d) *Ius* from the twelfth to the sixteenth century.

(1) The Glossators and Commentators.

Little advance on the Roman texts.

Gloss "*ius quid sit*" on rubric to Sext, De reg. iur.; Johannes Andreae on rubric to Sext, De reg. iur.; Bartolus on Dig. i, 1, 1.

(2) The scholastic philosophers.

Thomas Aquinas, Summa Theologica, II–II, q. 57, arts. 2–4.

No clear setting off of "a right," but suggestion of a just claim as a distinct conception.

(3) The Humanists.

I Donellus, De iure civili, 3, 2–4 (1589).
Ius as "a right" distinctly set off as a different conception from *ius* as "right-and-law."

(e) "Right" in medieval law.

Rectum as equivalent to *ius* with most of its meanings, tending to become "that which is right as applied to my case."
See Du Cange, Glossarium ad scriptores mediae et infimae Latinitatis, sub voc. *Rectum*; Fleta, vi, c. 1, § 1. See also Co. Lit. 158b, 266a, 345a, b.

(f) Natural rights.

The transition from natural law to natural rights.

Grotius, De iure belli ac pacis, i, 1, 4; Hobbes, Leviathan, chap. 14; Dunning, Political Theories from Luther to Montesquieu, 272–276; Ritchie, Natural Rights, chaps. 1–2.

(g) The system of the Pandectists.

I Windscheid, Pandekten, § 37a; Regelsberger, Pandekten, § 13.

(h) Jhering's setting off of the recognized interest from that which secures it.

III^i Jhering, Geist des römischen Rechts, §§ 60–61.

(i) The system of the English analytical jurists.

I Austin, Jurisprudence, lects. 12, 14–16; Holland, Jurisprudence, chap. 7.

(j) Recent German analyses.

Somló, Juristische Grundlehre, 439–485. See Thon, Rechtsnorm und subjectives Recht, chaps. 4–6; II Bierling, Kritik der juristischen Grundbegriffe, 128–149.

(k) Hohfeld's analysis — see *infra* 5 (b).

4. Theories of "a right."

(a) The natural-law conception — a right as a recognized and secured quality.

Jus has another signification [i.e. than "law"] derived from the former which refers to the person. In this sense *jus* (a right) is a moral quality by which a person is competent to have or to do a thing justly. — Grotius, De iure belli ac pacis, i, 1, 4 (1625).

That moral quality by which either we rightly command persons or hold things, or by force of which something is owed to us. — I Pufendorf, De iure naturae et gentium (1672) 1, 30.

The moral justification of one human being in controlling for his own benefit the volition of another. — Phillips, Jurisprudence (1863) 6–8, 27.

That quality in a person which makes it just or right for him either to possess certain things or to do certain actions. — I Rutherforth, Institutes of Natural Law, 2, § 3.

(b) A right as a policy — the general security put in terms of "a right."

"The law punishes the larceny of property, not solely because of any rights of the proprietor, but also because of its own inherent legal rights as property." — Shaw, C. J. in Commonwealth v. Rourke, 10 Cush. (Mass.) 397, 399 (1852).

(c) Metaphysical — a right as deduced from the fundamental datum of free will.

A power over an object which, by reason of the right, is subjected to the will of the person entitled. — II Puchta, Cursus der Institutionen (9 ed.) § 207.

A moral power over others residing in one's self. — I Stahl, Philosophie des Rechts (5 ed.) 279.

See Kant, Rechtslehre (2 ed.) xliv-xlvii, 55–56 (Hastie's transl. 55–59, 61–62); Miller, The Data of Jurisprudence, 50–51, 131–132.

(d) Jural relations — a right as a relation.

If we consider the jural and legal order, which surrounds us and presses on us from every side, we see first of all the power belonging to the individual person; a sphere in which his will rules, and rules with our concurrence. We call this power a right of that person, meaning the same thing as authority. Many call it *Recht* in the subjective sense. . . . But a more precise consideration shows us . . . the need of a deeper foundation. We find this in the jural relation (Rechtsverhältniss). — I Savigny, System des heutigen römischen Rechts, § 4.

Each particular jural relation [is] . . . a relation between person and person, determined by a rule of law. But this determination by a rule of law consists herein: that a sphere is assigned to the individual will in which it may govern independent of the wills of others. — Id. § 52.

A relation between persons, concerning an object, created by a particular fact, determined by a principle or rule of law, for an end of human life. — I Ahrens, Cours de droit naturel, § 23.

A relation sanctioned and protected by the legal order. — Kohler, Einführung in die Rechtswissenschaft, § 6.

Wigmore, Summary of the Principles of Torts (Cases on Torts, vol. 2, app. A) §§ 4–8; Korkunov, General Theory of Law (transl. by Hastings) §§ 27–29; Kocourek, Jural Relations, chaps. 1, 3 (reprinted with some changes from Basic Jural Relations, 17 Illinois L. Rev. 515, and Various Definitions of Jural Relation, 20 Columbia L. Rev. 394).

I Savigny, System des heutigen römischen Rechts, §§ 4, 52–53; Puntschart, Die fundamentalen Rechtsverhältnisse des römischen Privatrechts, §§ 7–8; Herkless, Jurisprudence, 84–88; Stammler, Theorie der Rechtswissenschaft (2 ed.) 124–126, 135–138; I Kohler, Lehrbuch des bürgerlichen Rechts, §§ 44–46.

(e) A right as liberty.

Right consisteth in liberty to do or to forbear; whereas law determineth and bindeth to one of them: so that law and right differ as much as obligation and liberty. — Hobbes, Leviathan, chap. 14.

Right is liberty, namely, that liberty which the civil law leaves us. — Id. chap. 26.

A liberty to follow my own will in all things where that rule [i.e. a standing rule applicable to all and made by the legislative authority] prescribes not. — Locke, Two Treatises of Government, bk. ii, chap. 4.

By private civil right we can mean only the liberty every man possesses to preserve his existence, a liberty limited by the edicts of the sovereign power and preserved only by its authority. — Spinoza, Tractatus Theologico-Politicus, chap. 16.

A permission to exercise certain natural powers and upon certain conditions to obtain protection, restitution, or compensation by the aid of the public force. Just so far as the aid of the public force is given a man, he has a legal right. — Holmes, The Common Law, 214.

(f) A right as what is right put subjectively.

The legal order (*Recht* in the objective sense, objective right), on the basis of a concrete situation of fact, puts forth a command, requiring conduct of a certain sort, and puts this command at the free disposition of the one for whose benefit it was issued. It leaves it to him whether or not he will make use of the command and in particular whether or not he will put in action the means afforded by the legal order against those who disobey it. His will is determining for the carrying out of the command issued by the legal order. The legal order has made its command his command. What is right has become his right. . . .

A right is a power or authority of the will conferred by the legal order. — I Windscheid, Lehrbuch des Pandektenrechts, § 37.

I Windscheid, Lehrbuch des Pandektenrechts, §§ 37–37a; Schuppe, Begriff des subjektiven Rechts, chap. 2; Affolter, Untersuchungen über das Wesen des Rechts, 36–43; Jellinek, System der subjektiven öffentlichen Rechte (2 ed.) 54–93; Pagel, Beiträge zur philosophischen Rechtslehre, 85–123 (critique of Schuppe).

Capitant, Introduction à l'étude du droit civil (4 ed.) no. 74; I Roguin, La science juridique pure, §§ 87–93; I Duguit, Traité de droit constitutionnel (1 ed.) no. 1, cf. id. (2 ed.) 6–11; Tasic, Sul concetto di diritto soggettivo (1928) 8 Revista internazionale di filosofia del diritto, 240; II Gorovtseff, Études de principiologie du droit, Théorie du sujet de droit (1928).

(g) A right as a secured interest.

An interest protected by law. — III Jhering, Geist des römischen Rechts, § 60.

A moral or natural right is an interest recognized and protected by the rule of natural justice — an interest the violation of which would be a moral wrong, and respect for which is a moral duty. A legal right . . . is an interest recognized and protected by the rule of legal justice — an interest the violation of which would be a legal wrong to him whose interest it is, and respect for which is a legal duty. — Salmond, Jurisprudence, § 72.

There has been a controversy whether right is power or interest. The word suggests both; a power to exact a particular act or forbearance, service, or benefit, and a particular interest on account of which the power exists, from which it derives its value, with respect to which its form is determined, and which it serves to protect. But the right in itself is power. It is related to the interest as the fortification to the protected land. — Merkel, Juristische Encyklopädie (2 ed.) § 159, note.

Salmond, Jurisprudence, §§ 70–74.

Korkunov, General Theory of Law (transl. by Hastings) § 22; Gareis, Science of Law (transl. by Kocourek) 31–35.

(h) A right as a power or capacity.

The capacity or power of exacting from another or others acts or forbearances.

A party has a right when another or others are bound or obliged by the law to do or forbear towards or in regard of him. — I Austin, Jurisprudence, lect. 16.

A capacity in one man of controlling, with the assent and assistance of the state, the actions of others. — Holland, Jurisprudence, chap. 7.

I Austin, Jurisprudence, lect. 12; Gray, Nature and Sources of the Law, §§ 22–62; Holland, Jurisprudence, chaps. 7, 8, to subdiv. I; Pollock, First Book of Jurisprudence (5 ed.) 61–72; Markby, Elements of Law (6 ed.) §§ 146–160; Hearn, Theory of Legal Duties and Rights, chap. 8; Terry, Leading Principles of Anglo-American Law, §§ 113–127.

Amos, Science of Law, 89–97; Rattigan, Science of Jurisprudence, §§ 11a–20b; Miller, The Data of Jurisprudence, 131–132; Brown, The Austinian Theory of Law, 192–193.

(i) A right as a legally assertable claim.

Thon, Rechtsnorm und subjektives Recht, chap. 5; II Bierling, Kritik der juristischen Grundbegriffe, 49–73; Somló, Juristische Grundlehre, §§ 125–126, 131–135.

(j) The conception of social functions.

In what, then, does this notion of social function consist? It comes to this: The individual man has no rights, nor has the collectivity rights. To speak of the rights of the individual and of the rights of society, to say that we must reconcile the rights of the individual with those of the collectivity, is to speak of things which do not exist. But every individual has a certain function to perform in society, a certain task to carry out. He cannot be allowed not to perform this function, he cannot be allowed not to carry out this task, because a derangement or at least a prejudice to society would result from his refraining. Moreover, every act which he does, contrary to the function which devolves upon him, will be socially repressed. But conversely, everything which he does to accomplish the mission which is his because of the place he occupies in society will be socially protected and guaranteed. — Duguit, Les transformations générales du droit privé depuis le Code Napoléon, 24.

Duguit in Progress of Continental Law in the Nineteenth Century (11 Continental Legal History Series) 74–75; Duguit, Objective Law, 20 Columbia L. Rev. 817, 822–825 (as to this, see 41 Harv. L. Rev. 174, 195).

(k) Wrong made the elementary concept, instead of right and duty.

Voegelin, Kelsen's Pure Theory of Law, XLII Political Science Q. 268, 270, 272.

See Kelsen, Hauptprobleme der Staatsrechtslehre (2 ed.) 567–579, id. Reine Rechtslehre (1934) 40–46; id. The Pure Theory of Law (1934) 50 L. Q. Rev. 474, 491–496.

5. Analysis of the nineteenth-century conception.

(a) German analyses.

Windscheid (1862) —

Subjective right $\begin{cases} \text{right,} \\ \text{power.} \end{cases}$

Thon (1878) —
Anspruch (claim).
Genuss (liberty).
Befugung (power).

Bierling (1883) —
Anspruch (claim).
Dürfen (liberty).
Können (power).

(b) Anglo-American analyses.

Salmond (1902) —

Legal advantages
(rights in the wider sense): $\begin{cases} \text{rights in the stricter sense,} \\ \text{liberties,} \\ \text{powers.} \end{cases}$

Legal burdens: $\begin{cases} \text{duties,} \\ \text{disabilities,} \\ \text{liabilities.} \end{cases}$

Hohfeld (1913) —

Jural opposites: $\begin{cases} \text{right,} \quad \text{privilege,} \quad \text{power,} \quad \text{immunity,} \\ \text{no-right;} \text{duty;} \quad \text{disability;} \text{liability.} \end{cases}$

Jural correlatives: $\begin{cases} \text{right,} \quad \text{privilege,} \quad \text{power,} \quad \text{immunity,} \\ \text{duty;} \quad \text{no-right;} \quad \text{liability;} \quad \text{disability.} \end{cases}$

Kocourek (1927) —

Advantage: $\begin{cases} \text{claim,} \\ \text{immunity,} \\ \text{privilege,} \\ \text{power.} \end{cases}$

Disadvantage: $\begin{cases} \text{duty,} \\ \text{disability,} \\ \text{inability,} \\ \text{liability.} \end{cases}$

Beale (1935) —
   primary rights:
      static rights,
      dynamic rights.
   Secondary rights:
      rights of redress or restoration,
      remedial rights.

The wider sense —

Recognized and delimited interest plus the complex of conceptions securing it.

The stricter sense —

Capacity of asserting a recognized claim, having a correlative duty.

Hohfeld, Fundamental Legal Conceptions as Applied in Judicial Reasoning (reprint of papers in 23 Yale L. J. 16, 30, and 26 id. 712); Kocourek, Jural Relations, chaps. 1, 4, 6; id. The Hohfeld System of Fundamental Legal Concepts, 15 Illinois L. Rev. 24; Husik, Hohfeld's Jurisprudence, 68 U. Pa. L. Rev. 263; Corbin, Rights and Duties, 33 Yale L. J. 501; Randall, Hohfeld on Jurisprudence, 41 L. Q. Rev. 86; Pound, Fifty Years of Jurisprudence, 50 Harv. L. Rev. 557, 571–576; Radin, A Restatement of Hohfeld, 51 Harv. L. Rev. 1141, 1147–1153, 1156–1160, 1163–1164.

I Savigny, System des heutigen römischen Rechts (1840) §§ 4, 52–63; I Windscheid, Lehrbuch des Pandektenrechts (1862) § 37; III Jhering, Geist des römischen Rechts (1865) §§ 60, 61; I Austin, Lectures on Jurisprudence (3 ed. 1869) lect. 16; Thon, Rechtsnorm und subjektives Recht (1878) chap. 5; Holland, Elements of Jurisprudence (1880) chaps. 7, 8; Holmes, The Common Law (1881) 214; II Bierling, Zur Kritik der juristischen Grundbegriffe (1883) 49–73; Hearn, Theory of Legal Duties and Rights (1883) chap. 8; Terry, Some Leading Principles of Anglo-American Law (1884) chap. 6; id. Duties, Rights, and Wrongs (1924) 10 A. B. A. J. 123; Merkel, Juristische Enzyklopädie (1885) §§ 146–170; Puntschart, Die fundamentalen Rechtsverhältnisse des römischen Privatrechts (1885) §§ 7–8; Schuppe, Der Begriff des subjektiven Rechts (1887) chap. 2; Salmond, Jurisprudence (1902) §§ 70–74; I Kohler, Lehrbuch des bürgerlichen Rechts (1906) §§ 44–46; I Bierling, Juristische Prinzipienlehre, § 12 (pp. 183–206); Somló, Juristische Grundlehre, §§ 127–129; I Cosack, Lehrbuch des deutschen bürgerlichen Rechts, §§ 16–20; Gray, The Nature and

Sources of the Law (1909) §§ 22–62; Wigmore, A Summary of the Principles of Torts, app. A, §§ 4–8, in II Select Cases on the Law of Torts (1912); Pound, Introduction to the Study of Law (1912) § 6; id. Readings on the History and System of the Common Law (2 ed. 1913, 3 ed. 1927) chap. 8; id. Legal Rights (1915) 26 Internat. Journ. of Ethics, 92; Hohfeld, Some Fundamental Legal Conceptions as Applied in Judicial Reasoning (1913) 23 Yale L. J. 16, reprinted in Hohfeld, Fundamental Legal Conceptions as Applied in Judicial Reasoning and Other Legal Essays (ed. by Cook, 1923); I Beale, Conflict of Laws (1935) 58–86, but first published 1916; Cook, The Alienability of Choses in Action (1916) 29 Harv. L. Rev. 816, and (1917) 30 id. 449; id. Privileges of Labor Unions in the Struggle for Life (1918) 27 Yale L. J. 779; id. Hohfeld's Contribution to the Science of Law (1919) 28 id. 721; Corbin, Offer and Acceptance, and Some of the Resulting Legal Relations (1917) 26 id. 169; id. Legal Analysis and Terminology (1919) 29 id. 163; id. Jural Relations and Their Classification (1921) 30 id. 226; id. Terminology and Classification in Fundamental Jural Relations (1921) 4 Am. L. School Rev. 607; id. What is a Legal Relation? (1922) 5 Illinois L. Q. 50; id. Rights and Duties (1924) 33 Yale L. J. 501; Kocourek, The Hohfeld System of Fundamental Legal Concepts (1920) 15 Illinois L. Rev. 24; id. Various Definitions of Jural Relation (1920) 20 Columbia L. Rev. 394; id. Plurality of Advantage and Disadvantage in Jural Relations (1920) 19 Mich. L. Rev. 47; id. Tabulae Minores Jurisprudentiae (1921) 30 Yale L. J. 215; id. Polarized and Unpolarized Legal Relations (1921) 9 Kentucky L. J. 131; id. Basic Jural Relations (1923) 17 Illinois L. Rev. 515; id. Non-Legal-Content Relations Recombated (1923) 5 Illinois L. Q. 150; id. Jural Relations (1927) Goadby, Introduction to Law (3 ed. 1921) 58, 250 (the 1 ed. 1910 and 2 ed. 1914 suggest no analysis); Page, Terminology and Classification in Fundamental Jural Relations (1921) 4 Am. L. School Rev. 616; Clark, Relations, Legal and Otherwise (1922) 5 Illinois L. Q. 26; Goble, Affirmative and Negative Legal Relations (1922) 4 Illinois L. Q. 94; id. Negative Legal Relations Re-examined (1922) 5 Illinois L. Q. 36; id. A Redefinition of Basic Legal Terms (1935) 35 Columbia L. Rev. 535; Green, The Relativity of Legal Relations (1923) 5 Illinois L. Q. 187; Farnum, Terminology and the American Law Institute (1933) 13 Boston Univ. L. Rev. 203; Vinogradoff, The Foundations of a Theory of Rights (1924) 10 Virginia L. Reg. (N. S.) 549; Husik, Hohfeld's Jurisprudence (1924) 72 U. Pa. L. Rev. 263; Brown, Re-Analysis of a Theory of Rights (1925) 34 Yale L. J. 765; Randall, Hohfeld on Jurisprudence (1925) 41 L. Q. Rev. 86; Radin, L'analisi dei rapporti giuridici secondo il metodo di Hohfeld (1927) 7 Rivista internazionale di filosofia del diritto, 117; Keeton, Elementary Principles of Jurisprudence (1930) pt. 2, §§ 15–16; Allen, Legal Duties and Other Essays in Jurisprudence (1931) 156–220, also in (1931) 40 Yale L. J. 331; Jenks, The New Jurisprudence (1933) chap. 8.

6. Classification of rights.

I Austin, Jurisprudence, lects. 14–16; Salmond, Jurisprudence, §§ 78–85; Markby, Elements of Law (6 ed.) §§ 161–180; Terry, Leading Principles of Anglo-American Law, §§ 128–138; id. Arrangement of the Law, 15 Illinois L. Rev. 61; Hohfeld, Fundamental Legal Conceptions as Applied in Judicial Reasoning (1923) 64–114; Kocourek, Rights in Rem, 68 U. Pa. L. Rev. 322; id. Jural Relations, chap. 13; Radin, A Restatement of Hohfeld, 51 Harv. L. Rev. 1141, 1153–1156.

III Roguin, La science juridique pure, §§ 920–1195.

XXII. POWERS

Salmond, Jurisprudence, § 76; Miller, The Data of Jurisprudence, 63–70; Hohfeld, Fundamental Legal Conceptions, 50–63.

I Kohler, Lehrbuch des bürgerlichen Rechts, § 48; Thon, Rechtsnorm und subjektives Recht, chap. 7.

Ius disponendi.

Power of assignee to sue.

Powers to create or transfer title to another's property.
- Powers under the Statute of Uses.
- Power of pledgee to sell pledged property where he has possession but not ownership.
- Sale of chattels { of tenant / of third person } taken under distress for rent.
- Sale by disseisor of chattel severed from land.*
- Sale by mortgagor of chattel severed from mortgaged land.
- Power of tenant without impeachment of waste to become owner of wood cut.
- Sale in market overt.
- Transfer after unrecorded conveyance.
- Power of carrier to sell perishable goods.
- Power of finder without clue to sell.
- Powers of sale in admiralty.
- *Fructus perceptio, fructus consumptio.*
- Transfer by legatee under probated subsequent will where prior will is afterwards probated.
- Transfer by agent who has apparent general authority.
- Sale by trustee or by one who has legal but not equitable ownership.
- Power of cutting off equitable defenses by sale to purchaser for value.

* Branch v. Morrison, 5 Jones Law (N. C.) 16, 6 Jones Law (N. C.) 16; Lehigh Zinc Co. v. New Jersey Zinc Co., 55 N. J. Law 350, 357 and cases cited; Phelps v. Church, 99 Fed. 683, 685; Stockwell v. Phelps, 34 N. Y. 363; Page v. Fowler, 39 Cal. 412.

Power of promisor (at law) to transform duty to perform into duty to pay damages.*

Powers of representation.

Powers of acceptance.

Powers of rejection (election), termination(forfeiture), and revocation.

XXIII. CONDITIONS OF NON–RESTRAINT OF NATURAL POWERS

(Liberty and Privilege)

I Austin, Jurisprudence (5 ed.) 274–275, 356; Salmond, Jurisprudence, § 75; Miller, The Data of Jurisprudence, 96–100, 103–108; Bigelow, Torts (8 ed.) 13–16; Brown, The Austinian Theory of Law, 180–181 (note); II Bentham, Works (Bowring's ed.) 217–218; Hearn, Theory of Legal Duties and Rights, 133–134; Hohfeld, Fundamental Legal Conceptions, 38–50; Bohlen, Incomplete Privilege, 39 Harv. L. Rev. 307; Kocourek, Jural Relations, 125–128; id. "Privilege" and "Immunity" as Used in the Property Restatement, 1 La. L. Rev. 255.

Thon, Rechtsnorm und subjektives Recht, chap. 6; Somló, Juristische Grundlehre, §§ 128–129.

A. LIBERTY

E.g. the "right to pursue a lawful calling;" the *jus utendi, jus fruendi,* and *jus abutendi* of an owner; "liberty" under the V and XIV Amendments.

Field, J. in Butchers' Union Co. v. Crescent City Co., 111 U. S. 746, 756–757; Bradley, J. id. 762–763; Quinn v. Leathem [1901] A. C. 495, 534; Attorney General v. Adelaide Steamship Co. [1913] A. C. 781, 793.

Chatfield v. Wilson, 28 Vt. 49; Phelps v. Nowlen, 72 N. Y. 39; Letts v. Kessler, 54 Ohio St. 73; Allen v. Flood [1898] A. C. 1; Dig. 1, 17, 55; I Dernburg, Pandekten (8 ed.) § 34.

Harlan, J. in Adair v. United States, 208 U. S. 161, 174; Peckham, J. in Allgeyer v. Louisiana, 165 U. S. 578, 592; Holmes, J. in Aikens v. Wisconsin, 195 U. S. 194, 205; Black, J. in State v. Loomis, 115 Mo. 307, 315; O'Brien, J. in People v. Coler, 66 N. Y. 1, 14–17; Dodge, J. in State v. Kreutzberg, 114 Wis. 530, 536–537; Sutherland, J. in Adkins v. Children's Hospital, 261 U. S. 525, 545–546; McReynolds, J. in Meyer v. Nebraska, 262 U. S. 390, 399; Sutherland, J. in Tyson v. Banton, 273 U. S. 418.

B. PRIVILEGE

1. Recognized by law immediately.

Self-defense.

* See Clark v. Marsiglia, 1 Denio (N. Y.) 317.

Self-help.

Self-redress.

Prevention of felony.

Arrest for felony, affray, etc.

Privileges as to speech and writing.

    In legal proceedings.

    In administrative matters.

    In legislative assemblies.

    Reports of public proceedings.

    Comment on and criticism of public affairs, public officers and candidates.

    Private communications on privileged occasions.

Prevention of or defense against public peril — fire, flood, disease.

Defense against the public enemy.

Deviation where highway is impassable.

Emergency privileges.

2. Arising from legal transactions.

License.

Estate without impeachment of waste.

On necessity, see: Moriaud, Du délit nécessaire et de l'état de nécessité; De Hoon, De l'état de nécessité en droit pénal et civil, VI Revue de droit belge, 29, 79; Titze, Notstandsrechte; Oetker, Ueber Notwehr und Notstand; I Neubecker, Zwang und Notstand in rechtsvergleichender Darstellung, 1–14, 107–133; Goldschmidt, Der Notstand, ein Schuldproblem; Wolter, Das Notrecht, XXII Archiv für Rechts- und Wirthschaftsphilosophie, 66–83.

Compare Smith v. Stone, Style, 65; Gilbert v. Stone, Aleyn, 35; Cunningham v. Pitzer, 2 W. Va. 264; Ploof v. Putnam, 81 Vt. 471.

XXIV. DUTIES AND LIABILITIES

I Austin, Jurisprudence, lects. 17, 22–26; Holland, Jurisprudence, chap. 7; Salmond, Jurisprudence, § 77; Gray, Nature and Sources of the Law, §§ 45, 46, 59–61 (2 ed. 15–17, 23–25); Korkunov, General Theory of Law (transl. by Hastings) § 29; Hearn, Theory of Legal Duties and Rights, chap. 4; Miller, The Data of Jurisprudence, chap. 3; Terry, Leading Principles of Anglo-American Law, §§ 108–112; Hohfeld, Fundamental Legal Conceptions, 38; Corbin, Rights and Duties, 33 Yale L. J. 501; Kocourek, Jural Relations, 9–10 note; Pound, Introduction to the Philosophy of Law, lect. 3;

Goble, The Sanction of a Duty, 37 Yale L. J. 426; Allen, Legal Duties, 156–220.

Markby, Elements of Law (6 ed.) §§ 181–190; Pollock, First Book of Jurisprudence (5 ed.) 57–61; Rattigan, Science of Jurisprudence (2 ed.) § 20; Terry, Duties, Rights, and Wrongs, 10 A. B. A. J. 123.

I Bierling, Juristische Prinzipienlehre, § 11 (pp. 109–183); Somló, Juristische Grundlehre, §§ 123–124.

XXV. PERSONS

1. Legal units.

Subjects of rights? Holders or bearers of rights? Enjoyers of rights?

(a) In general.

Gray, Nature and Sources of the Law, §§ 63–148 (2 ed. pp. 27–64); Salmond, Jurisprudence, §§ 109–114; Korkunov, General Theory of Law (transl. by Hastings) § 28; Pollock, First Book of Jurisprudence (5 ed.) 111–129; Duguit in Progress of Continental Law in the Nineteenth Century (Continental Legal History Series, vol. 11) 87–100; Kocourek, Jural Relations, chap. 17; Kelsen, The Pure Theory of Law, 50 L. Q. Rev. 474, 496–498.

Demogue, Notions fondamentales du droit privé, 320–382; I Bierling, Juristische Prinzipienlehre, § 13; II Bierling, Kritik der juristischen Grundbegriffe, 74–85; Somló, Juristische Grundlehre, §§ 139–143; I Windscheid, Pandekten, § 49.

Miller, Lectures on the Philosophy of Law, lect. 11; Lasson, System der Rechtsphilosophie, § 41; Binder, Philosophie des Rechts, § 15.

II Roguin, La science juridique pure, §§ 620–799.

(b) "Natural" persons.

Holland, Jurisprudence, chap. 8, subdiv. I to ii; Markby, Elements of Law, §§ 131–135.

Capitant, Introduction à l'étude du droit civil (4 ed.) 133–192; I Dernburg, Pandekten (8 ed.) § 50; I Cosack, Lehrbuch des deutschen bürgerlichen Rechts, §§ 24–39; Stark, Die Analyse des Rechts, 236–269.

(c) Juristic persons.

Salmond, Jurisprudence, §§ 115–120; Holland, Jurisprudence, chap. 8, subdiv. I, ii; Markby, Elements of Law (6 ed.) §§ 136–145; Gierke, Political Theories of the Middle Ages, Maitland's Introduction, xviii-xliii; Maitland, Moral Personality and Legal Personality, III Collected Papers, 304; Gareis, Science of Law (transl. by Kocourek) 104–106; Machen, Corporate Personality, 24 Harv. L. Rev. 253, 347; Freund, The Legal Nature of Corporations; Laski, The Personality of Associations, 29 Harv. L. Rev. 404; Hohfeld, Fundamental Legal Conceptions, 197–202; Warren, Corporate Advantages Without Incorporation, 1–15, 841–846; Duff, Personality in Roman Law.

Dewey, The Historic Background of Legal Personality, 35 Yale L. J. 655; Vinogradoff, Juridical Persons, 24 Columbia L. Rev. 594; Geldart, Legal Personality, 27 L. Q. Rev. 90; Canfield, The Scope and Limits of the Corporate Entity Theory, 17 Columbia L. Rev. 128; Smith, Legal Personality, 37 Yale L. J. 283; Radin, A Restatement of Hohfeld, 51 Harv. L. Rev. 1141, 1160–1162; Dodd, Dogma and Practice in the Law of Associations, 42 Harv. L. Rev. 516; Radin, The Endless Problem of Corporate Personality, 32 Columbia L. Rev. 643; Latty, The Corporate Entity as a Solvent of Legal Problems, 34 Mich. L. Rev. 597; Hallis, Corporate Personality; Wolff, On the Nature of Legal Persons, 54 L. Q. Rev. 643; Foley, Incorporation, Multiple Incorporation, and the Conflict of Laws, 42 Harv. L. Rev. 516.

I Gierke, Deutsches Genossenschaftsrecht, 1; Gierke, Das Wesen der menschlichen Verbände, 33–34; id. Die Grundbegriffe des Staatsrecht und die neueste Staatstheorien, 30 Zeitschrift für die gesammte Staatswissenschaft, 304.

II Bierling, Kritik der juristischen Grundbegriffe, 85–118; Zitelmann, Begriff und Wesen der sogenannten juristischen Personen; Hölder, Natürliche und juristische Personen; Binder, Das Problem der juristischen Persönlichkeit; Rümelin, Methodisches ueber juristische Personen; Meurer, Die juristische Personen nach deutschen Reichsrecht; id. Der Begriff und Eigentümer der heiligen Sachen; Karlowa, Zur Lehre von den juristischen Personen, XV Grünhut, Zeitschrift für das privat und öffentliche Recht, 381; Haff, Institutionen der Persönlichkeitslehre und des Köperschaftsrechts; Stark, Die Analyse des Rechts, 270–310; I Dernburg, Pandekten (8 ed.) §§ 47–50; I Windscheid, Pandekten, § 57; I Kohler, Lehrbuch des deutschen bürgerlichen Rechts, § 131; I Schnorr von Carolsfeld, Geschichte der juristischen Person (1933); Wolff, Juristische Person und Staatsperson; I id. Organschaft und juristische Person (1933) 1–231.

Capitant, Introduction à l'étude du droit civil (4 ed.) 193–257; Vareilles-Sommières, Les personnes morales; Josserand, Essai sur la propriété collective, I Livre du centenaire du code civil français, 357; Saleilles, De la personnalité juridique, histoire et théorie; I Michoud, Théorie de la personnalité morale, §§ 1–74; Lévi, La société et l'ordre juridique, 245–343; Ferrara, Teoria delle persone giuridiche.

2. Personality.

Savigny, Jural Relations (transl. by Rattigan) § 75; Sohm, Institutes of Roman Law (3 ed. transl. by Ledlie) §§ 35–36; I Blackstone, Commentaries, 132; Town of Baltimore v. Town of Chester, 53 Vt. 315; In re Nerac, 35 Cal. 392; Avery v. Everett, 110 N. Y. 317; Bread v. Atlanta B. & C. R. Co., 241 Ala. 640.

3. Capacity.

Maine, Ancient Law (Pollock's ed.) 172–174, and Sir Frederick Pollock's note L (pp. 183–185); Holland, Jurisprudence, chap. 14, subdiv. II.

Ehrlich, Die Rechtsfähigkeit.

(a) Status.

II Austin, Jurisprudence, lects. 40–42; Cleveland, Status in Common Law, 38 Harv. L. Rev. 1074; Allen, Legal Duties, 28–70 (status and capacity); Stark, A Note on Status, 54 L. Q. Rev. 400.

Kohler, Lehrbuch der Rechtsphilosophie (1 ed.) 62–66 (and compare id. 3 ed. 112–116).

(b) Capacity for $\begin{cases} \text{rights,} \\ \text{legal transactions,} \\ \text{civil liability for acts,} \\ \text{criminal responsibility.} \end{cases}$

Gareis, Science of Law (transl. by Kocourek) 103.

I Dernburg, Pandekten (8 ed.) §§ 39–45; I Windscheid, Pandekten, §§ 54–56; Capitant, Introduction à l'étude du droit civil (4 ed.) 178–192.

XXVI. ACTS

I Austin, Jurisprudence, lects. 19–21; Holland, Jurisprudence, chap. 8, subdiv. III; Salmond, Jurisprudence, §§ 120–124, 133–144; Pollock, First Book of Jurisprudence (5 ed.) 141–171; Markby, Elements of Law (6 ed.) §§ 213–274.

Rattigan, Science of Jurisprudence, §§ 29–63; Hegel, Philosophy of Right (transl. by Dyde) §§ 115–126.

1. Conception and definition.

Salmond, Jurisprudence, § 128; Terry, Leading Principles of Anglo-American Law, §§ 77–81; Kocourek, Jural Relations, chap. 16 (reprinted from 73 U. Pa. L. Rev. 335).

I Kohler, Lehrbuch des deutschen bürgerlichen Rechts, § 216; II Binding, Die Normen und ihre Uebertretung, §§ 64–66.

2. Elements.

Salmond, Jurisprudence, § 128.

3. Representation.

Seavey, The Rationale of Agency, 29 Yale L. J. 859.

I Windscheid, Pandekten, §§ 73–74; Capitant, Introduction à l'étude du droit civil (4 ed.) 384–392; I Planiol, Traité élémentaire de droit civil (12 ed.) nos. 298–300; I Demogue, Traité des obligations en général, nos. 89–91, 147–155. See Baty, Vicarious Liability.

4. Legal transactions.

Salmond, Jurisprudence, §§ 121–123; Terry, Leading Principles of Anglo-American Law, §§ 172–180.

I Kohler, Lehrbuch des deutschen bürgerlichen Rechts, §§ 217–225; Capitant, Introduction à l'étude du droit civil (4 ed.) 294–299; I Demogue, Traité des obligations en général, nos. 11–15.

(a) Conception.

Karlowa, Das Rechtsgeschäft; I Windscheid, Pandekten, § 69; Enneccerus, Das Rechtsgeschäft.
Will-theory and declaration-theory: Holland, Jurisprudence (13 ed.) 262–268; I Williston, Contracts, §§ 18–21; III Savigny, System des heutigen römischen Rechts, § 140; Henle, Vorstellungstheorie und Willenstheorie; Deveux, L'interprétation des actes juridiques privés; I Demogue, Traité des obligations en général, nos. 156–158 *bis*; II id. nos. 539–541.

(b) Form.

I Dernburg, Pandekten (8 ed.) §§ 85–86; I Windscheid, Pandekten, § 72; I Kohler, Lehrbuch des deutschen bürgerlichen Rechts, §§ 235–237; German Civil Code, § 125; Swiss Code of Obligations, art. 11; Chinese Civil Code, art. 73; Civil Code of Soviet Russia, art. 29.

Historical forms.
In procedure.
In conveyances.
In contracts.

As to the old requirement of a seal in legal transactions of a corporation, see Bank of Columbia v. Patterson, 7 Cranch, 249, 305–306; Fleckner v. Bank of the U. S., 8 Wheat. 338, 357–359.

Modern forms.
Requirements of writing and signature.
Requirements of witnessing.
Requirements of acknowledgment before notary or magistrate.
Requirements as to wills.
(c) Avoidance.

I Dernburg, Pandekten (8 ed.) §§ 87–92, 107–109; I Windscheid, Pandekten, §§ 78–80; I Kohler, Lehrbuch des deutschen bürgerlichen Rechts, §§ 227–234; Capitant, Introduction à l'étude du droit civil (4 ed.) 333–360.

(d) Qualifications.

I Dernburg, Pandekten (8 ed.) §§ 93–104; I Windscheid, Pandekten, §§ 86–100; I Kohler, Lehrbuch des deutschen bürgerlichen Rechts, §§ 249–252; Capitant, Introduction à l'étude du droit civil (4 ed.) 360–384.

On conditions, see Langdell, Summary of the Law of Contracts, §§ 26–31; Pound, Legacies on Impossible or Illegal Conditions Precedent, 3 Illinois L. Rev. 1, 2–4; Simes, The Effect of Impossibility upon Conditions in Wills, 34 Mich. L. Rev. 909.

5. Wrongful acts.

Salmond, Jurisprudence, §§ 133–141; id. The Principles of Civil Liability, Essays in Jurisprudence and Legal History, 123–170; Holmes, The Common Law, lects. 3, 4; Pound, Introduction to the Philosophy of Law, lect. 4.

See Hasse, Die Culpa des römischen Rechts; I Binding, Die Normen und ihre Uebertretung, §§ 50–51; II id. §§ 76–91; V Egger, Kommentar zum schweizerischen Zivilgesetzbuch, 4–5; Schreiber, Schuld und Haftung als Begriffe der privatrechtlichen Dogmatik; Rümelin, Schadenersatz ohne Verschulden; Duguit in Progress of Continental Law in the Nineteenth Century (Continental Legal History Series, vol. 11) 124–128; Lundstedt, The General Principles of Civil Liability in Different Legal Systems; 2[II] Acta Academiae Universalis Jurisprudentiae Comparativae, 367; Lalou, La résponsabilité civile; Thayer, Liability Without Fault, 29 Harv. L. Rev. 801; Smith, Tort and Absolute Liability, 30 Harv. L. Rev. 241, 319, 409; Isaacs, Fault and Liability, 31 Harv. L. Rev. 954; Demogue, Fault, Risk and Apportionment of Loss in Responsibility, 15 Illinois L. Rev. 369; V Demogue, Traité des obligations en général, 1–5; Green, High Care and Gross Negligence, 23 Illinois L. Rev. 4.

(a) Causation.

Wigmore, Summary of the Principles of Torts, §§ 160–201; Smith, Legal Cause in Actions of Tort, 25 Harv. L. Rev. 103, 223, 303; Beale, The Proximate Consequences of an Act, 33 Harv. L. Rev. 633; Edgerton, Legal Cause, 72 U. Pa. L. Rev. 211, 343; McLaughlin, Proximate Cause, 39 Harv. L. Rev. 149; Hayting, The Proximate Cause in the Legal Doctrine of the United States and Germany, 2 Southern California L. Rev. 207; id. Proximate Causation in Civil Actions, 44 Juridical Rev. 239; Green, Judge and Jury, chaps. 6, 7, 8; Kahn-Freund, Remoteness of Damage in German Law, 50 L. Q. Rev. 512.

Müller, Der Kausalzusammenhang; Horn, Kausalitätsbegriff im Straf- und Zivilrecht; Rümelin, Verwendung der Kausalbegriffe im Straf und Zivilrecht; I Endemann, Lehrbuch des bürgerlichen Rechts, § 129; II Binding, Die Normen und ihre Uebertretung, §§ 92–98; Morton, Verschuldungsprinzip, Verursachungsprinzip (1926).

(b) Responsibility: Imputation.

Salmond, Jurisprudence, § 149; Terry, Leading Principles of Anglo-American Law, §§ 87–88.
Baty, Vicarious Liability.

XXVII. THINGS

I Austin, Jurisprudence, lect. 13; Holland, Jurisprudence, chap. 8, subdiv. II; Markby, Elements of Law, §§ 126–130; Pollock, First Book of Jurisprudence (5 ed.) 130–140; Korkunov, General Theory of Law (transl. by Hastings) § 30; Gareis, Science of Law (transl. by Kocourek) § 19; Buckland, Text Book of Roman Law, 182–184; Kocourek, Jural Relations, chap. 18.

I Dernburg, Pandekten (8 ed.) § 55; I Windscheid, Pandekten, §§ 42, 137–144; Birkmeyer, Das Vermögen im juristischen Sinn; I Bierling, Juristische Prinzipienlehre, § 14 (pp. 239–273); Fuchs, Grundbegriffe des Sachenrechts (1917) §§ 5–9; Capitant, Introduction à l'étude du droit civil (4 ed.) 259–283; I Gorovtseff, Études de principiologie du droit, Théorie de l'objet en droit.

Hegel, Philosophy of Right (transl. by Dyde) §§ 41–44; II Ahrens, Cours du droit naturel, § 54; Kohler, Lehrbuch der Rechtsphilosophie, 81–86.

The doctrine of the patrimony: See III Planiol et Ripert, Traité pratique de droit civil français, nos. 15–35; German Civil Code, § 419.

PART 8

THE SYSTEM OF LAW

XXVIII. DIVISION AND CLASSIFICATION

II Austin, Jurisprudence, lects. 43–47; Holland, Jurisprudence, chap. 9, last par. of chap. 7; Salmond, Jurisprudence, §§ 79, 81–83, 85, 86; Markby, Elements of Law (6 ed.) §§ 162–166; Pollock, First Book of Jurisprudence (5 ed.) 84–110; Korkunov, General Theory of Law (transl. by Hastings) §§ 32–34; Gareis, Science of Law (transl. by Kocourek) § 14; Pound, Classification of Law, 37 Harv. L. Rev. 933; II Proceedings, American Law Institute, 58–71, 381–425; Holdsworth, Charles Viner and the Abridgments (1923) 39 L. Q. Rev. 17, 37–39.

Holmes, Codes and the Arrangement of the Law, 5 American L. Rev. 1 (reprinted in 44 Harv. L. Rev. 725); id. The Arrangement of the Law — Privity, 7 American L. Rev. 46 (reprinted in 44 Harv. L. Rev. 738); Terry, The Arrangement of the Law, 17 Columbia L. Rev. 291, 365; Kocourek, Classification of Law, 11 N. Y. Univ. L. Q. 319; Ulrich, A Proposed Plan of Classification for the Law, 34 Mich. L. Rev. 226.

CLASSIFICATIONS FOR DISCUSSION AND REFERENCE

Gaius.
Public law.
Private law.
Persons.
Things.
Actions.

As to this, see Buckland, Text Book of Roman Law, 56–61, 599–601.
On Roman classification, see Affolter, Das römische Institutionen-System.

Modern Roman law (German).
Public law.
Criminal law.
Private law.
General part.
Persons.

Things.
Legal transactions.
Exercise and protection of rights.
Self-help and self-redress.
Special part.
Law of property.
Law of obligations.
Family law.
Law of inheritance.
French Civil Code (1804).
Persons.
Property.
Modes of acquiring ownership.
Succession.
Gifts *inter vivos* and wills.
Contracts.
Quasi contracts.
Delicts and quasi delicts.
Marriage.
Sale, exchange, bailment.
Partnership.
Agency.
Pledge and mortgage.
German Civil Code (1900).
General principles.
Persons $\begin{cases} \text{natural,} \\ \text{juristic.} \end{cases}$
Things.
Legal transactions.
Computation of time.
Prescription.
Exercise of rights.
Law of obligations.
Law of things.
Family law.
Law of inheritance.
Swiss Civil Code (1912).
Law of persons.
Natural persons.

Juristic persons.
Family law.
Law of inheritance.
Law of things.
Law of obligations.
Civil Code of Brazil (1917).
General part.
Persons.
Property.
Juridical facts.
Special part.
Family law.
Law of things.
Law of obligations.
Law of succession.
Blackstone.
Rights of persons.
Rights of things.
Private wrongs.
Public wrongs.
Committee on Classification of Law, American Bar Association (1902, XXV Rep. Am. Bar Assn. 474–475).
Municipal law.
Persons.
Public.
Private.
Several classes, i.e. citizens, aliens, corporations, etc.
Civil rights.
Domestic relations.
Things.
Personal.
Real.
Actions.
Crimes and criminal procedure.
International law.
Public.
Private.
Practical common-law classification (Century Digest, 1898).

Law of
   Persons.
   Property.
   Contracts.
   Torts.
   Crimes.
   Remedies.
   Government.
Jenks (Digest of English Civil Law, 1910–1917).
   General part.
      Persons.
      Things.
      Legal acts.
      Time.
      Limitation of actions.
      Self-help.
   Obligations.
   Property law.
   Family law.
   Succession.
Gareis (Encyklopädie der Rechtswissenschaft, 1 ed. 1887).
   Private law.
      Law of things.
         Rights relating to material things.
            Rights in one's own property.
            Iura in re aliena.
         Rights relating to incorporeal things.
      Mixed law of persons and law of things.
         Law of inheritance.
         Law of family property, i.e. property rights between husband and wife, parent and child, etc.
      Law of persons.
         Family law, i.e. marriage, parent and child, etc. except as to property rights.
      Law of obligations.
   Public law.
      Law of the state.
         Constitutional law.

Administrative law.

International law.

Kohler (Einführung in die Rechtswissenschaft, 1 ed. 1902, § 6).

Law relating to persons.

Law of persons.

Law of obligations.

Law relating to natural objects.

Hence:

Law of persons.

Law of property (including inheritance).

Law of obligations.

Cosack (Lehrbuch des bürgerlichen Rechts, 5 ed. 1910).

General part.

The holder of rights.

The objects of rights.

The origination, modification, and termination of rights.

Legal transactions.

Culpability and casualty.

Lapse of time.

Exercise of governmental power.

Exercise and securing of rights.

Special part.

Law of claims to performance.

Law of things.

Law of commercial paper.

Law of associations.

Law of juristic persons.

Family law.

Law of inheritance.

Planiol (Traité élémentaire de droit civil, 1 ed. 1905).

General principles.

Persons.

Things.

Obligations.

Matrimonial régimes.

Succession.

Gifts and testaments.

XXIX. PROPRIETARY RIGHTS: POSSESSION

Pollock, First Book of Jurisprudence (5 ed.) 171–206; Salmond, Jurisprudence, §§ 94–107; Holland, Jurisprudence, chap. 11, sub-div. V to "Ownership;" Markby, Elements of Law (6 ed.) §§ 347–399; Keeton, Elementary Principles of Jurisprudence, chap. 22; Pollock and Wright, Essay on Possession in the Common Law, introduction; Holmes, The Common Law, lect. 6; Shartel, Meanings of Possession, 16 Minnesota L. Rev. 611; Warren, Cases on Property (2 ed.) 1–3.

I Dernburg, Pandekten (8 ed.) §§ 142, 145–147; I Windscheid, Pandekten, § 148; II Cosack, Lehrbuch des bürgerlichen Rechts (7 & 8 ed.) §§ 4–18; III Planiol et Ripert, Traité pratique de droit civil français, nos. 143–170.

The literature upon the nature and elements of possession is very extensive. The following are important or useful: Savigny, Recht des Besitzes (7 ed. by Rudorff); Bruns, Recht des Besitzes im Mittelalter und in der Gegenwart; Bekker, Recht des Besitzes bei den Römern; Jhering, Der Besitzwille; Kuntze, Zur Besitzlehre; Stintzing, Der Besitz; Kniep, Der Besitz; Rohde, Studien im Besitzrecht; Kress, Besitz und Recht; Vermond, Théorie générale de la possession; Saleilles, Éléments constitutifs de la possession; id. La possession des meubles; Duquesne, Distinction de la possession et de la détention en droit romain; Cornil, Possession dans le droit romain; Schwab, La théorie possessoire objective.

Stewart, The Differences Between Possession of Land and Chattels, 11 Canadian Bar Rev. 651.

JURAL POSTULATE I.

In civilized society men must be able to assume that others will commit no intentional aggressions upon them.

JURAL POSTULATE II.

In civilized society men must be able to assume that they may control for beneficial purposes what they have discovered and appropriated to their own use, what they have created by their own labor, and what they have acquired under the existing social and economic order.

As to these postulates and those proposed in the following lectures, see Hocking, Present Status of the Philosophy of Law and of Rights, §§ 41–48. They were first formulated in Pound, Introduction to American Law (1919) but have since been revised. See Pound, Social Control Through Law (1942) 112–118.

Nature of proprietary rights in general.

Relation of possession to ownership.

Importance of theory of possession,

in Roman law,

in the common law.

The conception of possession. Physical custody plus an intention to exclude all others.

Law or fact?

Different connections in which the conception has been used and their effect upon it:

In Roman law,

usucapion,

interdicts.

In the common law,

adverse possession,

use of possessory actions to vindicate ownership,

larceny,

statutes.

The elements of possession.

Physical (*corpus*),

Mental (*animus*).

The physical element (*naturalis possessio*, detention, custody, *Inhabung*).

The mental element (juristic possession).

Difference between Roman and Germanic theories.

Animus domini.

Animus rem sibi habendi.

Animus possidendi.

Must it be a claim to control on one's own behalf, or for one's own purposes?

Servants and agents.

Mediate possession.

Representative — through agent or servant.

Through bailee — subject to demand,

for fixed term or subject to condition.

Derivative possession.

Possession is a matter of law and of fact equally. . . . Possession is a matter of fact in so far as a non-juridical conception of pure fact (detention) lies at its foundation. . . . But possession is a matter of law in so far as legal rights are bound up with the bare existence of a conception of fact. — Savigny, Recht des Besitzes, § 5.

To possess a thing means to have it in one's actual control. This actual control may have a foundation in right and law or not; for the conception of possession this is indifferent. When we speak of possession, we look away from the law. But while possession is not [an institution of] right and law, it has legal consequences. — I Windscheid, Pandekten, § 148.

It is merely a state of things, a fact, a mere *de facto* relation to a thing into which a man has brought himself; which, however, inasmuch as it may under certain circumstances bring about a right to the thing, enjoys in itself the protection of the law. — Wächter, Pandekten, § 122 (transl. by Moyle, Institutes, 2 ed. 336).

Possession is no [institution of] right and law, but a matter of fact. But it may be (a) the consequence of rights . . . [e.g. ownership]; (b) the originating cause of rights . . . [e.g. usucapion, adverse possession]; (c) in certain cases the mere matter of fact of possession is protected against disturbance. — Gareis, Encyklopädie der Rechtswissenschaft, § 17.

What is the ground of this protection? Must we not say that if possession is no [institution of] right and law, its violation is no violation of right, and hence affords no ground for its protection? — Bruns in Holtzendorff, Encyklopädie der Rechtswissenschaft (5 ed.) 473.

There has been much learned discussion of the question whether possession is a fact or a right. No doubt it differs from ownership in requiring a *de facto* relation between a person and an object, and to that extent it is a fact. But there is no doubt also that it has legal consequences, and if that is so it seems to be little less than quibbling to say it is not a right as well. — Moyle, Institutes (2 ed.) 336.

Every right is a consequence attached by the law to one or more facts which the law defines, and wherever the law gives any one special rights not shared by the body of the people, it does so on the ground that certain special facts, not true of the rest of the world, are true of him. When a group of facts thus singled out by the law exists in the case of a given person, he is said to be entitled to the corresponding rights; meaning, thereby, that the law helps him to constrain his neighbors, or some of them, in a way in which it would not, if all the facts in question were not true of him. Hence, any word which denotes such a group of facts connotes the rights attached to it by way of legal consequences, and any word which denotes the rights attached to a group of facts connotes the group of facts in like manner.

The word "possession" denotes such a group of facts. Hence, when we say of a man that he has possession, we affirm directly that all the facts of a certain group are true of him, and we convey directly or by implication that the law will give him the advantage of the situation. Contract or property, or any other substantive notion of the law, may be analyzed in the same way, and should be treated in the same order. The only difference is that, while possession denotes the facts and connotes the consequence, property always, and contract with more uncertainty and oscillation, denote the consequence and connote the facts. — Holmes, The Common Law, 214–215.

XXX. PROPRIETARY RIGHTS: OWNERSHIP

1. Conception and definition.

II Austin, Jurisprudence, concluding portion of lect. 47, lect. 48; Salmond, Jurisprudence, § 152; Markby, Elements of Law (6 ed.) §§ 307–314.

Simonton, Austin's Classification of Proprietary Rights, 11 Cornell L. Q. 277.
I Dernburg, Pandekten (8 ed.) §§ 155, 161; I Windscheid, Pandekten, §§ 167–168; Gareis, Science of Law (transl. by Kocourek) 139–144.
Ball, The Jural Nature of Land, 23 Illinois L. Rev. 45.
Husserl, Der Rechtsgegenstand: Rechtslogische Studien zu einer Theorie des Eigenthums.

The common-law doctrine of estates.

Markby, Elements of Law (6 ed.) § 333; Terry, Leading Principles of Anglo-American Law, § 45.

2. Analysis.

Markby, Elements of Law (6 ed.) §§ 307–345; Hearn, Theory of Legal Duties and Rights, chap. 10, § 1; Hohfeld, Faulty Analysis in Easement Cases, 27 Yale L. J. 66, reprinted in Fundamental Legal Conceptions as Applied in Judicial Reasoning, 11, 160.

I Baudry-Lacantinerie, Précis de droit civil (13 ed.) § 1332.

Incidents of ownership:
Rights —
Jus possidendi.
Jus prohibendi.

Power —
Jus disponendi.
Liberties —
Jus utendi.
Jus fruendi.
Jus abutendi.

3. Legal ownership and equitable ownership.

In Roman law:
Dominium ex iure Quiritium.
Dominium in bonis.

Gaius, ii §§ 40–41, 80; I Theophilus, Greek Paraphrase of the Institutes of Justinian, 5, § 4 (Ferrini's ed. I, p. 25); Code of Justinian, vii, 25; Buckland, Equity in Roman Law, chap. I.

In the common law:

Langdell, Brief Survey of Equity Jurisdiction (2 ed.) 5–10; Maitland, Equity, 106–152; Hanbury, Modern Equity, 54–62; Stone, The Nature of the Rights of the *Cestui Que Trust*, 17 Columbia L. Rev. 467; Hart, The Place of Trust in Jurisprudence, 28 L. Q. Rev. 290.

Huston, The Enforcement of Decrees in Equity, 87–148; Scott, The Nature of the Rights of the *Cestui Que Trust*, 17 Columbia L. Rev. 269; 1 Scott, Trusts, §§ 1, 130.

Lepaulle, Traité théorique et pratique des trusts (1932).

4. Classification of property.

Archaic Roman classification:
Res mancipi.
Res nec mancipi.
Maine, Ancient Law (9 ed.) 272–290.

See 2 Karlowa, Römische Rechtsgeschichte, 354–360; Bonfante, *Res mancipi e nec mancipi.*

Civil (modern Roman) law:
Movables.
Immovables.
Huebner, History of Germanic Private Law (transl. by Philbrick) 164–165.

See Schuster, Principles of German Civil Law, 60–61; French Civil Code, art. 516; Civil Code of Quebec, art. 374; Louisiana Civil Code, art. 461; Austrian Civil Code, § 291.

Common law:

Real property —
  freehold interests in land,
  incorporeal hereditaments.

Personal property —
  chattels real,
  chattels personal:
    choses in possession,
    choses in action.

See 2 Pollock and Maitland, History of English Law, 181–183; Plucknett, Concise History of the Common Law (3 ed.) 510–513; 7 Holdsworth, History of English Law, 515–544; Vinogradoff, Zur Geschichte der englischen Klassifikation der Vermögensarten, in Festschrift für Brunner (1910) 573–577.

5. Principal things and accessory things (*Pertinentia*).

I Dernburg, Pandekten, § 65; I Colin et Capitant, Précis de droit civil français, nos. 661–671; I Crome, System des deutschen bürgerlichen Rechts, § 60; I Planiol, Traité élémentaire de droit civil (12 ed.) no. 2213.

Digest, xli, 1, 7, § 10, xviii, 17, pr. and §§ 1–5, 7, xix, 1, 13, § 31, xix, 11, 14–16, xix, 1, 17, §§ 9–10.

French Civil Code, arts. 517, 524, 525; German Civil Code, §§ 93–98.

Yearworth v. Pierce, Aleyn, Select Cases, 31; Sawyer v. Twiss, 26 N. H. 345; Fay v. Muzzey, 13 Gray (Mass.) 53; Hopewell Mills v. Taunton Savings Bank, 150 Mass. 519; Teaff v. Hewitt, 1 Ohio St. 511; Hubbell v. East Cambridge Bank, 132 Mass. 447; Viscount Hill v. Bullock [1897] 2 Ch. 482; Miller v. Wilson, 71 Ia. 610; McFadden v. Crawford, 36 W. Va. 671.

6. Things incapable of private ownership.

I Dernburg, Pandekten (7 ed.) §§ 57–61; I Windscheid, Pandekten §§ 146–147; Kollath, Die Geltung der römischen Grundsatze über die *res extra commercium* in heutigen Recht; Pernice, Die sogennante *res communes omnium*.

Gaius, ii, §§ 1–8; Institutes, ii, 1, pr. and §§ 1–10; Digest, xvii, 1, 6, pr.

Krückmann, Lehrbuch des bürgerlichen Gesetzbuches, § 54; I Planiol, Traité élémentaire de droit civil (12 ed.) nos. 3059–3079.

Note that common-law writers have dealt with this subject partly as the property of public corporations and partly as "natural rights" of certain persons to the use of the things in question. See e.g. 2 Gray, Cases on Property, bk. V, chap. 2. See also French Civil Code, art. 538.

(a) The shore of the sea.

Digest, i, 8, 3–4, xviii, 6, 4, xli, 1, 14, pr., xlvii, 10, 13, § 7, 1, 16, 96, pr.

French Civil Code, art. 538.

Hale, De Jure Maris, chaps. IV–VI, De Portibus Maris, chaps. VI–VII, in Hargrave, Law Tracts, 10–37, 72–88; Blundell v. Catterall, 5 B. & Ald. 268; Weston v. Sampson, 8 Cush. (Mass.) 347; Packard v. Ryder, 144 Mass. 440; Gould, Law of Waters (3 ed.) §§ 167–178.

(b) Rivers and lakes (running water).

Digest, xliii, 12, 1, §§ 3–4, xliii, 14, 1, pr. and §§ 1–6, xliii, 20, 1, pr. and §§ 1–6.

French Civil Code, arts. 642–645; I Planiol, Traité élémentaire de droit civil (12 ed.) no. 2428; Bell, Principles of the Law of Scotland, §§ 1100–1109; Gierke, Grundzüge des deutschen Privatrechts (in I Holtzendorf, Encyklopädie der Rechtswissenschaft) § 52; Introductory Act to German Civil Code, § 65; Wolff und Herold, Wassergesetz (1913).

See Baudry-Lacantinerie et Chauveau, Traité des biens (2 ed.) §§ 854–877; Picard, Traité des eaux (2 ed.); Fabreguettes, Traité des eaux publiques et des eaux privées; Mazza, Dei diritti sulle acque; Costa, Le acque nel diritto romano; Ossig, Römisches Wasserrecht; Randa, Das Österreichische Wasserrecht; Kappeler, Der Rechtsbegriff des öffentlichen Wasserlaufs; Hesse, Grundzüge des Wasserrechts nach gemeinen Rechte, 5 Jhering's Jahrbücher, 179–317.

Wiel, Origin and Comparative Development of the Law of Water Courses in the Common Law and in the Civil Law, 6 California L. Rev. 245.

As to Spanish-Mexican water law see Lux v. Haggin, 69 Cal. 253, 315–334. As to Roman-Dutch water law, see Van Breda v. Silberbauer, L. R. 3 P. C. 94.

Embrey v. Owen, 6 Ex. 353; Atchison v. Peterson, 20 Wall. 507.

7. Common ownership.

Digest, xiii, 6, 5, § 15, 31, xiii, 66, § 2, viii, 2, 26, x, 2, 4, §§ 3, 5, 6, x, 3, 7, § 10, x, 3, 23, x, 3, 28, x, 2, 10, pr., x, 3, 1–3.

German Civil Code, §§ 741–753.

I Dernburg, Pandekten (8 ed.) §§ 158–160, 169a; I Planiol, Traité élémentaire de droit civil (12 ed.) nos. 2497–2505; II Cosack, Lehrbuch des bürgerlichen Rechts (7 & 8 ed.) §§ 284–290; Goeppert, Beiträge zur Lehre vom Miteigenthum; Seeler, Die Lehre vom Miteigenthum (1896).

See Wiggins v. Muscupiabe Land & Water Co., 113 Cal. 182, 190; Martin v. Martin, 170 Ill. 639; Brown v. Coddington, 72 Hun (N. Y.) 147; Coleman v. Harris, 19 Pa. St. 100; Haeussler v. Missouri Iron Co., 110 Mo. 188; Barr v. Lamaster, 48 Neb. 114.

8. Acquisition of ownership.

Holland, Jurisprudence (13 ed.) 316–322; Salmond, Jurisprudence, §§ 175–178; Ames, Lectures on Legal History, lect. 17.

I Dernburg, Pandekten (8 ed.) § 164; I Windscheid, Pandekten, § 170; II Cosack, Lehrbuch des bürgerlichen Rechts (7 & 8 ed.) § 195a; II Planiol, Traité élémentaire de droit civil (11 ed.) nos. 257–563; I Baudry-Lacantinarie, Précis de droit civil (13 ed.) §§ 1336–1337; Czyhlarz in Glück, Ausführliche Erläuterung der Pandekten, Serie der Bücher 41–42, I, 19–28.

Roman law	original	accretion	(*alluuio*).	
		occupation	*res nullius.* *res derelictae.* *res hostiles.* *thesaurus.*	
		confusion.		
		accession.		
		specification.		
		fructus perceptio.		
		adverse possession (prescription).		
	derivative	delivery (*traditio*).		
		adjudication.		
		entry upon inheritance.		
		legatum (gift by will).		
Common law	original	occupancy	[goods of an alien enemy.] abandoned chattels. wild animals. fruits of land.	
		accretion.		
		sale for taxes.		
		sale under judgment *in rem* (e.g. for forfeiture under revenue laws).		
		adverse possession.		
		accession.		
		confusion.		
	derivative	judgment.		
		[marriage.]		
		bankruptcy.		
		succession	intestate. testamentary.	
		gift.		
		sale.		
		conveyance.		

9. Loss of ownership.
Salmond, Jurisprudence, § 162.

Dobrin, English Assets of Pre-Revolutionary Russian Companies, 176 Law Times, 113.

10. Limited real rights (*iura in re aliena*).
II Austin, Jurisprudence, lect. 52; Salmond, Jurisprudence, § 83.

Landsberg, Das Recht des bürgerlichen Gesetzbuches, 579–583; I Wieland, Das Sachenrecht des schweizerischen Zivilgesetzbuches, 2, 200–201 (French transl. I, 3–4, 471–474); II Endemann, Lehrbuch des bürgerlichen Rechts (8 ed.) § 94.

The theory of "dismemberments" of ownership: I Planiol, Traité élémentaire de droit civil (12 ed.) § 2745.

For a different theory see III Crome, System des deutschen bürgerlichen Rechts, § 43.

(a) Servitudes.

II Austin, Jurisprudence, lects. 49–50; Holland, Jurisprudence (13 ed.) 224–232; Salmond, Jurisprudence, § 159; Markby, Elements of Law (6 ed.) §§ 400–430.

I Dernburg, Pandekten (8 ed.) §§ 198–201.

(1) Personal.

Roman law
{
usus.
usus fructus.
habitatio.
operae seruorum.
}

Common law
{
[easements in gross.]
profits in gross.
}

As to leases (which in the theory of the common law belong elsewhere) see Salmond, Jurisprudence, § 158.

As to the advisability of classing these as servitudes, see: I Planiol, Traité élémentaire de droit civil (12 ed.) § 2746; I Colin et Capitant, Droit civil français (7 ed.) 815–817.

(2) Real.

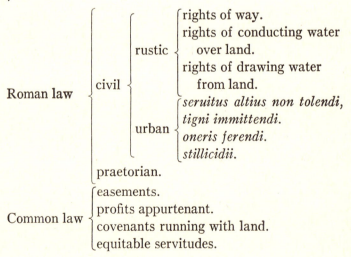

Roman law — civil — rustic {
rights of way.
rights of conducting water over land.
rights of drawing water from land.
}

urban {
seruitus altius non tolendi,
tigni immittendi.
oneris ferendi.
stillicidii.
}

praetorian.

Common law {
easements.
profits appurtenant.
covenants running with land.
equitable servitudes.
}

On equitable servitudes see Clark, Covenants and Interests Running With Land, 148–165; Maitland, Equity, 163–170; Stone, The Equitable Rights and Liabilities of Strangers to a Contract, 18 Columbia L. Rev. 291, 19 id. 177; Ames, Specific Performance Against Strangers to the Contract, 17 Harv. L. Rev. 174, also in id. Lectures on Legal History, 381; Pound, Progress of the Law — Equity, 33 Harv. L. Rev. 813–822.

In re Nisbet and Potts' Contract [1905] 1 Ch. 391, [1906] 1 Ch. 386.

Chafee, Equitable Servitudes on Chattels, 41 Harv. L. Rev. 945.

(b) Securities (liens, pledge-rights).

Salmond, Jurisprudence, § 160; Holland, Jurisprudence (13 ed.) 232–239; Markby, Elements of Law (6 ed.) §§ 443–481.

I Dernburg, Pandekten (8 ed.) §§ 224–225; I Windscheid, Pandekten, §§ 225–229.

```
                    ┌ fiducia.
                    │ pignus.
                    │ hypotheca      ┌ tacit.
Roman law           ┤                ┤
                    │                └ conventional.
                    │
                    └ antichresis.


                    ┌ contractual     ┌ pledge.
                    │                  ┤              ┌ general.
                    │                  └ hypothecation┤
                    │                                 └ particular.
                    │
                    │                              ┌ in favor of the fisc.
                    │                   ┌ general  │ against a guard-
                    │                   │          ┤   ian.
                    │                   │          │ for dos and para-
                    │                   │          └   phernalia.
                    │                   │          ┌ landlord's lien.
The civil law       ┤                   │          │ for money loaned
                    │                   │          │   to rebuild a
                    │   by operation    │          │   building.
                    │     of law        ┤          │ in favor of a pupil
                    │                   │          │   upon a thing ac-
                    │                   │ particular┤  quired with his
                    │                   │          │   money.
                    │                   │          │ in favor of a lega-
                    │                   │          │   tee against the
                    │                   │          │   heir who has
                    │                   │          │   withheld some-
                    │                   │          │   thing from the
                    │                   │          └   inheritance.
                    │                   │
                    └                   └ judicial.
```

Floating charges and preferences among creditors — see II Planiol, Traité élémentaire de droit civil (11 ed.) nos. 2542–2643.

Hypothecation (contractual pledge) in French law, see id. nos. 2644–2700.

Common law
$\left\{\begin{array}{l}\text{pledge.} \\ \text{mortgage.} \\ \text{common-law liens.} \\ \text{statutory liens.} \\ \text{equitable charges or liens.}\end{array}\right.$

11. Rights of neighbors.

Cicero, De legibus, I, 21, § 55; Institutes, iv, 17, § 6; Digest, xliii, 21, 1, x, 4, 9, § 1, xix, 5, 13, § 3, xliii, 27, 1, xlvii, 7, 6, § 2; Institutes, ii, 1, § 31.

I Dernburg, Pandekten (8 ed.) §§ 162–163; Hesse, Rechtsverhältnisse zwischen Grundstücksnachbarn; II Cosack, Lehrbuch des bürgerlichen Rechts (7 & 8 ed.) pt. 1, § 51; I Colin et Capitant, Droit civil français (7 ed.) 763–765; I Baudry-Lacantinerie, Précis de droit civil (13 ed.) §§ 1723–1786.

I Planiol, Traité élémentaire de droit civil (12 ed.) nos. 2504, 2506; German Civil Code, §§ 917–922.

Doderidge, J. in Millen v. Fawdry, Latch, 119, 120; Macneil, The Growing Lawlessness of Trees, Legal Essays in Honor of Orrin Kip McMurray, 375, 384–390; Bullard v. Harrison, 4 Maule & S. 387; Tracy v. Atherton, 35 Vt. 52; Ellis v. Blue Mountain Forest Assn., 69 N. H. 385; Clark v. Cogge, Cro. Jac. 170; Pomfret v. Ricroft, 1 Wms. Saund. 323a, n. 6; Pinnington v. Galland, 9 Ex. 1; Nichols v. Luce, 24 Pick. 102.

Humphries v. Brogden, 12 Q. B. 739; Birmingham v. Allen, 6 Ch. D. 284; Gilmore v. Driscoll, 122 Mass. 199.

12. Public rights.

(a) Deviation from highway where obstructed.

Campbell v. Race, 7 Cush. 408; Morey v. Fitzgerald, 56 Vt. 487.
Qu. Should this be treated here or under emergency privileges?

(b) Fishing.

Blundell v. Catterall, 5 B. & Ald. 268; Weston v. Sampson, 8 Cush. 347; Packard v. Ryder, 144 Mass. 440; People v. Platt, 17 Johns. 195; Carson v. Blazer, 2 Binney, 475.

(c) Bathing.

Blundell v. Catterall, 5 B. & Ald. 268.

(d) Boating.

Gould, Law of Waters (3 ed.) §§ 53–56.

(e) Floating logs.

Brown v. Chadbourne, 31 Me. 9; Moore v. Sanborne, 2 Mich. 519; Olson v. Merrill, 42 Wis. 203; Lewis v. Coffee County, 77 Ala. 190; Hubbard v. Bell, 54 Ill. 110.

(f) Taking seaweed.

Gould, Law of Waters (3 ed.) § 25.

(g) Taking ice.

Gould, Law of Waters (3 ed.) § 191.

(h) Towage.

Digest, xliii, 12, 1, § 14; Ubbelohde, Die Interdikte zum Schutze des Ge-
meingebrauches, 509–511; Pothier, Commentary on Digest, xliii, 12, 1, § 12 and
id. § 15, 17 Pandectes de Justinien (1823 ed.) 516, n. 4 and 517, n. 4; I Planiol,
Traité élémentaire de droit civil (12 ed.) no. 2907, 3.
Young's Case, 1 Ld. Raym. 725; Ball v. Herbert, 3 Durnf. & East, 253.

(i) Aerial navigation over land.

English Air Navigation Act (1920) — 10–11 Geo. V, chap. 80, § 9; Uniform
State Law for Aeronautics, §§ 4–5.

13. *Jura regalia* — royal mines.

Case of Mines, Plowd. 310; I Blackstone, Commentaries, 294–296; Moore v.
Smaw, 17 Cal. 200, 206–210, 219–222.

XXXI. OBLIGATIONS

DUTIES OF PERFORMANCE AND OF RESTITUTION

JURAL POSTULATE III.

In civilized society men must be able to assume that those with
whom they deal in the general intercourse of society will act in good
faith, and hence

(a) will make good reasonable expectations which their promises
or other conduct reasonably create;

(b) will carry out their undertakings according to the expectations which the moral sentiment of the community attaches thereto;

(c) will restore specifically or by equivalent what comes to them
by mistake or unanticipated situation whereby they receive, at another's expense, what they could not reasonably have expected to
receive under the actual circumstances.

Pound, Introduction to the Philosophy of Law, lect. 6.

1. History.

Maine, Ancient Law, chap. 9, and Sir Frederick Pollock's note R;
Kohler, Rechtsphilosophie und Universalrechtsgeschichte (in Holt-

zendorff, Encyklopädie der Rechtswissenschaft, 6 or 7 ed.) §§ 28–37; Berger, From Hostage to Contract, 35 Illinois L. Rev. 154.

2. Conception and definition.

Holland, Jurisprudence (13 ed.) 243–246; Salmond, Jurisprudence, § 165.

II Dernburg, Pandekten, §§ 1–3; II Windscheid, Pandekten, §§ 252–253.
Saleilles, Théorie générale de l'obligation (3 ed.) 7–37; I Demogue, Traité des obligations en général, nos. 1–10.
I Savigny, Obligationenrecht, §§ 2–4; II Bierling, Kritik der juristischen Grundbegriffe, 198 ff.; II Kohler, Lehrbuch des bürgerlichen Rechts, §§ 3–8; Stammler, Recht der Schuldverhältnisse, 1–35.

3. Classification.

Salmond, Jurisprudence, § 167; Holland, Jurisprudence (13 ed.) 646–647; Sohm, Institutes of Roman Law (transl. by Ledlie, 3 ed.) § 77; Gareis, Science of Law (transl. by Kocourek) 175.

$$
\text{Roman law}
\begin{cases}
\text{contractual}
\begin{cases}
\textit{ex contractu.}\\
\textit{quasi ex contractu.}
\end{cases}\\[2ex]
\text{delictal}
\begin{cases}
\textit{ex delicto.}\\
\textit{quasi ex delicto.}
\end{cases}
\end{cases}
$$

$$
\text{Common law}
\begin{cases}
\text{arising from legal transactions}
\begin{cases}
\text{contract}\\
\text{express trust.}
\end{cases}\\
\text{arising from office or calling.}\\
\text{arising from fiduciary relations.}\\
\text{arising from unjust enrichment.}
\end{cases}
$$

Is the Roman conception of obligations *ex delicto* expedient for our purposes?

4. Analysis of contract.

Salmond, Jurisprudence, §§ 122–124; Holland, Jurisprudence (13 ed.) 257–288; Markby, Elements of Law, §§ 603–624, 626–648, 651–658, 663; Morawetz, Essay on the Elements of a Contract, chap. 1; Langdell, Summary of the Law of Contracts (2 ed.) §§ 148–149, 1–17, 151–156, 178–182; Llewellyn, What Price Contract? 40 Yale L. J. 704; Cohen, The Basis of Contract, 46 Harv. L. Rev. 553; Gardner, An Inquiry Into the Principles of the Law of Contracts, 46 Harv. L. Rev. 1.

II Windscheid, Pandekten, §§ 305–318; II Dernburg, Pandekten (8 ed.) §§ 9–11.

(a) Parties.
(b) Declaration of will.

(c) Presupposition.

(d) Form.

"Abstract" promises.

Salmond, Jurisprudence, § 124, 6; II Dernburg, Pandekten (8 ed.) § 22; II
Windscheid, Pandekten, §§ 318, 319, 364; I Stampe, Grundriss der Wertbe-
wegungslehre, §§ 4–5; Capitant, De la cause des obligations (3 ed. 1927);
Lorenzen, Causa and Consideration in the Law of Contracts, 28 Yale L. J. 621;
Pound, Consideration in Equity, Wigmore Celebration Essays, 435; Lord Wright,
Ought the Doctrine of Consideration to be Abolished from the Common Law, 49
Harv. L. Rev. 1225; I Williston, The Law of Contracts (2 ed.) §§ 99–104.

Contracts for the benefit of a third person.

Hellwig, Verträge auf Leistung an Dritte, §§ 24, 40; II Dernburg, Pandekten
(8 ed.) § 18; II Windscheid, Pandekten, § 316; I Cosack, Lehrbuch des bürgerlichen Rechts (8 ed.) § 154; II Baudry-Lacantinerie, Précis de droit civil (13
ed.) §§ 60–85; II Colin et Capitant, Droit civil français (7 ed.) 122–128.
I Williston, The Law of Contracts (2 ed.) §§ 355–393.

Plurality of parties.

Salmond, Jurisprudence, § 166; II Dernburg, Pandekten (8 ed.) §§ 69–75;
II Windscheid, Pandekten, §§ 292–300; I Cosack, Lehrbuch des bürgerlichen
Rechts (8 ed.) §§ 178–179; II Baudry-Lacantinerie, Précis de droit civil (13 ed.)
§§ 266–307.

5. Classification of contracts.

(a) With respect to form.

Roman law	formal	verbal.
		literal.
	real	*mutuum.*
		commodatum.
		depositum.
		pignus.
	consensual	sale.
		letting and hiring.
		partnership.
		mandate.
	innominate	*do ut des.*
		do ut facias.
		facio ut des.
		facio ut facias.
	actionable pacts	*pacta adiecta.*
		pacta praetoria.
		pacta legitima.

Common law
- formal
  - recognizances.
  - instruments under seal.
  - mercantile specialties.
- real
  - debt.
  - bailment.
- simple
  - unilateral.
  - bilateral.

As to mercantile specialties see 2 Ames, Cases on Bills and Notes, 872–878.

(b) With respect to subject-matter.

See Holland, Jurisprudence (13 ed.) 289–313.

6. Obligations arising from office or calling.

Ames, Lectures on Legal History, 160–162; III Blackstone, Commentaries, 165; 1 Wyman, Public Service Companies, §§ 330–334.

7. Obligations arising from fiduciary relations.

1 Story, Equity Jurisprudence, §§ 307–324.

8. Duties of restitution.

Seavey and Scott, Restitution, 54 L. Q. Rev. 29.

Friedmann, Die Bereicherungshaftung im Anglo-Amerikanischen Rechtskreis in Vergleichung mit dem deutschen bürgerlichen Recht.

Institutes, iii, 27; Digest, l, 17, 206, xii, 6, 1, xii, 6, 52, xii, 5, 6, xii, 6, 66, xii, 5, 1–3; VI Planiol et Ripert, Traité pratique de droit civil français, no. 7, VII id. nos. 719–765; I Cosack, Lehrbuch des bürgerlichen Rechts (8 ed.) §§ 233–234.

Moses v. Macferlan, 2 Burr. 1005.

9. Transfer of obligations.

Holland, Jurisprudence (13 ed.) 314–316; Markby, Elements of Law (6 ed.) §§ 659–672; II Dernburg, Pandekten (8 ed.) §§ 47–53; I Cosack, Lehrbuch des bürgerlichen Rechts (8 ed.) § 176; II Planiol, Traité élémentaire de droit civil (11 ed.) §§ 389–398.

10. Extinction of obligations.

Holland, Jurisprudence (13 ed.) 316–322; II Dernburg, Pandekten (8 ed.) §§ 64–68; II Windscheid, Pandekten, §§ 341–361; I Cosack, Lehrbuch des bürgerlichen Rechts (8 ed.) §§ 172–175; II Planiol, Traité élémentaire de droit civil (11 ed.) §§ 399–400, 522–523, 529–609, 617–629.

OBLIGATION

The relation of one person to another whereby the one person is bound either to some performance or to forbear something. — Kohler, Einführung in die Rechtswissenschaft, § 28.

An obligatory right . . . is a right to require another person to do some act which is reducible to a money value. It is invariably directed against a determinate person. . . . Obligations are not designed to create any general control over all the acts of the debtor. A debtor can, in the last resort, rid himself of every obligation by sacrificing a corresponding portion of his property for the purpose of indemnifying his adversary. An obligation means a deduction, not from a man's liberty, but only from his property. — Sohm, Institutes of Roman Law (Ledlie's transl.) § 60.

CONTRACT

An expressed agreement of the wills of two or more persons for the purpose of producing an alteration in their spheres of rights. — Gareis, Encyklopädie der Rechtswissenschaft, § 23.

The declared agreement of two or more persons who desire to enter into an obligatory relation concerning an object of right. — II Ahrens, Cours de droit naturel, § 82.

The mutually expressed agreement of certain persons over a relation of law to be created between them. — II Stahl, Philosophie des Rechts (5 ed.) 412.

Those legal transactions which bring face to face several persons who have opposing interests are called agreements. They have special practical importance because, as men are compelled to live in community and are unable to do without mutual assistance, they must agree. Hence the transaction between persons with opposing interests — seller and buyer, hirer and letter, etc. — is likely to conform to the general interest and establish a wise mean.

These agreements may serve to create or to modify or to extinguish obligations.

Agreements which have for their end the creation of an obligation are known specially by the name of contracts. — I Demogue, Traité des obligations en général, no. 22.

A contract is a promise or set of promises to which the law attaches legal obligation. — I Williston, The Law of Contracts, § 1.

XXXII. WRONGS (DUTIES OF REPARATION)

COROLLARY OF JURAL POSTULATE I.

One who intentionally does anything which on its face is injurious to another must repair the resulting damage unless he can (1) justify his act under some social or public interest, or (2) assert a privilege because of a countervailing individual interest of his own which there is a social or a public interest in securing.

JURAL POSTULATE IV.

In civilized society men must be able to assume that others will act reasonably and prudently so as not, by want of due care under the circumstances, to impose upon them an unreasonable risk of injury.

JURAL POSTULATE V.

In civilized society men must be able to assume that others who maintain things or employ agencies, harmless in the sphere of their use but harmful in their normal action elsewhere, and having a natural tendency to cross the boundaries of their proper use, will restrain them or keep them within their proper bounds.

Hence one is liable in tort for

I. Intentional aggression upon the personality or substance of another (unless he can establish justification or privilege, according to the corollary of Postulate I).

II. Negligent interference with person or property — i.e. failure to come up to the legal standard of due care under the circumstances, while carrying on some course of conduct, whereby injury is caused to the person or substance of another.

III. Unintended non-negligent interference with the person or property of another through failure to restrain or prevent the escape of some thing or agency which one maintains or employs, such thing or agency having a tendency to get out of bounds and do harm.

Holland, Jurisprudence (13 ed.) 329–335; Terry, Leading Principles of Anglo-American Law, §§ 524–541; Wigmore, Responsibility for Tortious Acts: Its History, 7 Harv. L. Rev. 315, 383, 441; id. The Tripartite Division of Torts, 8 Harv. L. Rev. 200; id. A General Analysis of Tort Relations, 8 Harv. L. Rev. 377; id. Cases on Torts, Preface; Bigelow, Torts (8 ed.) 35–39; Salmond, Torts, §§ 1–14; Seavey, Principles of Torts (1942) 56 Harv. L. Rev. 72.

II Dernburg, Pandekten (8 ed.) § 129; I Cosack, Lehrbuch des bürgerlichen Rechts (8 ed.) §§ 147–148; II Baudry-Lacantinerie, Précis de droit civil (13 ed.) §§ 815–847.

Roman law
- Delicts
  - Wrongful appropriation of property — *furtum, rapina.*
  - Injury to corporeal property — *damnum iniuria datum.*
  - Injuries to personality — to the physical person or to honor, *iniuria.*
  - Injuries to personality whereby substance is impaired — *dolus, metus.*
- Quasi delicts
  - Liability of *iudex* who "makes a case his own."
  - Liability *de deiectis et effusis.*
  - Noxal liability.
  - Liability under the aedilician edict.

Common law
- Intentional aggression
  - a. Upon personality.
    - (i) Assault and battery.
    - (ii) Imprisonment.
    - (iii) Infringement of privacy (in dispute).
  - b. Upon personality and substance.
    - (i) Infringement of rights in the domestic relations.
    - (ii) Malicious prosecution.
    - (iii) Defamation,
      - (1) slander,
      - (2) libel.
  - c. Upon substance.
    - (i) Trespass upon possession,
      - (1) of land,
      - (2) of chattels.
    - (ii) Conversion of chattels.
    - (iii) Intentional interference with advantageous relations.
    - (iv) Deceit.
- Negligence.
- Failure to restrain or prevent escape of agencies or things likely to get out of hand and do harm.

As to the last category, see Smith Tort and Absolute Liability — Suggested Changes in Classification, 30 Harv. L. Rev. 241, 319, 409; Isaacs, Quasi Delict in Anglo-American Law, 31 Yale L. J. 571; Winfield, The Province of the Law of Torts, chap. 10.

In Roman law there was a contractual theory of delicts. A wrong gave rise to a claim on the part of the person injured to a penalty recoverable from the wrongdoer by the legal proceeding appropriate to collection of a debt. When the penalty came to be thought of as a penalty of reparation, the debt analogy had fixed the conception of an obligation *ex delicto*.

In the common law, on the other hand, for historical reasons, there is a tort theory of contracts. One sues for damages for non-performance of a promise instead of to exact performance.

XXXIII. EXERCISE AND ENFORCEMENT OF RIGHTS

1. Exercise of rights (i.e. of liberties).

See references under VII, 2, (5), i. Also Blümner, Lehre von böswilligen Rechtsmissbrauch.

2. Self help, self redress.

Vallimaresco, La justice privée en droit moderne.

Digest, iv, 2, 13, ix, 2, 45, § 4, xliii, 16, 1, § 27, xlviii, 7, 8, 1, 17, 176, pr.; Code, viii, 4, 1, viii, 4, 7; Wenger, Institutes of the Roman Law of Civil Procedure (transl. by Fisk) 8–11; I Dernburg, Pandekten (8 ed.) § 112; I Windscheid, Pandekten, § 123; I Cosack, Lehrbuch des deutschen bürgerlichen Rechts (1 ed.) § 78 (the last editions by Cosack and Mitteis are not so useful on this subject); Schuster, Principles of German Civil Law, 74–76; German Civil Code, §§ 227–231, 561, 859.

Schmitt, Die Selbsthilfe im römischen Privatrecht; von Tuhr, Der Nothstand im Civilrecht.

III Blackstone, Commentaries, 2–15, 18; Lagan Navigation Co. v. Lambeg Bleaching Co. [1927] A. C. 226, 244–246.

3. Private execution.

Demogue, Notions fondamentales du droit privé, 638–669.

4. Administrative enforcement.

Amos, Science of Law (2 ed.) chap. 11; Landis, The Administrative Process; id. Crucial Issues in Administrative Law, 53 Harv. L. Rev. 1077; Gellhorn, Federal Administrative Proceedings; Carr, Concerning English Administrative Law; Administrative Procedure in Government Agencies, Report of the Committee on Administrative Procedure, Appointed by the Attorney-General, Senate Document No. 8, 77th Congress, 1st Session; Montague, Reform of Administrative Procedure (1942) 40 Mich. L. Rev. 501; Dickinson, Administrative Justice and the Supremacy of the Law in the United States; Symposium on Administrative Law, 47 Yale L. J. 515–674; Functions and Procedure of Administrative

Tribunals, Report of the Cincinnati Conference, 12 Univ. of Cincinnati L. Rev. 117–286; Symposium on Procedural Administrative Law, 25 Iowa L. Rev. 421–620; Symposium, The Final Report of the Attorney-General's Committee on Administrative Procedure, 41 Columbia L. Rev. 585–645; Benjamin, Administrative Adjudication in the State of New York; Reports of the Special Committee on Administrative Law of the American Bar Association, 58 Rep. Am. Bar Assn. 407, 59 id. 539, 60 id. 136, 61 id. 720, 62 id. 789, 63 id. 331, 64 id. 231, 65 id. 215.

5. Judicial enforcement.

Holland, Jurisprudence, chap. 15; Salmond, Jurisprudence, §§ 172–176; Markby, Elements of Law (6 ed.) §§ 848–863; Amos, Science of Law, chap. 11; Gareis, Science of Law (transl. by Kocourek) § 50; Pound, The Causes of Popular Dissatisfaction with the Administration of Justice, 29 Rep. Am. Bar Assn. pt. I, 395, 40 American L. Rev. 729.

(a) Organization of courts.

Girard, L'Organisation judiciaire des Romains; Wenger, Institutes of the Roman Law of Civil Procedure (transl. by Fisk) 59–79; Ensor, Courts and Judges in France, Germany, and England; Pound, Organization of Courts; Bruce, The American Judge.

(b) Procedure.

Engelmann, History of Continental Civil Procedure (transl. by Millar).

(1) Mode of instituting a judicial proceeding.

Twelve Tables, Tab. I (Girard, Textes de droit Romain, 4 ed. 12); Gaius, iv, §§ 183–187; Digest, ii, 4, 2–3 and 4, pr., ii, 4, 18–21, ii, 5, 203, ii, 10, 1, pr. and §§ 1–3, xiii, 4, 7, § 1; Wenger, Institutes of the Roman Law of Civil Procedure (transl. by Fisk) 94–98, 269–284.

The Roman-Canon-law procedure: Engelmann, History of Continental Civil Procedure (transl. by Millar) 463–465; Lancelottus, Institutiones Iuris Canonici, lib. III, tit. 5, pr. and §§ 1, 2, tit. 6, pr. and §§ 1, 2.

The modern Roman law: I Windscheid, Pandekten, §§ 128–132.

Germanic law: Engelmann, History of Continental Civil Procedure (transl. by Millar) 125–126; Siegel, Geschichte des deutschen Gerichtsverfahrens, §§ 9–13; Laws of Hlothhaere and Eadric, § 8 (2 Thorpe, Ancient Laws of England, 31); Amira, Grundriss der germanischen Rechts (2 ed.) § 87.

France: Engelmann, History of Continental Civil Procedure (transl. by Millar) 668–671, 709–710, 755–756; Garsonnet et Cézar-Bru, Précis de procédure civile (7 ed.) §§ 355, 357, 368.

Germany: Stein, Grundriss des Zivilprozessrechts (3 ed.) § 51.

Italy: 2 Chiovenda, Istituzioni di diritto processuale civile, §§ 243–249.

Common law: III Blackstone, Commentaries, 279–292.

Equity: III Blackstone, Commentaries, 442–445.

England: Rules of the Supreme Court, Orders 5, 6, 8, 9.

Scotland: Manual of Practice in the Court of Session, chap. 23.

United States — Federal Practice; Federal Rules of Civil Procedure, rule 4.

(2) Actions.

Wenger, Institutes of the Roman Law of Civil Procedure (transl. by Fisk) 15–16; Gaius, iv, §§ 1–3, 5, 11–30, 34–37; Institutes, iv, 6, §§ 20, 28, 30, 31; Digest, xliv, 7, 25, pr., xlvii, 23, 1–3 and 8.

III Blackstone, Commentaries, 272–275; Maitland, The Forms of Action at Common Law; England, Supreme Court of Judicature Act (1873) Schedule I, rules 1, 2; New York, Code of Civil Procedure (1849) § 69; Federal Rules of Civil Procedure (1938) rules 1, 2.

(3) Ascertainment of the facts.
i. Pleadings.

Gaius, iv, §§ 39–44, 115–119, 130–133; Institutes, iv, 13–14; Digest, ii, 13, 1; Novel liii, cap. 3, §§ 1–2; Wenger, Institutes of the Roman Law of Civil Procedure (transl. by Fisk) 132–160, 275, 279; Buckland, Text Book of Roman Law (2 ed.) 664–665; I Dernburg, Pandekten (7 ed.) §§ 151–152.

Lancelottus, Institutiones Iuris Canonici, lib. III, tits. 7, 8, 10; Langdell, Summary of Equity Pleading, §§ 1–16.

Garsonnet et Cézar-Bru, Précis de procédure civile (7 ed.) §§ 356–392; 3 Hellwig, Lehrbuch des deutschen Zivilprozessrechts, §§ 141–146; Lewinski, Courts and Civil Procedure in Germany, 5 Illinois L. Rev. 193; Mackey, Manual of the Procedure of the Court of Session, chaps. 23, 28.

III Blackstone, Commentaries, 293–313; Langdell, Summary of Equity Pleading, §§ 54–69, 79–84, 85–89.

New York Code of Civil Procedure (1849) §§ 141–145, 149, 153; England, Rules of the Supreme Court of Judicature, order 19, rule 2; Federal Rules of Civil Procedure, rule 7.

Pound, Some Principles of Procedural Reform, 4 Illinois L. Rev. 388–491; id. Canons of Procedural Reform, 12 A. B. A. J. 541; Prozessreform: Vier Beiträge, von A. Mendelssohn-Bartholdy, G. Chiovenda, Roscoe Pound, und A. Tissier, 2 Rheinische Zeitschrift für Zivil- und Prozessrecht, 498.

ii. Proof: Trial and finding.

Digest, xi, 1, 1–8 and 21; Wenger, Institutes of the Roman Law of Civil Procedure (transl. by Fisk) 190–204, 293–303; Lancelottus, Institutiones Iuris Canonici, lib. III, tit. 14; Langdell, Summary of Equity Pleading, §§ 25–35, 167–173, 204; I Planiol, Traité élémentaire de droit civil (12 ed.) nos. 350–360; Garsonnet et Cézar-Bru, Précis de procédure civile (7 ed.) nos. 401–475; Stein, Grundriss des Zivilprozessrechts, §§ 77–90; III Blackstone, Commentaries, 325–385, 437–438; England, Rules of the Supreme Court, order 36, rules 2–9; New York Code of Civil Procedure (1849) §§ 251, 253, 254; Federal Rules of Civil Procedure, rules 38, 39, 43.

On general problems of proof see Wigmore, Principles of Judicial Proof (3 ed.); Arnold, Psychology as Applied to Legal Evidence. General reference may be made to Bentham, Rationale of Judicial Evidence; Wigmore, Treatise on the Anglo-American System of Evidence (3 ed.) I, §§ 1–36, II, §§ 475–479, IV, §§ 1171–1175, V, §§ 1360–1365, VI, §§ 1813, 1864, VII, §§ 1917–1929, 2032–2034, IX, §§ 2565–2570.

(4) Judgment.

Institutes, iv, 6, §§ 31–32; Digest, xv, 1, 3, § 11, xliv, 2, 14, § 2, xlii, 2, 1, xlii, 2, 4, xxvi, 7, 2; Wenger, Institutes of the Roman Law of Civil Procedure (transl. by Fisk) 206–208; I Windscheid, Pandekten, § 128; Stein, Grundriss des Zivilprozessrechts (3 ed.) §§ 64–65; III Blackstone, Commentaries, 395–399, 451–454.

i. The remedy.

I Dernburg, Pandekten (8 ed.) §§ 134–141.

Prevention: Digest, viii, 5, 2, pr. and § 1, viii, 5, 7, xxxix, 2, 2 and 2, 7, xxxix, 3, 1, pr. and §§ 1, 2, 8, 10, xxxix, 1, 1, §§ 11, 12, 16, 17; I Dernburg, Pandekten (7 ed.) §§ 193–196, 218–219; Baudry-Lacantinerie et Chauveau, Traité des biens (2 ed.) nos. 831–833; Garsonnet et Cézar-Bru, Précis de procédure civile (7 ed.) nos. 119–121.

Fitzherbert, Natura Brevium, 128 F; IV Blackstone, Commentaries, 251–254; Maitland, Equity, lect. 21.

Willoughby, Principles of Judicial Administration, 13–88; Borchard, Judicial Relief Against Peril and Insecurity, 45 Harv. L. Rev. 793, 33 Columbia L. Rev. 648; Arnold, Trial by Combat and the New Deal, 47 Harv. L. Rev. 913.

The declaratory judgment: Sunderland, A Modern Evolution in Remedial Rights, 16 Mich. L. Rev. 69; Borchard, The Declaratory Judgment, 27 Yale L. J. 1; Jennings, Declaratory Judgments Against Public Authorities, 41 Yale L. J. 407; Report of Committee on Jurisprudence and Law Reform, 45 Rep. Am. Bar Assn. (1920) 259, 260–263, 266–267; Torrey, The Declaratory Judgment, 8 Iowa L. Bull. 81; Hyde, Declaratory Judgments: Experience Under the Uniform Act, 26 Washington Univ. L. Q. 468; Note, The Declaratory Judgment in Public Law, 43 Harv. L. Rev. 1290; England, Rules of the Supreme Court, order 25, rule 5, order 54 A, rule 1, order 34, rules 1 and 2; Guaranty Trust Co. v. Hannay [1915] 2 K. B. 536; Liberty Warehouse Co. v. Grannis, 273 U. S. 70; Willing v. Chicago Auditorium Assn., 277 U. S. 274; Arizona v. California, 283 U. S. 423, 455–457; Uniform Declaratory Judgments Act, Proceedings of the Commissioners on Uniform State Laws (1922) 382 (as to the states which adopted this act, see id. (1939) 308). Compare II Vinogradoff, Historical Jurisprudence, 221–222.

Specific redress: Institutes, iv, 6, § 31; Wenger, Institutes of the Roman Law of Civil Procedure (transl. by Fisk) 147–153; VII Planiol et Ripert, Traité pratique de droit civil français, nos. 768–779, 775–781, 792–795; Maitland, Equity, lect. 20; Ames, Lectures on Legal History, 248–250.

Substitutional redress: Wenger, Institutes of the Roman Law of Civil Procedure (transl. by Fisk) 143–147; Ames, Lectures on Legal History, 142–145; III Blackstone, Commentaries, 434–435; Sedgwick, Elements of Damages, 216–218.

ii. Effect of the judgment.

Digest, xli, 1, 1, l, 17, 207, xlii, 1, 6, § 3, xliv, 2, 7, § 4; Wenger, Institutes of the Roman Law of Civil Procedure (transl. by Fisk) 147–153; I Windscheid, Pandekten, §§ 129–132; I Planiol et Ripert, Traité pratique de droit civil français, nos. 28–41; Stein, Grundriss des Zivilprozessrechts (3 ed.) § 66; von Moschzisker, Res Judicata, 38 Yale L. J. 299; Millar, The Premises of the Judgment as Res Judicata in Continental and Anglo-American Law, 39 Mich. L.

Rev. 1; Caterpillar Tractor Co. v. International Harvester Co., 120 Fed. (2d) 82, 84; American Law Institute, Restatement of Judgments, § 301.

See also cases and notes in Chafee and Simpson, Cases on Equity Jurisdiction and Specific Performance, 125–145.

(5) Review — appeal.

Pound, Appellate Procedure in Civil Cases, chaps. 1, 6.

(6) Execution.

Gaius, iii, §§ 77–80; Digest, xlii, 5, 12, pr., xxvii, 10, 5; Institutes, iii, 12, pr.; Digest, vi, 1, 68, xliii, 4, 3, pr.; Wenger, Institutes of the Roman Law of Civil Procedure (transl. by Fisk) 222–240; Garsonnet et Cézar-Bru, Précis de procédure civile (7 ed.) §§ 703–705; Stein, Grundriss des Zivilprozessrechts (3 ed.) §§ 127–396; Gloag and Henderson, Introduction to the Law of Scotland, chap. 46; III Blackstone, Commentaries, 412–425; Federal Rules of Civil Procedure, rules 69, 70.

(c) Costs.

Wenger, Institutes of the Roman Law of Civil Procedure (transl. by Fisk) 330–334; III Blackstone, Commentaries, 399–401; Federal Rules of Civil Procedure, rule 54(d).

6. Representation in litigation.
(a) Agents for litigation.

Bonner, Lawyers and Litigants in Ancient Greece, chap. 10; Wenger, Institutes of the Roman Law of Civil Procedure (transl. by Fisk) 88–93; Engelmann, History of Continental Civil Procedure (transl. by Millar) 338–341, 460–461, 123; 2 Holdsworth, History of English Law, 261, 265–267, 424–426; England, Solicitors' Act, 1932 (22 & 23 Geo. 5, c. 37); Cordery, Law Relating to Solicitors (4 ed.) chap. 1.

(b) Advocates.

Wenger, Institutes of the Roman Law of Civil Procedure (transl. by Fisk) 87–88, 322–323; Code, ii, 7, 14; Novel 122, cap. 6; Engelmann, History of Continental Civil Procedure (transl. by Millar) 341–343, 524, 671, 715, 779, 784–785; 2 Holdsworth, History of English Law, 261, 264, 408–412, 414–419, 421–431, 468–469, 486–490; Fortescue, De laudibus legum Angliae, chaps. 49–50; III Blackstone, Commentaries, 26–29; 2 Halsbury, Laws of England (2 ed.) §§ 648–686.

Warren, History of the American Bar.

(c) Legal aid.

Willoughby, Principles of Judicial Administration, 569–604; Smith, Justice and the Poor; Maguire, The Lance of Justice; id. Poverty and Civil Litigation, 36 Harv. L. Rev. 361.

BIBLIOGRAPHY

GENERAL BIBLIOGRAPHY

I. INTRODUCTIONS

Pollock, First Book of Jurisprudence (6 ed. 1929).

First ed. 1896. Part I, Some General Legal Notions. Written from the English analytical standpoint.

Korkunov, General Theory of Law (transl. by Hastings, 1909, 2 ed. 1922).

First ed. in Russian (1887). There is also a French translation by Tchernoff, Cours de théorie générale du droit (2 ed. 1914). Analytical-social-utilitarian.

Gareis, The Science of Law (transl. by Kocourek, 1911).

A translation of Gareis, Enzyklopädie und Methodologie der Rechtswissenschaft (3 ed. 1905). First ed. 1887, 5 ed. 1921, as Gareis und Wenger, Rechtsenzyklopädie und Methodologie.

Sternberg, Einführung in die Rechtswissenschaft (2 ed. 1912–1922).

First ed. as Allgemeine Rechtslehre (1904). Written from the social-utilitarian standpoint.

Kohler, Einführung in die Rechtswissenschaft (5 ed. 1919).

First ed. 1902. Written from the neo-Hegelian (i.e. historical social-philosophical) standpoint.

Grueber, Einführung in die Rechtswissenschaft (6 ed. 1922).

First ed. 1907. Written from the analytical standpoint.

Schmidt, Einführung in die Rechtswissenschaft (3 ed. 1934).

First ed. 1921. Written from a functional philosophical standpoint.

Radbruch, Einführung in die Rechtswissenschaft (5 ed. 1925).

First ed. 1910. Written primarily from a philosophical (neo-Kantian epistemological) standpoint.

Merkel, Juristische Encyklopädie (7 ed. 1922).

First ed. 1885. Written from the social-utilitarian standpoint.

Demogue, Les notions fondamentales du droit privé (1911).

Written from the standpoint of the revived natural law. Chaps. 1–12 are translated in chaps. 12–23 of Modern French Legal Philosophy (vol. VII, Modern Legal Philosophy Series).

Capitant, Introduction à l'étude du droit civil (4 ed. 1923).

First ed. 1898. Covers much the same ground as an English text on analytical jurisprudence, but with less of the comparative.

Jones, Historical Introduction to the Theory of Law (1941).

Courcelle-Seneuil, Préparation à l'étude du droit (1887).

Economic utilitarian.

May, Introduction à la science du droit (2 ed. 1925).

First ed. 1920. Written from an analytical-historical standpoint.

Bonnecase, Introduction à l'étude du droit (1926).

Written from a neo-idealist social-philosophical standpoint.

Burckhardt, Methode und System des Rechts (1936).

Written from a sociological standpoint.

Gjelsvik, Innleiding i Rettsstudiet (2 ed. 1924).

Hastie, Outlines of Jurisprudence (1887) is made up of translations from Puchta, Cursus der Institutionen, pt. 1, Encyklopädie (1841), Friedländer, Juristische Encyklopädie oder System der Rechtswissenschaft (1847), Falck, Juristische Encyklopädie (5 ed. 1851), and Ahrens, Juristische Encyklopädie (1855).

Mention may be made also of the following: Ahrens, Juristische Encyklopädie (1855–1857 — there is an English translation of parts in Hastie, Outlines of Jurisprudence, 1887); Arndts, Juristische Encyklopädie und Methodologie (10 ed. by Grueber, 1901); Del Giudice, Enciclopedia giuridica (2 ed. 1896); Den Tex, Encyclopaedia Jurisprudentiae (1839); Eschbach, Introduction générale à l'étude du droit (3 ed. 1856); Falck, Juristische Encyklopädie (5 ed. by Jhering, 1851 — there is a translation of the 4th ed. 1841, and an English translation of parts in Hastie, Outlines of Jurisprudence, 1887); Fischer, Einführung in die Wissenschaft von Recht und Staat (1920); Goldschmidt, Encyklopädie der Rechtswissenschaft (1862); Guelfi, Enciclopedia giuridica (5 ed. 1907); Hedemann, Einführung in die Rechtswissenschaft (1919); Hugo, Lehrbuch der juristischen Encyklopädie (5 ed. 1817); Krückmann, Einführung in das Recht (1912); Perassi, Introduzione alle scienze giuridiche (1922); Ratkowski, Encyklopädie der Rechts und Staatswissenschaften (1890); Warnkönig, Juristische Encyklopädie (1853); Zevenberger, Formeele Encyclopaedie der Rechtswetenschap (1925).

II. ANALYTICAL

1. *In English.*

Austin, Jurisprudence (5 ed. 1885, reprinted 1911).

The first six lectures were published in 1832 under the title of The Province of Jurisprudence Determined. The third edition (posthumous) 1863, or any subsequent edition, may be used. An abridgment by Campbell, styled Student's Edition (11 ed. 1909) is useful.

Holland, Elements of Jurisprudence (13 ed. 1924).

First ed. 1880. The ninth or any subsequent edition may be used.

Salmond, Jurisprudence (9 ed. by Parker, 1937).

First ed. 1902. The last edition is much altered by the editor. For many purposes the earlier editions, revised by the author, are preferable.

Markby, Elements of Law (6 ed. 1905).

First ed. 1871.

Brown, The Austinian Theory of Law (1906).

Gray, The Nature and Sources of the Law (1909, 2 ed. 1921).

The first edition is to be preferred.

Reference may be made also to Amos, Systematic View of the Science of Jurisprudence (1872); id. The Science of Law (2 ed. 1874); Heron, The Principles of Jurisprudence (1873); id. Introduction to the History of Jurisprudence (1860); Hearn, The Theory of Legal Duties and Rights (1884); Hibbert, Jurisprudence (1932); Lindley, Introduction to the Study of Jurisprudence (1854, 2 ed. 1890, a transl. of the general part of Thibaut, System des Pandektenrechts); Rattigan, The Science of Jurisprudence (3 ed. 1909); Dillon, The Laws and Jurisprudence of England and America (1894); Goadby, Introduction to the Study of Law (2 ed. 1914); Jenks, The New Jurisprudence (1933) (comparative analytical-historical, see review in 47 Harv. L. Rev. 890); Stone, Law and its Administration (1915); Harrison, Jurisprudence and the Conflict of Laws (1919, first published in 1878–1879); Wise, Outlines of Jurisprudence (revised by Winfield, 4 ed. by Oliver, 1925); Hexner, Studies in Legal Terminology (1941).

2. *In German.*

I Binding, Die Normen und ihre Uebertretung (2 ed. 1890).

Vol. I (1872, 2 ed. 1890), vol. II (1877, 2 ed. 1914–1916), vol. III (1918). The first 20 sections of vol. I are of general importance for the theory of the nature of law.

Bierling, Kritik der juristischen Grundbegriffe (1877–1883).

I Bierling, Juristische Prinzipienlehre (1894), vol. II (1898), vol. III (1905), vol. IV (1911).

Somló, Juristische Grundlehre (1917).

Friedrichs, Der allgemeine Teil des Rechts (1927).

See also Jellinek, Allgemeine Staatslehre (3 ed. 1914); Merkel, Elemente der allgemeinen Rechtslehre (5 ed. 1890); Müller, Die Elemente der Rechtsbildung und des Rechts (1877); Nicol-Speyer, Systematische Theorie des heutigen Rechts (1911); Puntschart, Die moderne Theorie des Privatrechts (1893); Schein, Unsere Rechtsphilosophie und Jurisprudenz (1899); Thon, Rechtsnorm und subjektives Recht (1878); Stern, Rechtsphilosophie und Rechtswissenschaft (1904).

Kelsen, Reine Rechtslehre (1934).

For a comparison of Kelsen's "pure theory of law" with English analytical jurisprudence, see Kelsen, The Pure Theory of Law and Analytical Jurisprudence, 55 Harv. L. Rev. 44. See also id. The Pure Theory of Law, 50 L. Q. Rev. 474, 51 id. 517. For a bibliography of Kelsen, see Pound, Fifty Years of Jurisprudence, 51 Harv. L. Rev. 444, 449 n. 2 (449–451).

3. *In French.*

Levy-Ullmann, Éléments d'introduction générale à l'étude des sciences juridiques. Pt. I, La définition du droit (1917).

Roguin, La règle de droit (1889); id. La science juridique pure (3 vols. 1923).

III. HISTORICAL

Savigny, Vom Beruf unsrer Zeit für Gesetzgebung und Rechtswissenschaft (1814, 3 ed. 1840, reprinted 1892).

Translated as The Vocation of our Age for Legislation and Jurisprudence by Hayward (1831).

Savigny, Geschichte des römischen Rechts im Mittelalter (6 vols. 1815–1831, 2 ed. 7 vols. 1834–1851).

There is a French translation by Guenoux, Histoire du droit romain au moyen âge (1839). The foreword to this translation is useful in connection with Savigny's life. There is an English translation (from the first edition) of vol. I by Cathcart (1829).

Savigny, System des heutigen römischen Rechts (8 vols. 1840–1849).

This book has been a quarry for the systematic part of treatises on analytical jurisprudence. Sections 1–14 of vol. I are important for the historical theory of the nature of law. There is an English translation of vol. I by Holloway (1867). There is also a French translation by Guenoux, Traité de droit Romain (1840–1851).

Puchta, Cursus der Institutionen (10 ed. by Krüger, 1893, bk. I, Encyklopädie).

First ed. 1841.

Maine, Ancient Law. New edition with introduction and notes by Sir Frederick Pollock (1906).

This book, first published in 1861, has gone through many editions in England and America. Pollock's edition is recommended.

Maine, Early History of Institutions (1874).

——, Early Law and Custom (1883).

——, Village Communities in the East and West (1871).

These works of Sir Henry Maine are at the foundation of all study of historical jurisprudence.

Bryce, Studies in History and Jurisprudence (1901).

Clark, Practical Jurisprudence (1883).

——, Roman Private Law: Jurisprudence (1914).

Carter, Law: Its Origin, Growth, and Function (1907).

Wigmore, Problems of Law (1920).

Lect. I, Problems of the Law's Evolution. Neo-historical, positivist-comparative.

I Vinogradoff, Historical Jurisprudence (1920).

Neo-historical, pluralist-ideological.

II Vinogradoff, Collected Papers: Jurisprudence (1928).

Reference may be made also to Pulszky, Theory of Law and Civil Society (1888); Lightwood, The Nature of Positive Law (1883); Adams, Economics and

Jurisprudence (1897). Hastie, Outlines of Jurisprudence (1887) contains a translation of Puchta's Encyklopädie (Cursus der Institutionen, I, §§ 1–61).

See also Bergbohm, Jurisprudenz und Rechtsphilosophie (1892); Beseler, Volksrecht und Juristenrecht (1843); Cogliolo, Saggi sopra l'evoluzione del diritto privato (1885); Löning, Ueber Wurzel und Wesen des Rechts (1907); Wieland, Die historische und die kritische Methode in der Rechtswissenschaft (1910).

IV. PHILOSOPHICAL

A convenient account of the history of philosophy of law and of the different philosophical schools may be found in Berolzheimer, The World's Legal Philosophies (transl. by Jastrow, 1913).

For statements of philosophical views as to law and the science of law from different recent standpoints, see My Philosophy of Law: Credos of Sixteen American Legal Scholars (1941).

1. *The forerunners of modern legal science.*

(Note: Only the books of prime importance are given here.
For the rest, see *ante*.)

(a) Scholastic Theological Jurisprudence.

Thomas Aquinas, Summa Theologica (ed. Migne, 1877).

Rickaby, Aquinas Ethicus (1896) is a convenient translation of the portions relating to law.

(b) The Law of Nature.

Grotius, De Iure Belli ac Pacis (1625).

Whewell's edition with an abridged translation (1853) is convenient.

(c) The Forerunners of the Analytical School.

Bodin, Les six livres de la république (1576).

Hobbes, Leviathan (1651).

Spinoza, Ethica (1674).

——, Tractatus Theologico-Politicus (1670).

Elwes' translation of Spinoza in Bohn's Libraries must be used with caution. There is a translation of the Ethica by Boyle (1910).

(d) The Forerunner of Sociological Jurisprudence.

Montesquieu, L'Esprit des Lois (1748).

Nugent's translation, revised by Prichard, in Bohn's Libraries, may be used conveniently.

(e) The English Utilitarians.

Bentham, Fragment on Government (1776, new ed. with introduction by Montague (1891, reprinted 1931).

——, A Comment on the Commentaries, first printed from the author's manuscript, with introduction and notes by Everett (1928).

——, Principles of Morals and Legislation (1780).

A convenient reprint published by the Clarendon Press (1876) may be recommended.

Bentham, Theory of Legislation (transl. by Hildreth, 1864, 5 ed. 1887; new ed. with introduction and notes by Ogden, 1931).

Originally published in French, 1820.

For a bibliography of Bentham's writings and of appreciations and critiques of Bentham, see Pound, Outlines of a Course on Legislation (1934) 55-56.

2. *Nineteenth-century philosophical (metaphysical)*.

Lorimer, Institutes of Law (1872, 2 ed. 1880).

Miller, Lectures on the Philosophy of Law (1884).

——, The Data of Jurisprudence (1903).

Herkless, Lectures on Jurisprudence (1901).

Green, Principles of Political Obligation (1911).

Reprinted from the Works of Thomas Hill Green, II, 335-553. These lectures were delivered in 1879-1880.

Reference may be made also to Phillipps, Jurisprudence (1863); Hutchison Stirling, Lectures on the Philosophy of Law (1873) — a mere outline of Hegel's philosophy; Watts, An Outline of Legal Philosophy (1893); Smith, Elements of Right and of the Law (2 ed. 1887); id. The Law of Private Right (1893); Lioy, Philosophy of Right (transl. by Hastie, 1891); Miraglia, Comparative Legal Philosophy (transl. by Lisle, 1912).

Kant, Metaphysische Anfangsgründe der Rechtslehre (2 ed. 1798).

Translated complete, anonymously, London, 1794; also in part by Hastie (1887) as Kant's Philosophy of Law.

Fichte, Grundlage des Naturrechts (1796, new ed. by Medicus, 1908).

Translated by Kroeger (1889) as Fichte's Science of Rights.

Hegel, Grundlinien der Philosophie des Rechts (1821; ed. by Gans, 1840; new ed. by Lasson, 1911, 2 ed. 1921).

Translated by Dyde (1896) as Hegel's Philosophy of Right.

The translation must be used with caution. A useful introduction for students is Reyburn, The Ethical Theory of Hegel, A Study of the Philosophy of Right (1921). See also Binder, Busse und Larenz, Einführung in Hegel's Rechtsphilosophie (1931).

Krause, Abriss des Systemes der Philosophie des Rechtes (1825).

Ahrens, Cours de droit naturel (1837, 8 ed. 1892).

This book went through twenty-four editions in seven languages. The German 6th edition (Naturrecht, 1870-1871) contains important matter not in the French editions.

Lasson, Lehrbuch der Rechtsphilosophie (1882).

Boistel, Cours de philosophie du droit (1870, new ed. 1899).

Mention may also be made of the following: Abate Longo, Principii di filosofia del diritto (1881); Acollas, L'idée du droit (1889); id. Introduction à l'étude du droit (1885); Affolter, Naturgesetze und Rechtsgesetze (1904); Anzilotti, La scuola del diritto naturale nella filosofia giuridica contemporanea

(1892); Arnold, Philosophische Betrachtungen eines Juristen (1908); Baumann, Abriss der Rechtsphilosophie (in Handbuch der Moral) (1879); Beaussire, Les principes du droit (1888); Bélime, Philosophie du droit (1844–1848); Beudant, Le droit individuel et l'état (1891, 3 ed. 1920); Bovio, Filosofia del diritto (2 ed. 1890); Carle, La vita del diritto (2 ed. 1890); id. La filosofia del diritto nello stato moderno (1903); Cogliolo, Filosofia del diritto privato (2 ed. 1881); Dahn, Rechtsphilosophische Studien (1883); De los Rios Urruti, La filosofia del derecho en Don Francisco Giner (1916) see bibliography on p. 65; Fouillée, L'idée moderne du droit (1878, 6 ed. 1909); Fabreguettes, Société, état, patrie (2 vols. 1898); Franck, Philosophie de droit civil (1886); Geyer, Geschichte und System der Rechtsphilosophie (1863); Giner de los Rios, Filosofia del derecho (1871); id. Principios de derecho natural (1873); Giner y Calderon, Filosofia del derecho (1898); Giner und Calderon, Zur Vorschule des Rechts, kurzgefasste Grundsatze des Naturrechts (transl. by Röder, 1907); Glinka, La Philosophie du droit (3 ed. 1863); Harms, Begriff, Formen und Grundlegung der Rechtsphilosophie (1889); Hennebicq, Philosophie de droit et droit naturel (1897); Herbart, Analytische Beleuchtung des Naturrechts und der Moral (1836); Jouffroy, Cours de droit naturel (5 ed. 1876); Kirchmann, Grundbegriffe des Rechts und der Moral (2 ed. 1873); Krause, Das System der Rechtsphilosophie (posthumous) ed. by Röder (1874); Lerminier, Introduction générale à l'histoire du droit (1856); Marino, Elementi di filosofia del diritto (1885); Miraglia, Filosofia del diritto (3 ed. 1903 — transl. by Lisle in Modern Legal Philosophy Series as Comparative Legal Philosophy); Raumer, Geschichtliche Entwickelung der Begriffe von Recht, Staat und Politik (3 ed. 1861); Röder, Grundzüge des Naturrechts oder der Rechtsphilosophie (2 ed. 1860); Rosmini, Filosofia del diritto (2 ed. 1865, first ed. 1841); Rothe, Traité de droit naturel théorique et appliqué (6 vols. 1885–1912) — Catholic; Schuppe, Grundzüge der Ethik und Rechtsphilosophie (1881); Stahl, Philosophie des Rechts (5 ed. 1878, first ed. 1829); Steudel, Kritische Betrachtungen über die Rechtslehre (1884); Tissot, Introduction historique et philosophique à l'étude du droit (1875); Trendelenburg, Naturrecht auf dem Grunde der Ethik (1868); Vareilles-Sommières, Les principes fondamentaux du droit (1889); Wallaschek, Studien zur Rechtsphilosophie (1889); Walter, Naturrecht und Politik im Lichte der Gegenwart (2 ed. 1871); Zeiller, Jus Naturae Privatum (3 ed. of Natürliches Recht, 1802, translated into Latin, 1839) — Kantian; Zoepfl, Grundriss zur Vorlesungen über Rechtsphilosophie (2 ed. 1879).

See Bonnecase, La notion du droit en France au dix-neuvième siècle (1919); id. La pensée juridique française de 1804 à l'heure présente (2 vols. 1933).

3. *Social-philosophical.*

(a) Transition from Utilitarian-Analytical.

Brown, The Underlying Principles of Modern Legislation (1912, 6 ed. 1920).

The third edition revised and enlarged, 1914, or any subsequent edition may be used.

(b) Social-Utilitarian.

Jhering, Der Zweck im Recht (1877–1883, 6–8 ed. 1923).

The first volume is translated by Husik under the title Law as a Means to an End (1913).

Jhering, Scherz und Ernst in der Jurisprudenz (1884, 13 ed. 1924).

See also Bekker, Ernst und Scherz über unsere Wissenschaft (1892); id. Grundbegriffe des Rechts und Missgriffe des Gesetzgebers (1909); Bentley, The Process of Government (1908); Bülow, Heitere und ernste Betrachtungen über die Rechtswissenschaft (2 ed. 1901); Grabowski, Recht und Staat (1908); Jhering, Der Kampf ums Recht (1872, 20 ed. 1921 — transl. by Lalor from 5 ed. as The Struggle for Law, 1879, 2 ed. by Kocourek, 1915; the book has gone through 30 editions in 18 languages); Krabbe, Die Lehre der Rechtssouveränität (1906); Parsons, Legal Doctrine and Social Progress (1911); Tanon, L'évolution du droit et la conscience sociale (3 ed. 1911).

Heck, Gesetzesauslegung und Interessenjurisprudenz (1914); id. Begriffsbildung und Interessenjurisprudenz (1932); id. Interessenjurisprudenz (1933); Schönfeld, Von der Rechtserkenntnis (1931); Wolf, Interessenschutz und allgemeine Rechtssätze (1932); Müller-Erzbach, Wohin führt die Interessenjurisprudenz? (1932).

(c) Neo-Kantian.

Stammler, Wirthschaft und Recht (1896, 5 ed. 1924).

——, Lehre von dem richtigen Rechte (1902, new ed. 1926).

The first edition is translated by Husik as The Theory of Justice (1925).

Stammler, Theorie der Rechtswissenschaft (1911, 2 ed. 1923).

——, Lehrbuch der Rechtsphilosophie (1922, 2 ed. 1923).

For bibliography of Stammler's writings and of critiques of Stammler, see Pound, Fifty Years of Jurisprudence, 51 Harv. L. Rev. 444, 448–449 n. 16; also note in 21 Mich. L. Rev. 623–624.

Stammler, Abhandlungen zur Rechtswissenschaft und zu Ihrer Method (3 vols. 1916, ed. by Joerges).

Del Vecchio, The Formal Bases of Law (transl. by Lisle, 1914).

A translation of I presupposti filosofici della nozione del diritto (1905); Il concetto del diritto (1906, reprinted 1912); Il concetto della natura e il principio del diritto (1908).

Del Vecchio, Lezioni di filosofia del diritto (1930, 3 ed. 1936); French translation as Leçons de philosophie du droit with preface by Le Fur (1936).

For bibliography of the writings of Del Vecchio, see Pound, Fifty Years of Jurisprudence, 51 Harv. L. Rev. 444, 451 n. 20.

See also Breuer, Der Rechtsbegriff auf Grundlage der Stammlerischen Sozialphilosophie (1912); Brütt, Die Kunst der Rechtsanwendung (1907) (criticalpositivist); Camus, Filosofia juridica contemporanea (1932); Del Vecchio, Il sentimento giuridico (1908); Nelson, Lehrbuch der philosophischen Rechtslehre (1920); Stammler, Ueber die Methode der geschichtlichen Rechtstheorie (1888) reprinted in I Rechtsphilosophische Abhandlungen, 1 (1925); id. Rechts und Staatstheorien der Neuzeit (1917); Sturm, Psychologische Grundlage des Rechts (1910); id. Die Materie des Rechts (1911); id. Die Form des Rechts (1911); id. Die Reaktion des Rechts (1914); Kantorowicz, Lehre vom richtigen Recht (1909).

See Vinogradoff, Common Sense in Law (1914) chap. 9; Kaufmann, Kritik der neukantischen Rechtsphilosophie (1926).

Reference may be made to: Zeitschrift für Rechtsphilosophie in Lehre und Praxis, ed. by Holldack, Joerges and Stammler, later by Holldack, Jung and Reichel (5 vols. 1914–1931); Rivista internazionale di filosofia del diritto, ed. by Del Vecchio and others (1921–1940, vols. 1–20).

(d) Neo-Hegelian.

Kohler, Rechtsphilosophie und Universalrechtsgeschichte, in I Holtzendorff, Enzyklopädie der Rechtswissenschaft (6 ed. 1904, 7 ed. 1913).

Not in prior editions.

Kohler, Lehrbuch der Rechtsphilosophie (1908, 3 ed. by Arthur Kohler, 1923).

The first edition is translated by Albrecht as Philosophy of Law (1914).

Kohler, Moderne Rechtsprobleme (1907, 2 ed. 1913).

For full bibliography of Kohler, see Arthur Kohler, Josef Kohler — Bibliographie (1931). For appreciations and critiques, see bibliography in Pound, Fifty Years of Jurisprudence, 51 Harv. L. Rev. 444, 453, n. 29.

Berolzheimer, System der Rechts- und Wirthschaftsphilosophie (1904–1907).

Vol. II, history of juristic thought, translated by Jastrow (somewhat abridged) under the title The World's Legal Philosophies (1912), vol. III, general system of legal and economic philosophy, vol. IV, philosophy of interests of substance, and vol. V, philosophy of criminal law, are important for our purpose.

See also Berolzheimer, Rechtsphilosophische Studien (1903); Barillari, Diritto e filosofia (1910–1912); Kohler, Recht und Persönlichkeit in der Kultur der Gegenwart (1914); Monasterio, L'elemento morale nelle norme giuridiche (1913).

Compare Munroe Smith, Jurisprudence (1908).

Reference may be made to Archiv für Rechts- und Wirthschaftsphilosophie, founded by Kohler and Berolzheimer, vol. 1 (1907–1908) to vol. 26 (1932–1933); continued under the name of Archiv für Rechts und Sozialphilosophie, ed. by Wenger and others, and later by Emge, vols. 27–32 (1933–1939).

(e) Neo-Idealist.

Hocking, The Present Status of the Philosophy of Law and of Rights (1926).

Tourtoulon, Principes philosophiques de l'histoire du droit (1908–1920).

Translated by Read as Philosophy in the Development of Law (1922). Neo-Kantian psychological-logical.

Reinach, Die apriorische Grundlagen des bürgerlichen Rechts (1913).

Neo-Kantian logical.

Huber, Recht und Rechtsverwirklichung (1921, 2 ed. 1925).

Radbruch, Rechtsphilosophie (3 ed. 1935). Spanish translation by Echavarría as Filosofia del derecho (1933).

1 ed. as Grundzüge der Rechtsphilosophie (1914). Neo-Kantian antinomic. For an exposition and critique of Radbruch see Gurvitch, Une philosophie

antinomique du droit — Gustav Radbruch (1932) Archives de philosophie du droit, 530; Pound, Fifty Years of Jurisprudence, 51 Harv. L. Rev. 444, 454–460.

Lask, Rechtsphilosophie (1905) in I Gesammelte Schriften (1923) 278–331.

Kaufmann, Logik und Rechtswissenschaft (1922).

Neo-Kantian logical.

Binder, Philosophie des Rechts (1925).

"An idealistic philosophy as a system of ideal propositions which find their fulfilment in the empirical world of the law, and according to which, therefore, we judge the structure of this law."

Binder, Grundlegung zur Rechtsphilosophie (1935).

——, System der Rechtsphilosophie (2 ed. 1937).

Mayer, Rechtsphilosophie (1922).

Miceli, Principii di filosofia del diritto (1914).

Logical psychological.

Recaséns Siches, Vida humana sociedad y derecho (1939).

See also Ssawalski, Grundlegung der Rechtsphilosophie im wissenschaftlichen Idealismus (1908); Binder, Rechtsbegriff und Rechtsidee (1915); Löwenstein, Der Rechtsbegriff als Relationsbegriff (1915); Salmon, Das Problem der Rechtsbegriffe (1907); id. Grundlegung zur Rechtsphilosophie (2 ed. 1925); Beling, Rechtswissenschaft und Rechtsphilosophie (1923); Kaufmann, Logik und Rechtswissenschaft (1922); id. Die Kriterien des Rechts (1924); A. Merkl, Die Lehre von der Rechtskraft (1923).

Compare Ravi, I comfiti della filosofia di fronte al diritto (1907); Alloggio, Le nuove teorie del diritto (1925); Gurvitch, L'idée du droit social (1932).

Reference may be made to Philosophie und Recht ed. by Emge and Raab (2 vols. 1920–1922).

Recaséns Siches, Los Temos de la filosofia del derecho (1934).

4. Phenomenology.

As to phenomenology see Reinach, Die apriorischen Grundlagen des bürgerlichen Rechtes (1922); Schapp, Die neue Wissenschaft vom Recht (1931–1932); Kaufmann, Logik und Rechtswissenschaft (1922); id. Die Kriterien des Rechts (1924); id. Die philosophischen Grundprobleme der Lehre von der Strafrechtsschuld (1929); Schreier, Grundbegriffe und Grundformen des Rechts (1924 — Spanish transl. as Concepto y formas fundamentales del derecho (1942) with introduction by L. Recaséns Siches); G. Husserl, Recht und Welt (1930); id. Der Rechtsgegenstand (1933); id. Rechtskraft und Rechtsgeltung (1925); Engisch, Zur phänomenologischen Methode im Strafrecht (1937) 30 Archiv für Rechts und Sozialphilosophie, 130; Nieto Arteta, Logica, fenomenologia y formalismo juridica (1942).

See also Spiegelberg, Gesetz und Sittengesetz (1934).

5. Revived natural law.

Fuller, The Law in Quest of Itself (1940).

Reference may be made to Modern French Legal Philosophy (1916) in the Modern Legal Philosophy Series; Jung, Das Problem des natürlichen Rechts

(1912). See also Cohen, Jus Naturale Redivivum (1916) XXV Philosophical Rev. 761.

(a) Neo-Metaphysical.

Demogue, Notions fondamentales du droit privé (1911, transl. in Modern French Legal Philosophy, 7 Modern Legal Philosophy Series, 347–572).

Sauter, Die philosophischen Grundlagen des Naturrechts (1932).

See also Boucaud, Qu'est-ce que le droit naturel? (1906); Charmont, La renaissance du droit naturel (1910, chaps. 5–12 are translated in Modern French Legal Philosophy where they are chaps. 5–12); id. Le droit et l'esprit démocratique (1908); Djuvara, Le fondement du phénomène juridique (1913); Fabreguettes, La logique judicaire et l'art de juger (1914).

For bibliography of Djuvara see Pound, Fifty Years of Jurisprudence, 51 Harv. L. Rev. 444, 463, n. 58.

(b) Neo-Scholastic.

Gény, Méthode d'interprétation en droit privé positif (1899, 2 ed. 2 vols. 1919).

A book of the first importance. Parts of the first edition are translated in Science of Legal Method, 9 Modern Legal Philosophy Series, 1–46. See Wortley, François Gény, in Modern Theories of Law, 139–159.

Gény, Science et technique en droit privé positif, vol. I (1913), vol. II, (1915), vol. III (1921), vol. IV (1924).

On Gény, see Pound, Fifty Years of Jurisprudence, 51 Harv. L. Rev. 444, 464–466; Jones, Modern Discussions of the Aims and Methods of Legal Science, 47 L. Q. Rev. 62, 67–73; Gurvitch, Le temps présent et l'idée du droit social, 216–227; Colmo, La tecnica juridica (1916); Dabin, La philosophie de l'ordre juridique positif (1929) 254–397.

Compare Cathrein, Recht, Naturrecht und positives Recht (1901).

(c) Positivist-Sociological.

As to the sociological basis see Durkheim, De la division de travail social (1896, 5 ed. transl. by Simpson as The Division of Labor in Society, 1933; review by Stone, 47 Harv. L. Rev. 1448).

Duguit, L'état, le droit objectif, et la loi positive (1901).

——, Le droit social, le droit individuel et la transformation de l'état (2 ed. 1911).

——, Les transformations générales du droit privé (1912).

Translated in 11 Continental Legal History Series, Progress of Continental Law in the Nineteenth Century, chap. 3.

Duguit, Les transformations du droit public (1913, transl. by Laski as Law in the Modern State).

——, Law and the State (transl. by De Sloovère, 1917).

——, Leçons de droit public général (1926).

See Leroy, La loi (1908). For appreciations and critiques of Duguit see Pound, Fifty Years of Jurisprudence, 51 Harv. L. Rev. 444, 466–471 and full bibliography on pp. 466–467, n. 69; Bonnard, Léon Duguit, 3 Revue internationale de la théorie du droit, 58–70 — complete bibliography; Gurvitch, Sociology of Law, 132–134.

V. THE ECONOMIC INTERPRETATION

Dicey, Lectures on the Relation between Law and Public Opinion in England in the Nineteenth Century (1905, 2 ed. 1914).

Note especially the preface.

Centralization and Law (1906).

Five lectures at Boston University Law School, with an introduction by M. M. Bigelow. Lect. I, Nature of Law, by Brooks Adams, and lect. II, Law under Inequality: Monopoly, by Brooks Adams, are important for our purpose.

Adams, The Modern Conception of Animus (1907) 19 Green Bag, 12.

Leist, Privatrecht und Kapitalismus im neunzehnten Jahrhundert (1911).

Croce, Riduzione della filosofia del diritto alla filosofia dell' economia (1907).

On the whole subject see Loria, Le basi economiche della costituzione sociale (1902, transl. by Keasbey as The Economic Foundations of Society, 1907); Pound, Interpretations of Legal History, lect. 5; id. The Economic Interpretation and the Law of Torts, 53 Harv. L. Rev. 365; Bohlen, Studies in the Law of Torts, 344, 368–377; id. Old Phrases and New Facts, 83 U. Pa. L. Rev. 305, 306–307; Albertsworth, Cases on Industrial Law, 1–5; Beard, An Economic Interpretation of the Constitution of the United States, 14–18, 156 ff.

VI. SOCIALIST

Menger, Das bürgerliche Recht und die besitzlosen Volksklassen (5 ed. 1927).

First published in 1889.

Menger, Ueber die sozialen Aufgaben des Rechts (3 ed. 1910).

First published in 1895.

Picard, Le droit pur (1899).

Reprinted 1908, 1916, 1920.

Picard, Les grandes fresques du droit (1919).

Panunzio, Il socialismo giuridico (2 ed. 1911).

Barasch, Le socialisme juridique (1923).

Contains a full bibliography.

Lévy, La vision socialiste du droit (1926).

——, Les fondaments de droit (1929).

For critique of Lévy see Gurvitch, Expérience juridique et la philosophie pluraliste du droit, 170–200; Gurvitch, Sociology of Law, 134–139.

Mention may be made also of Duchesne, La conception du droit et les idées nouvelles (1902); Fournière, L'individu, l'association, et l'état (1907); Platon,

Pour le droit naturel (1911); Salvioli, I difetti sociali delle leggi vigenti di fronte al proletario e il diritto nuovo (2 ed. 1906); id. Filosofia del diritto (1905).

See also Rossi, Observations sur le droit civil français (1840) XI Revue de Législation et de Jurisprudence, 1; Courey, Le droit et les ouvriers (1886); Glasson, Le code civil et la question ouvrière (1886).

Paschukanis, Allgemeine Rechtslehre und Marximus (transl. from 3 Russian ed. 1929).

See Pound, Fifty Years of Jurisprudence, 51 Harv. L. Rev. 777, 779–782; Dobrin, Soviet Jurisprudence and Socialism, 52 L. Q. Rev. 402; Gsovski, The Soviet Concept of Law, 7 Fordham L. Rev. 1.

VII. REALIST

Lundstedt, Superstition or Rationality in Action for Peace (1925).

——, Die Unwissenschaftlichkeit der Rechtswissenschaft (1932–1936).

See also Lundstedt, The General Principles of Civil Liability in Different Legal Systems (1934), 2^II Acta Academiae Universalis Jurisprudentiae Comparativae, 367.

Llewellyn, The Bramble Bush (1930).

Frank, Law and the Modern Mind (1931).

Arnold, The Symbols of Government (1935).

Robinson, Law and the Lawyers (1935).

Rodell, Woe Unto You Lawyers! (1939).

Garlan, Legal Realism and Justice (1941).

Seagle, The Quest for Law (1941).

Historical-realist, critical of philosophical jurisprudence and of skeptical realism.

For bibliography of different forms of juristic realism see Pound, Fifty Years of Jurisprudence, 51 Harv. L. Rev. 777, 779–799. See also Pound, The Call for a Realist Jurisprudence, 44 Harv. L. Rev. 697; Llewellyn, Some Realism About Realism, 44 Harv. L. Rev. 1222; Fuller, American Legal Realism, 82 U. Pa. L. Rev. 429; Kantorowicz, Some Rationalism About Realism, 43 Yale L. J. 1240; Llewellyn, A Realistic Jurisprudence — The Next Step, 30 Columbia L. Rev. 431; Pound, Contemporary Juristic Theory (1940); Fuller, The Law in Quest of Itself, 52–65.

VIII. COMPARATIVE

See also *post* 9 (2).

Meili, Institutionen der vergleichenden Rechtswissenschaft (1898).

Lambert, La fonction du droit civil comparé (1903).

——, L'enseignement du droit comparé (1919).

——, L'institut de droit comparé: son programme, ses méthodes d'enseignement (1921).

Buckland and McNair, Roman Law and Common Law: A Comparison in Outline (1936).

Introduction à l'étude du droit comparé: Recueil d'études en l'honneur d'Edouard Lambert (5 pts. in 3 vols. 1938).

In the first part there is a complete bibliography.

Roguin, Traité de droit civil comparé: Successions (5 vols. 1908-1912) is the best example of a comparative method applied to a large field of law and carried out with respect to Roman law, the modern codes, and English Law. In the studies publishing under the auspices of Professor Lambert, proceeding from the Institut de droit comparé of the University of Lyon (Bibliothèque de l'institut de droit comparé de Lyon) particular questions have been treated by comparison of French law and Anglo-American law.

See Del Vecchio, Sull' idea di una scienza del diritto universale comparato (1909) transl. in Kocourek and Wigmore, Primitive and Ancient Legal Institutions, 2 Evolution of Law Series, 61-70 (abridged) — French transl. by Francez as L'idée de droit universel comparé (1910), Spanish transl. by Castaño (1911), German transl. by Hellwig (1914); Kohler, Die Entwickelung im Recht (1887) XIV Grünhut's Zeitschrift für das privat- und öffentliche Recht der Gegenwart, 410, transl. as Evolution of Law in Kocourek and Wigmore, Primitive and Ancient Legal Institutions, 3-9; Pineles, Questions de droit romain, étudiées d'après la nouvelle méthode historique du droit comparé (transl. by Herzen, 1911); Saleilles, La fonction juridique du droit comparé (1909) Festgabe für Kohler, 164; Wenger, Römisches Recht und Rechtsphilosophie (1921) XIV Archiv für Rechts- und Wirthschaftsphilosophie, 1, 106.

Reference may be made to: Bulletin de la société de législation comparée (1869–); Zeitschrift für vergleichende Rechtswissenschaft (1878–); Jahrbuch der internationalen Vereinigung für vergleichende Rechtswissenschaft (1895-1914); Journal of the Society of Comparative Legislation (1896-1897); Journal of the Society of Comparative Legislation, New Series (1900–); Blätter für vergleichende Rechtswissenschaft (1905–); Revue de l'institut de droit comparé (1908-1914, vols. 1-7) continued as Bulletin trimestriel de l'institut belge de droit comparé (1922-1924, vols. 8-10) now Revue trimestriel de l'institut belge de droit comparé (1925– , vol. 11–). Compare Comparative Law Bureau of the American Bar Assn. (1907-1919) now the Section of Comparative Law. See also Acta Academiae Universalis Jurisprudentiae Comparativae (1927–); Galgano (editor) Annuario di diritto comparato e di studi legislativi (1928–).

Reference may be made also to Rechtvergleichendes Handwörterbuch des Zivil- und Handelsrecht der Zu- und Auslände (5 vols. 1927).

IX. SOCIOLOGICAL

1. *Mechanical and positivist.*

Spencer, Justice (1891).

See also Albuquerque, O direito e la sociologia (1906); Anzilotti, La filosofia del diritto e la sociologia (1907); Brugi, Introduzione enciclopedica alle scienze giuridiche e sociale (4 ed. 1907); Cosentini, Filosofia del diritto e sociologia (1905); id. Criticismo e positivismo nella filosofia del diritto (1912); Daguanno, La genesi e l'evoluzione del diritto civile (1890); Eleutheropoulos, Rechtsphilosophie, Sociologie und Politik (1908); Fragapane, Obbietto e limiti della filosofia del diritto (1897); Levi, Il diritto naturale nella filosofia di R. Ardigo (1904); Nardi Greco, Sociologia giuridica (1907); Porchat, Sociologia e direito (1902);

Ratto, Sociologia e filosofia del diritto (1894); Vadale Papale, La filosofia del diritto a base sociologica (1885); Vander Eycken, Méthode positive de l'interprétation juridique (1907).

Rueff, Des sciences physiques aux sciences morales (1922, transl. by Green as From the Physical to the Social Sciences, 1929).

2. *Biological and ethnological.*

Post, Der Ursprung des Rechts (1876).

Post, Bausteine für einen allgemeinen Rechtswissenschaft (1880).

——, Die Grundlagen des Rechts und die Grundzüge seiner Entwickelungsgeschichte (1884).

——, Grundriss der ethnologischen Jurisprudenz (2 vols. 1894–1895).

Kuhlenbeck, Natürliche Grundlagen des Rechts (1905).

A discussion of fundamental problems of jurisprudence from the Darwinian standpoint.

Richard, L'origine de l'idée de droit (1892).

Vaccaro, Les bases sociologiques de droit et de l'état (1898).

A translation of Le basi del diritto e dello stato (1893). A theory of law as the outcome of class struggles.

Mazzarella, Elementi irreduttibili dei sistemi giuridici (2 vols. 1918–1920).

See also Post, Ueber die Aufgaben einer allgemeinen Rechtswissenschaft (1891); Mazzarella, Les types sociaux et le droit (1908); Neukamp, Entwickelungsgeschichte des Rechts (1895); Seitz, Biologie des geschichtlich positiven Rechtes (1906–1910); San Gupta, The Evolution of Law (1925); Adam, Practical Ethnology in Modern Jurisprudence and Legislation, 9 Tulane L. Rev. 232.

For critiques see Tanon, L'évolution de droit et la conscience sociale (3 ed. 1911); Tourtoulon, Principes philosophiques de l'histoire du droit (1908–1920); Charmont, La renaissance du droit naturel (1910).

3. *Psychological.*

Tarde, Les transformations du droit (6 ed. 1909).

First published in 1894.

Vanni, Lezioni di filosofia del diritto (4 ed. 1920).

First published in 1901–1902.

See also Bonucci, L'orientazione psicologica dell' etica e della filosofia del diritto (1907); Bozi, Die Weltanschauung der Jurisprudenz (1907, 2 ed. 1911); id. Die Schule der Jurisprudenz (1910); id. Einführung in das lebende Recht (1912–1914); Cruet, La vie du droit et l'impuissance des lois (1908); de la Grasserie, Principes sociologiques du droit civil (1906); Jellinek, Die sozialethische Bedeutung von Recht, Unrecht und Strafe (1878, 2 ed. 1908); Lagorgette, Le fondement du droit (1907); Miceli, Le fonti del diritto dal punto di vista psichico-sociale (1905); id. Lezioni di filosofia del diritto (1908); Stark, Die Analyse des Rechts (1916).

For a history and critique of sociological ethics down to this point, see Cohn, Ethik und Soziologie (1916). As to social psychology see Geck, Sozialpsychologie in Deutschland (1929) XXII Archiv für Rechts- und Wirthschaftsphilosophie, 544, with full bibliography of works and papers in German till 1929, 606–615.

4. *Psychological intuitionist.*

Petrazycki, Methodologie der Theorien des Rechts und der Moral (1933) in Opera Academiae Universalis Jurisprudentiae Comparativae, Series 2, Studia, fasc. 2.

——, Ueber die Motive des Handelns und über das Wesen der Moral und des Rechts (transl. from Russian by Balson, 1907).

For bibliography see Pound, Fifty Years of Jurisprudence, 51 Harv. L. Rev. 777, 809, n. 104, n. 105.

5. *Experimental positivist.*

Vacca, Il diritto sperimentale (1923).

See Tourtoulon, Principes philosophiques de l'histoire du droit, 491–513 (English transl. Philosophy in the Development of Law, 416–441); Wigmore, Problems of Law, 48–61; Beutel, Some Implications of Experimental Jurisprudence, 41 Harv. L. Rev. 169.

6. *The stage of unification.*

On this stage in sociology see Durkheim, Les règles de la méthode sociologique (6 ed. 1912).

Holmes, The Path of the Law (1897) 10 Harv. L. Rev. 467.

Reprinted in Holmes, Collected Papers, 167–202.

——, Law in Science and Science in Law, 12 Harv. L. Rev. 443.

Reprinted in Holmes, Collected Papers, 210–243.

Ehrlich, Soziologie und Jurisprudenz (1903).

Wurzel, Das juristische Denken (1904) 98–102.

Transl. in The Science of Legal Method, 9 Modern Legal Philosophy Series, 421–428.

Gnaeus Flavius (Kantorowicz), Der Kampf um die Rechtswissenschaft (1906).

Brugeilles, Le droit et la sociologie (1910).

Kantorowicz, Rechtswissenschaft und Soziologie (1911).

Rolin, Prolégomènes à la science du droit (1911).

Kornfeld, Soziale Machtverhältnisse: Grundzüge einer allgemeinen Lehre vom positiven Rechte auf soziologischer Grundlage (1911).

Ehrlich, Erforschung des lebenden Rechts (1911) in XXXV Schmoller's Jahrbuch für Gesetzgebung, 129.

——, Grundlegung der Soziologie des Rechts (1913, 2 ed. 1929, transl. by Moll as Fundamental Principles of the Sociology of Law, 1936).

See critique by Vinogradoff, The Crisis of Modern Jurisprudence, 29 Yale L. J. 312; and reviews of the English version by Simpson, 51 Harv. L. Rev. 190 (1937), by Timasheff, 2 Am. Sociological Rev. 120 (1937) and by Rheinstein, 48

Internat. Journ. of Ethics, 232 (1937). Also critique by Gurvitch, Sociology of Law, 148–156; appreciation by Pound, Fifty Years of Jurisprudence, 51 Harv. L. Rev. 777, 805–806.

Ehrlich, Das lebende Recht der Völker von Bukowina (1913).

Page, Professor Ehrlich's Czernowitz Seminar of Living Law (1914) Proc. 14th Annual Meeting of Assn. of Am. Law Schools, 46.

Cosentini, Filosofia del diritto (1914).

Kjellén, Der Staat als Lebensform (1917).

Ehrlich, Die juristische Logik (1918).

Kornfeld, Allgemeine Rechtslehre und Jurisprudenz (1920).

Cardozo, The Nature of the Judicial Process (1921).

——, The Growth of the Law (1924).

——, Paradoxes of Legal Science (1928).

Queiros Lima, Principios de sociologia juridica (2 ed. 1931).

Pontes Miranda, Systema de sciencia positiva do direito (1932).

Cornil, Le droit privé: Essai de sociologie juridique simplifée (1924).

I Jerusalem, Soziologie des Rechts, Gesetzmässigkeit und Kollektivität (1925).

Burckhardt, Methode und System des Rechts (1936).

Sauer, Rechts und Staatsphilosophie (1936).

Bodenheimer, Jurisprudence (1940).

Cairns, The Theory of Legal Science (1941).
 Behaviorist sociological.

Niemeyer, Law Without Force (1941).
 Functionalist sociological.

Vale, Some Legal Foundations of Society (3 vols. 1941).
 Psychological sociological.
 See also Bunge, El derecho (5 ed. 1920); Cosentini, La réforme de la législation civile (1913, revised and augmented transl. of La riforma della legislazione civile, 1911); Kelsen, Ueber Grenzen zwischen juristischer und soziologischer Methode (1911); Letelier, Jénesis del derecho (1919); Levi, La société et l'ordre juridique (1911); id. Contributi ad una teoria filosofica dell' ordine giuridico (1914); Spiegel, Gesetz und Recht (1913); Ehrlich, The Sociology of Law, 36 Harv. L. Rev. 129 (La sociologia del diritto, II Rivista internazionale di filosofia del diritto, 111); Burckhardt, Die organisation der Rechtsgemeinschaft (1927); Fehr, Recht und Wirklichkeit (1927); id. Das Kommende Recht (1933); Legaz de Lecambra, Filosofia realista y derecho natural (1928); Du Pasquier, Modernisme judiciaire et jurisprudence Suisse (1929); id. Quelques réflexions sur la notion du droit (1933); Wurzel, Die sozialdynamik des Rechtes (1929); Schindler, Verfassungsrecht und soziale Struktur (1932); Gurvitch, L'idée du droit social (1932); id. L'expérience juridique et la philosophie pluraliste du droit (1935); Richard, La philosophie du droit et la sociologie en Angleterre (1933) Archives de philosophie du droit et de sociologie juridique, 377.

7. The methodological stage: sociology of law.

Weber, Rechtssoziologie in Wirthschaft und Gesellschaft (2 ed. in 2 vols. 1925, pt. II, chap. 7).

1 ed. 1922.

Horváth, Rechtssoziologie (1934).

See review by Wilson (1936) 52 L. Q. Rev. 138; Pound, Fifty Years of Jurisprudence, 51 Harv. L. Rev. 777, 806–807.

Timasheff, Introduction to the Sociology of Law (1939).

Sauer, Juristische Methodenlehre (1940).

Gurvitch, Sociology of Law (1942).

Supersedes the author's Éléments de sociologie du droit (1939).

Llewellyn and Hoebel, The Cheyenne Way: Conflict and Case Law in Primitive Jurisprudence (1941).

See also Llewellyn, On Reading and Using the New Jurisprudence, 40 Columbia L. Rev. 581; id. The Normative, the Legal, and the Law Jobs: The Problem of Juristic Method, 49 Yale L. J. 1355. See appreciation by Gurvitch in Sociology of Law, 178–183.

8. Neo-scholastic sociological jurisprudence.

Hauriou, La théorie de l'institution et de la fondation, in La cité moderne et les transformations du droit (1925).

Renard, La théorie de l'institution (1930).

See the papers in (1931) Archives de philosophie du droit et de sociologie juridique, especially Delos, La théorie de l'institution, 97–153, and Gurvitch, Les idées-maîtresses de Maurice Hauriou; Gurvitch, Sociology of Law, 139–147; Pound, Fifty Years of Jurisprudence, 51 Harv. L. Rev. 777, 807–809; Jennings, The Institutional Theory in Modern Theories of Law, 68–85.

Reference should be made also to Gil Robles, Ensayo de metodología jurídica (1893); Izquierdo, El derecho justo de Stammler y la ley justa de Santo Tomás (1926) and recent Spanish writings referred to in Recaséns Siches, Estudios de filosofía del derecho (1936) 489–492.

X. ENCYCLOPAEDIAS

Holtzendorff, Enzyklopädie der Rechtswissenschaft, systematisches Teil (7 ed. 4 vols. 1913–1915).

Birkmeyer, Encyklopädie der Rechtswissenschaft (1901).

Kohlrausch und Kaskel, Enzyklopädie der Rechts- und Staatswissenschaft, Abtheilung Rechtswissenschaft (1922–1937) appearing in parts, 36 parts thus far published.

Somló und Elster, Handwörterbuch der Rechtswissenschaft (6 vols. and 2 supplementary vols. 1926–1937 — the last vol., VIII, by Volkmar, Elster, and Küchenhoff).

XI. COLLECTIONS OF MATERIALS FOR STUDENTS

Keener, Selections on the Elements of Jurisprudence (1896).
  Chiefly analytical.

Hall, Readings in Jurisprudence (1938).

XII. MATERIALS FOR ANALYTICAL JURISPRUDENCE

The materials for analytical jurisprudence are drawn from the two developed systems of law:

A. The Roman or Civil law, beginning as the law of the city of Rome, became the law of the Roman empire and thus of the ancient world, and eventually, by absorption or reception from the twelfth to the eighteenth century, the law of modern Continental Europe. It is now the foundation or a principal ingredient of the law in Continental Europe (including Turkey), Scotland, Egypt, Central and South America, Quebec and Louisiana, and all French, Dutch, Spanish, or Portuguese colonies or countries settled by those peoples.

1. *Roman law.*

The authoritative form of the Roman law for the modern world is the *Corpus Juris Civilis*, or compilation of Roman law by the Emperor Justinian.

Corpus Juris Civilis (ed. by Mommsen, Krueger, and Schoell, vol. 1, Institutes by Krueger, Digest by Mommsen, revised by Krueger, 14 ed. 1922, vol. 2, Code by Krueger, 6 ed. 1895, vol. 3, Novels by Schoell, 1895).

The sources prior to Justinian may be found in convenient form in:
Girard, Textes du droit Romain (5 ed. 1923).

  This is the best edition of the pre-Justinian sources for students.

Bruns, Fontes iuris romani antiqui (7 ed. by Gradenwitz 1912).

  Covers the sources down to Justinian except the jurists.

Krueger, Mommsen, Studemund, Collectio librorum iuris anteiustiniani (3 vols. 1878–1905).

  A collection of the juristic remains before Justinian and of the remains of the compilations of legislation before the Theodosian Code.

Riccobono, Baviera et Ferrini, Fontes iuris romani anteiustiniani (1918).

  Covers the same ground as Girard's Textes.

There are good English translations of the Digest of Justinian (in part), the Institutes of Justinian, and the Institutes or Commentaries of Gaius:
Monro, The Digest of Justinian (2 vols. 1904–1909).

  This translation extends to book XV, title 4. Monro has published separate translations of other parts as follows: Book XVII, title 1, on mandate, XVII, title 2, on partnership, XIX, title 2, on letting and hiring, XLI, titles 1 and 2, on acquiring property and on acquiring and losing possession, XLVII, title 2, on theft (conversion of property).

Other translations of parts are: Book IX, title 2, on the Aquilian law, and XXIV, title 1, on gifts between husband and wife, by Thayer; XLI, titles 1 and 2 by de Zulueta (recommended in preference to Monro); XLVI, titles 1 and 2, on sureties and givers of mandates and on novations and delegations, by Robinson; XLVII, title 2, on theft, by Jolowicz.

Moyle, English translation of the Institutes of Justinian (5 ed. 1913).

Abdy and Walker, The Institutes of Justinian (transl. with notes, 1876).

Poste, Gai institutionum iuris civilis commentarii quatuor, or Elements of Roman Law by Gaius, with a translation and commentary (4 ed. by Whittuck 1904).

Muirhead, Institutes of Gaius and the Rules of Ulpian (with transl. and notes, 3 ed. 1904).

Abdy and Walker, The Commentaries of Gaius (transl. with notes new ed. 1880).

All editions and translations of Gaius before 1933 require to be supplemented by de Zulueta, Supplements to the Institutes of Gaius (1935).

Mention may be made also of Scott, The Civil Law (transl. of the remains of the XII Tables, Gaius, the Rules of Ulpian, the Opinions of Paul, the Institutes, Digest, Code, and Novels of Justinian, and the Constitutions of Leo, 17 vols. 1932). This work must be used with caution since the best texts were not used and at some points the translations are not reliable.

The following institutional books may be used:

Buckland, Manual of Roman Private Law (1925).

Sohm, Institutes of Roman Law (transl. by Ledlie 3 ed. 1905).

This is a translation of the 12 ed. 1905 of Sohm, Institutionen des römischen Rechts. The latter is now in its 17 ed. by Mitteis and Wenger, 1923.

Girard, Manuel élémentaire du droit romain (8 ed. by Senn 1929).

The best book for the student on all questions of the history of Roman legal precepts and doctrines.

Czyhlarz, Lehrbuch der Institutionen des römischen Rechts (18 ed. 1924).

A very useful book as an introduction to analytical jurisprudence by way of Roman law.

The most satisfactory treatise and work of reference for English-speaking students is Buckland, A Text-Book of Roman Law (1921, 2 ed. 1932).

2. *The civil law.*

For the modern Roman law (i.e. the Roman law of Justinian as systematized and interpreted for the legal purposes of western Europe from the twelfth to the nineteenth century) the best works of reference are:

Windscheid, Lehrbuch des Pandektenrechts (3 vols. 9 ed. by Kipp, 1906).

First ed. 1862–65. This book is of the first importance for the student of jurisprudence. It is the culmination of the analytical-historical systematic method of the nineteenth century.

Dernburg, System des römischen Rechts (2 vols. 8 ed. of Dernburg, Pandekten, 1911–1912).

Van Wetter, Pandectes (5 vols. 1909–1911).

Savigny, System des heutigen römischen Rechts (8 vols. 1840–1849).

Of the first importance. It has been a quarry for the systematic part of analytical jurisprudence.

Glück, Ausführliche Erläuterung der Pandekten (63 vols. 1790–1896, vols. 1–7 in 2 ed. 1797–1807 reprinted 1867).

Pothier, Oeuvres (ed. by Bugnet, 3 ed. 10 vol. and index 1890).

3. *Roman-Dutch law.*

Lee, Introduction to Roman-Dutch Law (2 ed. 1925, 3 ed. 1931).

Grotius, Jurisprudence of Holland (transl. by Lee, 1926).

Van der Linden, Institutes of the Laws of Holland (transl. by Juta, 5 ed. 1906).

Nathan, The Common Law of South Africa (4 vols. 1904–1907, vols. 1–2, 2 ed. 1913).

Maasdorp, Institutes of Cape Law (4 vols., vol. 1, 6 ed. 1938, vol. 2, 6 ed. 1936, vol. 3, 4 ed. 1932, vol. 4, 4 ed. 1932).

Pereira, The Laws of Ceylon (2 ed. 1913).

4. *Scots law.*

Bell, Principles of the Law of Scotland (10 ed. 1899).

Erskine, Principles of the Law of Scotland (21 ed. by Rankine 1911).

Gloag and Henderson, Introduction to the Law of Scotland (3 ed. 1939).

5. *Modern Greek law.*

As to the sources of law in modern Greece see I Theophanopoulos, Σύστημα ρωμαϊκοῦ δικαίου (1928) 4–6.

6. *The modern codes.*

ARGENTINA.

Argentine Civil Code (transl. by Joanini 1917).

Antokoletz, Código civil interpretado (2 vols. 1931).

Código civil de la República Argentina (new ed. 1931).

Código civil de la República Argentina y leyes complementarias (1930).

Bonet y Ramón, El anteproyecto de código civil Argentino (1933).

Gorostiaga, El código civil y su reforma ante el derecho civil comparado (1940).

Lacort, Proyecto de código civil Argentino; redactado por la commissión official (1938).

Llerena, Derecho civil: Concordancias y comentarios del código civil Argentino (3 ed. 10 vols. 1931).

Machado, Exposición y comentario del código civil Argentino (11 vols. 1922).

Ossorio, La reforma del código civil Argentino (1941).

Vélez Sarsfield, Código civil de la República Argentina con las notas de Vélez Sarsfield (new ed. 1939).

Iniguez, Comentarios al código civil, pt. I (1918).

Salvat, Tratado de derecho civil Argentino, Parte General (2 ed. 1922) Obligaciones (1923).

See Borchard, Guide to the Law and Legal Literature of Argentina, Brazil, and Chile (1917); Bunge, Historia del Derecho Argentino (2 vols. 1912–1913); Cabral-Texo, Historia del código civil Argentino (1919); id. Fuentes nacionales del código civil Argentino (1919); Martinez Paz, Dalmacio Vélez Sarsfield y el código civil Argentino (1916); Colmo, Tecnica legislativa del código civil Argentino (1917).

AUSTRIA.

Wolff, Grundriss des österreichischen allgemeinen bürgerlichen Rechtes (1923).

Krainz, System des österreichischen Privatrechts (5 ed. 1913–1917, 6 ed. 1920–1925 as Ehrenzweig, System des österreichischen allgemeinen Privatrechts, 2 vols. in 4 pts.).

Stubenrauch, Kommentar zum österreichischen allgemeinen bürgerlichen Gesetzbuch (2 vols. 8 ed. 1902–1903).

Krasnopolski, Lehrbuch des österreichischen Privatrechts (3 vols. not completed 1910–1914).

Festschrift zur Jahrhundertfeier des allgemeinen bürgerlichen Gesetzbuches (1911).

Gallaix, Remarks on the Revised Austrian Civil Code (1931).

Klang, Kommentar zum allgemeinen bürgerlichen Gesetzbuch (4 vols. in 6, 1930–1931).

There is a translation of the Austrian Civil Code by Winiwarter (1866).

BELGIUM.

Beltjens, Encyclopédie du droit Belge, code civil (6 vols. 3 ed. 1905–1907).

Servais et Mechelynck, Code Civil, précédé de la constitution Belge avec des notes de concordance utiles a l'interprétation des textes (1927).

See also Thiry, Cours de droit civil (4 vols. 1892–1893); Picard et Larcier, Bibliographie du droit Belge (1882–1890) continued as II Van Arenberg, Bibliographie générale et raisonnée du droit Belge (1913).

BOLIVIA.

Castillo, Código civil Boliviano, compilado con autorizacion del supremo gobierno (1939).

BRAZIL.

Civil Code of Brazil (transl. by Wheless 1920).

This translation must be used with caution.

Ferreira Coelho, Código civil do Estados Unidos do Brasil (20 vols. 1920–1930).

Bevilaqua, Código civil dos Estados Unidos de Brasil commentado (6 vols. 4 to 6 ed. 1937–1940).

Carvalho Santos, Código civil Brasileiro interpretado (25 vols. 1936–1938).

Goulé, Daguin et D'Ardenne de Tizac, Code civil des États-Unis du Brésil traduit et annoté (1928).

Heinsheimer, Brasilien Código civil, mit Übersetzung, Einleitung, und Anmerkungen (1928).

Lacerda, Código civil Brasileiro (15 ed. 1933).

See Borchard, Guide to the Law and Legal Literature of Argentina, Brazil, and Chile (1917); de la Grasserie, Lois civiles de Brésil (1897).

CHILE.

Otero Espinosa, Concordancias y jurisprudencia del código civil Chileno (6 vols. 1926–1930).

Barros Errázuriz, Curso de derecho civil (6 vols. 1907–1918).

I Claro Solas, Elementos de derecho civil (1912).

Claro Solar, Explicaciones de derecho civil Chileno y comparado (14 vols. 1898–1941).

de la Grasserie, Code civil Chilien (1897).

See Borchard, Guide to the Law and Legal Literature of Argentina, Brazil, and Chile (1917); Barriga Errazuriz, Observations critiques sur le code civil Chilien, titre préliminaire, liv. I: des personnes (1930).

CHINA.

Boulais, Manuel du code Chinois (1924).

Chu, Commentaries on the Chinese Civil Code, bk. I, General Principles (1935).

Ho, Code civil de la république de Chine, books I–III in one vol. (1930), books IV–V in one vol. (1931).

Hsia, Chow, and Chang, The Civil Code of the Republic of China, books I–III (1930).

See Escarra, Sources du droit positif actuel de la Chine in Balogh, Fontes Iuris Vigentis, I, i, 53.

COLOMBIA.

Rodriguez Piñeres, Código civil Colombiano y leyes que lo adicionan y reforman (11 ed. 1940).

Ministerio de Gobierno, Comisión de reforma del código civil: Proyectos de ley, exposiciones de motivos, actas correspondientes, 1939–1940 (1941).

Anzola, Lecciones elementales de derecho civil Colombiano (3 vols. 1918).

Mariño Pinto, Manual de derecho civil Colombiano (1918).

Rodriguez Piñeres, Curso elemental de derecho civil Colombiano (4 vols. 1919–1921).

Velez, Estudio sobre el derecho civil Colombiano (9 vols. 2 ed. 1926).

COSTA RICA.

Código civil (1916).

CUBA.

Translation of the Civil Code in Force in Cuba, Porto Rico and the Philippines (U. S. Government Publication, 1899).

Núñez y Núñez, Código civil concordado (10 vols. 1934–1936 with supplement 2 vols. 1938–1940).

CZECHOSLOVAKIA.

Mayr, Das allgemeine bürgerliche Gesetzbuch nach dem Stande der Gesetzgebung bis zum 15 Februar. 1931 bearbeitet (1931).

Melzer, Das allgemeine bürgerliche Gesetzbuch für die Czechoslovakische Republik samt den einschlägigen gesetzen und verordnungen mit erläuterungen aus der oberstgerichtlichen Rechtsprechung (1928).

DOMINICAN REPUBLIC.

Código civil de la Republica Dominicana (edición autorizada 1930).

ECUADOR.

Código civil de la Republica del Ecuador, edición hecta por la Academia de Abogados de Quito (1930).

EGYPT.

Bestawros, Code civil Égyptien mixte annoté (2 vols. 1929–1931).

Walton, The Egyptian Law of Obligations (3 vols. 2 ed. 1923).

Aziz, Concordance des codes Égyptiens avec le code Napoléon, code civil (2 vols. 1886–1889).

Grandmoulin, Traité élémentaire de droit civil égyptien indigène et mixte (2 vols. 1912).

See also Walton, Egyptian Law: Sources and Judicial Organisation in Balogh, Fontes Iuris Vigentis, I, i, 11.

FRANCE.

(a) The Civil Code.

Dalloz, Code civil annoté (4 vols. in 5, 1900–1907, with supplement 1919).

Sirey, Code civil annoté (3 ed. 1911–1920).

Fuzier-Hermann, Code civil annoté (new ed. in 4 vols. 1935–1938).

Bourdeaux, Code civil annoté d'après la doctrine et la jurisprudence (29 ed. 1928–1929).

Blackwood Wright, The French Civil Code (transl. 1908).

Other translations are Barrett (1811); A Barrister of the Inner Temple (1824, reprinted 1827 and 1841); Cachard (1895 revised ed. 1930). The latter must be used with caution.

See also Amirian, Dans quelle mesure le droit civil iranien s'est-il inspiré du code civil français? (1937); Gaudemet, L'interprétation du code civil en France depuis 1804 (1935); A. de Saint-Joseph, Concordance entre les codes civiles étrangers et le code Napoléon (2 ed. 1856); Livre centenaire du code civil français (1904).

(b) Institutional Books.

Capitant, Introduction à l'étude du droit civil (4 ed. 1923).

Planiol, Traité élémentaire de droit civil (3 vols. ed. by Ripert, vol. 1, 12 ed. 1932, vols. 2–3, 11 ed. 1928–1932).

A book of great value to the student of jurisprudence because of its keen analyses of dogmatic problems.

Baudry-Lacantinerie, Précis de droit civil (3 vols. 13 ed. 1922).

Colin et Capitant, Cours élémentaire de droit civil français (3 vols. 5 ed. 1929).

Bonnecase, Précis de droit civil (3 vols. 1934–1935).

Josserand, Cours de droit civil positif français (3 vols. 2 ed. 1933).

(c) Works of Reference.

Baudry-Lacantinerie, Traité de droit civil (26 vols. 2 ed. 1899–1905).

Two volumes of a supplement by Bonnecase have appeared 1921–1923.

Planiol et Ripert, Traité pratique de droit civil français (14 vols. 1922–1934).

Laurent, Principes de droit civil français (33 vols. 3 ed. 1878 and supplement of 8 vols. 1898–1903).

Aubry et Rau, Droit civil français (12 vols. 5 ed. 1897–1922).

Huc, Commentaire du code civil (15 vols. 1892–1903).

See Borchard and Stumberg, Guide to the Law and Legal Literature of France (1925).

GERMANY.

(a) The Civil Code.

Wang, The German Civil Code (transl. 1907).

There is also a translation by Loewy (1909) which must be used with caution. There is an official French translation (1923) and an annotated French translation by Bufnoir and others (4 vols. 1904–1914).

Achilles, continued by Greiff, Bürgerliches Gesetzbuch (15 ed. 1939).

Planck, Bürgerliches Gesetzbuch (7 vols. 4 and 5 ed. 1913–1933).

Staudinger and others, Kommentar zum bürgerlichen Gesetzbuch (7 vols. in 14, vols. 1 and 3 in 10 ed. 1935–1939, the rest in 9 ed. 1925–1931).

Oertmann and others, Kommentar zum bürgerlichen Gesetzbuch, General Part by Oertmann (2 ed. 1908); Law of Debt-Relations by Oertmann (3 ed. 1910); Law of Things by Biermann (3 ed. 1914); Law of Succession by Leonhard (2 ed. 1912); Family Law by Opt and von Blume (2 ed. 1906); Introductory Statute by Niedner (2 ed. 1901).

Das bürgerliches Gesetzbuch erläutert von Bessau, Hallamik, Lobe, Michaelis, Oegg, Schliewen, und Seyffarth (5 vols. 8 ed. 1934–1935).

Lindemann und Soergel, Bürgerliches Gesetzbuch (2 vols. 4 ed. 1929).

　See de la Grasserie, Code civil Allemand (2 ed. 1901).

(b) Institutional Books.

Schuster, Principles of German Civil Law (1907).

Krückmann, Institutionen des bürgerlichen Gesetzbuches (2 vols. 4 ed. 1912).

Cosack, Lehrbuch des deutschen bürgenlichen Rechts (2 vols., vol. 1, 8 ed. 1927; vol. 2, 7 and 8 ed. 1924).

Enneccerus, Kipp, und Wolff, Lehrbuch des bürgerlichen Rechts (3 vols. in 5 pts. 1926–1932).

　Vol. 1, pt. 1, 18–20 ed. 1928; vol. 1, pt. 2, 19–21 ed. 1928; vol. 2, 13 ed. 1931; vol. 3, 9 ed. 1931; vol. 4, 7 ed. 1931.

　Haff, Institutionen des deutschen Privatrechts auf rechtsvergleichender und soziologischer Grundlage (2 vols. 1927–1934).

(c) Systematic Treatises.

Goldman, Das bürgerliche Gesetzbuch systematisch dargestellt (vol. 1, 2 ed. 1903; vols. 2–3, 1912–1921).

Crome, System des deutschen bürgerlichen Rechts (5 vols. 1900–1912).

Endemann, Lehrbuch des bürgerlichen Rechts (vol. 1, 9 ed. 1903; vol. 2, 9 ed. 1905–1908; vol. 3, 7 ed. 1900).

Dernburg, Das bürgerliche Recht des deutschen Reichs und Preussens (vol. 1, 3 ed. 1906; vols. 2–4, 4 ed. 1908–1915; vol. 5, 3 ed. 1915).

Kohler, Lehrbuch des bürgerlichen Rechts (3 vols. 1905–1915).

　Very useful to the student of jurisprudence because of the critical and philosophical discussions of dogmatic problems.

　For bibliography see Fuchs, Juristische Bücherkunde (3 ed. 1928); Library of Congress, Guide to the Law and Legal Literature of Germany (1924).

GUATEMALA.

Secretaria de gobernacion y justicia: Constitutión de la Republica de Guatemala; ley constitutión del poder judicial; código civil de la Republica de Guatemala (1933).

　See Cruz, Instituciones de derecho civil patrio (2 vols. 1882–1888).

HAITI.

Léger, Code civil d'Haiti annoté (1931).

HONDURAS.

Código civil (tipografia nacional, 1906).

Quesada, Comentarios al código civil Hondureño (2 vols. 1924–1928).

HUNGARY.

Almási, Ungarisches Privatrecht (2 vols. 1922–1923).

ITALY.

(a) The Civil Code.

Fadda (and others), Giurisprudenza sul codice civile (5 vols. 1909–1919).

There are French translations of the Italian civil code by Orsier (1866) and by Gandolfi (1868).

Commissione Reale per la Riforma dei Codici: Sottocommissione per il Codice Civile, Codice Civile: Libro primo; progetto definitivo e relazione del guardasigilli (1936).

Secondo libro; cose e diritti reali (1937).

Terzo libro; successioni e donazioni (1936).

See Pandofelli et al., Codice civile: Libro I illustrato con i lavori preparatori (1939).

(b) Institutional Books.

Chironi, Elementi di diritto civile (1914).

——, Istituzioni di diritto civile italiano (2 vols. 2 ed. 1912).

(c) Systematic Treatises.

Pacifici-Mazzoni, Diritto civile italiano (16 vols. 6, 7 and 8 ed. 1927–1930).

Fiore (and others), Diritto civile italiano (59 vols. 1905–1936).

In course of publication.

Bianchi, Corso di codice civile italiano (12 vols. 1888–1922).

Vol. 2, 2 ed. 1922; vol. 6, pt. 2, 2 ed. 1908; vol. 7, 2 ed. 1909; vol. 8, 2 ed. 1911.

JAPAN.

De Becker, Elements of Japanese Law (1916).

——, Annotated Civil Code of Japan (4 vols. 1909–1910).

——, Principles and Practice of the Civil Code of Japan (1921).

Hozumi, Lectures on the Japanese Civil Code (2 ed. 1912).

The Civil Code of Japan translated by the Codes Translation Committee. Tentative drafts 1–4: bk. I, General Provisions (1936); bk. II, Real Rights (1937); bk. III, Obligations (1938); bk. IV, Relatives (1939).

See Oda, Sources du droit positif actuel du Japon in Balogh, Fontes Iuris Vigentis, I, i, 125.

LOUISIANA.

Saunders, Revised Civil Code of Louisiana (2 ed. by Marr 1920).

Merrick, Revised Civil Code of Louisiana (3 ed. 1925).

Dart, Civil Code of Louisiana (Revision of 1870 annotated, 1932).

See Fenner, The Jurisprudence of the Supreme Court of Louisiana, 133 La. lxi-lxvi; Saunders, The Law of Louisiana, prefixed to his Revised Civil Code (1909).

MEXICO.

Código civil del distrito y territorios federales (edicion oficial 1928).

Civil Code of the Mexican Federal District and Territories (transl. by Taylor 1904).

Contains a glossary and an account of the civil codes of the several Mexican states.

Wheless, Compendium of the Laws of Mexico (2 vols. 1910).

Pallares, Código civil vigente en el distrito y territorios federales. Edicion anotada y concordada con la legislatura vigente y la nueva ley sobre relaciones familiares (3 ed. 1923).

Santamaria, Código civil para el distrito y territorios federales, expedido en 30 Agosto de 1928; exposición de motivos de la comisión autora del proyecto, anotacion, concordancia y breve comento (1936).

Andrade, Nuevo código civil para el distrito y territorios federales y leyes complementarias (5 ed. 1939).

Mateos Alarcon, Estudios sobre el código civil del distrito federal (6 vols. 1885–1900).

Kerr, Handbook of Mexican Law (1909).

Verdugo, Derecho civil Mexicano (5 vols. 1885–1890).

Covers the law of persons only.

de la Grasserie, Code civil Mexicain (1895).

See Cruzado, Bibliografia juridica Mexicana (1905).

MONACO.

Code civil de la principauté de Monaco (1913).

MONTENEGRO.

See Dareste et Rivière, Code général des biens pour la principauté de Monténégro de 1888 in Collection des principaux codes étrangers (1892); Todaro della Galia, La seconda edizione del codice generale dei beni del Montenegro (1901).

NETHERLANDS

Haanebrink, Code civil Néerlandais (1921).

Opzoomer, Het burgerlijk Wetboek (3 vols. 3 ed. 1911–1918).

Land, Verklaring van het burgerlijk Wetboek (6 vols., vol. 1, 2 ed. 1914; vol. 2, 2 ed. 1901; vol. 3, 2 ed. 1902; vol. 4, 2 ed. 1907; vol. 5, 2 ed. 1915–1932 [in parts]; vol. 6, 2 ed. 1933).

Diephuis, Het nederlandsch burgerlijk Regt (13 vols. 1885–1890, vols. 1–9 are 2 ed.).

Veegens, Schets van het nederlandsch burgerlijk Recht, continued by Oppenheimer (3 vols., vol. 1, 3 ed. 1923; vol. 2, 3 ed. 1925; vol. 3, 4 ed. 1934 by Polak).

Wijnveldt, Burgerlijk wetboek, rechtspraak, literatuur en korte aanteekeningen (4 ed. 1933).

See van der Heijden, Het national karakter van ons burgerlijk wetboek (1938).

NICARAGUA.

Código civil de la República de Nicaragua (2 vols. 3 edición oficial 1931–1933).

Selva, Instituciones de derecho civil nicaragüense (1883).

PALESTINE.

See Goadby, Palestinian Law, Sources and Judicial Organisation in Balogh, Fontes Iuris Vigentis, I, i, 39.

PANAMA.

Código civil (edición oficial 1917).

Correa Garcia, Código civil de la República de Panama, anotado, concordado, con la jurisprudencia de la corte suprema de justicia (1927).

The Civil Code of the Republic of Panama and Amendatory Laws Continued in Force in the Canal Zone (transl. by Joannini 1905).

PARAGUAY.

Código civil de la República Argentina vigente en la República del Paraguay (1897).

Zubizarreta, Elementos de derecho civil (2 vols. 1899–1900).

PERU.

Rodriguez Llerena, Código civil promulgado por decreto supremo de 30 de Agosto de 1936 en uso de la autorización contenida en la ley no. 1805 (edición oficial 1936).

Vidaurre, Proyecto del código peruana dividido en tres partes (1935–1936).

Calle, Código civil del Peru anotado con las modificaciones que contendra el proyecto de nuevo código que en breve presentara al poder ejecutivo la comisión reformada creada por supremo decreto de 28 de Agosto de 1922 (1928).

De la Lama, Código civil anotado y concordado (6 ed. 1928).

Leguía y Martinez, Nuevo diccionario de la legislacion peruana (2 vols. 1915–1916).

Aparicio y Gómez Sánchez, Código civil: concordancias (9 vols. 1936–1941, vol. 2 in 2 ed. 1941).

Ortiz de Zevallos, Tratado de derecho civil peruano (1906).

Samanamú, Instituciones de derecho civil peruano (2 vols. 2 ed. 1919).

de la Grasserie, Code civil péruvien (1896).

PHILIPPINES.

Kincaid y Aldeguer, Código civil Español, anotado y concordado con la legislación y jurisprudencia de las Islas Filipinas (2 vols. 1921).

Willard, Notes to the Spanish Civil Code Showing Changes Effected by American Legislation with Citation of Cases from Philippines Supreme Court (1904).

Gamboa, Introduction to Philippine Law (1939).

POLAND.

Koschembahr-Lyskowski, Code civil de la République de Pologne, livre I, dispositions générales, projet et exposé des motifs (approved French transl. 1928).

See Lubliner, Concordance entre le code civil de Pologne et le code civil français (1848).

PORTUGAL.

Laneyrie et Dubois, Code civil portugais (1896).

Reforma de código civil e seu comentario oficial; decreto no. 19:126 de 16 de Dezembro de 1930 (1931).

Loureiro e Almeida, Código civil nos tribunais; actualização e anotações (3 vols. 1922–1924).

Vaz Serra, Código civil português (4 ed. 1939).

QUEBEC.

Beauchamp, Civil Code Annotated (English and French) (2 vols. in 3, 1904–1905 with supplements 2 vols. 1924, 2 vols. 1931).

Mignault, Droit civil canadien (9 vols. 1895–1916).

Langelier, Cours de droit civil de la province de Quebec (6 vols. 1905–1911).

ROUMANIA.

Vasilescu, Codul civil român; dupa editia oficiala din 1865, cu toate Modificarile ulterioare (1938).

The civil code has not been translated. It may be found also in vol. 1 of Legi Uzuale (Codul general al Romaniei, 1926). See Alexandresco, Droit ancien et moderne de Roumanie (1897); La vie juridique des peuples (vol. 5, Roumania, 1933).

RUSSIA.

(a) The Old Régime.

Lehr, Éléments de droit civil russe (2 vols. 1877–1890).

Todaro della Galia, Istituzioni di diritto civile russo (1894).

Klibanski, Handbuch des gesamten russischen Zivilrechts (3 vols. 1911–1918).

(b) The Soviet Régime.

Le premier code des lois de la République Russe Socialiste Fédérative des Soviets (Petrograd, 1919).

Freund, Das Zivilrecht Sowjetrusslands (1924).

I Les codes de la Russie soviétique (1925). Code de la famille (transl. by Patoillet), code civil (transl. by Patoillet and Dufour).

Hazard, Soviet Law: An Introduction (1937) 36 Columbia L. Rev. 1236.

SALVADOR.

Palacios, Código civil de la República de el Salvador (4 ed. revised by Castro, 1904).

SERVIA.

The code of 1844 is translated in III A. de St.-Joseph, Concordance entre les codes étrangers et la code Napoléon (1856) 447. But there was a revision in 1879.

SPAIN.

Fisher, The Civil Code of Spain with Philippine References and Notes (4 ed. 1930).

The official translation, United States War Department, Translation of the Civil Code in force in Cuba, Porto Rico, and the Philippines (1899), must be used with caution.

Walton, The Civil Law in Spain and Spanish America (1900).

Contains a translation of the civil code.

Lehr, Éléments de droit civil espagnol (2 vols. 1880–1890).

Sanchez Roman, Estudios de derecho civil español (6 vols. and supplement 1889–1911).

Falcón, Exposición doctrinal del derecho civil español (4 vols. 6 ed. 1902).

Valverde, Tratado de derecho civil español (5 vols. 3 ed. 1925).

Clemente de Diego, Instituciones de derecho civil español (2 vols. 1929–1930).

Manresa y Navarro, Comentarios al código civil español (12 vols. 1–7 in 5 ed. 8–12 in 4 ed. 1931–1932).

The standard commentary and book of reference.

Mucius Scaevola, Código civil concordado y comentado (24 vols. and supplement of 2 vols.; vols. 1, 3, 7, in 3 ed., vol. 2·in 4 ed., vols. 8–9 in 2 ed., vol. 1 of supplement in 2 ed., 1892–1909).

Barrachina, Derecho foral español (1911–1912).

Castán y Tobeñas, Derecho español foral (1922).

See Palmer, Guide to the Law of Spain (1915); Library of Congress, Guide to the Law and Legal Literature of Spain (1913).

SWITZERLAND.

Williams, Swiss Civil Code, I, Sources of Law (1923) II, English Version (1925).

Shick, The Swiss Civil Code (transl. 1915).

Rossel et Mentha, Manuel du droit civil suisse (3 vols. 2 ed. 1922).

Egger (and others), Kommentar zum schweizerischen Zivilgesetzbuch (6 vols. 1909–1916) with Supplement, Die Kantonalen Einführungsgesetze und Verordnunge zum schweizerischen Zivilgesetzbuch (2 vols. 2 ed. 1928–1941).

There is a French translation of vol. 4, Wieland, Les droits réels dans le code civil suisse (2 vols. 1913–1914).

Gmür, Kommentar zum schweizerischen Zivilgesetzbuch (6 vols. 1910–1934).

Vols. 1, 2 (in part), 4 (in part) and 5 (in part) in 2 ed. 1917–1927.

Schneider und Fick, Das schweizerische Obligationenrecht (2 vols. 4 ed. 1915–1916).

There is a French translation, Commentaire du code fédérale des obligations (2 vols. 1915–1916).

TURKEY.

Grigsby, The Medjellè or Ottoman Civil Law (transl. into English, 1895).

Young, Corps de droit Ottoman (7 vols. 1905–1906).

Code civil Turc, précédé d'un historique de la refonte du code civil Turc et du statut familial, de l'exposé des motifs, et du rapport de la commission judiciaire (Constantinople, 1926).

URUGUAY.

Código civil (official ed. 1914).

Guillot, Comentarios del código civil (2 ed. in 5 vols. 1926–1928).

Nin y Silva, Código civil de la República Oriental de Uruguay anotado y concordado (new ed. 1925, with supplement, 1937).

VENEZUELA.

Código civil de los Estados Unidos de Venezuela (edición oficial 1940).

de la Grasserie, Code civil de Venezuela (1896).

Semojo, Instituciones de derecho civil Venezolano (4 vols. 1873).

Bastidas, Comentarios y reparos al proyecto de código civil (1939).

See also on the more important countries, La vie juridique des peuples: bibliothèque de droit contemporain, sous la direction de H. Lévy-Ullmann et B. Mirkine-Guetzévitch (7 vols. 1931–1939).

7. *Commercial law.*

(a) Commercial Codes (in translation).

Mayer, The French Code of Commerce (1887).

Schuster, The German Commercial Code (1911).

Espiritu, The Code of Commerce of Spain (1919).

Yang, The Commercial Code of Japan (1911).

De Becker, The Commercial Code of Japan (1927).

Codes Translation Committee, The League of Nations Assn. of Japan, The Commercial Code of Japan, Annotated (2 vols. 1931–1932).

Contains a valuable historical introduction. The translation without the introduction and annotations was published separately in 1932.

Cheng and Allman, The Modern Commercial Legislation of China (1926).

(b) Institutional Books.

Lyon-Caen et Renault, Manuel de droit commercial (14 ed. 1924).

Thaller, Traité élémentaire de droit commercial (2 vols. 8 ed. 1931).

Lacour et Bouteron, Précis de droit commercial (2 vols. 3 ed. 1925, with supplement to vols. 1 and 2, 1933).

Lacour, Précis de droit commercial (7 ed. 1938).

Cosack, Lehrbuch des Handelsrechts (12 ed. 1930).

Esquivel Obregón, Latin-American Commercial Law (1921).

Molengraaff, Nederlandsche Handelsrecht (2 vols. 6 ed. 1930–1933).

Soares da Cunha Rego, Direito commercial portuguez (1886).

See Goirand, French Commercial Law (2 ed. 1898).

(c) Books of Reference and Systematic Treatises.

Lyon-Caen et Renault, Traité de droit commercial (8 vols. 5 ed. 1921–1936).

Bédarride, Droit commercial (30 vols. 1871–1896).

Ehrenberg, Handbuch des gesamten Handelsrechts (8 vols. 1913–1929).

Vivante, Trattato di diritto commerciale (4 vols. 5 ed. 1922–1926).

Navarrini, Trattato teorico-prattico di diritto commerciale (6 vols. 1913–1926, vol. 1 in 2 ed. 1931).

Alvarez, Bonilla, y Miñana, Códigos de comercio españoles y extranjeros (6 vols. 1909–1914).

Estasén, Instituciones de derecho mercantil (7 vols. 1912–1928).

Rodríguez Altunaga, Derecho mercantil, estudio sobre el derecho mercantil vigente en Cuba, España, Perú, y El Salvador (1917).

Hagerup, Omriss av den Norske handelsrett (9 ed. 1935).

De Becker, Commentary on the Commercial Code of Japan (3 vols. 1913).

Commercial Laws of the World (24 vols. 1911–1914).

Vols. 1–6, South America; vols. 7–10, North and Central America; vols. 13–14, North and Northwest Europe; vols. 15–18, British Dominions and Protectorates; vols. 19–20, North and Northwest Europe; vols. 21–22, 24–25, 28, Central Europe; vol. 32, South Europe.

8. *Countries with indigenous law and Roman legal science.*

Broecker, Privatrecht der gouvernements Liv- Est- und Courland (1902).

de la Grasserie, Les Codes suedois (1895).

Winroth, Svenska Civilrätt (5 vols. 1898–1909).

Munch-Petersen, Main Features of Scandinavian Law (1927).

Lehr, Éléments de droit civil scandinave (Danemark, Norvège, Suède, avec la collaboration de H. Munch-Petersen, Kristen Johansson, et Elsa Eschelsson (1901).

Areschoug, Berg, og Krieger, Nordisk retsencyklopaedi (5 vols. in 10, 1878–1899).

Munch-Petersen, Den borgerlige ret i hovedtraek (9 ed. 1934).

——, Den danske retspleje (5 vols. 2 ed. 1923–1926).

Knoph, Oversikt over Norges rett (1934).

As to the codes of the Scandinavian countries see A. de St. Joseph, Concordance entre les codes civiles étrangers et le Code Napoléon, II, 134, III, 1, 494; Angelot, Sommaire des législation des états du nord, Danemarck, Norvège, Suède, Finlande, et Russie pour servir à l'étude de la législation comparée (1834); Faurholt and Federspiel, Recent Danish Legislation on the Relation of Husband and Wife (1927); Hurtigkarl, Den danske og Norske private rets første grunde (4 vols. 1813–1820).

B. The common law, Germanic in origin, was developed by the English courts from the thirteenth to the nineteenth century, and has spread over the world with the English people. It now prevails in England and Ireland, the United States, except Louisiana and Porto Rico, Canada, except Quebec, India, except Ceylon and except over Hindus and Mohammedans as to inheritance and family law, and the principal British dominions and colonies except South Africa.

It is assumed that the student has a dogmatic knowledge of Anglo-American law.

The following will be of use to the student of jurisprudence:

Blackstone, Commentaries on the Laws of England (4 vols. Lewis's ed. 1897).

First ed. 1765–1769.

Kent, Commentaries on American Law (4 vols. 12 ed. by Holmes, 1873).

Stephen, Commentaries on the Laws of England (4 vols. 19 ed. 1928, vol. 1 in 20 ed. 1938).

Odgers, The Common Law of England (2 vols. 3 ed. 1927).

Terry, Leading Principles of Anglo-American Law (1884).

Jenks, Digest of English Civil Law (5 books in 2 vols. 2 ed. 1921).

———, The Book of English Law (1932).

Holmes, The Common Law (1882).

Pound, The Spirit of the Common Law (1921).

The Future of the Common Law, Harvard Tercentenary Publications (1937).

See Pollock, The Lawyer as a Citizen of the World. 48 L. Q. Rev. 40.

The student of jurisprudence may also refer profitably to the restatement of the law now in progress under the auspices of the American Law Institute.

Account must be taken also of two other systems:

C. The Canon Law — the law of the church during the Middle Ages.
Corpus Juris Canonici (ed. by Friedberg, 3 vols. 1876–1882).

See also Codex iuris canonici (1918); Sohm, Kirchenrecht (1892); Hinschius, Kirchenrecht (6 vols. 1896–1897); De Angelis, Praelectiones iuris canonici (4 vols. 1877–1884); Haring, Grundzüge des katholischen Kirchenrechts (2 ed. 1916); Gonzales Tellez, Commentaria perpetua in singulos textus quinque librorum Decretalium Gregorii IX (4 vols. 1673, there are also ed. 1690, 1699, 1713).

On the sources of the canon law see Schulte, Geschichte der Quellen und Literatur des canonischen Rechts (3 vols. 1875–1880); Tardif, Histoire des sources du droit canonique (1887); Cicognani, Canon Law (transl. by O'Hara and Brennan 1934) 60–403.

D. International Law — a system of adjusting the relations of states with one another so as to meet the approval of the moral sentiment of the community of nations; in great part an application of the principles of private law to the relations of states.

(a) History.

Walker, History of the Law of Nations (1899).

Westlake, Chapters on the Principles of International Law (1894).

Nys, Les origines du droit international (1894).

(b) Treatises.

Wheaton, Elements of International Law (8 ed. by Dana 1866, new ed. by Wilson 1936).

Hall, Treatise on International Law (8 ed. by Higgins 1924).

Anzilotti, Cours de droit international (transl. by Gidel, vol. I, 1929).

This work is of special importance for juristic theory.

Oppenheim, International Law (2 vols. ed. by Lauterpacht, vol. 1 in 5 ed. 1937, vol. 2 in 6 ed. 1940).

Westlake, International Law (2 vols. 1910–1913).

Hyde, International Law (2 vols. 1922 — a second edition is soon to appear).

Brierly, The Law of Nations (2 ed. 1936).

Wilson, Handbook of International Law (3 ed. 1939).

Fauchille, Traité de droit international public (2 vols. in 4, 1921–1926).

Liszt, Das Völkerrecht (12 ed. 1925).

(c) Works of Reference.

Calvo, Le droit international théorique et pratique (6 vols. 5 ed. 1896).

Pradier-Foderé, Traité de droit international (8 vols. 1885–1906).

(d) Source Materials.

Moore, A Digest of International Law (8 vols. 1906).

——, History and Digest of International Arbitrations to which the United States has been a party (6 vols. 1898).

——, International Adjudications, Ancient and Modern: Ancient Series (2 vols. 1936) Modern Series (6 vols. 1929–1933).

Hackworth, Digest of International Law (2 vols. 1940–1941).

American Digest of Public International Law Cases (8 vols. 1919–1937).

Hudson, International Legislation (7 vols. 1931–1941).

Scott, Hague Court Reports (1916, second series 1932).

Hudson, World Court Reports (3 vols. 1934–1938).

(e) Bibliography.

The Hague: Peace Palace. Bibliothèque du Palais de la Paix: Catalogue (1916 with three supplements and four indexes 1916–1937).

XIII. MATERIALS FOR HISTORICAL JURISPRUDENCE

The materials for historical jurisprudence are drawn from:

A. The history of the developed systems of law, Roman and Germanic; B. The systems of law which obtained among peoples of some degree of civilization which did not attain to maturity because of the spread of the Roman law, or of the English law; C. The Hindu and the Mahommedan law, which have a limited application today in British India; D. "Adatrecht" (the native customary law of the Dutch East Indies); E. Customary law of Nepal; and F. The institutions of social control among primitive and uncivilized peoples.

For general reference:

Kocourek and Wigmore, Sources of Ancient and Primitive Law (in Evolution of Law Series, 1915).

——, Primitive and Ancient Legal Institutions (in Evolution of Law Series, 1915).

——, Formative Influences of Legal Development (in Evolution of Law Series, 1918).

Dareste, Études d'histoire du droit (3 vols., vol. 1, 2 ed. 1908; vol. 2, as

Nouvelles études d'histoire du droit, 1902; vol. 3, as Nouvelles études d'histoire du droit, 3 series, 1906).

Kohler und Wenger, Allgemeine Rechtsgeschichte, I, Orientalisches Recht und Recht der Griechen und Römer (1914).

Kohler, Shakespeare vor dem Forum der Jurisprudenz (1883, 2 ed. 1919).

Vinogradoff, Historical Jurisprudence, I, Tribal Law (1920).

——, Collected Papers (2 vols. 1928).

See Hartland, Primitive Law (1923); Wilutzky, Vorgeschichte des Rechts (3 vols. 1903); Diamond, Primitive Law (1935).

A. HISTORY OF THE DEVELOPED SYSTEMS OF LAW.

1. *The legal institutions of Indo-European peoples.*

Fustel de Coulanges, The Ancient City (transl. by Small 1874).

Translation of La cité antique (1864, now in 9 ed. 1920).

Hearn, The Aryan Household, an Introduction to Comparative Jurisprudence (1878).

Leist, Altarisches Jus Civile (2 vols. 1892–1896).

——, Altarisches Jus Gentium (1889).

I Vinogradoff, Historical Jurisprudence, pt. 3 (1920).

2. *History of Roman law.*

Jolowicz, Historical Introduction to the Study of Roman Law (1932 reprinted with corrections 1939).

Declareuil, Rome the Law-Giver (transl. by Parker 1926).

Jhering, Geist des römischen Rechts (3 vols. in 4, 1856–1865, 7 and 8 ed. 1906–1924, French transl. by Meulenaere, L'esprit du droit romain, 1875).

A book of the first importance for the student of jurisprudence.

See Kuhlenbeck, Entwicklungsgeschichte des römischen Rechts (2 vols. 1910–1913); Karlowa, Römische Rechtsgeschichte (2 vols. 1885–1901); Cuq, Les institutions juridiques des Romains (2 vols. 1902–1904, vol. 1 in 2 ed.); von Mayr, Römische Rechtsgeschichte (4 vols. 1912–1913); Bonfante, Storia di diritto romano (1900); Costa, Storia del diritto romano privato (1925); Girard, Histoire de l'organisation judiciaire des Romains (1901).

As to Byzantine law, see Freshfield, translations of A Manual of Later Roman Law, I, The Ecloga, II, The Ecloga ad Procheiron mutata (2 vols. 1926); id. A Revised Manual of Roman Law (transl. of the Ecloga privata aucta, 1927). See also Mortreuil, Histoire du droit byzantin (3 vols. 1843–1847).

3. *Germanic law.*

von Amira, Grundriss des germanischen Rechts (2 ed. 1901).

Heusler, Institutionen des deutschen Privatrechts (2 vols. 1885–1886).

Hübner, Grundzüge des deutschen Privatrechts (1908, transl. as A History of Germanic Private Law by Philbrick 1918).

For fuller expositions, reference may be made to Gierke, Deutsches Privatrecht

(2 vols. 1895–1905); Brunner, Deutsche Rechtsgeschichte (2 vols. 1892–1906, vol. 2 in 2 ed. by von Schwerin 1928); Maurer, Altnordische Rechtsgeschichte (5 vols. 1907–1910).

A table of the principal sources may be found in Jenks, Law and Politics in the Middle Ages, 319–345.

See also The Earliest Norwegian Laws, being the Gulathing Law and the Frostathing Law (transl. by Larson 1935); Fairbanks, The Old West Frisian Skeltana Riucht with an Introduction, Translation, and Notes (1939).

(a) The Anglo-Saxon Laws.

Liebermann, Gesetze der Angelsachsen (2 vols. 1903–1912).

Thorpe, Ancient Laws and Institutes of England (text and transl. 2 vols. 1840).

Attenborough, The Laws of the Earliest English Kings (text and transl. 1922).

Does not go beyond Aethelstan.

Reference may be made also to Essays in Anglo-Saxon Law (by Adams, Lodge, Young, and Laughlin 1876).

(b) The French Coutumes.

Beaune, Droit coutumier français (4 vols. 1880–1889).

There is a full bibliography in I Chénon, Histoire générale du droit français public et privé (1926) §§ 220–221.

4. *History of English and Anglo-American law.*

Holdsworth, History of English Law (12 vols. 3 ed. 1922–1938).

Pollock and Maitland, History of English Law Before the Time of Edward I (2 vols. 2 ed. 1898).

Select Essays in Anglo-American Legal History (3 vols. 1907–1909).

Ames, Lectures on Legal History (1913).

Jenks, Short History of English Law (4 ed. 1925).

Potter, An Historical Introduction to English Law (2 ed. 1932).

See Winfield, The Chief Sources of English Legal History (1925); Holdsworth, Sources and Literature of English Law (1925). Also the Publications of the Selden Society.

Plucknett, Concise History of the Common Law (3 ed. 1940).

Radin, Handbook of Anglo-American Legal History (1936).

Walsh, History of Anglo-American Law (2 ed. 1932).

Pound, The Formative Era of American Law (1938).

5. *History of the modern law of Continental Europe.*

(a) General.

A General Survey of Events, Sources, Persons, and Movements in Continental Legal History, I Continental Legal History Series (1912).

Progress of Continental Law in the Nineteenth Century, XI Continental Legal History Series (1918).

Conrat, Geschichte des römischen Rechts im früheren Mittelalter (1891).

Savigny, Geschichte des römischen Rechts im Mittelalter (7 vols. 2 ed. 1834).

Vol. I is translated by Cathcart (1829) from 1 ed. The whole is translated into French by Genoux, Histoire du droit romain au Moyen Âge (1839).

Vinogradoff, Roman Law in Medieval Europe (2 ed. 1929).

Munroe Smith, The Development of European Law (1928).

(b) Academic and Juristic Development of the Law.

Stintzing, Geschichte der deutschen Rechtswissenschaft (3 vols. the 3d by Landsberg, 1880–1883).

Portions are translated in I Continental Legal History Series, General Survey, pt. IV, chaps. 2, 3.

(c) Commercial Law.

Goldschmidt, Universalgeschichte des Handelsrechts in 1 Handbuch des Handelrechts (1891).

(d) French Law.

Chénon, Histoire générale du droit français public et privé (vols. 1–2, 1926–1929).

Declareuil, Histoire générale du droit français (1925).

Brissaud, History of French Private Law (transl. by Howell 1912) III Continental Legal History Series.

Translation of Brissaud, Manuel d'histoire du droit privé (1908) a second edition of the latter part of Brissaud, Cours d'histoire générale du droit français public et privé (2 vols. 1904).

See also Esmein, Cours élémentaire d'histoire du droit français (15 ed. 1925); Viollet, Histoire du droit civil français (3 ed. 1905).

For French-Canadian law see Lemieux, Les Origines du droit franco-canadien (1901).

(e) German Law.

Brunner, Grundzüge der deutschen Rechtsgeschichte (8 ed. 1930).

Parts of an older edition are translated in I Continental Legal History Series, pt. IV.

Schroeder, Lehrbuch der deutschen Rechtsgeschichte (7 ed. 1932 by Schroeder und Künssberg).

Parts of an older edition are translated in I Continental Legal History Series, pt. IV.

Huebner, A History of Germanic Private Law (transl. by Philbrick, 1918) IV Continental Legal History Series.

A translation of Hübner, Grundzüge des deutschen Privatrechts now in 4 ed. 1922.

(f) Italian Law.

Salvioli, Storia del diritto italiano (8 ed. 1921).

Pertile, Storia del diritto italiano (7 vols. in 9, 1892–1903).

See also Besta, Storia del diritto italiano (2 vols. 1912–1914); Calisse, Storia del diritto italiano (3 vols., vols. 1–2 in 2 ed. 1901–1903, transl. in I Continental Legal History Series, General Survey, pt. I, chaps. 1–2, and pt. II).

(g) Roman-Dutch Law.

See Wessels, History of the Roman-Dutch Law (1908).

(h) Scandinavian Law.

Dahl, Geschichte der dänischen Rechtswissenschaft in ihren Grundlagen (transl. by Haff and Henningsen 1940).

Jørgensen, Udsigt over den danske retshistorie (3 ed. 1926).

Kolderup-Rosenvinge, Grundrids af den danske retshistorie (2 vols. 3 ed. 1860 — the 1 ed. transl. by Homeyer as Grundriss der dänischen Rechtsgeschichte, 1825).

Matzen, Foreläsninger over den danske retshistorie (3 vols. 1893–1895).

Ficker, Über nähere Verwandschaft zwischen gothisch-spanischem und norwegisch-isländischem Recht (1887).

Hermannsson, The Ancient Laws of Norway and Iceland (1911).

Taranger, Udsigt over den norske retshistorie (1898).

As to Lapland see Taranger, Lappiske Retsstudier (1933).

(i) Scots Law.

Stair Society, An Introductory Survey of the Sources and Literature of Scots Law by various authors (1936) with separate index (1939).

The publications of the Stair Society of which six volumes have appeared thus far are making accessible the materials for a history of the law in Scotland.

(j) Spanish Law.

See I Continental Legal History Series, General Survey, 579–702, and the bibliography, 579; Palmer, Guide to the Law and Legal Literature of Spain (1915) 36–38; Annuario de historia del derecho español, vols. 1–12 (1924–1935).

(k) Portuguese Law.

See Codinho e Caeiro, Historia do direito portugues (2 ed. 1915).

(l) Hungarian Law.

See Timon, Ungarische Rechtsgeschichte (1904).

B. LAWS OF CIVILIZED PEOPLES WHICH HAVE NOT COME TO MATURITY

1. *Babylonian law.*

Harper, The Code of Hammurabi (1904).

Johns, Babylonian and Assyrian Laws, Contracts and Letters (1904).

Kohler und Peiser, Hammurabis Gesetz (5 vols. 1904–1911).

——, Aus dem babylonischen Rechtsleben (5 pts. 1890–1898).

Kohler und Ungnad, Assyrische Rechtsurkunden (1913).

——, Hundert ausgewählte Rechtsurkunden aus der Spätzeit des babylonischen Schrifttums (1911).

Edwards, The World's Earliest Laws (1934).

See Dareste, Code Babylonien du roi Hammurabi in Nouvelles études d'histoire du droit (1906) 3 series, 1–36.

2. *Egyptian law.*

Revillout, Cours de droit égyptien (1884).

——, Les obligations en droit égyptien comparé aux autres droits de l'antiquité (1886).

——, La propriété, ses démembrements, la possession et leur transmissions en droit égyptien (1897).

——, Les actions publiques et privées en droit égyptien (1896–1897).

Dagalle, Institutions juridiques de l'Égypte ancienne (1914).

Pirenne, Histoire des institutions et du droit privé de l'ancienne Égypte (2 vols. 1932–1934).

3. *Jewish law.*

Kent, Israel's Laws and Legal Precedents (1907).

Mielziner, Introduction to the Talmud (3 ed. 1935).

Contains a bibliography.

Rabbinowicz, Législation civile du Thalmud, Nouveau commentaire et traduction critique (5 vols. 1880).

Beer und Holzmann, Die Mischna, Text, Uebersetzung und ausführliche Erklärung. In course of publication 1912–.

Epstein, The Talmud Translated into English (3 vols. 1935).

Smith, The Origin and History of Hebrew Law (1931).

Goodenough, The Jurisprudence of the Jewish Courts in Egypt (1929).

Rodkinson, The Babylonian Talmud (transl. into English, Section Jurisprudence, vols. 5–10, 1903, cannot be recommended); Goldin, Text of the Talmud: Mishna, Translated and Annotated (3 vols. 1933); Kadushan, Jewish Code of Jurisprudence (2 ed. 1919) must be used with caution.

See I Moore, Judaism, 134–160. For bibliography see Strack, Einleitung in den Talmud (5 ed. 1921).

4. *Greek law.*

II Vinogradoff, Historical Jurisprudence, The Jurisprudence of the Greek City (1922).

Contains a bibliography.

Bonner, Lawyers and Litigants in Ancient Athens (1927).

Weiss, Griechisches Privatrecht (1923).

Hermann, Lehrbuch der griechischen Rechtsaltertümer (4 ed. by Thalheim 1895).

Lipsius, Das attische Recht und Rechtsverfahren (3 vols. 1905–1915).

Leist, Gräco-Italische Rechtsgeschichte (1884).

Dareste, La science du droit en Grèce (1893).

Beauchet, Histoire du droit privé de la république athénienne (1896).

Mitteis, Reichsrecht und Volksrecht in den östlichen Provinzen des römischen Kaiserreichs (1891).

Caillemer, Études sur les antiquités juridiques d'Athènes (10 pts. 1865–1880).

Hruza, Beiträge zur Geschichte griechischen und römischen Familienrechts (2 vols. 1892–1894).

See also Dareste, Questions du droit grec in Nouvelles études d'histoire du droit (1902) 55–116. For bibliography see Calhoun and Delamere, A Working Bibliography of Greek Law (1927) and review by Schiller, 28 Columbia L. Rev. 523. For bibliography of Hellenistic Egyptian Law see also Schiller, Ten Coptic Legal Texts (1932).

5. *Celtic law.*

Cameron, Celtic Law in Stair Society, Introductory Survey of the Sources and Literature of Scots Law (1936) 333–355 with bibliography.

D'Arbois du Jubainville, Études sur le droit celtique (1895).

(a) Irish Law.

Ancient Laws of Ireland (3 vols. 1865–1873).

Ginnell, The Brehon Laws (1894).

Dareste, Le droit celtique — L'Irlande, in Études d'histoire du droit (2 ed. 1908) 356–381.

(b) Welsh Law.

Ancient Laws and Institutes of Wales (2 vols. 1841).

Wade-Evans, Welsh Medieval Law (1909).

Ellis, Welsh Tribal Law and Custom in the Middle Ages (2 vols. 1926).

6. *Slavonic law.*

Sigel, Lectures on Slavonic Law (1902).

Kovalevsky, Modern Customs and Ancient Laws of Russia (1891).

Macieiowski, Slavische Rechtsgeschichte (2 vols. 1835–1839).

Ewers, Das älteste Recht der Russen (1826).

Goetz, Das russische Recht (3 vols. 1910–1912).

Krauss, Sitte und Brauch der Südslaven (1885).

——, Slavische Volkforschungen (1908).

See Dareste, L'ancien droit slave in Études d'histoire du droit (2 ed. 1908) 158–247.

As to Poland see von Ostrowski, Civilrecht der polnische Nation (2 vols. 1797–1802).

As to Balto-Slavonic law see Bunge, Altlivlands Rechtsbücher (1879); id. Beiträge zur kunde der Liv-, Esth-, und Curlandischen Rechtsquellen (1831); id. Geschichte des Gerichtswesen und Gerichtsverfahren in Liv-, Est-, und

Curland (1874); Bunge und Madai, Erörterungen aus den in Liv-, Est-, und Curland geltenden Rechten (5 vols. 1840–1853).

7. *Old Japanese law.*

Wigmore, Materials for the Study of Private Law in Old Japan (supplement to 20 Transactions of the Asiatic Society of Japan, 1892).

Kanazawa, Grundlagen der Japanischen Rechtsgeschichte, 31 Archiv für Rechts und Sozialphilosophie, 38.

8. *Old Chinese law.*

Wu, Readings from Ancient Chinese Codes and other Sources of Chinese Law and Legal Ideas, 19 Mich. L. Rev. 502.

The Book of Lord Shang: A Classic of the Chinese School of Law (transl. with introduction and notes by Duyvendak 1928).

C. HINDU AND MOHAMMEDAN LAW

Markby, Introduction to Hindu and Mahommedan Law (1906).

1. *Hindu law.*

Gautama (transl. by Bühler 1879).

Vasishtha (transl. by Bühler 1882).

Vishnu (transl. by Jolly 1880).

Manu (transl. by Bühler 1886).

Narada (transl. by Jolly 1876).

Jolly, History of the Hindu Law (1895).

——, Hindu Law and Customs (1928).

Mayne, Treatise on Hindu Law and Usage (10 ed. 1938).

Cowell, Short Treatise on Hindu Law (1895).

Colebrooke, Digest of Hindu Law (2 vols. 4 ed. 1874).

West and Bühler, Digest of Hindu Law (4 ed. under name of West and Majid 1919).

Sarkar, Hindu Law (5 ed. 1924).

Ghose, Principles of Hindu Law (2 ed. 1906).

2. *Mohammedan law.*

The Hedaya or Guide, a Commentary on the Mussulman Laws (transl. by Hamilton 4 vols. 1791).

There is an abridged edition by Grady 1870.

Vesey-Fitzgerald, Mohammedan Law, An Abridgment According to the Various Schools (1931).

Wilson, Introduction to the Study of Anglo-Muhammadan Law (1894).

——, Digest of Anglo-Muhammadan Law (6 ed. 1930).

Abdur Rahim, Muhammadan Jurisprudence (1912).

Ameer Ali, Mohammedan Law (2 vols. 5 ed. 1929).

Ruxton, Maliki Law (1916).

Morand, Études de droit musulman algérien (1910).

——, Droit musulman algérien (1916).

Kohler, Rechtsvergleichende Studien über islamitisches Recht, das Recht der Berbern, das chinesische Recht und das Recht auf Ceylon (1889).

Abdur Rahman, Eine kritische Prüfung der Quellen des islamitischen Rechts with complete bibliography (1914).

There is an Italian translation of Abdur Rahim, Muhammadan Jurisprudence by Cimino, I principi della giurisprudenza musulmana which contains a useful bibliography (1922).

D. ADATRECHT — THE NATIVE CUSTOMARY LAW OF THE DUTCH EAST INDIES

Pandekten van het Adatrecht (7 vols. 1912–1924).

E. CUSTOMARY LAW OF NEPAL

See Adam, Sitte und Recht in Nepal: Angaben und Schilderungen von Angehörigen der Gurkha-Regimenter (1934) 49 Zeitschrift für vergleichende Rechtswissenschaft, 1–269.

F. LEGAL INSTITUTIONS OF PRIMITIVE AND UNCIVILIZED PEOPLES

I Vinogradoff, Historical Jurisprudence, Tribal Law (1920).

Contains a bibliography.

Post, Grundriss der ethnologischen Jurisprudenz (2 vols. 1894–1895).

——, Afrikanische Jurisprudenz (1887).

These books of Post's and the older books of the descriptive sociology must be used with caution.

Goldenweiser, Early Civilization (1922); Lowie, Primitive Society (1920); Malinowski, Crime and Custom in Savage Society (1925); Rivers, Social Organization (1924); Schurtz, Altersklassen und Männerbunde (1902); Hogbin, Law and Order in Polynesia (1934).

See also Kohler, Zur Urgeschichte der Ehe, 12 Zeitschrift für vergleichende Rechtswissenschaft, 187.

Llewellyn and Hoebel, The Cheyenne Way (1941).

PERIODICALS OTHER THAN IN ENGLISH OF CHIEF INTEREST IN THE STUDY OF JURISPRUDENCE

I. PERIODICALS DEVOTED TO PHILOSOPHICAL AND ANALYTICAL JURISPRUDENCE

AUSTRIA.

Oesterreichische Vierteljahrschrift für Rechts- und Staatswissenschaft (18 vols. 1858–1866). Founded by Haimerl.

Zeitschrift für soziales Recht (6 vols. 1928–1934). Founded by Bauer, Grünberg, Kelsen, Radbruch, and Sinzheimer.

BELGIUM.

Revue catholique sociale et juridique (29 vols. 1898–1925). Until 1920 Revue catholique du droit.

CZECHOSLOVAKIA.

Rechts- und Staatswissenschaftliche Abhandlungen (11 vols. 1931–1937). Edited by Englander, Foltin, and Weizsacker.

Revue internationale de la théorie du droit (12 vols. 1926–1938). Founded by Duguit, Kelsen, and Weyr. Neo-Kantian analytical.

GERMANY.

Arbeiten aus dem juristisch-staatswissenschaftlichen Seminar der Universität Marburg (19 vols. 1904–14).

Archiv für Rechts- und Wirthschaftsphilosophie (33 vols. 1907–1940). Published since 1932 as Archiv für Rechts- und Sozialphilosophie. Founded by Kohler and Berolzheimer. Neo-Hegelian.

Philosophie und Recht (2 vols. 1920–1923). Founded by Emge.

Sozialrechtliches Jahrbuch (4 vols. 1930–1934). Founded by Brauer, Eckert, Lindemann, and von Wiese.

Zeitschrift für Rechtsphilosophie im Lehre und Praxis (6 vols. 1914–1934). Founded by Holldack, Joerges & Stammler. Neo-Kantian philosophical.

ITALY.

Archivio di studi corporativi (12 vols. 1930–1941). Founded by Bottaie.

Rivista internazionale di filosofia del diritto (20 vols. 1921–1940). Founded by Del Vecchio, Sforza, Pagano, and Vacca.

II. PERIODICALS DEVOTED TO JURISPRUDENCE IN ITS RELATIONS WITH THE OTHER SOCIAL SCIENCES

ARGENTINE.

Revista de ciencias juridicas y sociales (2 vols. 1923–1924).

Revista juridica y de ciencias sociales (54 vols. 1884–1937). Founded by Munoz, Labos, and Bidau.

FRANCE.

Annales du droit et des sciences sociales (3 vols. 1933–1936). Founded by Gouet and others.

Archives de philosophie du droit et de sociologie juridique (9 vols. 1931–1939). Founded by Le Fur, Davy, Gény, Lévy-Ullman, Matte, Morin, Renard, Richard, and Teissier.

Revue du droit public et de la science politique en France et à l'étranger (46 vols. 1894–1939). Founded by Larnaude.

Sciences politiques (54 vols. 1886–1939). Formerly Annales de l'école libre etc., Annales des sciences politiques, and Revue des sciences politiques. Founded by Boutmy.

GERMANY.

Annalen für soziale politik und Gesetzgebung (6 vols. 1912–1919). Founded by Braun.

Archiv für Sozialwissenschaft und Sozialpolitik (69 vols. 1888–1933, vols. 1–18, 1888–1903 under the title Archiv für Soziale Gesetzgebung und Statistik with supplements 1–18, 1911–1923). Founded by Braun.

Recht und Wirtschaft (11 vols. 1911–1922). Founded by Reichel, Riss, and Rumpf.

INTERNATIONAL.

Jahrbuch für Soziologie (3 vols. 1925–1927). Founded by Salomon.

ITALY.

Annali dell' istituto di scienze giuridiche economiche, politiche e sociali della R. Università di Messina (8 vols. 1927–1935).

Annali del seminario giuridico economico della Università di Bari (20 vols. 1927–1937, later volumes as Annali della Facoltà di Giurisprudenza, Nuova serie, vol. 1, 1938). Founded by Barillari.

Annuario delle scienze giuridiche sociali e politiche (4 vols. 1880–1883). Founded by Ferraris.

Lo Stato, Revista de scienze politiche e giuridiche (11 vols. 1930–1940). Founded by Rosboch and Costamagna.

Nuovi studi di diritto, economia e politica (8 vols. 1927–1935). Founded by Spirito and Volpicelli.

Studi economici giuridici R. Università di Cagliari (26 vols. 1909–1938).

PARAGUAY.

Revista de derecho y ciencias sociales (13 vols. 1927–1941). Founded by Creydt.

POLAND.

Zeitschrift für polnisches Recht- und Wirtschaftswesen (3 vols. 1928–1931). Founded by Langrod.

SPAIN.

Revista de ciencias juridicas y sociales (19 vols. 1918–1936). Founded by Smenjand.

URUGUAY.

Revista del derecho y ciencias sociales (9 vols. 1914–1921, continued as Revista de derecho jurisprudencia y administracion). Founded by De los Reyes Pena.

III. PERIODICALS DEVOTED TO HISTORICAL JURISPRUDENCE

FRANCE.

Revue historique de droit français et étranger (84 vols. 1855–1939). Founded by De Laboulaye, de Rozière, Dareste and Ginoudhiac (4 series 15 vols. 1855–1870, 6 vols. 1870–1877, 45 vols. 1877–1921, 18 vols. 1922–1939).

GERMANY.

"Gaius" Zeitschrift für Rechtsgeschichte (2 vols. 1907–1912).

Freiburger Rechtsgeschichtliche Abhandlungen (6 vols. 1931–1937).

Münchener Beiträge zur Papyrusforschung und antiken Rechtsgeschichte (31 vols. 1915–1940, ed. by Wenger).

Rheinisches Museum für Jurisprudenz, Philologie, Geschichte und griechische Philosophie (7 vols. 1827–1835). Founded by Hasse, Boeckh, Niebuhr, and Brandis.

Zeitschrift der Savigny-stiftung für Rechtsgeschichte (72 vols. 1861–1939). Founded by Rudorff, Bruns, Roth, Merkel.

ITALY.

Annuario dello istituto di storia del diritto romano (18 vols. 1891–1933). Founded by Zocco-Rosa.

Bullettino dell' istituto di diritto romano (46 vols. 1888–1939). Founded by Scialoja.

Rivista di storia del diritto italiano (14 vols. 1928–1941). Founded by Tamassia, Calisse and Brandileone.

Studi e documenti di storia e diritto, Publicazione . . . dell' Accademia di Conferenze Storico-Guiridiche (25 vols. 1880–1904).

IV. PERIODICALS DEVOTED TO COMPARATIVE LAW

BELGIUM.

Revue trimestrielle de l'institut belge de droit comparé (25 vols. 1908–1939). Founded by Busschere, Vauthier, Vauthier and Wauwermans.

FRANCE.

Annales de l'institut de droit comparé de l'Université de Paris (3 vols. 1934–1938).

Annuaire de législation étrangère publié par la Société de Législation Comparée (62 vols. 1870–1936).

Bulletin de la Société de Législation Comparée (68 vols. 1869–1939).

Revue de droit français et étranger (17 vols. 2 series, 1834–1843 and 1843–1850). Founded by Foelix.

Revue de droit international et de législation comparée (third series 20 vols. 1920–1939, second series 16 vols. 1899–1914, first series 30 vols. 1869–1898).

Revue générale du droit de la législation et de la jurisprudence en France et à l'étranger (62 vols. 1877–1938). Founded by Barthelon, Boistel and others.

GERMANY.

Blätter für vergleichende Rechtswissenschaft und Volkswirthschaftslehre (19 vols. 1906–1926). Founded by Meyer.

Kritische Zeitschrift für Rechtswissenschaft und Gesetzgebung des Auslandes (28 vols. 1829–1855). Founded by Mittermaier and Zachariä.

Zeitschrift für ausländisches öffentliches Recht und Völkerrecht (7 vols. 1929–1937). Founded by Bruns.

Zeitschrift für ausländisches und internationales Privatrecht (12 vols. 1927–1939). Founded by Rabel.

Zeitschrift für Ostrecht (8 vols. 1927–1934). Founded by Schott, Schöndorf, Bochmann and Warschauer and others.

Zeitschrift für vergleichende Rechtswissenschaft (53 vols. 1878–1939). Founded by Bernhöft and Cohn.

INTERNATIONAL.

Acta Academiae Universalis Jurisprudentiae Comparativae (2 vols. in 5 1928–1935).

Studia Opera Academiae Jurisprudentiae Comparativae (2 fascicules, series 2, 1933).

ITALY.

Annuario di diritto comparato e di studi legislativi (14 vols. 1927–1940). Founded by Galgano.

Bollettino dell' istituto di diritto comparato annesso alla R. Università Commercial di Trieste (3 vols. 1927–1929).

Rivista di legislazione comparata (3 vols. 1903–1905). Founded by Todaro della Galia.

NETHERLANDS.

Tijdschrift voor Rechtsgeschiedenis — Revue d'histoire du droit (16 vols. 1918–1939). Founded by de Blécourt, Van Kuyk, Van Kan, and Meijers.

V. UNSPECIALIZED LEGAL PERIODICALS OF INTEREST IN JURISPRUDENCE

AUSTRIA.

Magazin für Rechts und Staatswissenschaft (16 vols. 1850–1857). Founded by Haimerl.

Oesterreichisches Centralblatt für die juristische Praxis (41 vols. 1883–1923, continued as Zentralblatt für die juristische Praxis, 14 vols. 1924–1938). Founded by Geller.

Oesterreichische Zeitschrift für öffentliches Recht (continued as Zeitschrift für oeffentliches Recht) (21 vols. 1914–1938). Founded by Bernatzik, von Heinlein, Lammasch, and Menzel.

Zeitschrift für das privat- und öffentliche Recht der Gegenwart (42 vols. 1874–1916). Founded by Grünhut.

BRAZIL.

Revista do instituto da ordem dos advogados da Bahia (1927).

Revista do instituto da ordem dos advogados brasileiros (19 vols. 1862–1907).

COSTA RICA.

Revista de ciencias jurídicas y sociales; director lic. Hector Beeche (4 vols. 1936–1939).

FRANCE.

Bulletin de la Société d'Études Législatives (35 vols. 1901–1939).

Revue catholique des institutions et du droit (68 vols. 1873–1939). Founded by Victor Nicolet.

Revue critique de législation et de jurisprudence (96 vols. 1851–1939).

Revue trimestrielle de droit civil (38 vols. 1902–1939). Founded by Esmein, Massigli, Saleilles, and Wahl.

GERMANY.

Archiv des öffentlichen Rechts (31 vols. 1886–1939). Founded by Laband and Stoerk.

Archiv für bürgerliches Rechts (43 vols. 1889–1919). Founded by Kohler and Ring.

Archiv für die civilistische Praxis (145 vols. 1818–1839). Founded by von Löhr, Mittermaier and Thibaut.

Centralblatt für Rechtswissenschaft (33 vols. 1882–1912). Founded by Kirchenheim.

Die Justiz (8 vols. 1925–1933). Founded by Kroner, Mittermaier, Radbruch and Sinzheimer.

Gruchot's Beiträge zur Erläuterung des deutschen Rechts (73 vols. 1857–1933).

Jahrbuch des öffentlichen Rechts der Gegenwart (25 vols. 1907–1938). Founded by Jellinek, Laband, and Piloty.

Jhering's Jahrbücher für die Dogmatik des heutigen römischen und deutschen Privatrechts (88 vols. 1857–1939). Founded by Jhering and Gerber.

Kritische Vierteljahresschrift für Gesetzgebung und Rechtswissenschaft (66 vols. 1859–1939). Founded by Pözl, Arndts, and Bluntschli, etc.

Kritische Zeitschrift für die Gesamte Rechtswissenschaft (5 vols. 1853–1859). Founded by Brinckmann, Dernburg, and others.

Kritische Zeitschrift für Rechtswissenschaft und Gesetzgebung (6 vols. 1826–1829). Founded by Mohl, Rogge, Scheurlen, Schrader, etc.

Kritische Zeitschrift für Rechtswissenschaft und Gesetzgebung des Auslandes (28 vols. 1829–1856). Founded by von Mittermaier and Zachariä.

Schmoller's Jahrbuch für Gesetzgebung Verwaltung und Volkswirthschaft (64 vols. 1877–1940). Founded by Schmoller.

ITALY.

Il pensiero giuridico-penale (13 vols. 1929–1941). Founded by Penso.

La scienzia del diritto privato (4 vols. 1893–1896). Founded by Tortori.

Lo stato corporativo — Rivista di diritto e di studi sindacali corporativi (5 vols. 1933–1937). Founded by Viglietti and Tricarico.

Rivista italiana per le scienze giuridiche (2 series, vols. 1–66, 1886–1921, vols. 1–16, 1926–1941). Founded by Schupfer and Tucinato.

MEXICO.

Revista de derecho y ciencias sociales; mensual de cultura jurídica y social. (1936).

TURKEY.

Revue des sciences juridiques (6 vols. 1926–1931).

VI. ACADEMIC AND LAW SCHOOL PERIODICALS

ARGENTINE.

Revista de estudos juridicos; orgão do Centro academico de estudos juridicos. (2 vols. 1930–1931).

Revista de ciencias jurídicas y sociales (vols. 1–2, 1922–1925).

Revista de la Facultad de derecho y ciencias sociales (2 vols. 1907–1909).

Revista del Centro estudiantes de derecho, 1907/08–1917/18. (11 vols. in 19).

BRAZIL.

Revista academica da Faculdade de direito do Recife (35 vols.).

Revista academica; publicaçao do diretorio academico da Faculdade de direito do Piauí (nos. 1–4, 1935–1936).

Revista da Faculdade de direito de Sao Paulo, anno de 1893–1938 (vols. 1–34, 1893–1938).

ECUADOR.

Revista de derecho y ciencias sociales; órgano de la Facultad de jurisprudencia de la Universidad Central (vols. 1–2, 1933–1934).

GERMANY.

Bonner Rechtswissenschaftliche Abhandlungen (41 vols. 1928–1938).

Greifswalder Rechtswissenschaftliche Abhandlungen (4 vols. 1932–1933).

Heidelberger Rechtswissenschaftliche Abhandlungen (25 vols. 1929–1940).

Kölner Rechtswissenschaftliche Abhandlungen (30 vols. 1932–1939).

Leipziger Rechtswissenschaftliche Studien (123 vols. 1922–1940).

Rechtswissenschaftliche Studien (84 vols. 1919–1940). Published by Ebering.

ITALY.

Messina: Università; Istituto di scienze giuridiche, economiche, politiche e sociali (nos. 1–11, 1935–1939).

MEXICO.

Revista jurídica de la Escuela libre de derecho (3 vols. 1914–1921).

Revista jurídica de la Escuela libre de derecho, creada por acuerdo de la junta general de profesores de la misma (4 vols. 1921–1928).

Revista de la Escuela nacional de jurisprudencia; director general: lic. Augustín García López (3 vols. 1939–1941).

PERU.

Revista de derecho y ciencias políticas; organo de la Facultad de derecho y ciencias políticas de la Universidad Mayor de San Marcos (4 vols. 1936–1940).

SWITZERLAND.

Basler Studien zur Rechtswissenschaft (14 vols. 1932–1940). Edited by Wieland, Ruck, Simonius, Haab, and Germann.